The Permissive Society
America, 1941–1965

The Permissive Society points to the emergence of a liberalizing impulse during the Truman and Eisenhower years in contrast to those who see the 1950s as a conservative period and who view the 1960s as a time of rapid moral change. The book shows how a traditionalist moral framework was beginning to give way during the 1950s to a less authoritarian approach to moral issues as demonstrated by a more relaxed style of childrearing, the rising status of women both inside and outside the home, the increasing reluctance of Americans to regard alcoholism as a sin, loosening sexual attitudes, the increasing influence of modern psychology, and the declining influence of religion in the personal lives of most Americans.

Alan Petigny, the son of West Indian immigrants, is an Assistant Professor of History at the University of Florida. He graduated with honors from the University of South Florida and received his master's and doctorate degrees from Brown University. Before becoming an academic, Petigny worked as a policy analyst for the U.S. Congress's Joint Economic Committee. He was also an award-winning reporter for a public radio station based in Tampa, Florida, contributing material to both Florida Public Radio and National Public Radio.

"In the past few years, historians have begun to disassemble the stereo-types of the 1950s, rejecting the descriptions of a uniformly rigid, con-servative, and dour society. With Alan Petigny's astute and surprising book, this demolition project hits with full force. Focusing on liberal religion and the widespread popularity of psychology, counseling, and the ideals of identity-fulfillment, the author describes a very different society in the making, in which permissive behavior rejected the stri-dent calls for Cold War conformism. Contrarian in the very best sense of the term, this remarkable book transforms what we thought we knew about the postwar world, restoring balance, common sense, and dispassionate perspective to the history of the period."

– James Gilbert, University of Maryland

"In *The Permissive Society*, Petigny finds new indicators of behavioral change in sources neglected by cultural historians. His documentation of a permissive turn in the 1940s and 1950s provides a marvelous anti-dote to the naïve narratives of social change that clutter the canon of post–World War II cultural history. Both conservatives and progres-sives will benefit from careful study of this fascinating lesson in how cultural norms changed in response to new social realities."

– James Reed, Rutgers University

"With *The Permissive Society*, Alan Petigny gives revisionist history a good name. With freshness of perspective, deftness of design, and ingenuity of research, he proposes to find in the 1950s the seeds of the democratic change associated with the 1960s – and thus makes both decades more intriguing. *The Permissive Society* is a work that social and cultural historians of the postwar era will have to reckon with, and that anyone interested in a cogent scholarly argument is bound to enjoy."

– Stephen J. Whitfield, Brandeis University

The Permissive Society

America, 1941–1965

ALAN PETIGNY
University of Florida

CAMBRIDGE
UNIVERSITY PRESS

CAMBRIDGE UNIVERSITY PRESS
Cambridge, New York, Melbourne, Madrid, Cape Town, Singapore,
São Paulo, Delhi, Dubai, Tokyo

Cambridge University Press
32 Avenue of the Americas, New York, NY 10013-2473, USA

www.cambridge.org
Information on this title: www.cambridge.org/9780521757225

First published 2009

Printed in the United States of America

A catalog record for this publication is available from the British Library.

Library of Congress Cataloging in Publication data

Petigny, Alan Cecil, 1970–
The permissive society : America, 1941–1965 / Alan Cecil Petigny.
p.   cm.
Includes bibliographical references and index.
ISBN 978-0-521-88896-7 (hbk.) – ISBN 978-0-521-75722-5 (pbk.)
1. United States – Social conditions – 1945– 2. Social change – United States –
History – 20th century.   3. Liberalism – Social aspects – United States – History –
20th century.   4. United States – Moral conditions – 20th century.   I. Title.
HN58.P46 2009
306.0973'09045 – dc22   2008049123

ISBN 978-0-521-88896-7 Hardback
ISBN 978-0-521-75722-5 Paperback

This book is dedicated to the memory of my father,
Rene Petigny.

Contents

Acknowledgments   *page* ix

    Introduction: World War II, the Ascendancy of Science,
    and the Prologue to the Permissive Turn   1

1 Psychology: Benjamin Spock, Carl Rogers, and the
    Liberalizing Impulse in the 1950s   15

2 Religion: Ballrooms, Bingo, Blue Laws, and Billy Graham –
    Piety and Secularization in 1950s America   53

3 Sex: Ingrid Bergman, Elizabeth Taylor, and the Sexual
    Revolution in the Postwar Period   100

4 Feminism: The Rising Status of Women in the Age
    of Eisenhower   134

5 Youth Culture: Rock 'n' Roll, Blue Jeans, and the Myth
    of Opposition   179

6 The Self: From Original Sin to Self-Actualization – Jackson
    Pollock, Charlie Parker, and New Notions of Identity
    in Postwar America   224

7 Denouement: The Normative Lag and the Role of Religion in
    the Transformation of American Culture   249

Archives   283
Index   285

Acknowledgments

Many people helped bring this book to fruition. Foremost among them is my dissertation committee at Brown University which comprised James T. Patterson, Jack Thomas, and Howard Chudacoff. Jim Patterson, in particular, deserves credit for molding me into an historian, not an easy task. Graduate students are notoriously thin-skinned but Jim was patient with me and I hope he is pleased with the final product. Two senior scholars, Donald Critchlow and Larry Friedman, external to Brown and not part of my dissertation committee, acted as mentors and spent hours reading drafts and pushing me to think harder about the issues I raised. Likewise, Howard University's Daryl Scott spent more than 25 hours over 10 days reading aloud with me every word of my dissertation and offering his critique. It was an act of generosity for which I will always be grateful.

Early in my graduate student career, a daylong workshop was held at the George Mason University School of Law where several scholars provided feedback on one of my early chapters. This workshop featured an All Star lineup of Donald Critchlow, Alan Brinkley, Francis Fukuyama, James Jones, James Gilbert, Roy Rosenzweig, and Leo Ribuffo. It was an incredible experience, and I would like to thank them again for their generosity.

I also appreciate the support and constructive criticism I received from the community of graduate students at Brown University. They included Jim Sparrow, Ray Douglas, Robert Fleegler, Joshua Zietz, Peter Baldwin, Dan Williams, David Farbman, Margaret Crosby, Kevin Cloud, Alyssa Lodewick, Mark Herlihy (a true mental giant), and Julie Des Jardins. At the University of Florida, I was given critical feedback by my colleagues Jeff Adler, Robert McMahon, Eldon Turner, Matt Gallman,

John Sommerville, Betty Smocovitas, Louise Neman, Mitch Hart, Bertram Wyatt-Brown, Richard Horner, Jay Langdale, Randall Stephens, and Ken Wald. My undergraduate professors, Stephen Lawson and Nancy Hewett, also read and commented on sections of my manuscript. At Princeton University there was Robert Wuthnow of the Center for the Study of Religion, Andrew Jewett, Healan Gaston, as well as Rutgers University's James Reed, Gerald Grob, and Kieth Wailoo, and the University of Denver's David Ciepley. Brandeis University's Stephen Whitfield and University of Alabama's David Beito, two exceptional scholars and friends, took time to read and comment on draft chapters. Finally, due to my modest mathematical skills, I turned to three very capable economists to help me crunch numbers: William Doerner, Garth Brazelton, and my old racquetball partner John Bowblis, currently on the faculty of the Economics Department at Miami University in Ohio.

With respect to my prose, freelance editors Henry Butler, Michael Garvin, Michael Bagen, Dona Perkins, Matt Walker, and my former master's student Ryan Boyle, helped make this book more readable. Brown professors Patricia Herlihy, Karl Jacoby, and Hilary Silver showered me with many helpful suggestions. I also received assistance from Peter Levin, Mitch Bainwol, Jeff Styles, Mark Henrie, Steven Brust, Wilfred McClay, Leonard Liggio, Doug Den Uyl, Ingrid Gregg, Lyn Downey, Kathleen Laughlin (who helped me develop my chapter on women in the 1950s), Sherill Sunseri, and Oneshin Aiken. Additionally, this list would not be complete without mentioning the patience, understanding, and support of my editor, Eric Crahan, and his team at Cambridge Press.

On a final note, I would like to thank my mother Pearl, older brothers Arthur and Ludlow, and sisters Michelle and Sheila for their encouragement as I pursued my love of history.

Alan Petigny
March 2008

Note: Material appearing in Chapters 3 and 6 was previously published in the *Journal of Social History* (Fall 2004) and *The Mailer Review* (Fall 2007), respectively.

Introduction

World War II, the Ascendancy of Science, and the Prologue to the Permissive Turn

Images can be deceiving. Once time has passed, the complexities of every-day life are often simplified and idealized. Unfortunately, the price paid for this kind of nostalgia is a profound misunderstanding of past events, and one need look no further than the decade of the 1950s to discover innumerable examples. In the imagination of most Americans, the fifties were a solidly conservative era – we see images of June Cleaver perform-ing housework in pearls, nuclear families inhabiting long rows of near identical tract housing, and glib ad men espousing the benefits of a tailfin on every car and a television in every home. These are the reels of memory that remain with us, perpetuated by retrospective television sitcoms and professors of history alike. Even though a majority of scholars acknowl-edge the importance of subversive figures like Jack Kerouac, Elvis Presley, and Martin Luther King, Jr., they have been reluctant to depict these indi-viduals – or the movements from which they emerged – as representative of the general cultural trend, preferring instead to re-imagine a bygone world of crew cuts and manicured lawns.

Although scholars readily concede that the 1950s bore witness to the rise of the Beatniks, rock 'n' roll, and the civil rights movement, they are generally quick to characterize these oppositional developments as undercurrents – mere rumblings – that went against the dominant mood. In this way, they are regarded as seeds of discontent sown during the 1950s, only to blossom in the ensuing turmoil of the 1960s.[1]

---

[1] Chafe, William H. *The Unfinished Journey: America since World War II* (New York: Oxford University Press, 1986), pp. 164–5; Evans, Sara. *Personal Politics: The Roots of Women's Liberation in the Civil Rights Movement and the New Left* (New York:

It is this divide between the nominally conservative fifties and the socially liberal sixties that has shaped our general understanding of the early postwar years. As Daniel Yankelovich puts it, "The campus upheavals of the sixties gave us the first premonitory sign that the plates of American culture, after decades of stability, had begun to shift."[2] Some observers of the American scene attribute the social changes of the 1960s to a generation gap, others credit the civil rights and antiwar movements, some point to the rise of second-wave feminism, and still others to the formation of a counterculture. Whatever the primary cause, the proposition that a transformation in moral values truly began during the 1960s would appear to be a settled question.[3]

But this is bad narration. It is bad fiction, not fact and certainly not history. Over the years, this complacency narrative has been perpetuated by liberals and conservatives alike. Their analysis is virtually identical – the only difference in the positions they espouse are the values, or the meanings, they attach to the narrative. So when conservatives look back to the 1950s, they see an era of sexual reticence, a time when conservative Christianity was on the march, a halcyon era of order and tradition untarnished by the turmoil that would come. Conversely, liberals often vilify this time for its hypocrisy and repression. In both cases, the Complacency Narrative of the 1950s is held as fact, admitting debate only over the meaning of what happened.

However, this is not so. In establishing the case for the dramatic liberalization of values during the Truman and Eisenhower years, this book points to the emergence of a Permissive Turn. It argues that during the latter half of the 1940s, and continuing throughout the 1950s, the popular ingestion of modern psychology, coupled with significant changes in

Vintage Books, 1979), pp. 3–23; Chalmers, David. *And the Crooked Places Made Straight: The Struggle for Social Change in the 1960s* (Baltimore: The John Hopkins University Press, 1991), pp. xv, 12–14, 168; Diggins, John Patrick. *The Proud Decades: America in War and Peace, 1945–1960* (New York: W. W. Norton & Company), p. 295.

[2] Yankelovich, Daniel. *New Rules: Searching for Self-Fulfillment in a World Turned Upside Down* (New York: Bantam Books, 1981), p. 173.

[3] Two exceptions to this general trend can be found in Yankelovich, Daniel. *New Rules* (New York: Bantam Books, 1981); and Frum, David. *How We Got Here: The 70's: The Decade that Brought You Modern Life (For Better or Worse)* (New York: Basic Books, 2002). Although both books treat the 1970s as the time when social upheaval reached its peak, they also see the 1960s as a time of great social change, particularly among the young.

child-rearing and religious practices, constituted an unprecedented challenge to traditional moral constraints.

In the course of relating this story, the succeeding chapters will confront what we might regard as the four great myths of the 1950s – interpretations with which we are all acquainted and the veracity of which we have, generally, taken for granted. These myths – in the order in which they will be addressed – are as follows:

1) The belief that religious piety, as demonstrated by the popularity of Reverend Billy Graham and the climbing rates of church attendance, was on the rise during the 1950s.
2) The proposition that as far as sex is concerned the 1950s were a relatively stable period, and it was not until the 1960s that the sexual revolution actually began.
3) The claim that with the celebration of domesticity and the more general affirmation of "traditional values," the status of women was losing ground or – at best – remaining stagnant in the fifteen years following World War II.
4) The belief that the youth culture of the 1950s represented a vigorous challenge to the values of the adult world.

Although behaviors were loosening during the middle decades of the twentieth century, it is imperative to see these changes not as a tectonic shift, but as an acceleration of trends initiated earlier. Well before the Scopes Monkey Trial of 1925, the rise of science in general, and Darwinism in particular, posed a serious challenge to the intellectual and cultural dominance of traditional Protestant belief. Further undermining the influence of conservative Protestantism was the rise of the Social Gospel movement that had considerable influence before the nineteenth century. Likewise, the enormous success of Freud's celebrated visit to the United States in 1909 bears witness that psychology was making impressive inroads during the earliest days of the twentieth century. Therefore, rather than representing a break with all that came prior, the Permissive Turn imparted momentum to a process that had been unfolding for well over five decades.[4]

---

[4] In other important areas of life such as sex, consumerism, and popular entertainment, there are compelling reasons to believe that traditional constraints were becoming somewhat more relaxed during the closing years of the nineteenth century. See Meyerowitz, Joanne, "Sexual Geography and Gender Economy: The Furnished-Room Districts of

The World War II experience intensified the challenge to established values: it helped precipitate a collective backlash against sacrifice, and it also imbued the sciences with a prestige that, in turn, expanded the authoritative role of experts. A consideration of each development provides a new way of understanding the sweeping upheavals at work during the latter half of the twentieth century.

Repercussions of the War Effort

In 1945, as hostilities in Europe and the Pacific were drawing to a close and with an artificially large pool of savings available, Americans were in no mood for yet another round of renunciation and denial.[5] After fifteen years of depression and war, struggle and sacrifice, people sought to shake off years of public asceticism by a widespread "renunciation of renunciation."[6]

This pattern was perfectly illustrated by the meat crisis of 1946. Owing to continuing price controls, meat and other foodstuffs remained scarce and expensive. In dozens of cities, consumers staged buyers' strikes – sometimes revolving around chain phone calls and in other instances

Chicago, 1890–1930," in Ruiz, Vicki L. and DuBois, Ellen Carol (ed.), *Unequal Sisters: A Multicultural Reader in U.S. Women's History* (New York: Routledge, 2000), pp. 307–23; Leach, William. *Land of Desire: Merchants, Power, and the Rise of a New American Culture* (New York: Pantheon Books, 1993); Nasaw, David. *Going Out: The Rise and Fall of Public Amusements* (New York: Basic Books, 1993); Levine, Lawrence W. *Highbrow/Lowbrow: The Emergence of Cultural Hierarchy in America* (Cambridge, Mass.: Harvard University Press, 1988). Also, as Steven Mintz and Susan Kellogg point out, the American family at the turn of the century was experiencing enormous change. "A rapidly rising divorce rate, an alarming fall in the birthrate, a sexual revolution, and a sharp increase in the numbers of women continuing their education, joining women's organizations, and finding employment – each of these worked to transform the middle class family." See Mintz, Steven and Kellogg, Susan, *Domestic Revolutions: A Social History of American Life* (New York: The Free Press, 1988), pp. 108–9.

[5] Higgs, Robert. "Wartime Prosperity? A Reassessment of the U.S. Economy in the 1940s," *Journal of Economic History*, Vol. 52 (1992), pp. 41–60; and Bureau of Economic Analysis, *Survey of Current Business*, Vol. 74, No. 9 (September 1994), p. 46.

[6] The "sacrifice" of Americans on the home front during World War II requires some qualification. As a result of wartime prosperity, personal income went up significantly. However, due to rationing, shortages, higher taxes, and considerable pressure to buy war bonds, Americans were forced to curtail their consumption. As historian Mark Leff puts it: "In common parlance, sacrifice did not require the suffering of terrible loss. It instead comprehended a range of activities – running the gamut from donating waste paper to donating lives – in which narrow, immediate self-interest was subordinated to the needs of the war effort." See Leff, Mark H. "The Politics of Sacrifice on the American Home Front in World War II," *The Journal of American History* (March, 1991), p. 1296.

around picketing – to protest rising food costs.[7] Public outrage reached such a pitch that President Truman ultimately reversed his policy by gutting the Office of Price Administration (OPA) and terminating price controls on meat. Of all the issues in the congressional races, popular indignation over this issue was perhaps the most intense, prompting Democratic Congressman Sam Rayburn to refer to the 1946 congressional contests as simply the "Beef steak election."[8]

The meat crisis demonstrates that although Americans had dutifully accommodated themselves to wartime shortages, their willingness to continue enduring privations plummeted once Hitler and Tojo were vanquished. For most voters, the meat crisis involved more than the mere search for sirloins and pot roasts. It was symbolic of something larger, for it dramatized the major economic problems of the day: postwar inflation, economic mismanagement, and – above all else – an egregious failure on the part of Democrats to bring a timely end to wartime shortages.

The proliferation of labor strikes in 1946 likewise illustrated a natural frustration with continued sacrifices. Although there had been some labor disturbances throughout the war, union–management relations had been relatively peaceful. However, with the end of hostilities, restraint became more difficult to maintain as real incomes eroded due to rising prices and reduced overtime hours. Accordingly, beginning January 1946, steel-workers left the mills for more than ten weeks. In April of the same year, John L. Lewis launched a crippling strike with approximately four hundred thousand members of the United Mine Workers (UMW) behind him. All told, nearly five thousand strikes occurred in 1946, at a cost of approximately 160 million man-hours of work – four times the previous record.[9]

The combination of the meat crisis and work stoppages – both beginning in the immediate aftermath of World War II – suggests that in 1945

[7] See Jacobs, Meg. "'How About Some Meat?: The Office of Price Administration, Consumption Politics, and State Building from the Bottom Up," *Journal of American History* (December 1997), pp. 910–43; *New York Times*, October 20, 1946 (8:1); October 21, 1946 (2:3, 6); October 23, 1946 (1:1); October 27, 1946 (IV, 8:4).
[8] Jacobs. "'How About Some Meat?" pp. 910–41; Donovan, Robert J. *Conflict and Crisis: The Presidency of Harry S. Truman, 1945–1948* (Columbia, Missouri: University of Missouri Press, 1977), pp. 235–7; "President: Election Eve Price Retreat," *Newsweek* (October 21, 1946), pp. 31–34; Hamby, Alonzo L. *Man of the People: A Life of Harry S. Truman* (New York: Oxford University Press, 1995), pp. 382–4; and McCullough, David. *Truman* (New York: Simon & Schuster, 1992), p. 520.
[9] Bureau of the Census, U.S. Department of Commerce, *Historical Statistics of the United States: Colonial Times to 1970*, Part I, (Washington, D.C.: Bureau of the Census, 1975), p. 179.

(and possibly as early as 1944, when victory was within grasp) Americans were no longer willing to forgo basic food staples or long-awaited pay raises as a sacrifice to patriotic sentiments. From the perspective of most Americans, they had subordinated their private interests to a larger cause for long enough. Now that the war was won, it was their chance – indeed, it was their right – to catch up on the art of living.

Hastening the renunciation of selflessness was a harvest of corporate advertisements tailored to fit the needs of a long-suffering public. During the latter stages of World War II, when total victory seemed imminent, corporations promoted the prospect of postwar abundance. A magazine advertisement from Nash Motors typified the simple messages that flooded the airwaves and popular publications: "When victory comes Nash will go on...from the building of instruments of war to the making of two great new cars designed to be the finest, most comfortable, most economical, most advanced automobiles ever produced in their respective fields...And we will build these cars in numbers three times greater than our 1941 peak."[10] This advertisement was quite typical for its time, as dozens of other products, from the Ford Mercury and Sunbeam Coffeemaster, to vacuum cleaners and General Electric ranges, assured consumers that once peace arrived, production lines would flow with new products that surpassed their prewar equivalents in both style and affordability.[11]

A unique combination of forces ensured a high level of advertising during the war years. First, lucrative government contracts brought manufacturing companies high returns for producing war materials, even while limiting the production of consumer goods. As a result, corporations found themselves in a perplexing situation: Although earning record profits, they harbored serious doubts about their economic futures because military spending would eventually decline and consumer loyalty could not be guaranteed. Whereas in 1940 businesses spent only $216 million on radio ads, annual expenditures on radio commercials easily topped $400 million five years later.[12] By advertising so heavily, businesses hoped to encourage brand loyalty, burnish their public image, and heighten the thirst for consumer goods.[13]

---

[10] *The Saturday Evening Post*, (March 17, 1945), page not numbered.
[11] *The Saturday Evening Post*, (June 23, 1945), pp. 76, 52, 43; *The Saturday Evening Post* (December 1944), pp. 5, 76.
[12] U.S. Department of Commerce, *Historical Statistics of the United States, Colonial Times to 1970, Part 2* p. 797.
[13] Chappell, John D. *Before the Bomb: How America Approached the End of the Pacific War* (Kentucky: The University Press of Kentucky, 1996), p. 55.

Concentrating on the marvels of technology wrought by warfare, articles in the popular press further fanned the expectations of a postwar boom. Writing in *The New York Times Magazine*, Walter Teague argued as early as 1943 that peacetime progress had "in many respects" been "far outstripped." Due to the war, he explained, "there have been advances in chemistry, in metallurgy, technology, and machinery design which would have needed years at the tempo of peace." Consequently, "American industry, while it devotes all of its plants and manpower to turning out the weapons of this war, is boiling with plans for what it will do when it can get back to its regular job... I wouldn't bank on anything being just the same after the war as it was before."[14]

From the perspective of the typical American consumer, the promises of industry still seemed credible if perhaps a little exaggerated. Readers of *The Saturday Review of Literature* learned that because "housing has made more progress during the five years of war than in the two preceding decades," it was perfectly plausible that during the postwar years homes would be "erected on leased land and moved to a new site like the furniture when the lease expires." Regaled with predictions smacking of science fiction, readers were told about "ultra-violet bacterial lamps" that were capable of sterilizing dirty dishes, and new machines that would make cooking "all but automatic."[15] Subscribers to *Better Homes & Gardens*, a monthly magazine directed at middle-class housewives, received a similarly upbeat message. After hostilities ended, the magazine predicted families could expect to tread on scuffless floors, recline on flyweight furniture, relax under bladeless fans, and enjoy warm vacuum-packaged meals "delivered once a day like your milk."[16]

There is some evidence to suggest that consumer desires also changed dramatically during the war. From the moment the war broke out, Americans en masse seemed to accept an ethic of sacrifice. Thanks to their enthusiastic purchase of war bonds, an unprecedented level of savings were acquired – not just in absolute terms, but also as a percentage of their personal income. As the end of the war drew closer, the expectations

---

[14] Teague, Walter Dorwin. "Is It Just a Dream, Or Will It Come True," *New York Times Magazine* (September 26, 1943), pp. 15, 34.

[15] Kaempfert, Waldemar. "Green Light for the Age of Miracles," *The Saturday Review of Literature* (April 22, 1944), p. 14.

[16] "Quick Looks at Things to Come," *Better Homes & Gardens* (May 1943), p. 22; "Things to Come," *Better Homes & Gardens* (March 1944), p. 30; "Previews of Things You'll Wear, Drive, Eat, and Live with Tomorrow," *Better Homes & Gardens* (October 1943), p. 28.

of many Americans rose accordingly: by fall 1945, a *Woman's Home Companion* poll showed that more than four out of five Americans considered an apartment or even a "used house" to be an unacceptable place to call home.[17]

The reality of American economic might, along with the prospect of a technological utopia and the promise of postwar opulence, exerted a profound effect on the American psyche.[18] On the eve of the U.S. entry into World War II, more than three-fourths of Americans believed "after the present war" the nation would face another depression.[19] However, by spring 1945, six out of ten Americans believed the war would be followed by an extended period (five to seven years) of prosperity, while only 28 percent believed otherwise.[20]

Remarkably, civilian wages rose by an astounding 29 percent during World War II. At no other period in the nation's history had civilian income risen so quickly.[21] However, due to the collective efforts of industry admen and government propaganda, many Americans – apparently believing the band would keep playing – anticipated even sunnier economic times once peace arrived. In short, as the United States came out of World War II, expectations were unusually high, and prosperity came to be seen simultaneously as an opportunity, a right, and an affirmation of the American Way. Needless to say, such an atmosphere had little sympathy for a continued ethic of sacrifice.

Just how did rising expectations contribute to a Permissive Turn – or a more secularized frame of mind? The answer lies in the attitudes they fostered and the values they cultivated. Rising expectations and the rejection of austerity encouraged increasing numbers of people to embrace a materialistic outlook that stressed securing life's pleasures in the "here and now." Reinforcing this development was a consumerist ethos that

---

[17] Cited from Gitlin, Todd. *The Sixties: Years of Hope, Days of Rage* (New York: Bantam Books, 1987), p. 14.

[18] *Survey by Gallup Organization, April 20–April 25, 1945*. Retrieved August 19, 2008, from the iPOLL Databank, The Roper Center for Public Opinion Research, University of Connecticut. Online at http://www.ropercenter.uconn.edu/ipoll.html.

[19] In the Gallup Poll only 14 percent of respondents believed "Prosperity" was likely to follow the war. See *Survey by Gallup Organization, July 31–August 4, 1941*. Retrieved August 19, 2008, from the iPOLL Databank, The Roper Center for Public Opinion Research, University of Connecticut. Online at http://www.ropercenter.uconn.edu/ipoll.html.

[20] *Survey by Gallup Organization, April 20–April 25, 1945*. Retrieved August 19, 2008, from the iPOLL Databank, The Roper Center for Public Opinion Research, University of Connecticut. Online at http://www.ropercenter.uconn.edu/ipoll.html.

[21] U.S. Department of Commerce, *Historical Statistics of the United States, Colonial Times to 1970*, Part I, p. 125.

encouraged Americans to yield to the influence of the popular culture and, in so doing, take less of their cues from their neighbors and family. Indeed, in its catering to the new and the fleeting, its celebration of luxury and discouragement of thrift, its prompting of people to "keep up with the Joneses," and its glorification of style and fashion, a consumerist ethos compelled many to look to the world – and to the ways of the world – as the key to molding behavior, shaping identity, and finding meaning. Although most people did not translate this orientation into a reckless hedonism, it did succeed in nudging large numbers – especially those from the middle class, as well as the millions of adolescents entering the ranks of a consumer-driven youth culture – away from the repressive worldly asceticism that had long undergirded a conservative moral outlook.

The Continuing Liberalization of Values

The enormous faith placed in the possibilities of science helped lead to the liberalization of values in other ways. Besides cultivating a heightened sense of economic optimism, science – or, more precisely, the vast hope placed in the possible applications of science – gave greater cultural authority to "scientific" voices. As a result, various individuals who invoked the authority of science when addressing social questions were better able to challenge the traditional moral framework.

The government led the way in reshaping popular attitudes. Emboldened by wartime success in developing the atomic bomb, perfecting radar, and mass-producing penicillin, federal authorities became the country's chief peacetime patron of the sciences for the first time.[22] Thus, in 1946, Congress created the Atomic Energy Commission, passed the National Mental Health Act, and, four years later, established the National Science Foundation (NSF). In his 1949 inaugural address, President Truman hailed science as one of the leading solutions to the problems of a war-torn world. "Greater production," asserted Truman, "is the key to prosperity and peace. And the key to greater production is a wider and more vigorous application of modern scientific and technical knowledge."[23]

---

[22] For a discussion of wartime production of penicillin see Neushul, Peter. "Science, Government and the Mass Production of Penicillin," *Journal of the History of Medicine and Allied Sciences* 1993 Vol. 48 No. 4: 371–95; for a discussion of radar, see van Keuren, David K. "Science Goes to War: The Radiation Laboratory, Radar, and Their Technological Consequences," *Reviews in American History* (Fall 1997), pp. 643–7.

[23] Truman, Harry S. *The Inaugural Addresses of the Presidents*, Hunt, John Gabriel. (ed.) (New York: Random House, 1995), p. 407.

With the increased prestige of science, old stereotypes began to decline and the caricature of the scientist as an absentminded genius impervious to the pressing issues of the day gave way to a more positive appraisal. In the aftermath of Hiroshima, a new image – that of the socially conscious scientist – emerged in the national consciousness. With the creation of the Doomsday Clock in 1947, the editors of *The Bulletin of Atomic Scientists* were able to solidify their position as an authoritative voice on the Left with respect to issues of international peace. Likewise, physicists experienced a rapid ascent in their social status. Samuel Allison, the scientist who had led the Manhattan Project's Metallurgical Laboratory, recalled how physicists like himself were suddenly "exhibited as lions at Washington tea parties," welcomed at "conventions of religious orders," and "invited to conventions of social scientists, where their opinions on society were respectfully listened to by lifelong experts in the field."[24]

Advances in the social sciences paralleled the ascendancy of the physical and natural sciences, although somewhat more modestly. As Paul Starobin correctly observed, during the latter half of the 1940s "there was a naïve faith that social sciences could be a precision tool to solve the world's problems." Thus, in *An American Dilemma* (1944), a book that sought to end the systematic subjugation of African Americans, the author called for the "reconstruction of society" through "social engineering" grounded in "fact-finding and scientific theories."[25] Instead of turning off readers, such language helped turn *An American Dilemma* into a near-instant social science classic, and elevated Gunnar Myrdal, its lead author, to ever higher levels of celebrity status. Similarly, in 1944, when the American Jewish Committee (AJC) decided to sponsor a series of books on the causes of intolerance and bigotry, it did so under the auspices of its newly created Department of Scientific Research.[26] "Our aim is not merely to describe prejudice, but to explain it in order to help in its eradication," explained the series' editors. "Eradication means re-education, scientifically planned on the basis of understanding scientifically arrived at."[27]

---

[24] Ibid.
[25] Starobin, Paul. "Word Warriors Destroying Debate in Washington," *The Denver Post* (August 24, 1997), p. 6J.
[26] Svonkin, Stuart. *Jews Against Prejudice: American Jews and the Fight for Civil Liberties* (New York: Columbia University Press, 1997), p. 32.
[27] Adorno, T.W., Frenkel-Brunswik, Else, Levinson, Daniel J., and Sanford, R. Nevitt. *The Authoritarian Personality* (Abridged Edition) (New York: The American Jewish Committee, 1950), p. ix.

By the end of the fifties, writes historian Godfrey Hodgson, social scientists at leading American universities were bristling with a new found excitement. "It came from the feeling that, for the first time, the academic world seemed thoroughly integrated into the life and purposes of the nation." Although natural scientists, he continues, were the first to be patronized by federal authorities, "It was not long before sociologists, political scientists, even historians were being called into service by the government – all of the social sciences received from the relationship an injection of adrenaline, as well as money."[28]

Philanthropic organizations followed the lead of the federal government and became major sponsors for the furtherance of social scientific research. As the work of Roger Geiger reveals, shortly after the war senior officers in the Carnegie Corporation, the Rockefeller Foundation, and – a little later – the Ford Foundation decided to drastically increase their support for the social sciences. And increase it they did. Between the late 1940s and the late 1950s, foundation support for the nation's leading sixteen universities for social science had soared more than ninefold, rising from just under $4.5 million for the years 1946–9 to more than $43 million for the years 1955–8.[29]

Newfound confidence in the social sciences and humanities even affected government policy. Economically, World War II established Keynesianism as accepted wisdom, with its towering level of federal spending and stellar rates of economic growth. Accordingly, in the years between World War II and the late 1970s there arose a general consensus that encompassed many of the basic ideas of John Maynard Keynes. As Herbert Stein documents in *The Fiscal Revolution in America*, although conservatives and liberals continued to battle over tax and spending priorities, the vast majority held common assumptions, believing that during recessions "of some exceptional degree of severity" it may be obligatory to "take affirmative steps to enlarge the deficit."[30] Arthur Burns, the head of Eisenhower's Council of Economic Advisors,

---

[28] Hodgson, Godfrey. *America in Our Time: From World War II to Nixon, What Happened and Why* (New York: Random House, 1976), pp. 96–7.
[29] Geiger, Robert L. "American Foundations and Academic Social Science, 1945–1960," *Minerva* (Autumn, 1988), pp. 317, 318, 335. The list of the sixteen universities are Columbia University, Cornell, Harvard, Johns Hopkins, M.I.T., Northwestern, the University of Pennsylvania, Princeton, Stanford, Yale, the University of California, the University of Illinois, the University of Michigan, the University of Minnesota, the University of North Carolina, and the University of Wisconsin.
[30] Stein, Herbert. *The Fiscal Revolution in America* (Washington: The AEI Press, 1990), p. 240.

was more succinct. "It is no longer a matter of serious controversy," he observed, "whether the government shall play a positive role in helping to maintain a high level of economic activity."[31] In short, during the 1950s some of the most important assumptions of Keynesian thinking had become articles of faith among liberals and conservatives alike.[32]

There is polling data that lend support to the claim that Americans during the 1950s had an enormous level of faith in the promise of science compared to more recent times. In 1985, the National Science Board conducted an extensive examination of popular attitudes toward science. One of the questions put to respondents was: "Overall would you say that science and technology do more good than harm, more harm than good, or about the same amount of each?" In response, some 58 percent of Americans indicated that they believed science and technology had done more good than harm. Apparently, the National Science Board was pleased with the survey's results. "The generally positive pattern shown... may be viewed as a continuation of long-term popular support for science and technology in the United States," it concluded in its biannual report.

As impressive as the 1985 numbers were, they pale in comparison to the survey results gathered a generation earlier. When Americans were asked a similar question in a 1957 survey ("All things considered, would you say the world is better off or worse off because of science?") eight in ten respondents said they thought the world was better off due to the rise of science.[33] What the survey data suggest is that Americans during the late 1950s were roughly one-third more likely to have a positive appraisal of science than their counterparts during the 1980s.

The heightened prestige of postwar social science is not a very difficult matter to explain. The Permissive Turn of the 1940s and 1950s hastened the challenge to inherited values, and in the vacuum scientific experts came to the fore. The increasing respect accorded to psychologists, sociologists, economists, and social workers enabled a battery of experts to

[31] Cited from Hodgson. *America in Our Time* (New York: Random House, 1976), p. 72.
[32] For a fairly in-depth discussion of the extent to which the Eisenhower administration accepted key aspects of Keynesian thinking, see Stein, *The Fiscal Revolution in America*, pp. 282–98. Adams, Sherman. *Firsthand Report: The Story of the Eisenhower Administration* (New York: Harper & Brothers, 1961), pp. 153–79.
[33] Beveridge, Andrew A., and Rudell, Fredrica. "A Review: An Evaluation of 'Public Attitudes Toward Science and Technology' in Science Indicators: The 1985 Report," *The Public Opinion Quarterly* (Autumn, 1988), p. 382.

better challenge the traditional or religious view of the way life should be ordered. As Chapter 1 will show, a new breed of child-rearing experts was able to insist, with greater legitimacy, that a less authoritarian style of parenting would lead to fewer psychological problems in the future. Likewise, with greater confidence and effectiveness, proponents of the so-called disease model could argue that efforts to portray the alcoholic as sinful or weak were unscientific and closed-minded.

In earlier times, when seeking moral guidance many Americans would have turned to the faith of their fathers and asked, "What does the Bible say?" Alternatively, others might have turned to the authority of tradition and asked, "What would my parents say?" However, with the increasing stature of the social sciences, a new oracle had taken a seat at the table. Now, more Americans were apt to inquire, "What do the experts say?"[34] The enormous faith the public ascribed to the seemingly endless possibilities of science made the country increasingly susceptible to the claims of experts. This enhanced receptivity, in turn, undermined the rigid, pre-scientific truths of a religiously oriented tradition.

The Permissive Turn

Another factor that facilitated the rise of more liberal attitudes during the 1950s was the expansion of higher education. As Chapter 4 discusses in greater detail, college enrollment – hitherto, the providence of the privileged – boomed in the fifteen years following World War II. Besides producing a more educated workforce, the dramatic expansion of educational opportunities helped alter the way Americans thought about a host of sensitive issues, including attitudes toward psychology, sex, religious faith, and the role of women in society.

With the postwar "renunciation of renunciation," the heightened prestige of science, and the unprecedented accessibility of college, all of the pieces for a Permissive Turn were in place by the mid-1940s. As a result of the World War II experience, Americans were more likely to indulge their consumer impulses and enjoy life in the moment. They were more inclined to defer to experts on a host of issues ranging from intolerance and child rearing to alcoholism and sex. And due in part to the GI Bill,

---

[34] In her examination of the Kelly Longitudinal Survey, an extensive study of public opinion during the mid-1950s, historian Elaine Tyler May observed: "So pervasive was the therapeutic approach to life that respondents quoted, cited, and discussed experts in their anonymous questionnaires." May, *Homeward Bound*, p. 187.

college became a viable possibility for millions of Americans. Thus the stage was set for a Permissive Turn, a phenomenon that pushed back the many constraints arising out of a more restrictive, more conservative, religiously oriented past and – by so doing – accelerated a pattern of liberalization that had been on the march for at least half a century.

I

Psychology

Benjamin Spock, Carl Rogers, and the Liberalizing Impulse in the 1950s

In an article written more than a decade ago, essayist Joseph Epstein waxed nostalgic about his coming of age during the 1950s. In his day, he recalled, a young man would walk into a drugstore to buy a pack of cigarettes – and timidly ask to be slipped a packet of prophylactics. However, today the procedure is precisely the reverse.[1]

Few dispute that American values underwent a process of liberalization during the latter half of the twentieth century, but just how and when it happened is a far more vexing question. Today most historians are quick to argue while there were cultural rumblings during the 1950s, it was not until the 1960s that moral values began to shift in a fundamental way.[2] This book takes issue with the foregoing perspective, arguing that by mid-century a liberalizing impulse had become visible in four crucial areas: psychology, religion, childrearing, and popular attitudes toward addiction. Although leading thinkers of the time were aware of these cultural developments, they failed to appreciate their full implications. However, a closer analysis reveals that instead of simply "anticipating" the 1960s, these changes challenged and helped alter an older, more traditional morality and, as such, should not be relegated to the status of prologue.

In exploring the shift in postwar values, why should we give special attention to psychology, parenting, and religion? The social landscape

[1] Epstein, Joseph. "My 1950s." *Commentary* (September 1993), p. 40.
[2] See Patterson, James T., *Grand Expectations: The United States, 1945–1974* (New York: Oxford University Press, 1996); Mintz, Steven, and Kellogg, Susan, *Domestic Revolutions: A Social History of American Family Life* (New York: The Free Press, 1988); and Lytle, Mark Hamilton, *America's Uncivil Wars: The Sixties Era from Elvis to the Fall of Richard Nixon* (New York: Oxford University Press, 2006).

of any era is replete with moral indices, from general levels of civic engagement to changing rates of suicide, crime, fertility, divorce, single motherhood, and charitable giving. However – within the ethical realm – psychology, parenting, and religion are of an entirely different order. They are not merely barometers of social attitudes but, rather, integral parts of a person's moral universe: inherent in any school of psychology is an understanding of man's natural dispositions, at the heart of a parent's child-rearing philosophy is a particular evaluation of human nature, and at the center of all monotheistic religion lies a conception of the individual's intrinsic worth. In other words, psychology, child rearing, and religion – and all that they entail – touch directly on issues that relate to the self. Linked to a series of moral assumptions, they provide the basis on which one renders a thousand moral judgments.

The Democratization of Psychology

The democratization of psychology offers what is perhaps the most striking evidence for a Permissive Turn during the late 1940s. As numerous theologians have indicated, modern psychology's deemphasis of faith and its indictment of guilt as a guiding sentiment stand in tension with an older, more religiously oriented ethic. While Christians traditionally regarded guilt as an essential ingredient of man's spiritual makeup, Freud characterized guilt as not just a "problem," but as the foremost problem facing modern man. As the father of psychoanalysis himself conceded, the goal in writing *Civilization and Its Discontents* was to "represent the sense of guilt as the most important problem in the development of civilization and to show that the price we pay for our advance in civilization is a loss in happiness through the heightening of the sense of guilt."[3]

However, guilt was not the only issue distinguishing Freud and his disciples from the traditional Christian model. Another point of departure centered on the nature of religious faith. As with many psychologists, Freud was very critical in his assessment of religious belief. In *The Future of an Illusion*, for example, he likened faith to a juvenile desire for protection. "Religious ideas," claimed Freud, "have arisen from the same needs as have all the other achievements of civilization: from the necessity of defending oneself against the crushing superior force of nature."[4]

---

[3] Freud, Sigmund. *Civilization and Its Discontents*. Strachey, James (ed.). (New York: W.W. Norton & Company, 1961), p. 81.

[4] Freud, *The Future of an Illusion*. (New York: Norton, 1927, 1962), p. 21.

To the Freudian mind-set, modern psychology had sweeping implications, repercussions that went beyond a metaphysical stance. As psychiatric social worker Ella Van Hille explained, a secular worldview was amenable to modern psychology and tended to generate "more tolerant" and "more permissive" attitudes. By contrast, those adhering to a traditionally religious outlook were likely to espouse a "stern philosophy" that induced people to have "an identification of pleasure with sin."[5]

In describing the cultural shift during the postwar period as a "permissive turn," a qualification is in order. During the 1940s, 1950s, and even into the first half of the 1960s, *permissive* did not have a negative connotation. As Webster's *New International Dictionary* defined it in 1957, permissive meant "granting liberty; allowing, permitting"; and as late as 1961, *The Oxford English Dictionary* rendered permissive in neutral and, perhaps, even slightly positive terms. According to its definition, permissive meant "having the quality of permitting or giving permission; that allows something to be done or to happen; not forbidding or hindering." It is especially telling that in the context of the 1950s, such "granting of liberty" or "giving permission" did not imply unbridled hedonism. It was only during the late 1960s and early 1970s, in reaction to campus unrest and the emergence of a counterculture – and as part of a barrage of attacks from such conservative cultural warriors as Spiro Agnew and James Dobson – that permissive became associated with the near total absence of restraint. In seizing upon the term permissive – as in the "permissive turn" – this book is not assuming the rise of a reckless licentiousness. It is, instead, employing the term permissive in its older, narrower meaning: free from moral baggage, intending to simply convey the sense of loosening traditional constraints.

In spite of the hostility of conservatives, Freud's status among the pantheon of modern thinkers was rising, and the discipline of psychology was thriving as a result of World War II. Early in the conflict, during the North African campaign, the U.S. Army treated psychiatric casualties in a traditional manner, sending them to rear echelon hospitals as far as five hundred miles away. This practice yielded some major unintended consequences. The time spent transporting soldiers such long distances frequently led to delays in treatment. Moreover, the habit of completely separating soldiers from their units further isolated and depressed the psychologically wounded. In the end, only about 10 percent of

[5] Van Hille, Ella. "What is the Meaning of the Word 'Social' in Psychiatric Social Work?" *Journal of Psychiatric Social Work* (Winter, 1948–9), p. 122.

psychiatric casualties in the North African theater ever returned to the field.[6]

By contrast, toward the end of the war a revised strategy of prompt psychiatric treatment, offered only miles from the battlefield, yielded far more favorable results. The ability to provide soldiers with warm meals, immediate counseling, a shower, a shave, and a sedative-induced sound night's sleep proved very effective. Typically, within five days, approximately 60 percent of psychiatric casualties were able to return to the field; and most of those unable to return to the front lines nonetheless remained capable of serving in a noncombatant role.[7] "More than any other element," observed historian Gerald Grob, "the success in returning servicemen who experienced psychological problems to active duty renewed a spirit of therapeutic optimism and activism, which was subsequently carried back to civilian life."[8]

Members of the media dutifully reported on these psychiatric success stories. Through such popular magazines as *Time, Newsweek, Science Digest,* and *Collier's,* those back home learned of the incredible psychiatric breakthroughs occurring on the battlefront. "There is No Such Thing as Shell Shock: Soldiers Cured and Restored to Duty by Army Psychiatrists," read the headline of an October 1943 article in *Reader's Digest.* Another article, featured in *Science Digest,* claimed as its title "They're Beating Battle Breakdown."[9] The clear implication, in these and other stories, was that the psychiatric discoveries born on the battlefield would be applied to the home front once the war came to an end. As an article in *Collier's* concluded: "Any doubts about the efficacy of psychiatric treatment have been dissipated in the heat of war. Thousands of men have been returned to normal life and even to combat life by uses of the new therapy."[10]

[6] Grob, Gerald N. "World War II and American Psychiatry." *Psychohistory Review,* 19(1) (Spring 1990), pp. 56–7.

[7] Ibid, p. 58.

[8] Ibid, p. 59.

[9] Maisel, A. "They're Beating Battle Breakdown." *Science Digest* (September 1944), pp. 27–32; Painton, F. C. "There is No Such Thing as Shell Shock; Soldiers Mentally Shaken by War's Ordeals are Being Cured and Restored to Duty by Army Psychiatrists." *Reader's Digest* (October 1943), pp. 59–63. Also see "Spit It Out Soldier; Modern Treatment of Shell Shock or Traumatic War Neurosis." *Time* (September 13, 1943), pp. 60; Van De Water, M. "Mental Combat Causalities: Eight of Ten Can Get Back." *Science* (June 17, 1944), p. 391; "Squawk that Cures; Preventative Psychiatry." *Newsweek* (April 17, 1944), p. 93; Crichton, K. "Repairing War-Cracked Minds." *Collier's* (September 23, 1944), pp. 22–3.

[10] Crichton, "Repairing War-Cracked Minds," *Collier's,* p. 54; for an extended discussion of the media's coverage of psychiatric breakthroughs on the battlefront, see Hale, Jr.,

Accordingly, when the war came to an end, psychology and psychiatry continued to grow rapidly. Between 1945 and 1950, membership within the American Psychological Association (APA) grew from fewer than 4,200 to more than 7,200.[11] If examined in the twenty years between 1940 and 1960, the APA's growth was even more astounding, rising from approximately 3,000 to more than 18,000 members – an increase of more than sixfold.[12] Almost as significant as the growing number of psychologists was the increasing emphasis on clinical treatment. In 1940, only 272 members of the APA were engaged in clinical work of any kind, but by 1950 the total number of clinical psychologists soared to more than 2,500.[13]

The larger point of these figures is to show that after World War II, the professional counseling of "normal" folks expanded exponentially as waves of psychiatrists, psychoanalysts, psychologists, and even psychiatric social workers began offering therapy to average Americans.

In the postwar years, a time when psychology was truly coming into its own, the gulf separating cultural conservatives from mental health experts grew even wider. This growing chasm occurred because most psychiatrists and psychologists, finding Freud too pessimistic, sought to tone down some of the gloomier elements of Freudian thought. Consequently, whereas moral traditionalists might have objected to Freud on the grounds that he had gone too far in pushing the culture away from the notion of original sin, the response from most counselors was that Freud had failed to go far enough.

A brief survey of the literature illustrates this point. When it came to psychological counseling at midcentury, the most prominent thinkers on the American scene were Erich Fromm, Karen Horney, Harry Stack Sullivan, and Carl Rogers. In their respective approaches, there was a general downplaying of the severe limitations and the unavoidable neuroses inherent in Freudian theory. Fromm and Horney, for example, took issue with the claim that man was forever at war with himself. Rather than focusing on the Freudian clash between the Id and the Superego, Fromm

Nathan G., *The Rise and Crisis of Psychoanalysis in the United States: Freud and the Americans, 1917–1985* (New York: Oxford University Press, 1995), pp. 277–81.

[11] Cited from *American Psychological Association Year Book* for the appropriate years (Washington, D.C.: Library of the American Psychological Association).

[12] Ibid.

[13] Herman, *The Romance of American Psychology*, 84, 247. Among psychiatrists, a similar transformation was under way. Whereas before the war four out of five psychiatrists worked with seriously ill patients in mental hospitals, by 1947 fewer than 1,800 of the 4,765 APA members had any hospital affiliation. See Greene, *The Role of the Psychiatrist in World War II*, p. 497.

and Horney argued that the major source of psychological problems in modern times was the nature of the social structure itself. If people could restructure society properly, many of the neuroses of modern man would disappear.[14]

Emerging from a non-Freudian tradition, Harry Stack Sullivan was even more critical of Freudian theory. Rejecting free association and dream analysis, Sullivan adopted a strong empirical approach discounting much of Freud's thought as insufficiently grounded and unverifiable. By the early 1930s, Sullivan's clinical success with schizophrenics led him to believe that – far more than an examination of the subject's childhood experiences – a healthy interpersonal environment between doctor and patient was the key to psychic healing.[15] As the sociologist David Riesman correctly noted, "Sullivan's very insistence on the importance of interpersonal relations" caused him to believe "much more than Freud, in the adaptability of men and the possibilities of social science and harmony."[16]

Although not an intimate of Sullivan, Horney, or Fromm, Carl Rogers was probably the most vehemently anti-Freudian of the lot, and he was arguably the most influential therapist of the past half-century.[17] While

[14] See Fromm, Erich, *Escape From Freedom* (New York: Farrar & Rinehart, 1941), passim; and *Man For Himself: An Inquiry Into the Psychology of Ethics* (New York: Rinehart, 1947). Horney writes: "When we realize the great import of cultural conditions on neuroses the biological and physiological conditions, which are considered by Freud to be their root, recede into the background." See Horney, Karen, *The Neurotic Personality of Our Time* (New York: W.W. Norton & Company, 1937), p. viii. Of course, Horney and Fromm were immigrants, but their most productive work and their greatest influence occurred in the United States, their adopted country.

[15] Chapman, A. H. *Harry Stack Sullivan: His Life and His Work* (New York: G. P. Putnam and Sons, 1976), pp. 38–49; 230–41.

[16] Riesman, David, Glazer, Nathan, and Denney, Reuel. *The Lonely Crowd: A Study of the Changing American Character* (New York: Doubleday & Company, 1950), p. 47. It should also be noted that the common ground shared by Fromm, Horney, and Sullivan went beyond their rejection of orthodox Freudian teachings. All three were close colleagues who encouraged each other's work. During the mid-1930s, Horney and Fromm were members of the so-called Zodiac Club, an informal group of dissenting psychoanalysts, headed by Sullivan, which met periodically to explore various psychological issues. When Sullivan formed the William Alanson White Institute in the 1940s, Fromm joined him. In fact, Fromm made the institute his professional home until 1950, when he moved to Mexico. Fromm's association with Horney was even closer than his relationship with Sullivan. Besides being close collaborators, Fromm and Horney were lovers for a number of years. See Paris, Benard J., *Karen Horney: A Psychoanalyst's Search for Self-Understanding* (New Haven: Yale University Press, 1992), p. 138.

[17] One survey of 800 clinical psychologists named Carl Rogers the most influential psychotherapist of all time, surpassing even Freud. See Warga, Claire, "You Are What You Think; Profile of Psychologist Elbert Ellis," *Psychology Today* (September 1988).

Freudianism saw human beings as fundamentally conflicted, and behaviorism viewed man as essentially passive and plastic, the humanistic school of psychology – best exemplified by Rogers (but also advanced by Abraham Maslow and Rollo May) – elevated the self to a more exalted position. At the core of the person, wrote Rogers, stripped of his inhibitions, manners, acculturation, and prejudices, lies the actualizing tendency. Rogers described this phenomenon as an internal mechanism, present in everyone, that impels the individual toward self-improvement and psychological healing.[18]

Rogers labeled his approach to counseling "nondirective" and, later, "client-centered" therapy. He argued that the purpose of an analyst is not primarily to diagnose, certainly not to preach, but to be little more than a guide or facilitator. By listening empathetically, the therapist should attempt to put the client in touch with him or herself. As the reasoning went, through honest introspection would come self-acceptance, leading to self-realization and, ultimately, the unleashing of the actualizing tendency.[19]

In the mid-1950s, psychology professor Joseph Adelson sought to explain the cultural influence of Fromm, Horney, Sullivan, and Rogers. The sharp contrast between Freudian thought and the dominant trends in American psychology, he argued in a 1956 article, was attributable to what Tocqueville had called "the idea of the infinite perfectibility of man." While Freud believed that "Man's biology orders the human situation, in which the use of reason is, for most of us, severely limited," American psychology subscribed to a far more optimistic vision: "We tend to emphasize the ego's resources, its ability, somehow, to drive its way to health." The one quality "Rogers, Horney, and Sullivan have in common [is] the explicit assumption that the organism autonomously moves forward to growth."[20]

During the latter half of the 1940s, it was manifestly clear that psychological theories such as these were weaving themselves into the fabric of mainstream culture. This was particularly evident in American cinema. By 1947, the film industry was producing more than twenty films per year that the Motion Picture Association characterized as psychological

[18] Rogers, Carl R. "Significant Aspects of Client-Centered Therapy." *The American Psychologist* (June 1946), pp. 415–21; and Rogers, Carl R., and Becker, Russell J. "A Basic Orientation for Counseling," *Pastoral Psychology* (February 1, 1950), pp. 26–34.
[19] Rogers, "Significant Aspects of Client-Centered Therapy."
[20] Adelson, Joseph. "Freud in America: Some Observations." *The American Psychologist* (September, 1956), pp. 467–70.

in narrative theme.[21] Among the most successful of these films was *The Snake Pit*, a movie about a troubled housewife who, with the help of her sympathetic therapist, overcomes severe psychological problems. This film became one of the five most popular box-office draws of 1949 and for her role Olivia De Havilland received an Academy Award nomination for Best Actress.[22]

At midcentury, even a medium as pedestrian as comic books reflected the rise of psychiatry. In 1955, for example, EC Comics – the publisher of *MAD* magazine – introduced a new line of comics called *Psychoanalysis*. Instead of scuffling with kidnappers, mad scientists, and similar purveyors of evil, the hero of *Psychoanalysis* did battle against human neuroses, arguably the oldest foe of humankind. "You are going to meet three troubled and tormented people," explained the editors in an introductory note to readers. "You will see how the subconscious bases for their emotional disorders are discovered ... This is the method of psychoanalysis."[23]

In each issue, the bespectacled protagonist offered compassion, insight, and understanding to his emotionally ravaged clients; but in the mold of his muscle-bound counterparts, the psychoanalyst-hero exhibited a great measure of firmness. To the parents of his teenage patient, he yells: "There are no delinquent children ... only delinquent parents!"[24] In a later issue, when fifteen-year-old Freddy Carter is physically prevented from leaving the psychiatrist's office, the boy cries out: "L-LET ME GO! YOU HAVE NO RIGHT TO KEEP ME HERE! YOU'RE NOT MY FATHER!" The psychoanalyst is not intimidated. While restraining the boy he responds sternly: "NOR YOUR MOTHER EITHER! BUT I'M

---

[21] Holifield, E. Brooks. *A History of Pastoral Care in America* (Nashville: Abingdon Press, 1983), p. 265.

[22] Magill, Frank N. *Magill's Survey of Cinema, Volume 3* (Englewood Cliff, NJ: Salem Press, 1980), pp. 1009–11. More acclaimed than *The Snake Pit* was Alfred Hitchcock's thriller *Spellbound*, which debuted in 1945. In the movie, Ingrid Bergman plays a talented and courageous psychiatrist whose patient (Gregory Peck) suspects himself of murder. Like *The Snake Pit*, *Spellbound* portrayed psychiatry with reverential respect; and like *The Snake Pit*, it received critical acclaim, winning Academy Award nominations for Best Picture, Best Director, and Best Cinematography. See Brown, Jay A., *Rating the Movies: For Home Video, TV, and Cable* (Lincolnwood, IL: Publications International, 1990), p. 469.

[23] *Psychoanalysis* No. 2 (June 1955), box 290a, Comic Book Collection (hereafter referred to as CBC), Library of Congress, Serial and Government Publications Division, Washington, D.C.

[24] *Psychoanalysis* No. 1 (March/April 1955), box 290a, CBC.

GOING TO HELP YOU WHERE THEY CANNOT! I'M NOT GOING
TO YELL AT YOU LIKE YOUR FATHER ... OR PAMPER YOU LIKE
YOUR MOTHER! I'M GOING TO MAKE YOU SEE WHAT YOU'RE
DOING TO YOURSELF."[25]

As in most comic book adventures, the story ultimately ends on a
positive note. After four sessions of therapy – over the course of four
comic book issues – Freddy finally realizes that for years he had sought
to turn his parents against each other to monopolize the affections of
his mother. For their part, Freddy's parents come to recognize that they
had been using the boy as a pawn in their struggle against each other.
In the final scene – in what is portrayed as a most fortunate development – Freddy's parents are persuaded to seek psychoanalysis for themselves.[26]

There is reason to believe that during the 1950s, psychology became
popular not just among comic book writers and Hollywood produc-
ers, but also among ordinary folks. According to one major survey conducted by the University of Michigan in 1957, one in seven Americans
admitted to consulting with a professional counselor (a cleric, psycholo-
gist/psychiatrist, doctor, or marriage counselor) to help cope with a problem of a psychological nature.[27] Although impressive in itself, the figure
of one in seven Americans seeking psychological counseling is almost
certainly understating the level of popular support for the mental health
profession. The University of Michigan survey – which became the basis
of three subsequent books – showed that another 9 percent of respondents admitted that they could have benefited from professional help in
the past, and an additional 27 percent indicated that they could conceive
of circumstances where they might seek professional help in the future.
Hence, by the late 1950s, a slight majority of respondents accepted the
legitimacy of professional psychological services.[28]

[25] *Psychoanalysis* No. 2 (June 1955), box 290a, CBC.
[26] *Psychoanalysis* No. 2 (September 1955), box 290a, CBC.
[27] Herman, *The Romance of American Psychology*, p. 262. Likewise, in her examination
of the Kelly Longitudinal Survey – an extensive study of public attitudes during the
mid-1950s – historian Elaine Tyler May found that one in six Americans admitted to
consulting a psychologist, even though the overwhelming majority of those seeking help
did not consider their problems "severe." See May, Elaine Tyler, *Homeward Bound:
American Families in the Cold War* (New York: Basic Books, 1988), p. 27.
[28] Veroff, Joseph, Kulka, Richard A., and Douvan, Elizabeth. *Mental Health in America: Patterns of Help-Seeking from 1957 to 1976* (New York: Basic Books, 1981),
p. 79.

The Mental Health Profession and Psychotropic Drug Use

Contributing further to the prestige of the mental health profession was the rise of psychotropic drugs. Spurred by the Food and Drug Administration's (FDA) approval of the tranquilizer Miltown® in 1955, psychotropic drugs (i.e., medication aimed at ameliorating psychological problems) sparked a revolution that eventually led to the displacement of psychoanalysis as the ruling paradigm in American psychiatry. Earlier in the decade, with the introduction of such drugs as reserpine and chlorpromazine, notable headway had been made in the treatment of schizophrenia and other mental illnesses.[29] However, for American psychiatry, the key moment was not the introduction of drugs for the seriously ill, but rather the development of medication for the relatively normal. With the debut of Miltown, psychiatry entered a new era. In the first month, sales of Miltown amounted to only about $7,500 nationally. Yet shortly thereafter, as word of the drug spread, Americans realized that by taking a pill they could ease some of the anxieties and pressures of daily life. Sales exploded. By the end of August 1955 monthly sales had reached $85,000, and in September 1955 they exceeded $200,000.[30]

In less than two years, tranquilizers would become familiar to millions of American families. An estimated thirty million prescriptions were written for tranquilizers in 1956, and an estimated forty million prescriptions were written in the following year, accounting for four of the top ten prescriptions written by doctors.[31]

Before long, the national craze over tranquilizers attracted the attention of comedians. Milton Berle was soon referring to himself as "Miltown Berle." In one of his acts, Red Skelton told audiences how one of the Miltowns in his pillbox had said to the other Miltown, "I feel so terrible I think I'll take a Perry Como." And columnist Mike Connolly, quoted in a *Newsweek* article, quipped he "just heard about a mother who is so considerate of her child that she gives him Miltown before she spanks him."[32]

In the 1950s, the popularity of Miltown was driven in large measure by the aggressive marketing campaigns of pharmaceutical companies.

[29] "Onward and Upward with the Arts: Getting There First with Tranquility," *The New Yorker* (May 3, 1958), p. 95.

[30] Ibid, p. 109.

[31] "Ups and Downs with Pills," *The New York Times Magazine* (February 3, 1957).

[32] "Pills vs. Worry – How Goes the Frantic Quest for Calm in Frantic Lives?" *Newsweek* (May 21, 1956), p. 68.

In advertising and promotional literature, drug firms touted the effectiveness of their products in treating such conditions as nervousness, anxieties, the problem child, and even the colicky infant. According to Gallup, within ten years of Miltown's release, 25 percent of American adults admitted to having used tranquilizing drugs at one time or another.[33]

By embracing tranquilizers, Americans helped usher in a new era when millions of seemingly normal Americans would seek relief for their troubles in the form of a pill. However, beneath the simple veneer, the psychotropic turn in American psychiatry represented a genuine challenge to a traditionally Protestant vision. In the case of Freudianism, neo-Freudianism, and humanistic psychology, a frequent criticism of conservative religious figures was that all three schools seemed to gloss over the inherently sinful nature of man. Accordingly, they each rejected repression and downplayed traditional notions of guilt. However, all three approaches called for introspection – and, of course, introspection is the first step toward moral reflection. By contrast, introspection did not naturally follow the ingestion of prescribed tranquilizers. As physician Ian Stevenson noted in an article he penned for *Harper's Magazine*, "The prescription of a sedative or tranquilizer to a person only mildly or moderately anxious moves treatment in the wrong direction. It transfers attention from the mind to the body instead of the reverse." As for those who would insist that tranquilizers and introspection are not mutually exclusive, Stevenson had a ready response. "A physician makes little sense to his patient if he says, 'Your symptoms arise in your troubled thoughts and emotions and in your relations with other people. Have this prescription.'"[34]

Alcoholism and the Secularization of American Religion

The popularization of psychology proved to be significant in two other respects: it contributed to changes in established attitudes toward alcoholism and, to an even greater extent, it accelerated the secularization of modern American religion. During the late 1940s and 1950s, mainstream views toward the nature of addiction underwent a fundamental shift. In 1944, for example, a national survey found only 6 percent of those

[33] Lexis-Nexis, Reference (Polls & Surveys), Accession number: 0039723 for April 28, 1965, conducted by Gallup.
[34] Stevenson, Ian. "Tranquilizers and the Mind," *Harpers* (July 1957), p. 26.

FIGURE 1.1. Marty Mann, preeminent advocate of the disease model for addiction, at her desk in the early 1950s. (Reproduced by permission of the National Council on Alcoholism and Drug Dependence, Inc.)

surveyed considered chronic inebriation to be an illness. Yet by 1949, a Roper poll found that one-third of the respondents held this view.[35]

Probably no single organization did more to bring about this shift of opinion than the National Committee on Alcohol Education (NCA).[36] Spearheaded by Marty Mann, the so-called First Lady of the alcoholism movement, the NCA portrayed alcoholics as the victims not of their own behavior, but of a genetic predisposition. As Mann, recounting her early experiences with alcohol, stated in a 1947 interview: "One thing I did not realize then – I did not learn of it until years later – was that I, like three-quarters of a million others who are known and countless others who are not known, may be called allergic to alcohol. We are the unfortunates who are not immune to it."[37]

After joining Alcoholics Anonymous (AA) and attaining sobriety, Mann sought to erase the shame associated with alcoholism, the strong stigma of which discouraged problem drinkers from seeking treatment.[38]

[35] Rothe, Anna, (ed.), *Current Biography* [under the entry: "Mann, Marty"] (New York: H. W. Wilson Company, 1949), pp. 398–9.

[36] The name was later changed to the National Council on Alcoholism and, subsequently, to the National Council on Alcoholism and Drug Dependency.

[37] Woolf, S. J. "The Sick Person We Call an Alcoholic," *New York Times Magazine* (April 21, 1946), p. 22.

[38] Mann, Marty. "What Shall We Do About Alcoholism," *Vital Speeches of the Day* (February 8, 1947), p. 255. In her remarks, Mann states: "Not until the stigma is removed and alcoholism is discussed as freely and as openly as any other illness, will these people dare to seek help. We must remove this stigma if we are to save thousands from unnecessary deaths."

"I am an alcoholic," she wrote in 1946. "I no longer mind that appellation for I have learned that I have a disease like several million other Americans who are victims of alcoholism. I am no more ashamed of it than if I had diabetes."[39]

During the 1940s, the shame felt by alcoholics seemed to erode as more and more problem drinkers came forward to receive treatment. When Mann founded the NCA in 1944, approximately ten thousand people were members of AA, which at the time was only nine years old. By the close of the 1940s, AA claimed a membership of more than ninety-six thousand.[40]

As executive director and chief spokesperson, Marty Mann brought special talents to the NCA. With an extensive background in public relations, Mann was able to arouse a high level of media attention. Thus, when she first announced the creation of the NCA in October 1944, nearly four dozen reporters attended the New York press conference. Less than a month later a photograph of Mann and a description of her efforts appeared in the pages of *Time* magazine.[41]

Mann's social background proved an invaluable asset in furthering her cause. At a time when alcoholism was associated with male degeneracy – when the popular image of the alcoholic was that of the disheveled, unshaven drunk on skid row – Marty Mann forced people to reconsider old stereotypes. Here was a sophisticated woman, the daughter of a wealthy Chicago executive, who had attended various boarding schools in the United States before going on to finishing school in Florence, Italy. Surely if such a person could become an alcoholic, virtually anyone could.

Mann's appearance on the public stage created a double shock. Almost as arresting as the spectacle of a female alcoholic was that of one who was willing to shed her anonymity and announce her condition publicly. Until midcentury, most alcoholics – including those in AA – confided the details of their affliction to a select few, such as members of their families and support groups. Thus, Mann's decision to go public and encourage fellow alcoholics to seek treatment took many by surprise.

---

[39] Rothe, *Current Biography*, p. 399.
[40] Membership listed in the *World Directory*, published annually by the General Service Office of Alcoholics Anonymous, Inc., as cited in Johnson, Bruce Holey, *The Alcoholism Movement in America: A Study in Cultural Innovation* (University of Illinois, Urbana, Ph.D. dissertation: 1973), p. 287.
[41] Johnson, *The Alcoholism Movement in America: A Study in Cultural Innovation*, pp. 273, 275; also see *Time* (October 23, 1944), pp. 72, 75.

In short order, the NCA became an ever more insistent voice on the issue of alcoholism.[42] Within a year of its founding, five NCA chapters appeared in various cities throughout the country. Three years later, there were thirty-nine local affiliates in such disparate communities as Boston, Portland, the District of Columbia, and Minneapolis.[43] Chapters were usually headed up by prominent members of the community. For instance, of the thirty-nine affiliates existing in 1948, four had judges for chairs, three had doctors, another three had clerics, college presidents chaired three more, female civic activists presided over two chapters, and local businesspeople chaired the remaining affiliates.[44]

Although she was hardworking, articulate, and well-connected, Mann's great visibility was not entirely of her own doing. Rather, it appears Mann's message was something the larger public was eager to hear. She herself seemed to have been cognizant of this possibility. In a 1949 report, in which she recounted the founding of the NCA, Mann described the efforts of a prominent journalist to line up speaking engagements on her behalf. "At the time," she explained, "it was thought that invitations to speak on alcoholism might be hard to come by – it was still a very taboo subject in most circles." In spite of the great stigma, a flood of media attention and unsolicited speaking invitations rolled in after Mann's appearance in *Time* magazine, rendering outside assistance unnecessary. "There was no doubt that public opinion had been aroused," recalled Mann, "and that the aroused public was turning to us for advice and assistance."[45]

Not surprisingly, the medicalization of alcoholism generated its share of critics. In his best-selling book *Peace of Soul*, Roman Catholic cleric Fulton Sheen referred to the alcoholic as simply "the drunkard," whose condition was essentially an "act of choice."[46] More significantly, E. M. Jellinek, in a survey of the scientific literature on alcoholism, found a moderate level of resistance within medical and scientific circles to the very notion of the disease model. Although believing alcoholism warranted

---

[42] NCA Scrapbook, Marty Mann Papers, Syracuse University Special Collections (hereafter cited as Mann Papers). In reviewing the NCA scrapbook, the author counted more than 120 articles about Marty Mann and the NCA within the first six months of the organization's creation.

[43] The National Committee for Education on Alcoholism (memo), January 1949, box 3, folder heading: NCA-Policies and Changes in Policies Reflected in Meetings of Board, 1944–1956, Mann Papers.

[44] Ibid.

[45] National Committee for Education on Alcoholism, January 1949, Mann Papers.

[46] Sheen, *Peace of Soul*, p. 29.

intervention on the part of doctors and compassion on the part of the public, Jellinek noted a substantial proportion of expert opinion regarded alcoholism as a symptom or a reflection of a deeper psychological problem.[47]

Fortunately for the NCA, the majority of journalistic and, in time, popular sentiment was partial to Mann's position. When Edward R. Murrow prepared a series of reports on the personal philosophies of ten living Americans in 1953, he included Marty Mann along with such prominent figures as Eleanor Roosevelt, Helen Keller, Ralph Bunche, and Bernard Baruch.[48] By 1954, Marty Mann had succeeded in convincing such notables as Eleanor Roosevelt, unionist Walter Reuther, Dr. Robert Felix (then chief of the National Institute of Mental Health) and African American activist Mary McLeod Bethune to become active boosters of the NCA.[49] Yet another sign of the growing respectability of the alcoholism movement was the funding the NCA received from such corporations as IBM, Revlon, and General Motors by the close of the decade.[50]

Most telling of all, by the mid-1950s the majority of Americans had come to share Mann's position that alcoholism was an illness. A 1954 Gallup Poll showed that more than six out of ten Americans (63 percent) – up from 33 percent in 1949 and a mere 6 percent in 1944 – viewed alcoholism as a disease. Equally surprising, respondents were three times more likely to blame "worries and problems" for heavy drinking than "weakness, cowardice, [and] self-pity."[51]

On one level, the medicalization of alcoholism seems far out of step with the optimistic character of Big Science, progressive child rearing, and

---

[47] Jellinek, E. M. *The Disease Concept of Alcoholism* (New Haven: College and University Press, 1961), pp. 57–9.

[48] Murrow, Edward R. "This I Believe," LP album, 1953, Broadcasting and Recorded Sound Division, Library of Congress.

[49] Decade in Progress (pamphlet), box 12, folder heading: NCA Annual Reports 1945–1946; 1946–1947; 1952–1953, Mann Papers.

[50] NCA Amicus Curiae–New York State, page 11, box 2, Mann Papers. Other supporters included Union Carbide, Shell Oil, General Foods, Johnson & Johnson, and Standard Oil of New Jersey. Another sign of the NCA's growing acceptance was evident in 1956. That year, when the NCA sponsored a workshop for hospital administrators, more than fifty health professionals from eighteen states, including twenty-three physicians and nineteen hospital directors and superintendents, attended the New York seminar National Committee on Alcoholism Institute for Hospital Administrators (booklet), March 31, 1956, box 7, Mann Papers.

[51] Gallup, George. *The Gallup Poll: Public Opinion, 1935–1971* (Wilmington, Delaware: Scholarly Resources, 1972), p. 1299.

postwar psychology. After all, the very concept of alcoholism assumes that there is a serious behavioral problem on the part of the habitual drinker. Despite this, the disease model for alcoholism presented the individual as optimistically as possible by transplanting causality out of the spiritual realm and rooting it firmly into the world of the biological. Thus, although the individual may be partially responsible for remaining an alcoholic, he was not – according to Mann – morally blameworthy for becoming an alcoholic. In other words, while the disease model did not promulgate – at least explicitly – an optimistic view of the self, neither was it pessimistic. Instead, the proponents of the disease model viewed the self as essentially innocent, the victim of a disease process beyond its own control and causation.

This stance proved too extreme for AA, an organization that championed a blend of traditional and liberal principles. Although its twelve-step program was therapeutically innovative, the spirituality of AA was decidedly conservative. It was because of Mann's secularized vision – the scant emphasis that she and her allies placed on the importance of God and self-transcendence – that AA remained so resistant to the disease model. As the historian Ernest Kurtz has shown, Bill Wilson, the cofounder and leader of AA, was reluctant to pronounce alcoholism a disease, preferring to describe it as an "illness," or as simply a "malady." The explanation Wilson offered seemed contrived. "We have never called alcoholism a disease," he began, "because, technically speaking, it is not a disease entity. For example, there is no such thing as heart disease. Instead there are many separate heart ailments, or combinations of them. It is something like that with alcoholism."[52]

A more compelling explanation for Bill Wilson's reticence stems from AA's strong religious underpinnings. From its earliest days, the call to surrender and the recognition of a higher power has been central to the AA message. This meant for Wilson and other AA leaders it was the self – specifically the uninhibited self – one not constrained by tradition, custom, God, or prevailing norms that ultimately was responsible for the plight of the alcoholic. "Selfishness – self-centeredness!" thundered Wilson. "That, we think, is the root of our troubles . . . the alcoholic is an extreme example of self-will run riot."[53]

[52] Kurtz, Ernest. *Not-God: A History of Alcoholics Anonymous* (Minnesota: Hazelden Educational Services, 1979), pp. 22–3.
[53] Ibid, pp. 34–5.

The distinction AA made between sobriety and "dry drunks" further attests to the strong religious orientation of Alcoholics Anonymous. To Wilson, sobriety involved more than just abstaining from liquor; it meant maintaining the proper spiritual balance of personal humility and continual surrender to God. Dry drunks, by contrast, may have ceased consuming alcohol but – in rejecting the spiritual principles upon which true sobriety rested – continued to "think alcoholically," remaining in a precarious state.[54] Contrasted with the more modern approach of Marty Mann, the spiritual focus of Bill Wilson illustrates how differing ideas of the self clashed in the postwar era. It is important to note, however, that in time AA altered its tone and eventually joined the American Medical Association and the majority of the American people in characterizing alcoholism as a disease.

Psychology had provided the groundwork for the popular acceptance of the disease model. It gave legitimacy to the notion that personal destructive behavior did not necessarily proceed from an act of volition. In addition, for those seeking to overcome their dependency, psychology played a critical role in the recovery process. It is not surprising, therefore, that in the formulation of the AA philosophy, and in the formation of the alcoholism movement, the role of psychology loomed large.

The medicalization of alcoholism proved to be a harbinger of things to come. With increasing rapidity during the postwar period, a wide range of so-called deviant behaviors – from child abuse and spousal violence to drug addiction and compulsive gambling – likewise became medicalized. In the process, a decidedly less judgmental approach dominated public discourse.

In the end, the story of Marty Mann and the NCA is more than a tale of the medicalization of alcoholism. Her success in persuading millions of Americans to accept the disease model provides us with a glimpse into the volatile moral climate of the early postwar years. Both before and during World War II, the majority of Americans regarded alcoholism as a sign of moral turpitude. Traditional notions of free will, self-discipline, and moral responsibility ensured such a verdict; but with the postwar liberalization of values – and, more specifically, the rise of modern psychology – it became easier to attribute destructive personal behavior to external forces over which the individual had little or no control.

[54] Ibid, pp. 94–5; 123.

Marty Mann was undoubtedly right in arguing that removing the stigma surrounding alcoholism would make it easier for problem drinkers to seek help. Yet from the perspective of cultural conservatives who sought to preserve the traditional moral order, the medicalization of alcoholism reflected a larger trend that minimized guilt and blame, and downplayed self-restraint.[55]

Psychology and Religion

During the 1940s, psychology extended its reach even further into the religious life of the country. A reflection of this postwar influence was the success of Rabbi Joshua Loth Liebman's book *Peace of Mind* in 1946. As earlier thinkers had sought to harmonize religion and science, *Peace of Mind* sought to reconcile God and Freud. According to Liebman, "Far from being antagonistic, religion and psychiatry are mutually supplementary . . . only in the mighty confluence of these two tides shall we find peace of mind." Accordingly, Liebman called on his readers to "engrave" into their hearts "the commandments of a new morality." Following the cadences – although certainly not the spirit – of the Book of Exodus, he reassuringly told the reader that "thou shalt not be afraid of thy hidden impulses," and "thou shalt transcend inner anxiety, recognizing thy true competence and courage."[56]

In what could pass as a line from a popular advice column, Liebman asserted, "Whatever aids mankind in the quest for self-improvement is a new revelation of God's working in history."[57] To the dismay of religious conservatives, this was a message the public proved eager to hear. Rebecca Alpert notes that the phrase *peace of mind* came into vogue shortly after the publication of the book.[58] In 1946 and 1947, *Peace of Mind* reigned at the top of the nonfiction best-seller list of *The New York Times* for a record-breaking fifty-eight consecutive weeks, a streak since surpassed by only one book.[59]

55 Sheen, Fulton. *Peace of Soul* (Garden City, New York: Garden City Books, 1949), p. 29.
56 Liebman, Joshua Loth. *Peace of Mind* (New York: Simon & Schuster, 1946), p. 202.
57 Ibid.
58 Alpert, Rebecca T. "Joshua Loth Liebman: The Peace of Mind Rabbi," in Libowitz, Richard, (ed.), *Faith and Freedom: A Tribute to Franklin H. Little* (New York: Pergamon Press, 1987), p. 181.
59 See Bear, John. "Who's No. 1?" *New York Times* (December 27, 1992), Section 7; p. 23.

FIGURE 1.2. Rabbi Joshua Loth Liebman speaking to a crowd. Liebman's *Peace of Mind* was a forerunner to a myriad of self-help guides that fused psychology and spirituality. (Reproduced by permission of the Howard Gotlieb Archive Research Center, Boston University.)

From the publication of *Peace of Mind* in 1946 until his untimely death in 1948, Liebman was a hot commodity. Speaking invitations arrived from Dartmouth, Cornell, Columbia, and numerous other universities and organizations across the nation.[60] Excerpts from his book appeared in *Reader's Digest* and *Cosmopolitan*, while profiles of Liebman ran in *Look* and *The Ladies Home Journal*.[61]

Although he had his share of critics, many seemed to perceive Liebman as a first-rate thinker with a provocative message.[62] Thus in the fall of 1947, New York's renowned Temple Emanu-El – the so-called national cathedral of Reform Judaism, and the largest synagogue in the

[60] Alpert, "Joshua Loth Liebman: The Peace of Mind Rabbi," pp. 177–91.
[61] Ibid.
[62] For example, Liebman was awarded honorary doctorates from Colby College, North-eastern University, and Hebrew Union College. Moreover, within months of his death, a committee was formed to create a memorial fund for Rabbi Liebman. Among those serving on the committee were the president of Harvard University, Israel's ambassador to the United States, and the head of the Federal Council of Churches.

world – offered Liebman its rabbinate.[63] When he died of a heart attack eight months later, Boston's public schools closed early as a sign of respect, and letters of condolence came in from across the country.[64] Among those who promptly sent off a letter or telegram to Liebman's widow were Secretary of State George Marshall, with whom Liebman had visited; CIO President Philip Murray; NAACP chief Walter White; and FBI Director J. Edgar Hoover.[65] According to Genna Rae McNeil's biography of Charles Houston – Thurgood Marshall's mentor, and predecessor as head counsel of the NAACP – in Houston's final days he read *Peace of Mind*, and arranged to have the book passed on to his son in the event of his death.[66] Even years after Liebman's voice fell silent, Hoover included *Peace of Mind* among his six favorite books.[67]

Despite Liebman's fame, his ideas contrasted greatly with those of contemporary religious figures like the Reverend Billy Graham and Monsignor Fulton Sheen. Although all three took to the airwaves at midcentury, Liebman's message differed from their comparatively doctrinaire stance. In Liebman's theology, guilt was neither a necessary nor even a desirable component of moral thinking–quite the reverse. In accordance with much of modern psychological theory, the heart of Liebman's message was a deemphasis of guilt. "The voice of conscience," he wrote, does not always manifest itself in a "high, healthful form of expression." Instead, he noted that more often than not, "Their cry is the cry of most western religions: 'Atone, you miserable human worm! Smite yourself with the rod of self-punishment. Lacerate your guilty soul with the knot of Conscience, else ye be not worthy of the sight of God.'" It was not God, but religion's misguided approach to the problem of evil that was to "blame for this morbid, guilt-ridden attitude."[68]

---

[63] "Liebman Declines Call to Emanu-El," *New York Times* (October 8, 1947), p. 9a.

[64] Searching Guide (for multimedia exhibit), April 24–June 12, 1988, p. 5, Joshua Loth Liebman Papers, Boston University Special Collections (hereafter Liebman Papers).

[65] Box 4, Liebman Papers. Those sending telegrams to Liebman's widow were Secretary of State George Marshall, labor leader Philip Murray, the president of the Congress of Industrial Organizations (CIO); and NAACP chief Walter White. FBI Director J. Edgar Hoover sent Liebman's widow a personal letter.

[66] McNeil, Genna Rae. *Groundwork: Charles Hamilton Houston and the Struggle for Civil Rights* (Philadelphia: The University of Pennsylvania Press, 1983), p. 210.

[67] Boston Public Library pamphlet, n.d., box 4, Liebman Papers. Actually, Hoover was asked to list the six books he would most want to possess if he was stranded alone on a desert island. Also included on Hoover's list was Norman Vincent Peale's *The Power of Positive Thinking*.

[68] Liebman, *Peace of Mind*, pp. 24–5. It is worth noting that the original working title of *Peace of Mind* was "Morale for Moderns." See Alpert, Rebecca T., "Joshua Loth

In sharp contrast, Sheen and Graham preached a traditional message of self-restraint, simple faith, and resistance to the temptations of the material world. "Unless souls are saved, nothing is saved," proclaimed Sheen in his 1949 best-seller.[69] The titles of Sheen's and Graham's works strongly suggest that they viewed their own writings as a necessary rebuttal to Liebman. Sheen's 1949 book *Peace of Soul* was an obvious echo of Liebman's *Peace of Mind*, as was the title of Graham's 1952 book *Peace with God*.

Today, cultural historians have largely forgotten Joshua Liebman.[70] Few of the standard surveys of the Truman and Eisenhower years, or of American religion in the twentieth century, ever mention his name.[71] Instead, Norman Vincent Peale's *Power of Positive Thinking* (1952), which still holds the record for the longest reign at the top of *The New York Times* best-seller list (ninety-eight consecutive weeks), has come to symbolize the increasing secularization of popular religion in postwar America.[72] While scholars have correctly noted Peale's importance, they have failed to give adequate weight to the earlier influence of Liebman.

At the time of his death at age forty-one, Liebman's sermons were being broadcast on several radio networks coast-to-coast, to a weekly audience well in excess of a million.[73] Moreover, the meteoric rise of *Peace of Mind*, which appeared six years before *The Power of Positive*

Liebman: The Peace of Mind Rabbi," in Libowitz, Richard, (ed.), *Faith and Freedom: A Tribute to Franklin H. Little* (New York: Pergamon Press, 1987), p. 181.

[69] Sheen, Fulton, *Peace of Soul* (Garden City, NJ: Garden City Books, 1949).

[70] A notable example of this trend is Heinze, Andrew R., *Jews and the American Soul: Human Nature in the Twentieth Century* (Princeton, NJ: Princeton University Press, 2004).

[71] See, for example, Halberstam, David, *The Fifties* (New York: Villard Press, 1993); McCullough, David G., *Truman* (New York: Simon & Schuster, 1992); Hunter, James Davison, *Culture Wars: The Struggle to Define America* (New York: Basic Books, 1991); Finke, Roger, and Stark, Rodney, *The Churching of America, 1776–1990: Winners and Losers in Our Religious Economy* (New Brunswick, NJ: Rutgers University Press, 1992); and Ellwood, Robert S., *The Fifties Spiritual Marketplace: American Religion in a Decade of Conflict* (New Brunswick, NJ: Rutgers University Press, 1997) – although Ellwood tries to discuss Liebman, he gets his name wrong, calling him "Joshua Loth Lieb." A notable exception to this trend is found in Marty, Martin E., *Modern American Religion: Under God, Indivisible, 1941–1960* (Chicago: University of Chicago Press, 1996), pp. 314–17; as well as Chalmers, David, *And the Crooked Places Made Straight: The Struggle for Social Change in the 1960s* (Baltimore: John Hopkins University Press, 1991), passim.

[72] See Bear, John, "Who's No. 1?" *New York Times* (December 27, 1992), Section 7, p. 23.

[73] Rote, *Current Biography*, p. 346.

Thinking, suggests that a secularized religious message that minimized traditional constraints in favor of personal growth resonated strongly with the public, not only during the prosperous decade of the 1950s, but also in the immediate aftermath of World War II.

Liebman's role as a spiritual counselor to millions was all the more remarkable when one considers his Jewish background. Although the rise of Nazism rendered the crudest forms of anti-Semitism unacceptable in America, an undercurrent of aversion to Jews and things Jewish persisted. Nonetheless, Liebman's appeal transcended traditional religious boundaries. "Even though we are Catholics we seldom miss your programs," wrote an admirer from Winthrop, Maine. "I could not help but think how God has so richly blessed you and has given you such a brilliant mind and [sic] capable of passing on your wisdom to others." A listener from Somerville, Massachusetts, was equally laudatory: "Even though I am a Protestant attending the Unitarian Church, I greatly enjoy your sermons and wish they came every Sunday."[74] Historian Andrew Heinze estimates that Liebman's radio program drew a weekly audience of between one to two million people, and of those listeners, somewhere between 70 to 80 percent were Christians.[75] That Liebman was able to attract a mass audience during this period of considerable anti-Jewish sentiment is testimony to the inherent appeal of his message and the public's openness to it.

Besides deemphasizing sin and guilt, Liebman – and, shortly thereafter, Peale – were significant in another way: to an extent greater than any of their predecessors, they succeeded in transforming theology into therapy. As sociologist Steve Bruce points out, religion has always had "latent functions" or "secondary consequences." At times, these subsidiary effects have come in the form of greater social cohesion. On other occasions, they have helped provide strength for the embattled and consolation for the grieving. However, from a traditional Protestant perspective, these "latent functions," no matter how welcome, were never the principal purpose behind religion. The establishment of an intimate relationship with God was the ultimate goal, and any temporal benefits derived from it were of secondary importance. However, with the rise of an earthbound theology, as exemplified by the popularity of Liebman and Peale, "religion as a relationship to the supernatural was replaced with

[74] Untitled pamphlet, box 4, Liebman Papers.
[75] Heinze, Andrew R., *Jews and the American Soul: Human Nature in the 20th Century* (Princeton, NJ: Princeton University Press, 2004), p. 205.

religion as personal therapy . . . Previously, one intended to worship God and accidentally maintained the cohesion of society. Now one pursues personal satisfaction and accidentally worships God."[76]

Psychology and Child Rearing

The practice of child rearing was another arena that bore the imprint of the increasing influence of psychology. As was the case with the medicalization of alcoholism, the rise of modern psychology, and the prominence of Liebman and Peale, this new style of parenting clashed with the customary approach propounded by advocates of the conservative Protestant vision. Although hardly the paean to permissiveness that conservatives have alleged, Benjamin Spock's *The Common Sense Book of Baby and Child Care* (1946) embraced a number of nontraditional child-rearing practices. Almost immediately following its release in the summer of 1946, this parenting guide became a national best-seller. To the surprise and delight of its publisher, Spock's book sold more than a million copies within a year of its debut, and those numbers almost certainly would have been greater had production not been hampered by an acute paper shortage.[77] By 1952, sales for *The Common Sense Book* reached four million; and throughout the remainder of the decade, it sold an additional million copies each year.[78]

Written in a simple, conversational style, Spock's work appealed to parents and physicians alike. A sign of its popularity was the flood of unsolicited letters directed to Benjamin Spock. "I would like to express some of the gratitude mothers have towards your book. It gives them confidence and reassurance," wrote a doctor from Ann Arbor. Another physician from Boston said, "I want to tell you that your book on baby and child care is, in my opinion, excellent, and find it useful in my practice."[79] Indeed, the response from physicians was so positive that Spock's publisher began targeting doctors for bulk sales – apparently believing that they would either sell or give away copies of the book to their patients.[80]

---

[76] Bruce, Steve. *Religion in the Modern World: From Cathedrals to Cults* (New York: Oxford University Press, 1996), pp. 144–5.

[77] Robert F. de Graft to Benjamin Spock, September 3, 1947, box 1, Benjamin Spock Papers, Syracuse University Special Collections.

[78] Jones, Landon Y., *Great Expectations: America and the Baby Boom Generation* (New York: Coward, McCann & Geoghegan, 1980), p. 54.

[79] Charles H. Duell to Spock, May 5, 1949, box 1, Benjamin Spock Papers.

[80] Wallis E. Howe Jr. to Spock, November 26, 1947, box 1, Benjamin Spock Papers.

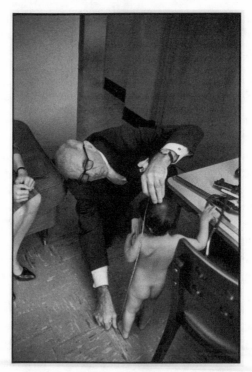

FIGURE 1.3. Dr. Benjamin Spock, August 1962, measuring two-year-old Linda, who had been coming to see him twice a week since her birth. His book *The Common Sense Book of Baby and Child Care* had a lasting influence on child-rearing practices. (Photographer: Henri Cartier-Bresson. Reproduced by permission of Magnum Photos, Inc.)

As expected, Spock's book proved to be especially popular among new parents. A 1961 survey commissioned by Pocket Books found nearly two-thirds of the more than one thousand new mothers queried had read Spock's work. Equally impressive, among those possessing the book, four out of five mothers said they referred to Spock's manual at least twice a month.[81]

Rather than promote traditional notions of discipline, Spock counseled parents to be more understanding and flexible. Thus, he discouraged parents who were dissatisfied with the neighborhood in which their child lived and played, or who were wary of the friends their child kept, from voicing these concerns. To do so, warned Spock, might cause the

---

[81] Cited from Maier, Thomas, *Dr. Spock: An American Life* (New York: Harcourt, Brace & Company), pp. 202, 468.

child to "grow up unable to mix with any group or to make a happy life. Then his high standards won't be of any use to the world or to himself."[82]

The manner in which Spock dealt with antisocial behavior is particularly revealing. With respect to theft, Spock recommended a couple of different approaches depending on the age of the child. For the youngster who stole, Spock implored parents "not to shame the child, since that will make him feel more lonely still." Instead, he urged mothers and fathers to "consider whether he needs more affection and approval at home, and help in making closer friendships outside."[83] In the same empathetic spirit, *The Common Sense Book* suggested that parents "make a present to the child of an object similar to the one he has stolen and returned." This gesture was "not a reward for stealing," Spock reassured his readers, "but a sign that the parent is concerned that the child not take what isn't his, and that he should have his heart's desire if it is reasonable."[84]

For larcenous adolescents, Spock's position was only slightly less permissive. Rather than giving such a child a present, Spock recommended an "understanding talk." In almost the same breath, however, he urged parents to avoid regarding their child's delinquent behavior as "vicious" or even as "a sign of maladjustment." After all, explained Spock, the adolescent who steals "as a result of peer pressure" – or because he "think[s] of swiping things as the daring and manly thing to do" – is "only obeying a normal instinct to make his place in the group."[85] Even in the case of the "aggressive child or adult" who steals, and who exhibits "little conscience," Spock refrained from advising parents to take a hard line. "A person gets this way only through a childhood quite lacking in love and security," he explained. "His only hope is in good psychiatric treatment and being able to live with kind, affectionate people."[86]

As these examples illustrate, Spock's stance toward punishment reflected a mild, nontraditional child-rearing approach. While willing to tolerate the occasional spanking (although quick to add that he personally opposed corporal punishment), Spock believed that any form of punishment should rarely be needed.[87] When it came to table manners,

---

[82] Spock, Benjamin. *The Common Sense Book of Baby and Child Care* (New York: Duell, Sloan & Pearce, 1946), p. 324. Hereafter, all citations attributed to Spock will be derived from his original 1946 edition.

[83] Ibid, p. 325.

[84] Ibid, pp. 324, 325.

[85] Ibid, pp. 325.

[86] Ibid.

[87] Ibid, p. 271.

truth-telling, common courtesy, and respect for others, explained Spock, punishment would have little effect on a child's behavior. "The thing that keeps us all from doing 'bad' things to each other," he confidently asserted, "is the feelings we have of liking people and wanting them to like us." The secret, therefore, to ensuring good behavior was for parents to have a clear sense of purpose. "If they are sure in their own minds how they expect him [the child] to behave," declared Spock, "and tell him reasonably, not too irritably, they will have all the control over him that they need."[88]

A final example of Spock's departure from more traditional child-rearing practices was his treatment of peer group interaction. In discussing the importance of peer acceptance for a child's emotional development, Spock advised parents to permit their children "to dress like, talk like, and play like" other children in their social group. He added that a child must "have the same allowances and privileges as the other average children in the neighborhood," even if the parents do not "approve of the way [such children] are brought up."[89]

Over the years, some scholars have sought to minimize the permissiveness of *The Common Sense Book of Baby and Child Care*.[90] Spock's conservatism with respect to gender roles partially accounts for this misplaced analysis on the part of academics. Implicit in Spock's conception of the good life was his belief that husbands went to work and wives tended to the home. So even when recognizing that in some cases it might be necessary for the mother to work, Spock could not conceal his general disapproval of such arrangements. "The important thing for a mother to realize," cautioned Spock, "is that the younger the child the more necessary it is for him to have a steady, loving person taking care of him . . . If a mother realizes clearly how vital this kind of care is to a small child, it may make it easier for her to decide that the extra money she might earn, or the satisfaction she might receive from an outside job, is not so important after all."[91] Notwithstanding Spock's attachment to traditional family forms and conservative gender roles, his stance on discipline, peer group

[88] Ibid.
[89] Cited in Zuckerman, Michael, "Dr. Spock: The Confidence Man," in Rosenberg, Charles E., ed., *The Family in History* (Philadelphia: University of Pennsylvania Press, 1975), p. 199.
[90] Jones, Landon Y., *Great Expectations: America and the Baby Boom Generation* (New York: Ballantine Books, 1996), pp. 55–6; Mintz, Steven, and Kellogg, Susan, *Domestic Revolutions: A Social History of American Family Life* (New York: The Free Press, 1988), pp. 187–8; and Maier, Thomas, *Dr. Spock: An American Life* (New York: Harcourt Brace, 1997), passim.
[91] Spock, *The Common Sense Book of Baby and Child Care*, p. 484.

interaction, and the innate goodness of children themselves was anything but conservative.

There is good reason to believe that the relaxation of parental discipline advocated by Spock reflected child-rearing practices in general, especially among the middle class. Spock's *Common Sense Book*, in other words, was more a reflection than the primary cause of less traditional parental attitudes. In 1958, sociologist Urie Bronfenbrenner published an analysis of more than a dozen studies examining the attitudes and practices of white middle- and working-class parents over the span of twenty-five years. In synthesizing the results of these various studies, Bronfenbrenner concluded: "middle-class mothers, especially in the postwar period," were "consistently more permissive toward the child's expressed needs and wishes."[92] For example, at the outset of the 1940s, strict feeding schedules were the rule of the day: only 4 percent of middle-class families "fed [the baby] when hungry" – which is to say, allowed the baby's hunger pangs to determine the mealtime. By the late 1940s, however, a virtual sea change had taken place. In line with the increasingly popular belief that children were self-regulating organisms who did not require strict oversight and governance, approximately 65 percent of middle-class families were allowing babies to determine their own feeding times.[93]

According to Bronfenbrenner's synthesis of the literature, these less exacting attitudes on the part of the parents were perpetuated beyond infancy. Over time, it was ascertained that American children were "less often treated by spanking and scolding," "less often disciplined for touching sex organs," and less likely to upset parents by thumb-sucking and the exhibition of poor table manners.[94] In other words, Bronfenbrenner's research suggested a permissive turn in child rearing was not solely confined to the middle class and elites who might have been consulting the *Common Sense Book*. Rather, the move away from a stern, disciplinary approach seemed to have been a widely diffused cultural phenomenon that influenced broad segments of society.

Attitudes of Other Groups

Although postwar changes in child rearing, alcoholism, and psychology helped reshape popular attitudes, not all groups were affected equally.

[92] Bronfenbrenner, Urie. "Socialization and Social Class Through Time and Space," *Readings in Social Psychology*; Maccoby, Eleanor E. et al., (ed.), (New York: Holt, Reinhart & Winston, 1958), pp. 400–25.

[93] Ibid, p. 408.

[94] Ibid.

According to Gallup's research, white-collar workers were more likely to
believe in the disease model as an explanation for alcoholism than either
manual workers or farmers. In fact, farmers were nearly twice as likely
to reject the medicalization of alcoholism as their white-collar counterparts. In addition, women were considerably more disposed toward the
disease model than men.[95] Notwithstanding these variations, among virtually all the demographic groups there appears to have been a dramatic
shift in public opinion in the ten years following World War II. By the
mid-1950s, men as well as women, manual laborers, and white-collar
workers had largely discarded their earlier prejudices in favor of the once
controversial disease model. Among American farmers – an especially
conservative group – opinions on that matter were split evenly, with
50 percent of respondents classifying "drunkenness" as a disease, and
most of the remainder (44 percent) objecting to such a designation.[96]

As a group, African Americans had experiences that significantly differed from their white counterparts. Although the empirical data are
limited, the evidence suggests that African Americans tended to be less
permissive in their child-rearing approach than whites who hailed from
similar socioeconomic backgrounds. Nonetheless, the parenting strategies
of most black families apparently became more moderate over time.

With respect to the larger white population, the sociological literature
relating to parenting is more fragmented and, therefore, more impressionistic than the public opinion data relating to alcoholism. Nonetheless, a
few general patterns are discernible. In synthesizing the results of some
twenty different child-rearing studies, Bronfenbrenner detected sharp differences between white middle- and working-class parents. During and
prior to World War II, it was found that white middle-class families
tended to be more strict with their children than working-class parents.
"After World War II, however, there has been a definite reversal in direction," observed Bronfenbrenner. "Now it is the middle-class mother who
is the more permissive...."[97]

Bronfenbrenner attributed this class divide to a lower degree of sophistication on the part of working-class families. As he put it, "Child-rearing
practices are likely to change most quickly in those segments of society
which have closest access and are most receptive to the agencies or agents
of change (e.g., public media, clinics, physicians, and counselors)."[98] All

[95] Gallup, *The Gallup Poll: Public Opinion, 1935–1971 Volume 2*, p. 1299.
[96] Ibid.
[97] Bronfenbrenner, "Socialization and Social Class Through Time and Space," p. 424.
[98] Ibid, p. 411.

TABLE 1.1. *Educational background and gender*

Has Used or Could Have Used Psychological Help		
Grade school	Men: 11%	Women: 20%
High school	Men: 18%	Women: 30%
College	Men: 30%	Women: 32%

of these differences notwithstanding, when child-rearing practices were examined during the late 1950s, he detected a permissive trend within nonelite households – and thus a general convergence in the child-rearing patterns of white middle- and working-class families. "As Mrs. Johnson, down in the flats, puts away the hairbrush and decides to have a talk with her unruly youngster 'like the book says,'" wrote Bronfenbrenner, "Mrs. Thomas, on the hill, is dutifully striving to overcome her guilt at the thought of giving John the punishment she now admits he deserves."[99]

In the 1950s, popular attitudes toward psychology were even more discernable than general sentiments toward child-rearing practices or the disease model for alcoholism. Thanks to an in-depth survey of nearly twenty-five hundred adult Americans, conducted in 1957, a great deal of data exists surrounding the receptivity of Americans to psychological treatment. As in the case of the medicalization of alcoholism, gender and class would appear to have been important considerations. Women with only a grade school education were almost twice as likely to have sought professional help for a mental health problem – or to have admitted to having formerly been in a psychological state where they could have benefited from professional help – than their male counterparts. Compared to men with only a high school education the disparity shrank somewhat, with high school educated women about 60 percent more open to the promise of psychology than high school educated men. However, among the college educated, the differences between men and women had largely evaporated (see Table 1.1).[100]

The University of Michigan study revealed several other differences along religious, regional, and generational lines. As one might expect, Roman Catholics and mainline Protestants were more likely to have a positive assessment of psychology than Baptists; and American Jews were even more likely to be favorably inclined toward psychology than

---

[99] Ibid, p. 423.
[100] Gurin, Gerald, Veroff, Joseph, and Feld, Sheila. *Americans View Their Mental Health* (New York: Basic Books, 1960), p. 121.

mainline Protestants. Similarly, according to the 1957 survey, young people (ages 18 to 29) were nearly twice as likely as older Americans (i.e., ages 65 or older) to view psychology in a positive light. Surprisingly, not a great deal of variation was uncovered along residential and racial lines. Inhabitants of rural areas were almost as receptive to the promise of psychology as those living in either cities or suburbs. Perhaps most astonishing of all, the study found African Americans were no less receptive to psychology than their white counterparts. Given the educational discrepancies that existed between the races, one would have expected to see similar discrepancies in popular attitudes toward psychology. For some odd reason, however, this apparently was not the case.

As in the case of the medicalization of alcoholism, where the more tradition-minded elements of society (e.g., farmers) tended to be less inclined toward the disease model, we correspondingly witness middle-class Americans becoming more liberal in their child-rearing approaches and more accepting of psychology than their working-class counterparts. However, it is noteworthy that in each case the general trend was affecting men and women, middle- and working-class families alike, in the direction of greater permissiveness. In short, insofar as liberalizing attitudes toward alcoholism, child rearing, and psychology were concerned, not all the groups were moving at the same pace – but all seemed to be headed in the same general direction.

The Permissive Turn

Of all the various influences that aided the Permissive Turn, the rise of psychology must be regarded as the most significant. It is not that the cultural influences of Spock, Mann, and Liebman were modest, but on the most basic level, their prominence during the 1940s and 1950s was a reflection of psychology's postwar ascendance. It is, therefore, hardly a coincidence that prior to 1945, when few private citizens contemplated psychotherapy, Marty Mann, Benjamin Spock, and Rabbi Liebman had all undergone counseling.[101] In their minds, psychotherapy was not only for the deranged and seriously disturbed: it also had vital applications for respectable, highly functioning people like themselves.

[101] Marty, Martin E. *Modern American Religion: Under God, Indivisible, 1941–1960* Volume 3 (Chicago: University of Chicago Press, 1996), p. 315; Heinze, Andrew H. "Peace of Mind (1946): Judaism and the Therapeutic Polemics of Postwar America," *Religion and American Culture.* Volume 12, No. 1 (2002), p. 36; Maier, *Dr. Spock,* p. 135.

Mann, Spock, and Liebman promoted modern psychological theories not only in their personal lives, but also in their public works. Besides contributing an article to the *Journal of Pastoral Psychology*, Mann frequently praised AA's twelve-step program in both her writings and public remarks. Mann even dedicated her book, *A New Primer on Alcoholism*, to Dr. Harry Tiebut, a psychiatrist who had previously treated her, and to the legendary Bill Wilson, co-founder of Alcoholics Anonymous.[102]

Liebman's relationship with psychology was equally strong. In addition to emphasizing the importance of psychology in his writings, Liebman organized one of the earliest conferences on psychology and religion in 1946.[103] It is noteworthy that in their biography of Marty Mann, authors Sally and David Brown report that, as a recovering alcoholic, Mann regarded *Peace of Mind* as a source of much inspiration and insight.[104] Finally, throughout *The Common Sense Book of Baby and Child Care*, Spock advised parents to take their children to a psychologist, a psychiatrist, or a child guidance clinic for problems ranging from stealing and stuttering to exhibiting symptoms of anxiety and unsociable behavior.[105]

Besides the transforming influence of modern psychology, Mann, Spock, Liebman, and Carl Rogers shared another characteristic in common: each person came from a liberal religious background. Both Mann and Spock were Episcopalians, one of the more progressive of the mainline denominations. Rabbi Liebman, as a Reform Jew, came out of a more quasi-secularized branch of Judaism than his conservative or orthodox counterparts; and prior to his enrolling in Columbia University to pursue a degree in psychology, Carl Rogers had studied at Union Theological Seminary, one of the leading bastions of liberal Protestantism.

The liberal theological backgrounds of these four individuals are neither surprising nor accidental. Postwar changes in child rearing, religion, psychology, and attitudes toward alcoholism relaxed many of the

---

[102] Mann, Marty. *A New Primer on Alcoholism: How People Drink, How to Recognize Alcoholics, and What to Do About Them* (New York: Holt, Reinhart, & Winston, 1958), acknowledgment page. Although Mann's acceptance of the disease model was in tension with AA, she credited AA and Bill Wilson with having rescued her from her addiction earlier in her life. Consequently, Mann remained a strong booster of AA until her death.

[103] Hall, Charles E. *Head and Heart: The Story of the Clinical Pastoral Education Movement* (Decatur, GA: Journal of Pastoral Care Publications, 1992).

[104] Brown, Sally, and Brown, David R. *A Biography of Mrs. Marty Mann: The First Lady of Alcoholics Anonymous* (Center City, Minnesota: Hazelden Pittman Archives Press, 2001), p. 130.

[105] Spock, *The Common Sense Book of Baby and Child Care*, pp. 288, 325.

restrictions and controls that had long been allied with an older, more restrictive ethic. The orthodox vision – which blamed alcoholics for their alcoholism, regarded children as "scaled-down savages," and dismissed psychology for its light treatment of sin and guilt – was itself shaped by conservative theological concepts.[106]

A former boy prodigy and well versed in philosophy, Rabbi Liebman was especially eloquent in drawing the connection between theological pessimism on the one hand, and an ethical moralism on the other. In a sermon delivered in 1944, Liebman castigated the conservative Protestant tradition for its "contempt for sins of the flesh" and its "preoccupation with the sensual instincts of man as evil and degrading." As Liebman explained it, believing the world is inherently depraved makes it seem only natural for the "Puritan-minded" to stress petty injunctions, exacting discipline to repel the temptations abounding in this earthly realm. Liebman traced this "rigid Puritanism" to the Apostle Paul and his disciples, "who came under the influence of Greek philosophy" and, accordingly, "regarded lust and adultery as the cardinal sins in the calendar of life."[107]

Carl Rogers seemed to share Liebman's general sentiments. "Religion, especially the Protestant Christian tradition," wrote Rogers in 1952, "has permeated our culture with the concept that man is basically sinful, and only by something approaching a miracle can his sinful nature be negated." Such pessimism was wholly unwarranted, explained Rogers, because clinical experience had shown that "the innermost core of man's nature, the deepest layers of his personality, the base of his 'animal nature,' is positive in nature – is basically socialized, forward-looking, rational, and realistic."[108]

Neither liberal Protestantism nor Reform Judaism could imbibe the twin notions of Original Sin and innate human depravity. Therefore, the challenge to the traditional, conservative ethic was most likely to come from the likes of a Marty Mann, a Benjamin Spock, a Joshua Liebman, or a Carl Rogers – individuals who did not subscribe to the conservative Protestant tradition.

---

[106] The term *scaled-down savages* is borrowed from Zuckerman, Michael, "Dr. Spock: The Confidence Man," in Rosenberg, Charles E. (ed.), *The Family in History* (Philadelphia: University of Pennsylvania Press, 1975), p. 186.

[107] What are the Real Moral Issues of our Day: Reflections Suggested by the Banning of "Strange Fruit," April 14, 1944, box 69, Liebman Papers.

[108] Rogers, Carl. *On Becoming a Person* (Boston: Houghton Mifflin Company, 1961), p. 91. Although published in 1961, Rogers was drawing on articles and speeches he had penned during the 1950s.

The Early Postwar Years

Considering the economic boom of the 1950s, it is understandable that many would see the prosperity of the age as the driving force behind changing moral values. In fact, even those scholars given to portraying the Eisenhower years as essentially sedate have often pointed to the affluence of the postwar years as the critical factor leading to the emergence of the generation gap and the subsequent rise of the counterculture. According to this view, while the 1960s ushered a "new morality" into being, it was the prosperity of the 1950s that planted the seeds of rebellion. Elaine Tyler May, for example, argues that the demographic explosion of the forties and fifties – a process that led to larger families and a more conservative culture – lasted only until the baby boomers reached maturity: "The parents, having grown during the depression and war, had begun their families during years of prosperity. Their children, however, grew up amid affluence during the cold war; they reached adulthood during the 1960s and 1970s, creating the counterculture and a new women's liberation movement."[109]

In *Great Expectations*, Landon Jones is explicit in portraying the early postwar years as a time of considerable economic prosperity. The fertility boom of the late 1940s, he argues, "coincided with the greatest economic expansion this country has ever seen." In *True Stories from the American Past*, William Graebner argues that the direction taken by American culture during the 1950s was largely set by the prosperity that emerged during the latter half of the 1940s. "Beginning in 1946," he writes, "an unanticipated baby boom helped sustain high rates of economic growth while fostering a new family-based domesticity in the rapidly expanding suburbs."[110]

May, Jones, and Graebner are partially correct. Undoubtedly, the affluence of the 1950s hastened the demise of the traditional moral framework. As Daniel Bell has argued, over time the maturation of consumer capitalism undermined older virtues of hard work, thrift, and delayed gratification. "The cultural transformation of modern society," he maintained, "is due, singularly, to the rise of mass consumption, or the diffusion of

---

[109] May, Elaine Tyler. *Homeward Bound: American Families in the Cold War Era* (New York: Basic Books, 1998), p. 9.
[110] Graebner, William, (ed.), *True Stories from the American Past* (New York: McGraw-Hill, 1973), p. 179.

what were once considered luxuries to the middle and lower classes in society."[111]

The issue taken with this interpretation is that in subscribing to the notion of a "postwar boom," the latter half of the 1940s is essentially conflated with the economic buoyancy of the 1950s. Upon closer inspection, we see the accelerated challenge to the traditional moral framework began not during the fifties, but in the immediate aftermath of World War II – a time when Marty Mann, Benjamin Spock, and Joshua Loth Liebman were becoming household names.[112] However, notwithstanding the higher expectations that emerged in the war's aftermath, the pivotal years between 1946 and 1949 could hardly be described as "booming." Until the outbreak of the Korean War, President Truman was confronted with serious economic problems. Because of demobilization, the gross national product spiraled downwards – falling more than 10 percent in 1946, and slipping slightly in 1947. More disturbingly, the removal of price controls caused inflation to soar to more than 8 percent in 1946, and another 14 percent in the following year.

Inflation struck working people with particular severity. Although annual earnings increased 10 percent between the years 1945 and 1947, once adjusted for inflation, real earnings of the average worker actually fell by 11.4 percent. Indeed, Americans would have to wait until 1950 to see real earnings for civilian workers catch up to 1945 levels. When inflation is taken into account, we see that between 1950 and 1960, the average earnings for the average American employee grew by 32 percent. During the war years of 1941 to 1945, real earnings grew by more than 29 percent. However, sandwiched between the explosive growth of the wartime years and the brisk expansion of the 1950s were the closing years of the 1940s (1946–9). During this period, real wages grew by less than 1 percent.*

The foregoing statistic is not intended to portray the four years following World War II as a postwar depression, but neither was it a postwar boom. Instead, during the latter half of the 1940s, Americans seemed conflicted as optimism and unease pushed and pulled them in different directions. Thus, while housing starts shot up, the Dow Jones index stayed flat.

[111] Bell, Daniel. *The Cultural Contradictions of Capitalism* (New York: Basic Books, 1976), p. 65.

[112] Psychology, of course, had already attained a sizable following by the mid-1940s. However, in the immediate postwar years, the experience of World War II provided the fields of psychology and psychiatry with a significant boost.

* U.S. Department of Commerce, *Historical Statistics of the United States, Colonial Times to 1970*, Part 1, pp. 164, 210, 224.

In addition, although Americans seemed surprisingly supportive of union demands, they remained hostile and suspicious of unions themselves. Finally, notwithstanding the frequent predictions of economic depression looming on the horizon, Americans embarked on an unprecedented consumption binge.

The Permissive Turn, therefore, emerged not during the "fat fifties," but during the early, leaner Truman years when economic anxieties coexisted with higher expectations. Although the democratization of psychology, the medicalization of alcoholism, the rise of a therapeutic theology, and the liberalization of child-rearing practices continued well into the 1950s, they all began – or, more precisely, their rapid acceleration began – during the 1940s. Accordingly, the postwar liberalization of values was less a product of material conditions than the consequence of a growing materialistic mind-set. Stamped with the experience of the Great Depression and World War II, this new worldview facilitated the acceptance of progressive parenting, modern psychology, a "softer" theology, and the disease model, with all their concomitants. Thus, in an inversion of the classic Marxist formulation, the ideological superstructure took precedence over the material base. At the most fundamental level, instead of flowing from prosperity, changing cultural attitudes actually preceded, reinforced, and helped guide prosperity.

None of this implies that prosperity was unconnected to the liberalization of values. Yet a great deal more was at play – particularly in the five years following World War II – than simply economic expansion. No less potent than prosperity was the psychology of prosperity, which galvanized America to live life in the moment and partake in the accoutrements of the here and now. Hence, what one sees in the postwar period are higher levels of consumption entwined with more gambling, more drinking, more sex (which we will explore at length in Chapter 3), and more therapy.

Thriving Conservative Conventions

Notwithstanding the enormous successes of Rogers, Mann, and Spock, conservative conventions did thrive during the early postwar period. In the fifteen years following World War II, the baby boom began, church attendance climbed, President Eisenhower's moderate conservatism supplanted President Truman's moderate liberalism, the Cold War commenced, and – with the defeat of Henry Wallace in 1948 – the Progressive Left found itself relegated to the outer fringes of the political landscape.

From either a cultural or political standpoint, there were few overt signs to suggest that Americans at midcentury were experiencing any sort of revolution.

This seeming paradox – characterized by the accelerated rise of permissive ideas on the one hand, and an increasingly conservative political order on the other – is not as difficult to reconcile as it might appear. During the 1950s, while the country was moving to the right politically, social values liberalized. In other words, many of the same people who were applauding the efforts of Senator Joseph McCarthy, casting ballots for Dwight Eisenhower, and heading off to church each Sunday were also raising their children along increasingly "progressive" lines and adopting a sympathetic stance toward psychology and the alcoholic disease model. It would be hard to submit a more apt example than Norman Vincent Peale. Perceived as a conservative, Peale forged a close relationship with Billy Graham's National Association of Evangelicals (NAE), a religious organization with a decidedly conservative tenor.[113] Peale's closeness to Republicans in general, and the Eisenhower administration in particular, prompted Adlai Stevenson to formulate one of his more memorable puns. When asked by a reporter whether it would be appropriate to compare Peale to the apostle Paul, Stevenson told the journalist that he thought "Paul is appealing, and Peale is appalling."[114] On racial issues, as well, Peale showed signs of conservatism. In a well-publicized incident during the late 1950s, Peale advised an African American woman to avoid crossing the color line by refraining from marrying the young white man with whom she was in love.[115]

However, in spite of Peale's political conservatism, he epitomized the therapeutic approach to religion. In *The Power of Positive Thinking* (1952), for example, Peale's chapters included such titles as "Try Prayer Power," "Expect the Best and Get It," "How to Use Faith in Healing," and "How to Get People to Like You."[116] Moreover, as early as

[113] George, Carol V. R. *God's Salesman: Norman Vincent Peale and the Power of Positive Thinking* (New York: Oxford University Press, 1993), pp. 191–2, 200–2.
[114] Diggins, John Patrick. *The Proud Decades: America in War and Peace, 1941–1960* (New York: W. W. Norton & Company, 1989), p. 127.
[115] Workman, William D. *The Case for the South* (New York: Devin-Adair Company, 1960), pp. 214–15. Workman, a sophisticated segregationist who served as a correspondent for the *Charleston News and Courier* and *Newsweek* magazine, used the negative reaction of the African American community to Peale's remarks to highlight what he (Workman) thought to be the potential threat of interracial sex.
[116] Peale, Norman Vincent. *The Power of Positive Thinking* (Greenwich, Conn.: Fawcett Publications, 1952), pp. 51, 93, 144, 190.

FIGURE 1.4. Norman Vincent Peale, author of the best-selling book *The Power of Positive Thinking*, was a leading advocate of pastoral psychology. (Reproduced by permission of The Peale Center for Christian Living.)

1950, Peale was enthusiastically touting the disease model for alcoholism, as well as the twelve-step recovery program already made famous by Alcoholics Anonymous.[117] At that very moment, Peale took a page out of Spock's handbook, urging parents to avoid hemming in their children with "a maddening barrage of 'do's' and 'don't's'" and advising mothers and fathers about the hazards arising from "stern discipline," "harsh commands," and sexual repression.[118] Finally, through his radio program "The Art of Living," a regular advice column in *Look* magazine, and a syndicated column carried in nearly a hundred newspapers nationwide, Peale established himself as one of the country's leading proponents of psychological counseling.[119]

That so few Americans were cognizant of a widening breach between their ideological vision and their personal values – or between Peale's conservative politics and his liberal theology – occurred because these unfolding cultural changes were viewed as neither "permissive" nor "liberal." During the 1950s, as today, many were blinded by the human tendency

[117] Peale, Norman Vincent, and Blanton, Smiley. *The Art of Real Happiness* (New York: Prentice-Hall, 1950), pp. 194–5, 198.
[118] Ibid, p. 37, 56. With respect to sexual repression, Peale writes: "More than one marriage has foundered on the reef of sexual inhibitions unwittingly instilled during childhood."
[119] A detailed account of Peale's promotion of psychological counseling appears in Chapter 3.

to conflate moral rebellion with the cultural fringe. Yet it was precisely their respectability that made the teachings of Benjamin Spock, the disease model for alcoholism, secularized theology, and postwar psychology so threatening to more traditional moral views. They each succeeded in commanding a large and enthusiastic following while fostering attitudes at odds with an older, more restrictive morality. Moreover, these postwar changes were not merely the products of the consumer culture. Instead, they touched on fundamental ideas that were capable of both challenging and redefining the worldview of individuals.

The new literature on child rearing, with its undeniably permissive bent, both reflected and helped change the way parents related to their children. The early success of Liebman and Peale, and the rise of pastoral counseling, both reflected and helped change the way people related to their faith. In addition, the democratization of postwar psychology, along with the medicalization of alcoholism, reflected and helped change the way people thought about themselves. Together, these postwar developments deemphasized sin, guilt, and shame – important bulwarks against permissiveness. What emerged, in short, could be seen as a kind of subversive consensus – the new values Americans were coming to esteem were incompatible with, and undermining of, a conservative moral outlook. Given these conditions and their far-reaching implications, it seems likely that a new postwar vision reflected in the midcentury rise of Spock, Mann, Liebman, and Peale effectively went further in challenging the "old morality" than all the Elvis Presleys, Hugh Hefners, and Jack Kerouacs combined.

So, notwithstanding the nostalgic recollections of essayist Joseph Epstein, it would appear that, at midcentury, the challenge to the traditional moral framework went well beyond the quest for cigarettes and prophylactics on the part of certain youngsters who were underaged and oversexed. From child rearing to theories of addiction, the morals of the country were being contested in all corners thanks to the ascendancy of the sciences and, in particular, the growth of what Philip Rieff called "Psychological Man."[120] These early challenges would bear fruit in the coming decade, when even the most conservative institution of all – the church – would feel the full weight of the Permissive Turn.

---

[120] Rieff, Philip. *The Triumph of the Therapeutic: Uses of Faith After Freud* (Chicago: University of Chicago Press, 1966).

2

Religion

Ballrooms, Bingo, Blue Laws, and Billy Graham – Piety and Secularization in 1950s America

In 1957, when the State Baptist Convention in North Carolina reaffirmed its prohibition of social dancing, students at Wake Forest College, a small Baptist school about seventy-five miles from the Blue Ridge Mountains, responded by going on the proverbial warpath. As *Life* magazine reported, students – on the evening of the convention vote – "tooted bugles, shot firecrackers, burned the convention president in effigy, and danced the bunny hop across campus." The following morning, nearly two thousand students walked out of chapel in protest, whereupon they proceeded to gyrate and croon to "Wake Up, Little Susie" and "There's a Whole Lot of Shaking Going On." One female student stated dryly, "We ought to go and dance with those old men and see if they get all shook up."[1]

The incident at Wake Forest was one of many cultural skirmishes that littered the social landscape during the 1950s. These skirmishes – along with a number of other religious developments ranging from the secularization of Sunday and the dulling of sectarian differences to the growth of interfaith marriages and the reduced emphasis placed on proselytizing – show that the early postwar years were not a time when the religious faith of most Americans was deepening. Instead of being an age of intensified religious belief, the 1950s was a moment – to borrow a rhetorical phrase from German theologian Dietrich Bonhoeffer – when "cheap grace" was on the rise or, as conservative intellectual Richard John Neuhaus might

---

[1] "Students Pan a Dancing Ban: Wake Forest Rebels Against Taboo," *Life* (December 2, 1957), pp. 32–3.

53

otherwise put it, a decade when "a safely neutered Christianity" became a salient feature of modern life.² In other words, putting aside the polemics of Bonhoeffer and Neuhaus, the level of commitment required of believers was becoming less burdensome.

This interpretation is at odds with the standard historical narrative, which in depicting the fifties as a period of consensus, conformity, and conservatism has portrayed the 1950s as a time of religious revival. Surprisingly, many leading thinkers at midcentury were less convinced of the claim of a general religious resurgence than their counterparts of today. In an article written in 1954, William Lee Miller – a professor of religion at Smith College and himself a Presbyterian minister – railed against the shallow spirituality that he believed was becoming prominent in official Washington. "The greatest demonstration of the religious character of this administration," he wrote, "came on July Fourth, which the President [Dwight Eisenhower] told us all to spend [it] as a day of penance and prayer. Then he himself caught four fish in the morning, played eighteen holes of golf in the afternoon, and spent the evening at the bridge table."³

According to Miller, the flippant, unreflective celebration of God undermined genuine piety by promoting spiritual complacency in its stead. "Officialdom prefers religion which is useful for national purposes," observed Miller, "but undemanding and uncomplicated in itself. It also wants religion which is negotiable to the widest possible public. Therefore, the official faith is easily impressed with the spread of any simple external sign of religion, however empty of content."⁴

In his classic book *Protestant-Catholic-Jew*, Will Herberg – probably the most acclaimed religious sociologist of the 1950s – provided a more systematic examination of the fifties' religious scene. Like Miller, Herberg argued that despite surface appearances, the forces of secularization were advancing in the country. Yet, at the same time, Herberg believed that the three predominant faiths – Protestantism, Catholicism, and Judaism – were providing increasing numbers of Americans with a new sense of identity. Consequently, argued Herberg, religion at midcentury was becoming both more and less important. From a sociological standpoint, religion was emerging as an increasingly potent force in the

² Neuhaus, Richard John. "The Public Square," *First Things* (June/July 2006), p. 56.
³ Miller, William Lee. "Piety Along the Potomac," *The Reporter* (August 17, 1954), p. 27.
⁴ Ibid, p. 28.

lives of many Americans; yet from a theological standpoint, a secularizing process was steadily advancing.[5]

Within academia, the apogee of this type of thinking came in the 1960s with the articulation of the so-called secularization thesis. In the tradition of William Miller and Will Herberg, scholars believed that the forces of secularization were in ascendancy. For example, in such classics of religious sociology as Peter Berger's *The Sacred Canopy* and Harvey Cox's *The Secular City*, the authors equated secularization with the ineluctable process of modernization. "As there is a secularization of society and culture," wrote Berger, "so there is a secularization of consciousness. Put simply, this means that the modern West has produced an increasing number of individuals who look upon the world and their own lives without the benefit of religious interpretations." This process, he went on, "may be viewed as a phenomenon of modern societies."[6]

As the sixties came to a close, there was broad agreement among American sociologists that the days of a vibrant religious faith were numbered. It was not that they really thought that religion itself would become extinct, but as they peered into the future, they believed that religion as a force would become more and more marginalized. By the twenty-first century, predicted Berger, "religious believers are likely to be found only in small sects, huddled together to resist a worldwide secular culture."

During the 1970s, however, the errors of this kind of analysis became apparent. Regardless of what one personally thought of Billy Graham, his ability to attract worshipers by the tens of thousands made the predictions of religion's impending demise seem highly exaggerated. Even more damaging, close examinations of church attendance rates clearly shows a greater percentage of Americans were attending church during the 1870s than the 1770s. In keeping with this trajectory, more Americans were trotting off to a house of worship in the 1970s than a hundred years prior.[7] In other words, over the long haul the American people were becoming churched. If religion was on the brink of extinction, then why were church construction, church-sponsored revivals, church finances, and church attendance rates doing so well?

[5] Herberg, Will. *Protestant, Catholic, Jew: An Essay in American Religious Sociology* (Garden City, New York: Doubleday & Company, 1956), passim.
[6] Berger, Peter L. *The Sacred Canopy: Elements of a Sociological Theory of Religion* (New York: Anchor Books, 1967), pp. 107–8.
[7] Finke, Roger, and Stark, Rodney. *The Churching of America, 1776–1990: Winners and Losers in Our Religious Economy* (New Brunswick, NJ: Rutgers University Press, 1992).

FIGURE 2.1. Worshipers gathering in front of small churches such as this one reflect rising rates of church attendance in the 1950s. (Reproduced by permission of the Mississippi Valley Collection, The University of Memphis.)

Adding to these already sizable doubts was the increasing skepticism toward modernization theory. The belief that the Western model of development was ipso facto the most advanced stage of civilization, and the concomitant hope that the nations of the developing world evolve from their "backwardness" by emulating the West, strongly resonated in public policy and academic circles in the quarter century after World War II. Among proponents of secularization theory, writes sociologist Rodney Stark, there was a near universal concordance that "modernization, and especially the rise of science, is the causal engine dragging the gods into retirement."[8] However, during the 1970s modernization theory began to

---

[8] Stark, Rodney. "Secularization: The Myth of Religious Decline," *Fides et Historia* (Summer/Fall 1988), p. 3.

fall out of favor. Scholars increasingly came to see modernization theory as less the product of innovative thinking than the unfortunate offspring of ethnocentric assumptions. As its influence abated, secularization theory – whose association of secularism with modernity owed a great deal to modernization theory – began to decline as well.[9]

Indeed, by the close of the 1980s secularization theory was no longer simply declining, it was in a state of free fall. Through the innovative use of census data, Roger Finke and Rodney Stark were able to show that in the first decade of the twentieth century, religion was more robust in America's cities than in America's rural areas. This finding put secularization theory on its head, because urban areas – the locus of science, modernity, and pluralism – should have been the place where religion was at its lowest ebb.[10] Yet as Finke and Stark observed, contrary to the claims of various social scientists, "The city is surprisingly sacred and pluralism is a friend, not a foe, to religious mobilization."[11]

In a nutshell, sustained research on church attendance rates and the effects of religious pluralism, combined with the decline of modernization theory and a recognition of the Graham phenomenon, convinced historians and sociologists to spurn the claims of secularization. Yet in their justifiable rejection of secularization theory, many scholars have been too indiscriminate. Simply put, they have failed to adequately distinguish between secularization theory and a secularization process.[12] Although scholars are correct in rejecting Berger's earlier claim that religion would soon become a marginal aspect of the life of the West, these same scholars

---

[9] Tipps, Dean C. "Modernization Theory and the Comparative Study of Societies: A Critical Perspective," *Comparative Studies in Society and History* (March 1973), pp. 199–226; Hoover, Dwight. "The Long Ordeal of Modernization Theory," *Prospects* 11 (1986), pp. 407–51; Greeley, Andrew M. *Unsecular Man: The Persistence of Religion* (New York: Schoken Books, 1972); Greeley, Andrew M. *The Denominational Society: A Sociological Approach to Religion in America* (Glenview, Ill.: Scott, Foreman & Company, 1972), pp. 128–55.

[10] This is precisely the point made by Harvey Cox in his classic work, *The Secular City*. As Cox states, secularization began "only when the cosmopolitan confrontation of city living exposed the relativity of the myths and traditions men once thought were unquestionable... In our day the secular metropolis stands as both the pattern of our life together and the symbol of our view of the world." See Cox, Harvey, *The Secular City: A Celebration of its Liberties and an Invitation to its Discipline* (New York: MacMillan Company, 1965), p. 1.

[11] Finke and Stark. "Religious Mobilization in American Cities, 1906," *American Sociological Review* (February, 1988), p. 47.

[12] Stark. "Secularization, RIP," *Sociology of Religion* 60 (1999), pp. 249–73; Ellwood, *The Fifties Spiritual Marketplace*, pp. 1–14.

TABLE 2.1. *Survey of young evangelicals (Behavior considered "always wrong")*

Behavior	1951	1961
Studying on Sunday	13%	2%
Playing pool	26%	4%
Playing cards	77%	33%
Social dancing	91%	66%
Folk dancing (tango, waltz, etc.)	59%	31%
Attending "Hollywood-type" movies	46%	14%
Drinking alcohol	98%	78%

Source: Hunter James Davison, *Evangelicalism: The Coming Generation* (Chicago: The University of Chicago Press, 1987), p. 59.

were amiss in maintaining that religious belief – or, more precisely, the robustness of religious faith – was intensifying during the middle decades of the twentieth century.

Dancing, Smoking, Drinking, and Card Playing

Two surveys of Evangelical students, the first conducted early in the fifties, and the second conducted ten years later in 1961, furnish some anecdotal evidence for the gradual moderation of traditional Christian attitudes that Will Herberg proposed, and that the dancing controversy at Wake Forest College reflected.[13] Both surveys inquired of seniors at Bethel College whether certain behaviors – such as dancing, drinking, or playing cards – were always morally wrong. The results of these survey questions are shown in Table 2.1.

Of course, dancing, smoking, drinking, and card playing are not, in themselves, antithetical to religious belief. However, historically, an important element of American piety has been a general reluctance to embrace the things of this world. "The pleasures of the world have Satan in every corner," warned a magazine article targeted at Adventist teenagers. "The joys that Seventh-Day Adventist youth have are far beyond the fake pleasures of the night-life world."[14] Although doctrinally heterodox, Seventh-Day Adventists espoused a view that resonated

---

[13] Hunter, James Davison. *Evangelicalism: The Coming Generation* (Chicago: The University of Chicago Press, 1987), p. 59.
[14] Fonn, Bel. "Dancing and Feet," *The Youth's Instructor* (May 22, 1956), p. 14.

with conservative Christians. Thus, in 1959, when the Baptist Children's Home in Round Rock, Texas, allowed its students to take part in a school dance, the state convention dismissed the home's administrative board.[15]

Despite the considerable resistance toward dancing, conservative Christian attitudes were softening by midcentury, and, consistent with this process, jeremiads against worldliness were beginning to fall on deaf ears. During the late 1950s, for example, *The Lariat*, the student newspaper at Baylor University (a Baptist institution) featured advertisements for dances that were being sponsored by campus clubs. During this same period, a few conferences within the Lutheran Church (Missouri Synod) passed resolutions that effectively reversed their traditional opposition to social dancing.[16]

Evolving attitudes toward movies were also indicative of a gradual softening of traditional attitudes. As the surveys of Bethel College students indicate, the patronage of "Hollywood movies" remained a sensitive subject to many conservative Christians. Hollywood, after all, was almost synonymous with sex, drugs, and Babylonian excess. Yet just as there was a loosening, in some quarters, of religious attitudes toward dancing, one also saw a growing tolerance of motion pictures in postwar America. Whereas in 1924 Methodist leaders were warning their parishioners "against attendance" of "theatrical or motion picture performances... all of which have been found to be antagonistic to vital piety, promotive of worldliness, and especially pernicious to youth," by the late 1940s *The Christian Advocate* – the official magazine of the Methodist Church – began carrying short reviews of the latest movies.[17] Indeed, even the creation of the Legion of Decency, a Roman Catholic organization that sought to suppress vulgarity in films, can be seen not as an

[15] Brewer, Anita. Baptist Replace Board in School Dance Fuss, dancing file, Southern Baptist Convention Library and History Archives.

[16] Van Zandt Baptist Association Resolution, February 25, 1960, dancing file, Southern Baptist Historical Association. Also see "Protestant Panorama," *Christianity Today* (February 16, 1959), p. 28.

[17] Berckman, Edward M. "The Changing Attitudes of Protestant Churches to Movies and Television," *Encounter* (Summer 1980), p. 296. Berckman also points out that, in time, this loosening attitude toward Hollywood would moderate the perspective of Billy Graham. Where Graham would declare in a 1960 speech: "The main themes of radio, television, and motion pictures center largely in selfishness, materialism, revenge, greedy manipulation, and worldliness in all its phases, things with no spiritual, permanent value. They all pass away quickly"; he would later appear as a guest on Johnny Carson's *Tonight Show*, and by 1971, "he contributed to the satirical merriment of *Laugh-In*," a satirical television program (see same article, pp. 299–300).

outright rejection but as the Church's reluctant acceptance of Hollywood. Founded in 1934 and reaching the height of its influence during the early postwar years, the Legion claimed some measure of success in making films consistent with wholesome entertainment.[18]

The Weakening Hold of Religion in America

Admittedly, during the 1950s, prohibitions against dancing, drinking, movies, and makeup seldom touched those belonging to mainline denominations. The intended recipients of such messages tended to be Christians of a more conservative stripe. Yet among the larger population of Christians, including members of mainline churches, other prohibitions against worldly pleasures were shrugged off with increasing ease. The proliferation of bingo – described by *Newsweek* in 1954 as a "national craze" – is illustrative of the weakening hold of religion in American private life.[19] Although its roots hearken back to the nineteenth century, the modern game of bingo, and even the term *bingo*, was born during the early days of the Great Depression thanks to the efforts of New York entrepreneur Edwin S. Lowe.[20] In 1931, a Catholic priest in Pennsylvania – desperately needing to raise money for his church – received assistance from Lowe in introducing the game to his congregation. The game was an instant hit and word of its success quickly spread to other parishes. By the end of the 1930s, bingo had become an important source of revenue for Catholic parochial schools and charities throughout the country.[21]

The popularity of this simple game continued to grow during the 1940s. However, it was not until the Eisenhower years that bingo became so large that it began to emerge as a divisive political issue. By the mid-1950s, *Reader's Digest* was describing bingo as "big business," and telling its readers that, according to moderate estimates, "Americans pay nearly a billion dollars a year to play the game – more than they pay to watch baseball, football, basketball, and boxing combined."[22]

---

[18] Black, Gregory D. *The Catholic Crusade Against the Movies, 1940–1975* (Cambridge, UK: Cambridge University Press, 1998); Corliss, Joseph. "The Legion of Decency," *Film Comment* (Summer 1968), pp. 25–54.

[19] "Bingo's Shadow Over Politics: Game Widely Outlawed, Widely Played – What to Do?" *U.S. News & World Report* (March 18, 1955), p. 40.

[20] Daley, Robert. "Bingo!: An Account of its Discovery and History, but Not of its Prevention or Cure," *Catholic Digest* (March 1958).

[21] Ibid, p. 20.

[22] Davidson, Bill. "Bingo is Getting too Big," *Reader's Digest* (March 1955), p. 102.

The growth of bingo gave rise to new controversies. Although the game was illegal in all but a handful of states, hundreds of thousands of Americans flouted the law every day. With their newspaper ads, outdoor signs, and chartered bus service, operators of bingo games – usually Catholic parishes and veterans' groups – made no attempt to mask their efforts. In 1954, when authorities in Campbell, Ohio, began cracking down on church bingo, the community went into an uproar. Within days Mayor Michael Kovach ordered his police chief "not to interfere or make an arrest of any bingo game or other type of lottery operated by a church or charitable organization...."[23] The same year, Deputy New York Police Inspector Louis Goldberg began initiating crackdowns against church bingo games. Despite receiving support from both *The New York Times* and the Protestant Council of Churches, Goldberg was soon reprimanded by his superiors, and then, for his labors, demoted to captain. Shortly thereafter, Goldberg resigned from the police force, bringing his thirty-six-year career in law enforcement to a close.[24]

The political fallout over bingo proved even more explosive in neighboring New Jersey. In the 1953 contest between Democratic candidate Robert Meyner and Republican nominee Paul Troast, bingo became a major issue in the race for governor. In the campaign, Meyner came out strongly behind bingo, employing such catchy slogans as "Vote for Meyner for Sure Bingo" and "You Shall Always Play."[25] The strategy apparently succeeded. As an article in *Newsweek* put it: "Meyner told the Bingo-conscious people that a vote for him was a vote for Bingo. Bingo and Meyner both won heavily."[26] In discussing the aftermath of the Meyner-Troast race, *U.S. News & World Report* described bingo as "the principal issue in that campaign."[27]

In Connecticut the issue of gambling may, once again, have played a pivotal role in a gubernatorial election. Thanks to a 1939 law, bingo – although legalized – was severely restricted in the prizes it could award to its winners. As a result, devotees of bingo remained a fairly small cadre, with few if any "high rollers" within its ranks. In 1951, partially in response to these restrictions, a coalition of citizens – composed of

---

[23] Parish Hold Bingo Game Despite Police Raid Earlier in Week, May 3, 1954, Bingo vertical file, Catholic News Service, Washington, D.C.

[24] "Gambling: Bing, Bang, Bingo," *Newsweek* (September 20, 1954), p. 32.

[25] Olsen, Eddie. "Bingo Making a Comeback after Long Decline," *The Bergen Record* (April 9, 1996), p. a8.

[26] "Gambling: Bing, Bang, Bingo," *Newsweek* (September 20, 1954), p. 33.

[27] "Bingo's Shadow Over Politics," p. 40.

veterans' groups, firefighters, and Roman Catholics – lobbied the legis-
lature to pass a bill that would liberalize the state's gambling laws.[28]
However, Connecticut Governor John Lodge refused to sign on. When
the governor sought reelection in 1954, the gambling issue resurfaced.
While Lodge stayed true to form and opposed the extension of gambling,
his opponent Democrat Abraham Ribicoff indicated his willingness to
sign a "good bill" if elected. In the end, Ribicoff defeated Lodge by a
razor-thin margin of less than 2,800 votes – and if *The Christian Century* is to be believed, Ribicoff's surprising strength in some traditionally
Republican strongholds was largely due to the gambling issue.[29]

Today, it is hard to understand how a game as innocuous as bingo
could provoke such heated controversy; but during the 1950s, when
religious conservatism – although in decline – remained a formidable force
in American life, the battle over bingo became a small campaign within a
larger cultural war. From the perspective of most Protestant leaders, bingo
was a deceptively banal incarnation of gambling, and gambling under
any other name was still a sin. The fact that the proceeds were typically
channeled toward such noteworthy purposes as funding hospitals and
supporting parochial schools meant little to these social crusaders. As
Reverend John Spradley elaborated in 1953 upon learning that twenty-
seven members of his Pontiac, Michigan, congregation had been caught
playing bingo, "Our church is against all forms of gambling, no matter
how small the gain," because gambling would likely lead "to other forms
of worldliness."[30]

Although bingo temporarily deepened the already extant chasm
between Protestant and Catholic leaders – with most Catholic priests
firmly in favor of bingo and most Protestant ministers implacably
opposed – it would be mistaken to believe that so clear a division existed
among the laity. In most referenda, bingo received strong support from
ordinary Catholic and Protestant voters. In 1953, for example, New Jersey voters backed a measure permitting local communities to legalize
bingo games by an overwhelming three to one margin. Several years

---

[28] Savino, Guy. "Rigid Law, No Cash Prizes Curb Bingo in Connecticut," *New Jersey
Evening News* (December 6, 1954). NJEN Collection.
[29] "Did the Gamblers Oust Gov. Lodge?" *The Christian Century* (November 24, 1954),
p. 1443.
[30] "Parson Raps Women Gambler," (April 13, 1953), Bingo Vertical File, *Boston Herald-
Traveler* Newspaper Morgue, Beebe Communications Library, Boston University (hereafter cited as BHTN Morgue).

later, in New York State, a similar measure passed by a comfortable six hundred thousand votes.[31]

On one level, the legalization of bingo – and even the toleration of illegal bingo – should not be construed as a sign of secularization. The deinstitutionalization of religion – that is, the decoupling of religion from law – is not incompatible with a high, or even an increasing, degree of religious piety. Thus, what is most important about the bingo battles of the 1950s was not the decline of legal barriers, but the ever-growing popularity of bingo itself. Far from simply tolerating it, more and more Americans partook in this game of chance. While 7 percent of Americans in 1945 admitted to playing bingo for money, by 1950 the proportion doing so had soared more than threefold to 22 percent, making bingo more popular than such pastimes as horse racing, sports gambling, and card playing.[32]

On the one hand, the increased willingness of the seniors at Bethel College to partake in forbidden pleasures does not easily lend itself to a sweeping generalization. The experiences of Christians attending a religious college during the fifties obviously differed from the experiences of the larger population. However, in important ways, both groups – the Bethel students and the larger population – underwent a similar process of moderation as the hold of an earlier, more orthodox piety was slowly losing its grip. The increasing acceptance among young Christian conservatives of dancing, card playing, alcohol drinking, and "Hollywood movies" suggests that the strict, "otherworldly" component of the Christian message was probably waning during the fifties. Moreover, on the other hand, the explosive growth of bingo among millions of Americans parallels a similar dynamic at work within the larger population.

The Blue Laws and the Sabbath

Consistent with the secularization of play was an increased defiance of Sunday blue laws and the steady erosion of Sabbath-day observance. A legacy from the nineteenth century, blue laws were implemented to encourage religious observance by curbing commercial activity on

---

[31] "526 Areas Ask Bingo," *The New York Times* (November 13, 1958), p. 26.

[32] Lexis-Nexis, Reference (Polls & Surveys), Accession number: 0033229 for May 1950. By contrast, only 8 percent of Americans in 1950 admitted betting on horses, 18 percent admitted to betting on sport events, and 21 percent of respondents admitted to playing cards or dice for money.

Sundays.[33] However, due to the proliferation of suburban-based dis-
count stores, along with the emergence of less traditional attitudes toward
Sabbath-day observance, the fifties saw businesses and consumers increasingly willing to conduct their affairs on Sundays. In Lincoln, Nebraska,
when a new Hinky Dinky supermarket first opened it doors on a Sunday in 1952, more than twelve hundred people stood waiting in a line.[34]
"The growing trend toward Sunday business has become one of the most
controversial issues in retailing," noted a 1956 article in *The New York
Times*. "In most Eastern states the openings have been confined to small
shops, particularly suburban highway stores. In the Middle and Far West,
however, some major department stores have been opening their ware-
houses to Sunday sales."[35]

Surveys sponsored by the Chicago-based Super Market Institute corroborated the popular impression that Sunday shopping was replacing
the prohibition. In 1950, only about 5 percent of all supermarkets were
open on Sundays. Four years later, that figure had tripled to 16 percent;
and of the approximately twelve hundred supermarkets opening in 1957,
more than a quarter (27 percent) did business on Sunday.[36]

Of course, the only reason Sunday hours caught on with merchants
was because Sunday shopping proved popular with consumers. Accordingly, those supermarkets that kept their doors open seven days a week
found Sunday to be their third best day.[37] In Paramus, New Jersey, the
three dozen retailers affiliated with the Suburban Merchants Association
reportedly received 25 to 40 percent of their weekly volume on Sunday.[38]

Predictably, traditionalists reacted to the secularization of Sunday
with alarm. The Third Order of St. Francis, a mixed community of

[33] For a history of blue laws, see Raucher, Alan, "Sunday Business and the Decline of
Sunday Closing Laws: A Historical Overview," *Journal of Church and State* 36 (Winter
1994), pp. 13–33.
[34] "Sunday Afternoon Open House Best Grand Opening We've Ever Had," *The Progressive
Grocer* (March 1953), p. 92.
[35] "Sunday Business Embroils Stores," *The New York Times* (May 20, 1956), Section III,
p. 1.
[36] Cited from Kenny, Thomas, "Sunday Selling Spreads," *Dun's Review and Modern Industry* (February 1958), p. 38.
[37] Cited from unpublished internal reports of the Super Market Institute, now called the
Food Market Institute. (Food Market Institute, Washington, D.C.). Pamphlet titled
"Facts About New Super Markets" for the years 1954–8; and "The Super Market
Industry Speaks" for years 1950 and 1958.
[38] Kenny, Thomas. "Sunday Selling Spreads," *Dun's Review of Modern Industry* (February
1958), p. 40

both lay Catholics and ordained priests, distributed hundreds of thousands of posters and stickers featuring the slogan: "Stop! Don't Shop on Sunday."[39] In a flourish of hyperbole, Reverend Melvin M. Forney, leader of the Lord's Day Alliance, called Sabbath-breaking the "No. 1 problem in America today."[40]

Despite such complaints, the secularization of Sundays continued. Even President Eisenhower was chided by a local newspaper for having gone turkey hunting on his Gettysburg farm in violation of local blue laws. And although Eisenhower subsequently refrained from Sunday hunts, more Americans than ever regarded blue laws as little more than the anachronistic legacy of a moralistic past.[41] Although not putting it quite so brashly, most seemed to agree with a Midwestern home builder who declared, "It would be practically un-American to deny the public the right to view homes on Sundays. It has become a national family habit: go to church, grab a bite to eat, and go out together and see about one of the most important investments they'll ever make."[42]

The Waning Influence of Religious Doctrine

The dulling of sectarian differences and, concomitantly, the rise of explicit interfaith cooperation offers us additional evidence of the waning influence of religious doctrine. The growth of Brotherhood Week, an interdenominational celebration, was an obvious indication of this burgeoning ecumenical spirit during the early Cold War years. Sponsored by the National Conference of Christians and Jews (NCCJ), and composed of clergy from Jewish, Catholic, and Protestant faiths, Brotherhood Week was first created during the mid-1930s. It was not until the immediate aftermath of World War II, however, that Brotherhood Week became a visible part of the national culture. Whereas in earlier years Presidents Roosevelt and Truman had done little more than issue annual proclamations on behalf of the weeklong observance, in 1946 Truman joined former Minnesota Governor Harold Stassen, a Republican, to serve as the chairman of Brotherhood Week. Supplementing these efforts were Supreme Court Justices Harlan Stone (a Protestant), Frank Murphy (a Catholic), and Felix Frankfurter (a Jew). In front of a battery of journalists

---

[39] Shea, James M. "Trafficking on the Lord's Day," *America* (August 28, 1954), p. 517.

[40] "On the Seventh Day?," *Newsweek* (April 21, 1958), p. 72.

[41] As cited by Ecenbarger, William, "Blue Laws: It was the Day Our Nation Stood Still," *Chicago Tribune* (July 5, 1987), p. 1C.

[42] "On the Seventh Day?," *Newsweek* (April 21, 1958), p. 72.

at the U.S. Supreme Court building, the three Justices praised the efforts of Stassen, Truman, and others to turn Brotherhood Week into a national celebration.[43] In the three succeeding years, James Winant, the wartime ambassador to Britain; Robert P. Patterson, the former Secretary of War; and Nelson Rockefeller, an heir to the Rockefeller fortune and a future vice president of the United States, assumed the chairmanship of the annual interfaith drives.[44]

Hollywood was keen to join the effort. Under the supervision of studio executive Spyros Skouras, the NCCJ produced a short film titled "The American Creed" in 1946. Featuring such celebrities as Ingrid Bergman, Jimmy Stewart, Katherine Hepburn, and Shirley Temple, the newsreel urged members of the moviegoing audience to sign a "Brotherhood Pledge" and participate in Brotherhood Week activities. In 1946, "The American Creed" appeared in more than ten thousand movie houses to an estimated audience of eighty-five million.[45]

Further assistance for Brotherhood Week came from Madison Avenue. The Advertising Council began promoting Brotherhood Week in 1946, and a handful of radio executives – including William Paley, president of the Columbia Broadcasting System (CBS), as well as the heads of the National Broadcasting Company (NBC), the American Broadcasting Company (ABC), and the Mutual Broadcasting System (MBS) – joined in the publicity effort. By the end of the year, stories about the Brotherhood Campaign had appeared on twenty-seven network programs, more than two thousand local programs, and "via 15,452 spot announcements." Equally impressive, by the close of the 1940s the nation's advertisers had dedicated, in airtime and advertising space, an estimated $3.5 million per year to the promotion of Brotherhood Week.[46]

This joint mobilization of public officials and public relations proved enormously successful. Whereas in 1942 only eight hundred communities held activities in honor of Brotherhood Week, just six years later Brotherhood Week was being celebrated in all fifty states – six thousand communities in all – as religious pluralism became a national priority.[47]

[43] Ashworth, Robert A. "Brotherhood Week in 1946" (Unpublished article), pp. 1–6, box 5, Papers of the National Conference of Christians and Jews, Social Welfare History Archives, University of Minnesota (hereafter cited as NCCJ Papers).

[44] Ibid.

[45] Ibid.

[46] Ashworth, *The Story of the National Conference of Christians and Jews* (unpublished history), box 7, NCCJ Papers.

[47] "Churches to Stress Brotherhood Aim," *The New York Times* (February 19, 1949). President Truman, in 1951, would serve as the Honorary Chairman of the National

Religious pluralism, of course, is not synonymous with secularization. This is to say, pluralism and traditional belief are capable of flourishing side by side, provided that significant theological differences are
not glossed over or trivialized. However, as sociologist Will Herberg
observed, America's postwar conception of pluralism demanded that
communicants mute their religious distinctiveness. In this country, he
explained, "controversial discussion of religion in which each participant
confesses and bears witness to his convictions, is felt to be undesirable
and 'un-American,' since it might seem to accentuate 'ideological' differences rather than stress commitment to the shared values and ideals of
the American Way of Life."[48] Accordingly, the Brotherhood Week program explicitly cautioned celebrants against engaging in discussions of
theology or church policy.

Indeed, in the immediate postwar period, the deemphasis of religious
doctrine had become so great that in 1946 more than four out of ten delegates at the Federal Council of Churches (FCC) – at the time, the largest
religious organization in the country – voted to award full membership
to the Universalist Church of America. From a theological standpoint,
full membership raised a very thorny issue. The FCC was a self-described
Christian federation. The preamble to its constitution required belief in
"Jesus Christ as . . . divine Lord and Savior."[49] Yet the Universalists did
not accept the divinity of Christ as doctrine. As such, it could not be
regarded as a truly Christian religion.[50] Nonetheless, many Protestant
leaders – indeed, nearly half of the delegates to the FCC – were willing to overlook these doctrinal differences for the sake of civility and
united action. During the fifties, this very generalized civic faith was
perhaps best expressed by none other than President Eisenhower. "Our
form of government makes no sense," he famously declared, "unless
it is founded on a deeply felt religious faith, and I don't care what
it is."[51]

Conference of Christians and Jews. In a message to celebrants in 1950, Truman stated,
"We are a united people of diverse origins. Our united strength enables us to face with
confident hope the evil forces that have been unleashed in the world." (See "Interfaith
Amity is Hailed at Rally," *The New York Times* [September, 25, 1950], p. 20).

[48] Herberg, *Protestant, Catholic, Jew: An Essay in American Religious Sociology* (New
York: Anchor Books, 1955, 1960), p. 245.

[49] Miller, Russell E. *The Larger Hope: The Second Century of the Universalist Church in
America, 1870–1970* (Boston: Unitarian Universalist Association, 1985), pp. 617.

[50] Ibid, pp. 608–22.

[51] Silk, Mark. "Notes on the Judeo-Christian Tradition in America," *American Quarterly*
(Spring 1984), p. 65.

The Rise in Interfaith Marriage

During the postwar years, interfaith cooperation extended out of the public square and into the private sphere. This process was most clearly seen
in the rise of interfaith marriages. Certainly, interfaith nuptials existed
prior to the 1940s, but during the postwar period they seemed to have
occurred more often. Precisely how frequently they were happening is
something that we probably will never know. However, the best evidence
to date suggests that the intermarriage rate between Catholics and non-
Catholics had been climbing briskly, from the 1920s through the 1980s.[52]

During the forties and fifties, Catholic–Protestant unions received the
most attention. Then, as today, the Catholic Church sanctioned mixed
marriages – but with certain qualifications. First, prior to marriage the
non-Catholic partner would have to promise not to try to convert his or
her spouse to a religion outside of the Catholic faith. Second, and more
significantly, both partners would be obliged to raise any as yet unborn
offspring within the Catholic Church. At a time when it was deemed impo-
lite to underscore fundamental religious differences, the Catholic determination to perpetuate the faith seemed divisive and autocratic. Hence, in
May 1950 the Northern Baptist Convention passed a resolution that repu-
diated "the Roman Catholic claim to authoritarianism in marriage and
declare it an invasion of the principle of religious and social freedom."[53]
Similarly, the Southern Baptists, in a resolution they approved in June
1951, called on their members to "maintain their own religious freedom
and guarantee the religious freedom of their children."[54] The Disciples
of Christ and the United Church of Christ soon followed suit, issuing
similar statements.[55]

Especially revealing was a pastoral letter issued by the Southern Presbyterian Church. In accordance with the prevailing spirit of postwar pluralism, the pastoral letter's hostility toward Presbyterian–Catholic marriages
stemmed not from intolerance per se but rather from the offense Presbyterians took toward what they perceived to be Catholic intolerance. For
Southern Presbyterians – as for most other Protestant denominations that
spoke out on the issue – the problem with Protestant–Catholic marriages

---

[52] Kalmun, Matthus. "Shifting Boundaries: Trends in Religious Educational Homogony,"
American Sociological Review, Vol. 16, No. 6 (1991), pp. 786–800.

[53] Pike, James A. *If You Marry Outside Your Faith: Counsel on Mixed Marriages* (New
York: Harper & Row, 1959), p. 82.

[54] Ibid, p. 78.

[55] Ibid, pp. 78–9; 83–7.

seemed to be less the prospect of two people from divergent religious traditions coming together in matrimonial union than from the prospect that the Catholic partner would hold a greater say in the religious upbringing of any future child. "In view of these facts," stated the pastoral letter, "the General Assembly counsels Presbyterians to refrain from marriage with Roman Catholics as long as the demands and rulings of that Church remain unchanged."[56]

Conspicuously absent from most of the resolutions and pastoral letters of the leading Protestant churches were warnings against interdenominational marriages, nuptials that bonded a member of one Protestant denomination with a member of another. To be sure, most denominations expressed opposition to marrying outside the church, but to the majority of Protestants, "marrying outside the church" actually meant "marrying outside" the Protestant faith. Although denouncing Protestant–Catholic marriages, most denominations expressed little concern over Methodist–Congregationalist marriages, or Lutheran–Baptist or Presbyterian–Quaker marriages. In fact, were it not for the insistence that future children be raised within the Catholic faith, it is likely that most denominational leaders would have had few qualms with Catholic–Protestant marriages.[57] In other words, within the large tent of American Protestantism, doctrinal differences, at least when it came to holy matrimony, were generally downplayed, evaded, or ignored.

When it came to mixed religious marriages during the 1950s, it is likely that the most rapid growth occurred not among Catholics but among Protestants. For example, according to an internal study conducted in the mid-1950s by the United Lutheran Church in America, the proportion of Lutherans marrying outside the denomination rose considerably, "especially after World War II." Grouped in five-year periods, the study found that "the percentage of all such mixed marriages" remained essentially flat between 1936 and 1945 (rising from 46 to 47 percent). However, the latter half of the 1940s witnessed a significant increase, with the percentage of Lutherans marrying non-Lutherans rising from 47 to 58 percent – an increase of nearly a quarter.[58]

---

[56] Ibid, p. 82.

[57] A notable exception to that trend would be the Lutheran Church (Missouri Synod), which, in its Resolution on mixed marriages, passed in June 1953, refers to the Roman Catholic faith as "the soul-destroying religion of the antichrist." See Pike, *If You Marry Outside Your Faith*, p. 82.

[58] Bossard, James H. S., and Letts, Harold C. "Mixed Marriages Involving Lutherans – A Research Report," *Marriage and Family Living* (November, 1956), pp. 308–10.

Unfortunately, the Lutheran study stands as the only systematic examination during the early postwar years of intermarriage involving a Protestant denomination. The dearth of such studies, coupled with a corresponding lack of interest on the part of the religious press, is revealing. It suggests that at midcentury interdenominational marriages were less stigmatized, and probably more frequent, than Protestant–Catholic unions. Therefore, it would seem that increasing numbers of Americans during the 1950s were really taking pluralism to heart. On the subject of marriage – one of life's most important questions – religious doctrine seemed to be less essential to Protestant and Catholic alike.

The Revised Standard Version of the Bible

The publication in 1952 of the Revised Standard Version (RSV) of the Bible was an enormously successful endeavor and, as such, could be seen as the counterevidence to the basic argument of this chapter. However, upon closer examination, one could argue that what the RSV signified – or, more precisely, what its enormous popularity signified – was the paucity of a deeply rooted attachment to Holy Scripture. In itself, the release of the newly revised Bible was not particularly novel. Fifty-one years earlier, in 1901, the Church of England had published a contemporary translation of the Bible. Two decades later, the Smith-Goodspeed Bible Translation appeared on the shelves of American bookstores, and, during the 1930s, a translation of the New Testament by Biblical scholar Charles B. Williams became available.[59] However, these earlier tinkerings had never resonated with the American public, leaving the King James Version in a virtually unassailable position. However, with the release of the RSV Bible in 1952 it quickly became obvious that the King James Version would finally be up against a worthy contender.

Contributing to the success of the RSV Bible was what, up to that time, may have been the most ambitious promotional campaign in the history of American publishing. On the evening of September 30, 1952, more than three thousand congregations across the nation, involving approximately two million people, celebrated the release of the RSV Bible.[60] In Pittsburgh more than fifteen thousand people gathered at Forbes Field

[59] "This Century's Bibles," *The Saturday Review* (November 10, 1956), p. 54.
[60] "New Bible Issued; Churches Hail It," *The New York Times* (October 1, 1952), p. 31; "Millions Hail New Version Bible," *The Christian Century* (October 15, 1952), p. 1181.

for an interdenominational service.[61] The promotional campaign for the RSV Bible cost an astounding half-million dollars, and involved television and radio commercials, 1.5-million circulars, and the services of a Madison Avenue public relations firm.[62] Within two days of the publication date, the first printing of the RSV Bible – one million copies in all – had sold out.[63] John Wesley Lord, the Boston-area bishop of the Methodist Church, praised the new translation for "rendering what may well prove to be the most significant contribution of the twentieth century to the religious peoples of the earth." Dr. James Muilenburg of Yale Divinity School was more succinct but no less effusive; he declared it to be "the greatest development in the century for Christianity."[64] Over the next few years, acceptance of the new Bible grew rapidly. By the close of 1956, the RSV had sold nearly three million copies. "No other regular book edition, religious or otherwise, has ever come close to this two-year record," boasted the National Council of Churches in a public statement.[65] By 1956, more than two dozen Protestant denominations, representing some thirty-million worshipers, were using the RSV Bible in their church schools and lesson plans.[66]

Although extensive, support for the RSV Bible was less than unanimous. Less than one month after the date of publication, a Gallup survey asked respondents, "From what you have heard or read, do you approve or disapprove of the new changes in wordings in the new edition of the Bible?" According to the results, 28 percent of respondents were favorable; 22 percent were unfavorable; 17 percent held no opinion; and the remainder, 33 percent, were ignorant of the controversy.[67]

The strongest source of opposition came from a comparatively small group of Christian newspapers and conservative ministers. The Indiana-based *Ambassador For Christ*, a conservative Christian journal with a

---

[61] Thuesen, Peter J. *In Discordance with the Scriptures: American Protestant Battles over Translating the Bible* (New York: Oxford University Press, 1999), p. 90.

[62] Fey, Harold E. "The New Best-Seller," *The Saturday Review* (December 20, 1952), p. 98.

[63] "Sales of New Bible Reported a Record," *The New York Times* (November 30, 1952), p. 85.

[64] "New Bible Issued," p. 31.

[65] "For Release: Thursday, Sept. 30, 1954." Princeton Theological Seminary. RSV Papers. Box 15. Folder: "1956: RSV Publicity, Criticism, and Praise."

[66] "Denominational Use of Revised Standard Version in the Curriculum." RSV Papers. Box 15. Folder: "1956: RSV Publicity, Criticism, and Praise."

[67] Chew, Peter. "The Great Bible Controversy," *Look* (February 10, 1953), p. 97.

national distribution, claimed the new translation "most flagrantly slants, twists, deletes, assaults, and mistranslates God's Word." It went on to characterize the work as "a plain fraud, a real weapon to be used by Satan."[68] Reverend Martin Luther Hux, a Baptist minister from North Carolina, went even further demonstrating his outrage. He ripped a page from the revised Book of Isaiah and burned it.[69]

However, the most sustained criticism came from fundamentalist minister Carl McIntire, the founder of the 200,000-member American Council of Christian Churches. In his widely distributed pamphlet "The New Bible, Revised Standard Version: Why Christians Should Not Accept It," McIntire insisted that the translators of the RSV Bible had "consistently removed or toned down references to Christ's deity." In other tirades, McIntire charged that "it would be nothing short of a calamity of infinite proportions if the book should be accepted by the English-speaking world."[70]

For all of the noisy protests and scorched-earth rhetoric, the most important fact about the RSV controversy was neither the level nor the intensity of the organized opposition but, rather, the relatively "smooth sailing" that the translation received. Indeed, many mainline Protestants seemed to be amused by all the fuss Fundamentalists were making of the RSV translation. For instance, in October 1953, an article in *Motive*, a publication targeted to Methodist college students, poked fun at the supposed paranoia of the RSV critics. It featured a photograph of a minister and six well-scrubbed young people sitting around a table. The caption beside the picture read, "The panel agrees that the Revised Standard Version was not written by communists."[71] That President Truman, in a highly publicized ceremony, was awarded the first official copy of the revised Bible was an indication of the high esteem in which leading cultural figures held the new Bible.[72]

In their classic "Middletown" study, Robert and Helen Lynd observed that during the late 1920s, there was "a general feeling in Middletown

[68] Farmer, William R. "The RSV Arrives in Coatesville," *Union Seminary Quarterly Review* (March 1953), pp. 19–20.
[69] "Burns Page of New Bible: North Carolina Baptist Minister Brands the Book 'Fraud,'" *The New York Times* (December 1, 1952), p. 69.
[70] "Sales of New Bible Reported a Record," *The New York Times* (November 30, 1952); Farmer, "The RSV Arrives in Coatesville," *Union Seminary Quarterly Review* (March 1953), p. 18.
[71] "Student Night Life," *Motive* (October, 1953), p. 25.
[72] "President Truman Gets First Copy of New Revised Version from National Council of Churches," *The New York Times* (September 27, 1952), p. 12.

that the book [the Bible] is perfect and free from inconsistencies." Such reverence for the "Good Book" was prevalent among old and young alike. In surveying the town's high school students, the Lynds found about two-thirds of the youngsters agreed with the statement, "The Bible is a sufficient guide to all the problems of modern life."[73]

Although apparently widespread during the twenties, such sentiments probably were not reflective of general attitudes during the 1950s. According to a 1954 survey, for example, fewer than half of Americans polled were able to name even one of the first four books of the New Testament.[74] Less than half of the respondents could correctly name the first book of the Bible, and a minority of respondents were able to correctly name two prophets from the Old Testament.[75] Even more amazing, only about one-third of Americans (34 percent) knew who delivered the Sermon on the Mount.[76] While no survey data indicate whether this sort of scriptural ignorance was rising or declining during the 1950s, or whether it was higher or lower than it had been during the 1920s, the sheer volume of Biblical illiteracy is revealing. It suggests that for all of the prayer breakfasts and popular religious programming, and despite the higher levels of church attendance, the masses of Americans at midcentury were not faithfully reading their Bibles.[77] In 1952, when Ben Gaffin and Associates asked a nationally representative sample "Do you believe in the Trinity – the Father, Son and Holy Ghost?" nine out of ten Americans said they did. However, twenty-nine months later, when Americans were asked "What is the Holy Trinity?" roughly four out of ten could answer correctly.[78]

73 As cited in Hunter, James Davison, *Evangelicalism: The Coming Generation* (Chicago: University of Chicago Press), p. 22.
74 Herberg, *Protestant, Catholic, Jew: An Essay in American Religious Sociology* (New York: Doubleday & Company, 1955), p. 14; and Reeves, Thomas C. *The Empty Church: The Suicide of Liberal Christianity* (New York: The Free Press, 1996), p. 124.
75 *Survey by Gallup Organization, November 11–November 16, 1954.* Retrieved July 20, 2008, from the iPOLL Databank, The Roper Center for Public Opinion Research, University of Connecticut. Online at: http://www.ropercenter.uconn.edu/ipoll.html.
76 Reeves, *The Empty Church*, p. 124.
77 During the 1950s, Bishop Fulton Sheen's "Life is Worth Living" was one of the most popular television programs on the air, reaching as many as thirty million viewers a week and, in one year, beating out "Milton Berle's Texaco Star Theatre" in their ratings war. See Bernstein, Jacob, "Father Albert's Pulpit Show," *Miami New Times* (September 16, 1999), 1 Features. Sheen also made the covers of *Time*, *Life*, and *Look* magazines as reported in Ruehlmann, Bill, "Find Food for Thought on the Menu in Works by Sheen, Rice, Cairns," *The Virginia Pilot* (October 11, 1998), p. J3.
78 *Survey by Ben Gaffin and Associates, June, 1952.* Retrieved March 10, 2009, from the iPOLL Databank, The Roper Center for Public Opinion Research, University

Needless to say, conservative Christians were inclined to take their
Bible-reading more seriously than the general population. As an article in
Newsweek reported, in the summer of 1955 the Southern Baptist Convention held its annual "Sword Drill" – a competition that drew its name
from a passage in Ephesians 6:17: ". . . the sword of the Spirit, which is
the Word of God." On the referee's instruction to "Draw Swords!" Baptist youth would brandish their Bibles, awaiting the next command. The
referee would toss out a trivia question, and then – upon yelling the order
"Charge!" – the youthful competitors were granted eight seconds to find
the appropriate passage in the Bible. On the day the *Newsweek* reporter
showed up, one girl, a high school junior from Knoxville, Tennessee,
needed only three seconds to answer the question: "Where in the Bible
is it written that all people have sinned?" The correct passage, located in
Isaiah 53:6, read: "All we like sheep have gone astray."[79]

Then, as today, the Biblical familiarity needed to excel at the "Sword
Drill" is most impressive; and in the summer of 1955, some five hundred
thousand Bible-toting youths took part in the annual competitions.[80]
Inasmuch as the overall membership of the Southern Baptist Convention
stood at nearly 8.5 million people in 1955, that meant one in seventeen
members – and certainly a substantial portion of Southern Baptist teens –
had competed in the annual "Sword Drill" competition.[81]

However, outside the world of religious conservatives, detailed knowledge of the Bible was not as highly prized. Indeed, a pejorative term arose
during the forties and fifties among some theological liberals to describe
avid Bible-reading fundamentalists: "bibliolatry."[82] As the expression
implies, a Christian guilty of bibliolatry was essentially guilty of wor-
shiping the Bible, thereby violating the First Commandment. From the
perspective of mainline Protestants, the severe veneration of the Bible by
fundamentalists – their insistence that it was without error and must be

of Connecticut. Online at: http://www.ropercenter.uconn.edu.proxy.lib.fsu.edu/ipoll.
html. *Survey by Gallup Organization, November 11–November 16, 1954.* Retrieved
March 10, 2009, from the iPOLL Databank, The Roper Center for Public Opinion Research, University of Connecticut. Online at: http://www.ropercenter.uconn.edu.
proxy.lib.fsu.edu/ipoll.html.
[79] "Armed with the Gospel," *Newsweek* (September 26, 1955), p. 102.
[80] Ibid.
[81] Landis, Benson Y., (ed.), *Yearbook of American Churches*, edition for 1957 (New York:
National Council of Churches, 1956), p. 251. The official tally of Southern Baptists
living in America in 1955 was 8,467,439.
[82] Niebuhr, Reinhold. *The Nature and Destiny of Man [Volume II]* (New York: Charles
Scribner's Sons, 1943), pp. 202, 229, 231.

interpreted literally, and the enormous effort they put into committing entire passages to memory – seemed to cross the thin line separating fervor from fanaticism.

Conservative Christians, however, saw the issue differently. From their perspective, the devotion to scripture was not only divinely commanded, but also emotionally fulfilling. Just as Shakespeare buffs would likely be skeptical of any attempt to bowdlerize the language of *Hamlet* or *Othello*, and just as the enthusiasts of cinema recoiled at the 1980s' colorization of classic black-and-white films, "Bible buffs" at midcentury were emotionally invested in preserving the King James Version.[83] From the viewpoint of fundamentalists and various conservative Christians, to alter the language of the Bible would necessarily detract from the majesty of Holy Scripture.

Among Christian conservatives, there was another reason why they were so reluctant to accept the RSV Bible. To do so and, thereby, allow the King James Version to be superseded by another translation, would be to admit the unthinkable: that one's understanding of the Bible may be in serious error. It would also mean that the scriptural comprehension of one's parents and grandparents might also have been mistaken. Most important of all, the acceptance of the RSV Bible would open the door to future alterations. It would mean that one's own understanding of the Bible – in principle, any chapter in the Bible – would be subject to future modifications of an unknown magnitude. In short, the RSV Bible called into question the sense of certainty and permanency that is so central to the belief of conservative Christians everywhere.

While the enormous success of the RSV Bible reflected a growing public interest during the early 1950s in matters pertaining to religion, it also revealed something of a very different nature. The RSV's rapid success suggests that during the 1950s, the mass of Americans lacked a deep-seated sentimental attachment to the older King James Bible. Moreover, it showed that in the doctrinal battles between conservative fundamentalists

---

[83] Mathews, "RKO Pictures Sues Over Colorization," *Los Angeles Times* (October 22, 1986), Part 6, p. 10; Joel Pisetzner, "Movie Colorization: The Spectrum of Views," *The Record* (Bergen County, New Jersey) (November 23, 1986), p. E1; Peter Osterlund, "Rukus Over Coloring Old Movies Reaches Halls of Congress," *The Christian Science Monitor* (May 14, 1987), p. 5: also see "Color Controversy," *The MacNeil/Lehrer NewsHour*, Transcript #2907 (November 18, 1986). On the program, Woody Allen says of Ted Turner's decision to colorize old movies; "I would say that it's a philistine notion conceived out of pure venality, with total disregard for the artist and total contempt for the audience."

and the more mainstream theological moderates, the former were in retreat while the influence of the latter was steadily advancing.

The Rise in Pastoral Counseling

Arguably, the most compelling evidence of the secularization of religion could be seen in the growing influence of modern psychology – in particular, the rising subfield of pastoral counseling. Seward Hiltner of the National Council of Churches noted that in 1939, "Seminary courses on pastoral counseling were rare... few conferences for the clergy included such material, and none made it a feature."[84] Yet by 1950, four out of five theological schools had one or more persons listed as "psychologists" on their faculty.[85]

In their book, *The Advancement of Theological Education* (1957), H. Richard Niebuhr, Daniel Day Williams, and James M. Gustafson went even further in charting the rise of pastoral counseling.[86] Instead of simply looking at the number of psychology professors hired, the authors focused on the establishment of clinical training programs – a decidedly higher standard. Whereas in 1943 only thirteen Protestant seminaries in America had clinical training programs, the authors found by 1952 that figure had more than tripled. More impressively, the authors reported that by 1955 some 75 percent of American seminaries either had their own clinical training program or were sending students to approved clinical training courses elsewhere.[87]

In addition to the advocacy of pastoral counseling by seminaries and divinity schools, a number of other organizations arose to provide ministers with basic instruction in modern psychological counseling. According to a survey in 1954, more than a dozen regional Councils of Churches, along with such groups as the Council for Clinical Training (CCT) and the Institute for Pastoral Care (IPC), were actively promoting pastoral psychology through seminars and conferences.[88]

---

[84] "Looking Forward – An Editorial," *Pastoral Psychology* (March 1950), p. 8.
[85] Queener, E. Llewellyn. "The Psychological Training of Ministers," *Pastoral Psychology* (October 1952), p. 30.
[86] Niebuhr, H. Richard, Williams, Daniel Day, and Gustafson, James M. *The Advancement of Theological Education* (New York: Harper, 1957), pp. 121–9.
[87] Ibid, p. 124.
[88] List prepared by the Department of Pastoral Services of the National Council of Churches. See "Opportunities for Study, Training, and Experience in Pastoral Psychology – 1954," *Pastoral Psychology* (January 1954), pp. 25–39.

The founding of professional journals was a notable facet of these changes in ministerial training. In 1947, both the *Journal of Clinical Pastoral Work* and the *Journal of Pastoral Care* were born; and 1950 saw the establishment of *Pastoral Psychology*, an influential publication that attracted articles from such notables as psychologists Carl Rogers and Rollo May, psychiatrist William Menninger, as well as theologians Paul Tillich and Joseph Fletcher. In short order *Pastoral Psychology* became the journal of record, boasting sixteen thousand subscribers, seven-eighths of whom were ministers.[89]

One would think that if forced to choose between humanistic psychology and Sigmund Freud, between the client-centered approach championed by Rogers and orthodox psychoanalysis, most Christian leaders would cast their lot in with the Freudians. Although Freud may have held most of man's anxieties arise out of sexual repression, he also believed much of man's repression – as well as the anguish that accompanies it – are a part of human existence and a necessary development for the functioning of civilization. Likewise, while Freud may have maintained that psychoanalysis could be helpful in some limited situations, he did not believe in the perfectibility of man – insisting that internal conflict was an inevitable part of the human experience. In short, traditional Christianity's understandings of the human condition and Freud's secularized vision of man were not altogether incompatible. In the case of the former, there stood the belief in original sin; in the case of the latter, there was a clear-eyed appreciation of humankind's limitations.

Humanistic psychology, however, had few of these restraints. Its emphasis was on man's ability to persevere, to overcome, to triumph. Throughout the writings of Carl Rogers, the themes of "potential" and "growth" are continually reappearing. Therefore, it would seem counterintuitive for Protestant churches to choose Rogers over Freud. However, embrace Rogers they did – and with surprisingly great enthusiasm. As *Pastoral Psychology* editor Seward Hiltner, arguably the most prominent postwar figure in the pastoral counseling movement, volunteered, Carl Rogers was "more concretely influential in American psychology than any other individual."[90]

According to a 1950 survey of theological schools, the most popular textbook for the teaching of psychology was Seward Hiltner's *Pastoral Counseling*. In this book, Hiltner repeatedly acknowledged his intellectual

---

[89] Holifield, *A History of Pastoral Care in America*, p. 274.
[90] Ibid, p. 300.

FIGURE 2.2. Carl Rogers, father of humanistic psychology. (Reproduced by permission of the Department of Special Collections, Davidson Library, University of California, Santa Barbara.)

debt to Rogers for illuminating some aspects of nondirective counseling. Indeed, even Hiltner's fictional transcript of a session between an emotionally disturbed woman and a skilled pastoral counselor amounted to little more than a dramatization of Rogers' nondirective approach.[91] The manual identified as the second most popular textbook for pastoral counseling was none other than Carl Rogers' *Counseling and Psychotherapy.*[92]

Seward Hiltner was similarly candid in describing the theological implications of pastoral counseling. Although conceding that it is possible for a minister to embrace Rogerian methods and still remain conservative "in the realm of faith and morals," he believed that, in a larger sense, client-centered therapy presented a legitimate threat to a conservative moral framework. This was due to what Hiltner termed the "democratic and antiauthoritarian implications of the nondirective approach."[93]

Although a minority position, there were some within the pastoral counseling movement who opposed Rogers' nondirective method. Doris Mode of the Institute for Rankian Psychoanalysis contrasted "Christian theory and critique" with Rogers' client-centered approach. "A permissive atmosphere where nothing occurs but an echo of the client's own

[91] Hiltner, Seward. *Pastoral Counseling* (Nashville: Abingdon Press, 1946).
[92] Queener, E. Llewellyn. "The Psychological Training of Ministers," *Pastoral Psychology* (October 1952), p. 30.
[93] Hiltner, *Pastoral Counseling*, pp. 273–4.

attitudes," stated Mode, "would indeed be empty of all value and judgment, and thereby of all therapy also." Her problem with Rogers was the passive role assigned to the therapist. By insisting that the counselor be nonjudgmental and "place no blame," Rogers was creating a situation where the therapist "abandons all values of his own."[94] The end result, insisted Mode, was a spiritual vacuum that effectively prevented the patient from becoming whole. "If God were not judgmental," wrote Mode, "there would be no meaning to life, and if he were not loving, there would be no fulfillment. Both of these concepts must flow through the therapist to the client if he is to become whole again."[95] Yet for all of Mode's criticism, it is important to realize that at midcentury her view was not dominant among pastoral counselors. What is more, the resonance of her critique would fade further with time.

From the early 1940s, two organizations – the Council for Clinical Training and the Institute for Pastoral Care, both dedicated to educating ministers about the latest innovations in clinical psychology – commanded the field of pastoral counseling. As even a cursory examination of their activities would evince, both organizations were profoundly influenced by modern psychological theory. As early as 1948, the CCT's pastoral counseling program was accredited by the Alanson White Institute of Psychiatry, an organization that had been established by none other than Harry Stack Sullivan. For a minister or a minister-in-training to graduate from the CCT's pastoral counseling program, an independent, secular psychiatric institute first had to certify that the student had acquired some measure of proficiency in the fundamentals of modern psychology.[96] In practical terms, this meant a para-religious organization had granted secular experts the prerogative to prevent aspiring clerics from advancing in their studies. Equally revealing, of the forty-one members serving on the CCT's Board of Governors in 1958, seventeen were psychologists or psychiatrists.[97]

At the rival Institute for Pastoral Care, the situation was little different. Because members of the pastoral counseling movement measured

---

94 Mode, Doris. "God-Centered Therapy: A Criticism of Client-Centered Therapy," *The Journal of Pastoral Care*, Volume 4, No. 1–2 (1950), p. 20.

95 Ibid, p. 23.

96 Minutes of the Council for Clinical Training's Meeting of the Board of Governors, February 28, 1949; Minutes of the Meeting of the Board of Governors, April 18, 1949, box 18, folder 274, Association of Clinical Pastoral Education Papers, Pitts Theological Library Archives, Emory University (hereafter cited as ACPE Papers).

97 Board of Governors – I.P.C., 1958, box 10, folder 170, ACPE Papers.

"legitimacy" by one's proximity to psychiatrists and psychologists, the IPC allowed doctors to play the leading role in the training of pastoral counselors. For example, an IPC seminar held in the spring and fall of 1944 attracted students from four seminaries and four denominations. Over the course of fourteen weeks, students participated in seminars that grappled with such topics as "Psychoanalysis," "Psychiatric Case Work," and "Recognizing Emotional Conflicts."[98] Although technically headed by an IPC official, members of Massachusetts General Hospital's psychiatric staff – all but one of whom were doctors – delivered all the lectures and directed all the seminars.[99]

In 1953, a new hybrid organization came on the scene. Founded by the indefatigable Norman Vincent Peale, and boasting an impressive list of donors, the American Foundation of Religion and Psychiatry (AFRP) quickly established itself as an active participant in the field of pastoral counseling. Thanks to its substantial financial resources, this new organization was equipped to take on two formidable tasks: providing psychological training for clerics and offering counseling to the public.[100]

Within the ranks of Peale's AFRP, mental health professionals – although ready to impart to ministers the fundamentals of psychology – appeared reluctant to subscribe to any body of religious dogma. As the minutes to the annual 1956 meeting tell, psychiatrist Iago Gladston, the chair of the Research Committee, confided to the board that he "dreaded to commit himself to another man's concept of God." Refusing to accept, automatically, the propriety of spiritual counseling, Gladston went on to reiterate that research, and research alone, "would give the answer as to whether spiritual therapy is a pious hope, or an actuality."[101]

If Gladston's vision did not completely hold sway, a non-doctrinaire approach resembling his appears to have triumphed. As the AFRP stated in an internal 1960 document: "[O]ur setting, that of a mental hygiene clinic and pastoral counseling center, allows the pastoral counselor to focus primarily, even completely, on the counseling aspect of his vocation. In other words, if the pastoral counselor chooses to be, he may discontinue

---

[98] Seminar in Psychiatry, box 10, folder 168, ACPE Papers.

[99] Ibid.

[100] American Foundation of Religion and Psychiatry: Joint Meeting – Members and Board Members (fact sheet), November 21, 1955, box 1, folder heading: Board of Directors Meeting, Institute of Religion Papers, Syracuse University Special Collections.

[101] The American Foundation of Religion and Psychiatry: Annual Meeting No. 3, October 22, 1956, p. 3, box 1, folder heading: AFRAP Charter Members, 1951–1958, IRH Papers.

all the usual pastoral duties connected with being a minister in a parish or an institution."[102]

In its vision of pastoral counseling and education, the AFRP was not far removed from the mainstream. In its willingness to heal souls "not overtly through the performance of religious acts such as prayer, scripture reading and the like, but intangibly and covertly,"[103] the AFRP, as well as the IPC and the CCT, simply reflected the cultural currents of the age. In America, at midcentury, psychology enjoyed considerable recognition, with its prestige penetrating even the fortress of the Christian religion.

One would expect pastoral psychology to be largely in vogue among the leading lights of liberal Protestantism. Yet it is clear that during the 1950s some of the more conservative denominations were also embracing the therapeutic. An examination of the course offerings of the three leading seminaries within the Southern Baptist Convention – namely, the Southern Baptist Theological Seminary, the New Orleans Baptist Theological Seminary, and the Southwestern Baptist Theological Seminary – tell much of the story. In 1949–50, the New Orleans Baptist Theological Seminary featured six psychology courses, all under the auspices of the Religious Education Department. Ten years later, the seminary was offering a dozen psychology courses through the recently created Department of Psychology and Counseling. In Louisville, Kentucky, at the Southern Baptist Theological Seminary, a total of eleven psychology courses were open to seminarians at the close of the 1950s – up from four in the 1946–7 school year, and only one in the 1941–2 school year. However the most impressive rate of growth occurred in Fort Worth, Texas, at the Southwestern Baptist Theological Seminary. There, the number of course offerings in psychology rose from five in the 1944–5 school year, to nine in the 1949–50 school year, and to a total of twenty in the 1957–8 academic year.[104]

[102] Some Observations, 1960, p. 4, folder heading: Foundation History, IRH Papers.
[103] Ibid.
[104] See "Bulletin of the Southwestern Baptist Theological Seminary" for the 1944–5 academic school year, the 1949–50 academic school year, and the 1957–8 academic school year; see "Curriculum Bulletin" of The *New Orleans Baptist Theological Seminary: Thirty-Second Session* for the 1949–50 academic year and the "Curriculum Bulletin" of *The New Orleans Baptist Theological Seminary: Forty-second Session* for the 1959–60 academic year; The Southern Baptist Theological Seminary: Ninety-eighth Session (April 1959), *Annual Catalogue of the Southern Baptist Theological Seminary* (1947), and *Annual Catalogue of the Southern Baptist Theological Seminary* (1942). All the material furnished to the author by The Southern Baptist Historical Library and Archive.

Pastoral counseling, of course, was hardly a postwar innovation. What distinguished the fifties was the extent to which pastoral counseling drew from the latest developments in psychological theory. The influence of these psychological theories is readily gleaned by a review of the movement's journals. In its first year of publication, *Pastoral Psychology* featured such articles as "Toward an Understanding of Anxiety," "The Locus of Responsibility in Counseling," and "Basic Concepts of Psychosomatic Medicine."[105] Likewise, *The Journal of Pastoral Care* and *The Journal of Clinical Pastoral Work* featured many articles with a heavy psychological emphasis. As religious historian E. Brooks Holifield notes, "It seems foolhardy to isolate one theme woven through the mass of pastoral writings. No single issue encompassed everything. But if any topic recurred consistently, as either an explicit issue or an implicit criterion, it was the theme of self-realization."[106]

The Softening Stance on Proselytizing

Like the growth of pastoral counseling, the waning emphasis on proselytizing speaks to the moderation of American Christianity during the 1950s. For centuries, a central feature of Protestantism was the injunction to "spread the faith" to all corners of the world. In practical terms this meant "witnessing," or proselytizing, on the assumption that unless unbelievers accepted Jesus Christ, they would have no avenue for salvation. Within the ranks of mainstream Protestantism this once ironclad commitment showed signs of compromise during the 1950s. Nowhere was this declining zeal for evangelization more evident than on the question of Jewish conversion.

In all likelihood, the fresh memory of gas chambers and living skeletons contributed to the Protestant churches' "softer" stance toward Jewish conversion. After all, if efforts were successful, three thousand years of Jewish culture would be threatened with near extinction. At a time when social critics and religious leaders were promoting the concept of a "Judeo-Christian" tradition, and when these very people were disturbed by the horrors of Nazi Germany, a Christian campaign to transform Jews into non-Jews caused some measure of discomfort. Yet despite these apprehensions, in the early years following World War II the traditional Christian emphasis on Jewish conversion remained essentially

---

[105] Cited from the first ten issues of *Pastoral Psychology*.
[106] Holifield, *A History of Pastoral Counseling*, pp. 275–6.

intact. Thus, at the First Assembly of the World Council of Churches, held in Amsterdam in 1948, there was little opposition to an official statement that enjoined the faithful to spread the gospel among Jews.[107]

However, this adherence to traditional Christian teachings was to be short-lived. In August 1954, the Second Assembly of the World Council of Churches gathered in Evanston, Illinois, where delegates from all over the world (including representatives from the leading mainline denominations in America) participated in the monthlong conference.[108] Again, a proposed statement that, in the words of *The Christian Century*, "stressed the importance of the conversion of the Jews in relation to the Second Coming of Christ" reached the floor of the Assembly. However, this time delegates voted the proposal down, with most of the American representatives aligning themselves with the majority of the Council in deciding to strike any language that stressed the importance of evangelizing among Jews.[109] Charles P. Taft, a delegate from America's Episcopal Church and the former president of the FCC, was the first delegate on the floor of the Assembly to voice opposition to the proposed statement.[110] If the motion passed, Taft warned, he and other Protestant leaders would needlessly "embarrass" their Jewish friends. In the end, the motion failed by a vote of 195 to 150, with most of the American delegates rejecting language that called on Christians to evangelize to Jews.[111]

Seymour Martin Lipset, reflecting on the Evanston Council a year later, found the whole incident to be a disturbing sign of American Protestantism's lack of religious commitment. Although conceding that the decision to downplay evangelizing would likely be welcomed by fellow Jews as a "sign of friendship," he also warned that the vote was "another example of how meaningless religion as anything more than a conventional set of brotherhood doctrines has become in this country." Lipset then cited the sociologist Will Herberg in arguing that a new "American Church," consisting of Protestant, Catholic, and Jewish branches, was

---

[107] Gaines, David P. *The World Council of Churches: A Study of Its Background and History* (Peterborough, Ontario: Richard R. Smith Company, 1966), pp. 310–12.

[108] Ellwood, Robert S. *The Fifties Spiritual Marketplace: American Religion in a Decade of Conflict* (New Brunswick: Rutgers University Press, 1997), p. 131.

[109] "Literalists Lose by Close Vote," *The Christian Century* (September 8, 1954), pp. 1073–4.

[110] The Federal Council of Churches, which Charles Taft headed in 1946, was absorbed by the National Council of Churches in 1950. However, during the 1940s, it was the largest organization of Christians in the United States.

[111] "Literalists Lose by Close Vote," *The Christian Century* (September 8, 1954), pp. 1073–4.

in the process of forming. "This religion," complained Lipset, "has few dogmas beyond belief in some vague abstraction called God."[112]

Judging from the religious press, Lipset's assessment appears to have been a minority position, at least among the mainline Protestant churches. *The Christian Century* seemed relieved by the decision of the Assembly. In its own words, the World Council of Churches had been "saved" from a formal commitment to the "conversion of the Jews."[113] Henry P. Van Dusen, the president of Union Theological Seminary and a delegate to the Evanston conference, expressed similar sentiments, describing the Assembly's decision as "sound, moderate, and constructive," and deriding those delegates who pushed for an affirmative statement on Jewish conversion as "biblical literalists."[114]

According to the research of historian Yaakov Ariel, by the 1940s and 1950s, Presbyterian efforts to convert Jews encountered mounting opposition within their own denomination. Although proselytizing efforts continued during these years, the Presbyterians' commitment to these efforts gradually faded into near oblivion. "By 1960," writes Ariel, "missions to the Jews as a denominational agenda were being phased out."[115] A year earlier, in 1959, Reinhold Niebuhr – the nation's foremost theologian – asserted in *Pious and Secular America* that the conversion of the Jews was neither necessary nor appropriate.[116]

This steady evaporation of missionary zeal continued into the 1960s. According to an extensive survey of Northern California church members, sponsored by the Anti-Defamation League during the mid-1960s, only one-third of Episcopalians, 29 percent of Methodists, and 21 percent of Congregationalists claimed that they personally approved of "converting Jews to Christianity."[117] Even more arresting, only 7 percent of Congregationalist clergy, 12 percent of Methodist clergy, and 13 percent of Episcopalian clergy agreed with the statement that "being of the

---

[112] "Second Round Table Conference: Discussion," *Jewish Social Studies* (July 1955), p. 236.
[113] "Literalists Lose by Close Vote," *The Christian Century*, pp. 1073–4.
[114] Van Dusen, Henry P. "Afterthoughts on Evanston," *Union Seminary Quarterly Review* (November 1954), p. 5.
[115] Ariel, Yaakov. *Evangelizing the Chosen People: Missions to Jews in America, 1880–2000* (Chapel Hill: University of North Carolina Press, 2000), p. 133.
[116] Niebuhr, Reinhold. *Pious and Secular America* (New York: Scribner's, 1958), p. 108.
[117] The same study found that 90 percent of Southern Baptists approved of "Converting Jews to Christianity." See Glock, Charles Y., and Stark, Rodney. *Christian Beliefs and Anti-Semitism* (New York: Harper & Row, 1966), p. 78.

Jewish Religion" would "definitely" or "possibly" prevent salvation.[118]
By 1973, Reverend Billy Graham issued a statement in which he dispelled
any lingering doubts about his commitment to religious pluralism by voicing his opposition to aggressive efforts aimed at proselytizing American
Jewry.[119]

However, the most telling sign of the Protestants' increasing reluctance
to evangelize is not to be found in the evolving relationship between Christians and Jews. The complicating issue of pluralism, coupled with the relatively small numbers of Jewish-Americans, render missionary efforts to
American Jewry an inadequate proxy with which to weigh the Christian
commitment to proselyte. Rather than looking at home, the best evidence
is to be found in the evangelism churches conducted abroad. When examined over time, these efforts reveal a gradually declining commitment to
"spreading the word of God."

In the years between 1950 and 1959, total contributions to foreign missions, the principal vehicle of overseas evangelism, rose from $56.6 million
to $86.9 million – a 30 percent hike for the forty-nine largest Protestant
dominations in the country. Yet during the same period, the overall level
of contributions to these forty-nine leading American churches increased
by 71 percent (from just under $1.3 billion to $2.35 billion). What these
numbers tell us is that as a proportion of total income, America's leading
Protestant churches were allocating 25 percent more to proselytization at
the beginning of the 1950s than they were at the decade's close.

The origins of this downward trend did not begin at midcentury. A
study of the finances of the ten leading Protestant denominations, conducted for the National Council of Churches in 1955, found that in the
years between 1913 and 1951, "total contributions reported for foreign
missions increased from $662,428 to $33,132,763, or 242.9 percent."
Yet during this same thirty-eight-year period, membership swelled by
more than 80 percent and inflation eroded the value of the dollar. When
the study considered the import of inflation and membership growth, it
found that "in purchasing power the per capita contribution [to overseas
proselytizing] declined by 29 percent" between 1913 and 1951.[120] Yet

---

[118] Ibid, p. 75.

[119] Healey, Robert M. "From Conversion to Dialogue: Protestant American Mission to
the Jews in the Nineteenth and Twentieth Centuries," *Journal of Ecumenical Studies*
(Summer 1981), p. 386.

[120] Study cited in Landis, Benson Y. *Yearbook of American Churches: Edition for 1955*
(New York: National Council of Churches, 1954), pp. 297–8.

during this same period, real per capita income rose by more than 80 percent (from \$1,351 to \$2,485) in 1958 dollars.[121] At a time when real per capita income shot up, per capita contributions for spreading the gospel fell quite dramatically; by nearly one-third in real terms. In short, this general deemphasis of proselytizing was nothing new. Indeed, it was part of a decades-long process beginning prior to World War I and stretching into the 1950s, marking a slow but significant change as Americans adapted Christianity to the mood of the twentieth century.

Reverend Billy Graham

The career of Reverend Billy Graham, the Southern Baptist evangelist who became the most recognizable religious figure of the postwar period, illustrates how the religious life of a society can be more moderate and less "traditional" than it appears on the surface. For all of the fire and brimstone emanating from his sermons, Reverend Graham was less theologically conservative than is widely assumed. It is true that when starting out in the 1940s, Graham had been a hard-liner. As the young college president at Northwestern Bible College in 1948, Graham issued a public apology to alumni when the school magazine inadvertently advertised the work of a liberal theologian. Neither he nor the college had forsaken the "orthodox, conservative theological position," he assured readers in a subsequent magazine issue. "We do not condone nor have fellowship with any form of modernism."[122] Later that year, when asked about his thoughts on the upcoming conference of the World Council of Churches, Graham replied grimly, "I believe they are going to nominate the anti-Christ."[123]

However, by 1949 Graham's words and deeds began to shift in a moderate direction. His metamorphosis began when he resigned as president of Northwestern Bible College and decided to dedicate his life to the ministry. To close observers it became increasingly apparent that, as an "ecumenical evangelist," Graham was far more tolerant of religious diversity than most of his fundamentalist colleagues. Whereas his conservative contemporaries opposed interdenominational cooperation in spreading

---

[121] *Historical Statistics of the United Sates: Colonial Times to 1970, Part I* (Washington, D.C.: U.S. Census Bureau, 1975), p. 224.

[122] Dalhouse, Mark Taylor. *An Island in the Lake of Fire: Bob Jones University, Fundamentalism and the Separatist Movement* (Athens, Georgia: University of Georgia Press, 1998).

[123] Ibid.

FIGURE 2.3. Reverend Billy Graham preaching to a vast crowd on Wall Street. (Reproduced by permission of the Billy Graham Evangelical Association.)

the gospel unless all parties involved subscribed to the essential tenets of the faith, Graham staked out a less rigid position. "The one badge of Christian discipleship is not orthodoxy, but love," he proclaimed before a Buffalo audience in 1957. "We evangelicals sometimes set ourselves up as judges of another man's relationship to God. We often think that a person is not a Christian unless he pronounces our shibboleths and clichés exactly the way we do."[124]

The spring of 1957 proved to be a momentous season for Billy Graham, when he permanently severed connections with such prominent Christian fundamentalists as Bob Jones and John Rice by inviting ministers from liberal theological backgrounds to cosponsor his New York Crusade.[125] This was a most significant step because it meant that Graham was willing to direct a proportion of the unchurched people who had attended his

[124] Cited from Butler, Farley P. *Billy Graham and the End of Evangelical Unity* (Dissertation: University of Florida, 1976), p. 206.
[125] In addition to being the editor of *The Sword of the Lord*, John Rice was the mentor of Moral Majority founder Jerry Falwell.

revival and desired further spiritual guidance to the good offices of liberal ministers. Since some of these ministers were "modernistic" in a doctrinal sense – rejecting the inerrancy of the Bible and, in some cases, they were dismissive of the virgin birth and even the bodily resurrection of Christ – Graham essentially agreed to promote biblical doctrines that were at loggerheads with his own.[126]

Indeed, in a 1960 interview, Graham admitted that his efforts in New York were not intended to persuade Roman Catholics to change their religion or modify their understanding of theological issues. As *Newsweek* magazine reported, "Despite their probable Roman Catholic background, some 50 percent of Spanish-speaking New Yorkers have no current church affiliation of any kind, according to Protestant churchmen. Dr. Graham made it clear that he and his fellow crusaders have no intention of doing any proselytizing." Graham emphasized, "The important thing to us is that these people are unchurched. We want them to accept Christ and they can do that whether they think of themselves as Catholics or Protestants."[127]

Fundamentalist minister William Ashbrook was especially scathing in his criticism of Graham. Such evangelists, he contended, were advancing a "new neutralism." Yet rather than leading to a workable truce, such accommodation was tantamount to a theological surrender. According to Ashbrook, true believers would be well advised to steer clear of "this New Neutralism" for it was a movement "born of compromise," "nurtured on pride of intellect," "growing on appeasement of evil," and "doomed by the judgment of God's Holy Word."[128]

In 1956, *Christianity Today*, a monthly magazine founded by Graham, began publication. Although marketed as a conservative alternative to the *Christian Century*, *Christianity Today* also sought to proffer itself as the moderate alternative to the fundamentalism of Bob Jones and John Rice. Accordingly, the new publication was willing to engage liberal Protestantism in a way that Jones, Rice, and the early Billy Graham would have flatly refused to do. When a decade earlier Graham had denounced the World Council of Churches in the most incendiary language, Graham's hand-selected editor of *Christianity Today* was soon serving as a consultant to a study sponsored by the World Council of Churches itself.[129]

[126] Butler, *Billy Graham and the End of Evangelical Unity*, pp. 210–27.
[127] *Newsweek* (October 17, 1960).
[128] Ibid, p. 222.
[129] Marty, *Modern American Religion*, p. 444.

When the Billy Graham of the late 1940s spoke frequently of the pains of hell and damnation, according to Howell Burkhead's extensive examination of Graham's sermons, the Billy Graham of the late 1950s was treating sin in a less personalized manner, frequently framing it as a manifestation of the nation's collective shortcomings. And whereas the Billy Graham of the mid 1950s was befriending Norman Vincent Peale, visiting the liberal Union Theological Seminary, and declaring his admiration for Reinhold Niebuhr, the earlier Graham scrupulously steered clear of liberal theologians – even once delivering a sermon entitled "The Sin of Tolerance."[130]

Even before the New York Crusade, there was foreshadowing that Graham was treating doctrinal differences with greater forbearance than his fundamentalist colleagues. In 1952 when Dwight Eisenhower asked Billy Graham what denomination he should join, the latter recommended the Presbyterian Church – advice that Eisenhower accepted.[131] The only problem was that Graham belonged to the Southern Baptist Convention, and the Presbyterian Church U.S.A. – a member of the National Council of Churches (NCC) – tended to be less theologically conservative than Southern Baptists. Indeed, on a wide gamut of issues, Presbyterians departed from conservative Christians – regarding it unnecessary to believe in the virgin birth of Christ, the inerrancy of the Bible, the literal existence of Hell, and the necessity of baptism.[132]

In addition to adopting a more fluid stance toward questions of doctrine, Reverend Graham apparently underwent a transformation – or, at the very least, a moderation – in his attitudes toward earthly pleasures. While president of Northeastern Bible College, Graham opposed any form of social dancing. However, by the mid-1950s, Graham was resisting conservative Baptist efforts to isolate and punish church institutions that, in any way, indulged dancing or the consumption of alcohol. As the historian Farley Butler has documented, this refusal helped create an early rift between Billy Graham and fundamentalist minister John Rice. Equally compelling, in a 1957 interview with *McCall's* magazine, Graham seemed to reject traditional exhortations against worldly indulges. "I know ministers who smoke, who have an occasional drink, dance, and

---

[130] Cited from Marty, *Modern American Religion: Under God, Indivisible, 1941–1960*, p. 329.

[131] Silk, Mark. *Spiritual Politics: Religion and America Since World War II* (New York: Simon & Schuster, 1988), p. 68.

[132] A worthwhile discussion of Presbyterian beliefs at midcentury appears in John Sutherland Bonnell's, "What is a Presbyterian?" *Look* (March 23, 1954), pp. 86, 88–90.

play a mild game of gin rummy," stated Graham, "This does not make them any less devout than I am."

Although Graham's 1957 crusade in New York infuriated his fundamentalist colleagues, by virtually all accounts – including Graham's – the New York Crusade was the most successful of all his evangelical campaigns.[133] However, of those who trotted off to Madison Square Garden to hear good gospel music and be electrified by the sermons of Reverend Graham, the overwhelming majority was almost certainly drawn from the ranks of the faithful.[134] Thus, of the approximately two million people who came to see Graham, only about fifty-seven thousand signed decision cards indicating that they desired to turn their lives over to the Lord. Yet according to William McLoughlin's survey of more than one hundred area ministers, of those fifty-seven thousand "converts," the overwhelming majority already belonged to a church![135] In fact, by McLoughlin's estimates, no more than seven thousand worshipers who signed the decision cards could be characterized as fresh converts. In other words, no more than 12 percent of the people who made "decisions for Christ" – or less than half of 1 percent of the total audience – became new church members.[136]

An investigation by *Life* magazine yielded similar results. It found that of those in the audience who heeded Graham's invitation to make a "decision for Christ," four-fifths already belonged to a church.[137] The theologically liberal *Christian Century* provided an even bleaker assessment of the event. On the first night of the New York Crusade, the magazine had its reporter interview people who made a "decision for Christ." It found that "of forty queried by our correspondent, only two were not already church members."[138]

Yet a fourth investigation – this one conducted by *The New York Times* several months after the New York Crusade ended – discovered

[133] Graham, Billy. *Just As I Am* (New York: Harper-Collins Publishers, 1997), pp. 361–83.
[134] According to an article in *Life* magazine, buses chartered by Protestant churches were bringing into the Graham revivals approximately eighty-five hundred church members every evening. See "Dedicated Deciders in Billy Graham Crusade," *Life* (1957), p. 91.
[135] McLoughlin, Jr., William G. *Billy Graham: Revivalist in a Secular Age* (New York: Ronald Press Company, 1960), p. 189.
[136] Ibid.
[137] "Dedicated Deciders in Billy Graham Crusade," *Life* (1957), p. 87. The *Life* article begins with the statement: "Billy Graham opened his New York Crusade in high hopes that it would 'soon be like a mighty river through the city.' But after 37 days of his 66-day stand in Madison Square Garden, the river has not been mighty."
[138] McLoughlin, *Billy Graham: Revivalist in a Secular Age*, p. 185.

that more than six in ten people who made a decision for Christ ended up attending churches to which they had already belonged.[139] The study also found that the interest of many of the "new" worshipers fell precipitously, as within a few months, many had ceased attending church altogether. "The 1957 Billy Graham Crusade gave the Protestant churches of New York a 'spiritual lift,'" the article conceded, "but otherwise it had little lasting impact on the city."[140]

The investigations of *The New York Times*, *Christian Century*, *Life* magazine, and historian William McLoughlin were unanimous in their conclusions. They found that although Graham succeeded in attracting vast multitudes, the overwhelming majority of worshipers were church-goers to begin with. Peering into the backgrounds of those who made "decisions for Christ," they all found that a distinct minority of these people could be categorized as unchurched. In short, it would seem that the New York Crusade – like most of Graham's crusades – was less a proselytizing campaign than a huge religious jamboree.[141]

Whatever one may think of Graham's conservative critics, they did recognize that his success as an ecumenical leader both reflected and rein-forced the decline of religious doctrine. In fairness to Graham, during the fifties he converted some and prevented many more from "backsliding." Yet equally significant was his ecumenical message, which had the effect of downplaying the importance of religious doctrine. In 1958 *The New York Times* noted that of the fifteen hundred congregations that cospon-sored Graham's New York Crusade, Marable Collegiate, the church of the theologically liberal Norman Vincent Peale, benefited the most from new recruits.[142] This was the price Graham had to pay to become a main-stream cultural figure who could fill up stadiums with worshipers, minis-ter to presidents, and earn the unofficial title of "America's Evangelist."

---

[139] Dugan, George. "Graham's Impact Termed Fleeting," *The New York Times* (January 26, 1958), p. 1. It should be noted that *The New York Times* survey did not track people who belonged previously to another congregation; it only counted those who returned to the church they had attended before the New York Crusade.

[140] Ibid, pp. 1, 61.

[141] McLoughlin, *Billy Graham: Revivalist in a Secular Age*, pp. 182–3. In looking at ear-lier Billy Graham crusades in Detroit (1953), Nashville (1954), New Orleans (1954), and Oklahoma City (1956), McLoughlin shows that a clear majority of those making "decisions for Christ" were already churched.

[142] Dugan, "Graham's Impact Termed Fleeting," p. 61. Shortly after the New York Cru-sade, on October 22, 1957, Peale thanked Graham, "Our church has profited in a wonderful way from the crusade." Quoted from Pollock, John, *Billy Graham: The Authorized Biography* (New York: McGraw-Hill, 1966), p. 186.

Secularization in Other Religions

The secularizing process discussed in this chapter was more than a Protestant phenomenon. As we have seen, religious intermarriage and the secularization of Sunday also applied to Roman Catholics. So too did the downplaying of sectarian differences. From medieval times, the dictum *extra ecclesiam nulla salus* – or "Outside the Church there is no salvation" – was a core part of the official teachings of the Catholic Church. However, when strictly interpreted, this formulation was problematic in an age when pluralism and tolerance had become the governing principles of the time. Many Catholics, who in the postwar period were moving into the ranks of the middle class, were unreceptive to exclusivist doctrines that painted Catholics as intolerant and rigidly dogmatic – qualities incompatible with the American way of life. The controversy surrounding Father Leonard Feeney, an accomplished poet and charismatic priest who ministered to Harvard students at midcentury, was a sign that a dominant faction within the Catholic Church wished to moderate its image and enter the American mainstream.

The Feeney Heresy, as it has come to be known, erupted in the late 1940s when the Jesuit priest and his committed band of followers began attacking some instructors at Boston College for propagating what was, in their eyes, false doctrine. More specifically, Feeney accused church officials and various instructors of abandoning the tenet that salvation was open only to those who accepted the authority of Rome. Through a magazine entitled *From the Housetops*, Father Feeney and his disciples lashed out against church leaders and so-called "Commonweal Catholics" for supposedly watering down the faith so as to enter the American mainstream. For a few brief moments, the Feeney controversy attracted national attention, becoming the focus of news stories in *The New York Times*, *Newsweek*, *Life*, and *Time* magazines.[143] In time, however, church leaders succeeded in destroying Feeney as a credible public figure. First, he was denounced by his Bishop, then he was expelled from the Jesuit Order and stripped of his priestly functions, and then, finally, Feeney suffered the ultimate chastisement: excommunication.

Upon closer inspection, it is clear that Feeney's transgression was not one of excessive laxity but quite the reverse: church authorities determined he was too militantly doctrinaire. Ironically, one could plausibly argue that Leonard Feeney was indeed "more Catholic than the Pope." What the

---

[143] Massa, Mark. "On the Uses of Heresy: Leonard Feeney, Mary Douglas, and the Notre Dame Football Team," *The Harvard Theological Review* (July 1991), p. 336.

Feeney controversy illustrates is that more than a decade before Vatican II, the deemphasis of religious dogma for the sake of civic peace was a strong impulse in America that extended to Catholics as much as to Protestants.

Probably the most significant sign of secularization among American Catholics was not the Feeney controversy, but the rise of pastoral psychology. Although the pastoral counseling movement was not as strong among Catholics as among Protestants, it was nonetheless gathering momentum throughout the 1950s. To be precise, in the immediate postwar period, the story had been very different. With the blessing of Rome, American clergy enforced an extremely harsh position toward psychoanalysis. For instance, in his widely publicized attacks on Freudianism, Monsignor Fulton Sheen assailed psychoanalysis as "a form of escapism" based on a poisonous mélange of "materialism, hedonism, infantilism, and eroticism." In contrast to the Catholic practice of confession, he exclaimed, "Psychoanalysis gives no norms or standards. There is no more disintegrated people in the world than the patients of Freudian analysis."[144] The sentiments expressed by Sheen were widespread among senior church authorities, whom as late as 1952, were adamant in their hostility toward psychoanalysis.

After 1953, however, the mood of American Catholics quickly shifted. In February of that year, Pope Pius XII gave his tentative approval to psychoanalysis. Thereafter, pastoral psychology made considerable headway within the American Church. In the following year, St. John's University in Minnesota inaugurated its first annual Summer Institute for the purpose of acquainting clergymen with the latest developments in modern psychology. In its first two decades of operation, twenty-five hundred clergy, the majority of whom were Catholic, had participated in a summer program. "Catholic writers have, in general, found their second look at psychoanalysis more reassuring than the original impression," observed a 1956 article in the Catholic journal, *America*. "Certain rather basic distinctions and reservations must be made, but it seems that they can be made; and once they are made, the fundamental tenets of psychoanalysis may be accepted by Catholics as by anyone else."[145]

It is only a minor exaggeration to say that within just a few years' time, the Catholic Church's receptiveness to psychology had undergone a virtual transformation. By the close of the 1950s, another mental health

[144] "Sheen Denounces Psychoanalysis," *The New York Times* (May 10, 1947), p. 18.
[145] Bier, William C. "Sigmund Freud and the Faith," *America* (November 17, 1956), p. 193.

training institute had been established at St. Catherine's College; *Pastoral Psychology*, the leading journal in the field, arranged for one of its issues to be entirely edited by Catholics involved in ministerial counseling; and such prominent conservatives as Boston Archbishop Richard Cardinal Cushing had characterized psychiatry "as an important collaborator with the church in its concerns for men's minds and souls."[146]

One notable countertrend – a development suggesting, that in at least certain religious circles, a growing intensity of faith had taken root – was the rise of religious vocations. Spurred, in part, by the publication of Thomas Merton's *Seven Story Mountain*, tens of thousands of Catholic men and women joined religious orders during the 1950s.[147] However, do vocations act as an accurate index to other forms of religious commitment? Or is it an index onto itself? Because the rise of vocations involved only a small portion of the total Catholic population, and because other indices of mass Catholic behavior – from the proliferation of Sunday shopping to the rise of religious intermarriage – reveal a relaxation of traditional religious attitudes, it is hard to see how the rise in vocations could have reflected a dominant trend within American Catholicism. In a word, the preponderance of evidence suggests that, in the post–World War II era, the intensified religiosity that spawned a generation of priests, brothers, and nuns proved to be the exception to a larger secular trend.

Among Jewish-Americans, the tale is more complicated. Compared with the 1930s, synagogue membership among American Jewry appears to have increased during the fifties. However, there is little indication that the force of belief became stronger. According to one 1953 study, only 37 percent of the board members of conservative Jewish congregations kept a "strictly kosher" home, while 27 percent kept a "partially kosher" home, and 36 percent were not kosher at all.[148]

The same survey, sponsored by the United Synagogue of America under the direction of Columbia University's Bureau of Applied Social Research, reported several findings that many would find startling. The report, "National Survey on Synagogue Leadership," studied the attitudes of

---

[146] Reverend A. Godin, S. J. "Twelve Months of Religious and Pastoral Psychology," *Bulletin of the Guild of Catholic Psychiatrists* (Vol. 5, No 2, 1959), p. 2.

[147] Allitt, Patrick. *Religion in America Since 1945: A History* (New York: Columbia University Press, 2003), pp. 19–20.

[148] Lehman, Emil. "National Survey on Synagogue Leadership," (New York: unpublished, 1953), pp. 14, 15. Although unpublished, this mimeographed study is available on microfilm at the New York Public Library.

nearly eighteen hundred board members from one hundred and fifty-five conservative Jewish congregations – people we can only assume tended to be more "religious" than the typical synagogue member.[149] Yet the level of religiosity among the respondents was surprisingly low. For example, when asked "Do you say your daily prayers regularly either at home or with your congregation?" only 13 percent answered in the affirmative, while 85 percent said they did not pray regularly, and 2 percent refrained from answering the question altogether.[150] In another question, congregational leaders were asked whether their children normally accompany them to the main Sabbath service. By a two to one margin, respondents confessed they did not typically bring their children along.[151] It should be kept in mind that the foregoing responses did not come from ordinary congregational members, but from the leaders – more specifically, the board members of conservative synagogues. As such, one can assume that the responses of rank-and-file members, who were not as vested in the religious life of the Temple, likely would have reflected an even lower level of observance.

Most surprisingly, when congregational leaders were asked to rank, in their order of importance, their reason for attending, only 16 percent of respondents said they did so because attendance at the synagogue "brings you closer to God." By contrast, 17 percent said their reason was that it "makes you feel better," while 20 percent attended because they felt "every Jewish person should go to synagogue," and 21 percent responded by saying they liked "the service and the atmosphere of the Synagogue."[152] The low level of spiritual enthusiasm on the part of most synagogue leaders would not have taken religious sociologist Will Herberg by surprise. "Nothing in the way of belief or practice," observed Herberg in a 1950 article, "not even the belief in God or the practice of the most elementary mitzvoth – may be taken for granted among synagogue members."[153]

Although the survey's findings are revealing in some respects, there are many questions left unanswered. We simply do not know if the comparatively low levels of religious fervency that existed among the board members of conservative Jewish congregations – and presumably

---

[149] Ibid, p. 3.
[150] Ibid, p. 12.
[151] Ibid, pp. 14, 15.
[152] Ibid, p. 12.
[153] Heinze, Andrew R. *Jews and the American Soul: Human Nature in the 20th Century* (Princeton, NJ: Princeton University Press, 2004), p. 232.

among the larger population of observant Jews – were more extensive, less extensive, or roughly equivalent to that of earlier times. Without a benchmark – which is to say, in the absence of comparable survey data for previous years – the question of declining religious fervency will remain unanswerable. Similarly, although synagogue membership rose in the aftermath of World War II, it is difficult to know what one should make of that fact. As the work of Eric Goldstein reminds us, during the 1950s, when the culture lauded the virtues of assimilation and, accordingly, cast a suspicious eye upon the ardent embrace of ethnic blood ties, synagogue membership – especially, for those moving into the new suburbs – became an acceptable way Jews could band together culturally as Jews.[154] Religion, in other words, became something of a "cover," or excuse, for greater ethnic solidarity.

This more secular outlook on the part of American Jews was reflected in the religious attitudes of Jewish adolescents. According to the Purdue Survey Panel, a sophisticated tracking of public opinion among American teenagers during the late forties and fifties, Jewish teenagers tended to have a less traditionally religious worldview than their Catholic and Protestant counterparts. When asked if they agreed with the statement: "Religious faith is better than logic for solving life's important problems," 57 percent of Protestant teens and 63 percent of Catholic teens said "yes." By contrast, only 23 percent of Jewish teens answered in the affirmative.[155] On another question, youngsters were asked whether "Our fate in the hereafter depends on how we behave on earth?" In their responses, more than two-thirds of Protestant and Catholic adolescents, while less than one-quarter of Jewish teenagers answered "yes." Likewise, on a host of other questions, such as whether "God knows our every thought and movement," whether he answers our prayers, and whether "Men working and thinking together can build a good society without any divine or supernatural help," Jewish teens were significantly more likely to take a secular position than their Protestant and Roman Catholic counterparts.[156]

In other words, the spiritual significance of increasing synagogue membership is open to question. However, what we can say with some measure of confidence is the level of fervent belief that was declining among

[154] Goldstein, Eric. *The Price of Whiteness: Jews, Race, and American Identity* (Princeton, NJ: Princeton University Press, 2006).
[155] Remmers, H. H., and Radler, D. H. *The American Teenager* (Indianapolis: Bobbs-Merrill Company, 1957), p. 171.
[156] Ibid, pp. 172, 173.

Catholics and Protestants at midcentury tended to be even lower among American Jews.

The Dichotomy of a Religious Nation

It is important to recognize that any suggestion of waning piety, or of a declining religiosity, does not necessarily mean that the America of today, or of the 1950s, ceased to be, in a meaningful sense, a religious country. It is true that in examining public responses to bingo, ballrooms, brides and bridegrooms, blue laws, Bibles, and Brotherhood Week it would appear that religious faith became less vigorous over time. However, it is also quite clear that by most cross-national comparisons, the citizens of the United States remain among the most religious people in the Western world.[157] Consequently, whatever winds were blowing over America's religious terrain at midcentury, it probably would be correct to state that, compared to her counterparts in Europe and Japan, the "typical" American did not seem very secular.

However, the critical question is not whether Americans at midcentury remained a religious people, but whether Americans during the 1950s became a *more* religious people. To be sure, church attendance – which appears to have been rising at midcentury – is an important index of the breadth of religious commitment.[158] Yet church attendance is merely one of many such indices. As sociologist Christian Smith noted, the implications of climbing rates of church attendance are anything but clear. "Hypothetically, a church's pews could be completely filled with regular attenders who are exceptionally uncommitted, uninformed, and apathetic

[157] Lipset, Seymour Martin. *American Exceptionalism: A Double-Edged Sword* (New York: W. W. Norton, 1996), pp. 63, 64. Lipset notes that according to cross-national survey data, 94 percent of Americans express faith in God compared to 70 percent of the British and 69 percent of West Germans. In addition, "86 percent of Americans surveyed believe in heaven; 43 percent say they attend church services weekly. The corresponding numbers for British respondents are 54 percent accepting the existence of heaven and only 14 percent indicating they attend church weekly. For West Germans, the numbers are also distinctly lower than for Americans, at 43 and 41 percent, respectively. A remarkable 69 percent of Americans say they believe the Devil exists, as compared to one-third of the British, one-fifth of the French, 18 percent of West Germans, 12 percent of the Swedes, and 43 percent of the Canadians." In the paragraph that follows, Lipset notes that more than 150 years ago, Tocqueville wrote: "There is no country in the world where the Christian religion retains a greater influence over the souls of men than in America."

[158] Finke and Stark, *The Churching of America, 1776–1990: Winners and Losers in Our Religious Economy* (New Brunswick, NJ: Rutgers University Press, 1992).

religiously – who perhaps want nothing more than a place to meet useful business contacts and the status they think is associated with being an upstanding, churchgoing citizen of their community. We wouldn't consider that a strong church."[159]

Smith's warning is more than mere conjecture. In 1960, a team of researchers completed a three-year study examining the attitudes of college students on a host of social issues. When queried about their spiritual lives, a clear majority expressed a need for religion. However, when researchers probed more deeply, and asked students why religion was so important to them, almost half cited such nonmystical reasons as "personal adjustment," "intellectual clarity," and "an anchor for family life." In other words, more than half of all the student respondents failed to identify the chief purpose of religion as a means of becoming closer to God.[160]

In his classic work *Islam Observed: Religious Development in Morocco and Indonesia* (1971), anthropologist Clifford Geertz draws an important distinction between the scope of religion and the force of religion. Were we to define "scope" as the weekly rates of church attendance, then the claim of a 1950s religious revival would probably be correct. However, by casting our net broadly, and looking at the kinds of behavior that go beyond mere church attendance, the picture that emerges is one of diminishing religious force.

The implications of this approach are potentially far-reaching. They suggest that Americans today are considerably less religious, in a personal sense, than their counterparts were during the early decades of the twentieth century. Despite the rise of religious conservatives and, with it, the strengthened bond between religion and politics, in the hearts and in the homes of most people of faith a transformation of just what it means to be religiously "conservative" had taken hold. As we have seen, Reverend Billy Graham of the late 1940s was a religious hard-liner who would scarcely recognize, let alone approve of, the Billy Graham of today. Likewise, if they were still among the living, the religious conservatives of the 1930s and 1940s would, with mouths agape, look at their counterparts in more recent times – people like the late Jerry Falwell and Pat Robertson, whose universities boast departments of psychology, whose religious ministries speak of the persistent consumption of pornography as "addictions," and in the case of Robertson, whose school's shops are

---

[159] Smith, *American Evangelicalism*, p. 20.
[160] "Uncommitted Minds," *Newsweek* (April 25, 1960), p. 104.

wide open for business on Sunday – with a combination of shock and disapproval. It is only by the relaxed standards of contemporary times that today's religious conservatives can truly be styled as "conservative."

Taken together, the downplaying of sectarian differences, the declining power of jeremiads against worldliness, the increasing frequency of religious intermarriage, the religious embrace of modern psychology, the waning emphasis on proselytizing, and the demise of Sabbath-day observance, all form a portrait of American piety during the age of Eisenhower that was less demanding than the alternative claim of an increasingly robust faith. In short, although increasing numbers of Americans could be categorized as "believers," the depth of such "belief" does not seem especially deep. To borrow from the imagery of historian Daniel Rodgers, American religion during the forties and fifties was akin to a nova about to enter its giant red phase: while expanding outwardly, the inner core was perceptively thinning out.[161]

[161] Rodgers, Daniel T. "Republicanism: The Career of a Concept," *Journal of American History*, Vol. 79 (January 1992), p. 11.

3

Sex

Ingrid Bergman, Elizabeth Taylor, and the Sexual Revolution in the Postwar Period

In examining public attitudes toward sex in the postwar era, two scandals involving movie stars and sexual impropriety provide us with a window into the shifting sensibilities of the American masses. In 1949, a torrent of public outrage forced the Swedish film star Ingrid Bergman to leave the United States and return to her native Europe. The reason for Bergman's sudden transformation from beloved celebrity figure to pariah was the disclosure of her plans to leave husband and daughter to be with Italian director Roberto Rossellini, whose child she was then carrying. In response to the scandal, the Federal Council of Churches, the largest religious organization in the country at the time, blasted the Rossellini–Bergman affair as the kind of "sex exhibitionism which is a symptom of the moral decay of the West."[1] Likewise, the Salvation Army promptly pulled all recordings Bergman had made on behalf of its annual fundraising drive. In addition, if author Donald Spoto is to be believed, from the fall of 1949 to the close of 1950 more than thirty-five thousand articles, essays, and editorials appeared in the American press dedicated to the Bergman controversy.[2]

For more than seven years Bergman remained essentially banished from the United States. During that time she did not set foot on American soil, nor did she appear in an American film. However, by 1956, when she completed *Anastasia* – a movie filmed in Europe but distributed in

[1] Spoto, Donald. *Notorious: The Life of Ingrid Bergman* (New York: Harper Collins, 1997), p. 292.
[2] Ibid, p. 283.

America – the public mood in the United States had changed noticeably. It was not that Americans had forgotten Bergman's behavior, but many seemed willing to put the incident behind them. On a brief visit to the United States in January 1957, many Americans welcomed Bergman with open arms. As an article in *Newsweek* described it, "For 36 hours last week, Ingrid Bergman back in the U.S. for the first time in eight years... trotted about New York while more than 60 reporters and photographers struggled mightily to keep up with her." It was clear that her exile had ended when, after Bergman and a friend finished lunching at The Colony, they were greeted by more than a thousand fans outside the restaurant.[3] That same year, Bergman won an Academy Award for Best Actress for her role in *Anastasia*, a clear sign that her pariah status in America had ended.

The Bergman–Rossellini controversy, which first erupted at the end of the 1940s, stands in sharp contrast to another scandal, which took place nine years later. Following the tragic death of film producer Michael Todd, celebrity crooner Eddie Fisher rushed to the side of Todd's even more famous wife, actress Elizabeth Taylor. In life, Todd and Fisher had been the closest of friends, so when Fisher offered his shoulder to Todd's grieving widow, few gave it any thought. However, as the months passed, the two carried on a very indiscreet love affair. The only problem was that Eddie Fisher was already a married man with two children. His wife was none other than actress Debbie Reynolds, generally regarded by the public as a paragon of innocence and virtue. By the end of 1958, less than ten months after Todd's death, Reynolds filed divorce papers, resulting in a torrent of articles in magazines including *Life* and *Newsweek*.[4]

Intense media coverage continued in 1959, when Fisher and Taylor married. According to Fisher's memoirs, at the height of the scandal he and Taylor were bombarded with approximately seven thousand angry letters per week. "Dear Eddie Fisher," began one letter, "You will never be allowed in our living room again. We will do everything in our power to tell all our friends not to buy your records or go to see your movies. You have brought shame upon your name and your people...." Some

---

[3] "Ingrid's Return," *Newsweek* (January 28, 1957), p. 63.

[4] Williams, Jeannie. "Eddie Dishes Dirt on Liz and Debbie," *USA Today* (September 8, 1999), p. 2D; Orchklin, Michele. "Books in Brief Non-Fiction: Eddie Fisher's *Been There, Done That*," *The New York Times* (September 26, 1999), Section 7, p. 21; Keck, William. "Scandal's History for 'These Old Broads,'" *Los Angeles Times* (February 12, 2001), p. 1F.

disgruntled fans went so far as to organize an "Eddie–Liz" boycott, and when Steve Allen announced that Eddie Fisher would appear on his show, the audience booed.[5]

However harsh the public's treatment of Fisher, Taylor's treatment was even worse. Once the scandal broke, the Theatre Owners of America promptly cancelled plans to name Taylor "Star of the Year" for her role in *Cat on a Hot Tin Roof*. Letters to gossip columnist Hedda Hopper revealed deep-seated hostility toward Taylor. Whereas fans depicted Fisher as weak-willed and disloyal, these same letter writers – the majority of whom were women – subjected Taylor to considerably sterner treatment. "Elizabeth Taylor is just no damn good," declared one Helen Moore, "Eddie never did have anything above his ears." Another fan, writing from Lompoc, California, complained that Taylor had "made herself sickening and disgusting to many people. It's too bad that Mr. Fisher is so weak minded as to be swayed by her."[6]

When Taylor went to the premiere of *Scent of a Mystery* – a movie produced by her late husband's company – she had to walk through a gauntlet of snarling fans who called her a "home-wrecker" and a "husband-stealer."[7] Yet for all of the negative publicity, the public backlash seemed quite tame when compared to the earlier Bergman–Rossellini scandal. Unlike Bergman, Taylor continued her career unhampered, receiving an Oscar nomination in 1959, and finally, in 1960, winning Best Actress for her performance in *Butterfield 8*. Less than three years after her affair with Fisher hit the papers, Taylor reached the high point of her career when she agreed to star in the title role of *Cleopatra*, becoming the first movie star – male or female – to receive $1 million to appear in a film.[8]

The Liberalization of Sexual Behavior

The difference in the way the public treated Ingrid Bergman in 1949 and Liz Taylor nearly a decade later fits very well within the popular understanding of American life at midcentury. Today, most scholars acknowledge that the culture was becoming sexualized during the 1950s.

---

[5] Fisher, Eddie. *Been There, Done That* (New York: St. Martin's Press, 1999), pp. 149–50.

[6] American Academy of Motion Pictures Arts and Sciences; Special Collections. Hedda Hopper File, "Letters About Liz – September 1958."

[7] Sheppard, Dick. *Elizabeth: The Life and Career of Elizabeth Taylor* (Garden City, New York: Doubleday & Company, 1974), pp. 251, 255.

[8] Leonard, William. "They Love Liz Taylor, Shocks and All," *Chicago Sunday Tribune Magazine* (June 12, 1960), p. 9.

Nevertheless, they still hold that insofar as behavior was concerned, the 1950s was by and large a conservative time. While acknowledging the earlier rise of Hugh Hefner's *Playboy* and an increasingly defiant youth culture, most scholars continue to portray these pre-1960s developments as mere rumblings or precursors to the liberalization of sexual behavior that emerged during the 1960s. Although many are aware of a general loosening of sexual attitudes during the forties and fifties – a loosening that we see in the starkly different treatments meted out to the exiled-then-redeemed Ingrid Bergman and the mildly rebuked Elizabeth Taylor – they fail to detect an appreciable upswing in premarital sexual behavior.

For instance, in *Embattled Paradise: The American Family in an Age of Uncertainty*, Arlene Skolnick argues that while the incidence of female premarital intercourse "leveled off in the 1940s and 1950s," it soared during the 1960s as "young women abandoned their desperate struggle to remain categorized as virgins."[9] Similarly, in *Him/Her/Self*, Peter Filene is adamant that "a 'revolution' in middle-class sexual behavior" did not occur during the 1950s.[10] During the past two decades, a string of scholars, including John D'Emilio and Estelle Freedman, Steven Mintz and Susan Kellogg, John Heindry, Elaine Tyler May, Steven Seidman, and Robert Francoeur have concurred with Filene and Skolnick in positing a virtual explosion of premarital intercourse during the decade of the 1960s.[11]

Thus, with the debut of rock 'n' roll and *Playboy* magazine, and with the publication of such novels as *Lolita* (1955) and *Peyton Place* (1956), the 1950s is seen as an era of increased sexual titillation, while the portrait of the sixties – with its free love, coed dorms, and oral contraceptives – is one of increased sexual activity. Such bifurcations between titillation and consummation, or between sexual suggestion and sexual license, have

[9] Skolnick, Arlene. *Embattled Paradise: The American Family in an Age of Uncertainty* (New York: Basic Books, 1991), p. 87.

[10] Filene, Peter G. *Him/Her/Self: Sex Roles in Modern America* (Baltimore: Johns Hopkins University Press, 1974), p. 12.

[11] D'Emilio, John, and Freedman, Estelle. *Intimate Matters: A History of Sexuality in America* (Chicago: University of Chicago Press, 1988); Mintz, Steven, and Kellogg, Susan. *Domestic Revolutions: A Social History of American Family Life* (New York: The Free Press, 1998); May, Elaine Tyler. *Homeward Bound: American Families in the Cold War Era* (New York: Basic Books, 1988); Francoeur, Robert T. "The Sexual Revolution: Will Hard Times Turn Back the Clock?," *The Futurist* (April 1980), p. 3; Seidman, Steven. *Embattled Eros: Sexual Politics and Ethics in Contemporary America* (New York: Routledge, 1992); and Heindry, John. *What Wild Ecstasy: The Rise and Fall of the Sexual Revolution* (New York: Simon & Schuster, 1997), pp. 66, 245.

enabled historians to depict the sixties as a morally tumultuous decade, while still holding fast to the view that the 1950s were a conservative time with respect to sexual behavior.

Admittedly, the evidence in support of such an interpretation is formidable. Notwithstanding an increased sexual candor in movies, music, theater, and literature, a family-oriented culture unquestionably prevailed throughout America during the Eisenhower years. People were marrying at younger ages – in fact, during the fifties, most women were marrying at an earlier age than their own grandmothers had. Couples begat more children, and for the first time in the twentieth century the divorce rate failed to rise.[12]

Technological innovation – what some would call "technology shock" – is believed by many to be one of the principal reasons sexual behavior in the 1960s became less repressed. According to this argument, when the Food and Drug Administration (FDA) approved the sale of the first oral contraceptive Enovid® in the summer of 1960, it helped usher in a new age of sexual freedom. By assuring women that they could have intercourse with little risk of conception, "the Pill" removed one of the most effective impediments to premarital sex: the fear of unwanted pregnancies.

Conventional wisdom has it that the effects of the Pill became so sweeping that even journalists began stating, as an unassailable fact, that the Pill paved the way to the sexual revolution. "In the beginning was the Pill," began an article in *Newsweek* in 1986, "then, it was the IUD. Together they started the sexual revolution of the 1960s, making sex both spontaneous and worry-free for the first time." More recently, an article in *Time* maintained that "the sexual revolution of the west" was "ignited by a technological breakthrough – the Pill."[13] And writing in *The New Republic*, during the late 1980s, Leon Kass asserted, "The Sexual Revolution that liberated (especially) female sexual desire from the confines of marriage, and even from love and intimacy, would almost certainly not have occurred had there not been available cheap and effective female birth control – the Pill – which for the first time severed female sexual activity from its generative consequences."[14]

[12] May, *Homeward Bound*, pp. 5, 8.
[13] Clark, Mike, and Springen, Karen. "Contraceptives: On Hold," *Newsweek* (May 5, 1986), p. 68.
[14] Kass, Leon R. "The Wisdom of Repugnance," *The New Republic* (June 2, 1987), p. 17; Spaeth, Anthony. "The Sexual Revolution," *Time* [International Edition] (March 25, 1996), p. 48.

For the most part historians, duly reluctant to embrace mono-causal explanations, have taken a more nuanced approach. Rather than characterizing the Pill as the ultimate cause, most historians have portrayed the sexual revolution as a critical breakthrough that, along with other developments (like the emergence of a generation gap), led to an avalanche of nonmarital sexual behavior. Yet for all of the differences between the standard journalistic account and the more modest claims of historians, both parties believe sexual behavior during the 1950s did not change dramatically. For journalists, time began with the introduction of the oral contraceptive. For most historians the sexual revolution, while not solely a creation of the Pill, truly came into its own during the Kennedy and Johnson years. However, in both cases the 1950s is marginalized: largely ignored by reporters and pundits, it tends to be treated as little more than a gestation period by scholars.

Of course, if either of these interpretations were correct then the very notion of a Permissive Turn would be in great peril. For if there was a dramatic "loosening" of values at midcentury, if – as I claimed earlier – Americans by the tens of millions were adopting a less traditional stance on fundamental moral questions, then surely we should be able to identify a significant upswing in premarital sex during the Eisenhower years.

This chapter seeks to challenge the traditional interpretation. Contrary to popular belief, the sexual revolution (on a behavioral level) did not start in the 1960s, it was not ignited by the introduction of the birth control pill, it was not significantly fanned by the baby boomers' coming of age, and – most important of all – the sexualization of the popular culture did not anticipate the liberalization of mass behavior. Through an examination of single motherhood and premarital pregnancy rates, and by carefully distinguishing between norms and values, it is possible to understand the sexual revolution in a way that departs sharply from the meta-narrative that now dominates the historiography and the journalistic accounts of the sexual revolution.

Premarital Sex

By its very nature, the frequency of premarital sex is a difficult phenomenon to measure. It is likely that those willing to respond to detailed questions about their sexual histories harbor fewer inhibitions than the larger population. In fact, in most sexual surveys a large proportion of people – sometimes as high as 90 percent of those initially approached – refuse to take any part in the study.[15] However, even when people are willing to answer inquiries about their sexual pasts, their truthfulness remains very questionable. An intriguing study, conducted in the mid-1960s, demonstrates the dangers of such self-reporting. Students at a university filled out a questionnaire asking them to disclose a number of nonnormative behaviors – such as masturbation, hitting one's girlfriend or wife, buying pornography, and having intimate relations with a person of the same sex. Students were then told that they would be compensated for their participation in the study, but only after they took a polygraph examination that probed the truthfulness of their responses. When given the opportunity to "correct" their answers, every student made revisions to the questionnaire – that is, they changed one or more of their original answers.[16] What this study suggests is that when sex is the central focus, the value of respondents' answers should be approached with a great deal of skepticism.

Yet in periodizing the sexual revolution, historians and sociologists have relied on these same kinds of studies pioneered by Alfred Kinsey and perpetuated by a later generation of social scientists. Fortunately, scholars need not solely depend on in-depth interviews or social science surveys when grappling with some important aspects of sexual behavior. With the help of vital statistics, it becomes possible to obtain clear and unambiguous information pertaining to nonmarital sexual activity during the 1960s, 1950s, and even the 1940s. Between 1940 and 1960, the frequency of single motherhood among white women increased more than 2.5-fold, rising from 3.6 newborns to 9.2 newborns per 1,000 unmarried women of childbearing age (see Graph 3.1). Among all women, single motherhood rose from 7.1 newborns to 21.6 newborns per 1,000 women of childbearing age.[17]

These increases would continue over the next several decades. However, the rate of acceleration would decrease so that by 1989 the rate of single motherhood among all women had risen to 41.8 newborns, and among white women it would climb to 29.2 newborns per 1,000 unmarried women of childbearing age. These were sizable increases, but when

---

[15] For a discussion of the high nonresponse rates that have plagued sexual surveys, see Michael, Robert T., Gagnon, John H., Laumann, Edward O., and Kolata, Gina, *Sex in America: A Definitive Survey* (New York: Little, Brown and Company, 1994), p. 23.

[16] See Clark, John P., and Tift, Larry L., "Polygraph and Interview Validation of Self-Reported Deviant Behavior," *American Sociological Review* (August 1966), pp. 516–23.

[17] Bureau of the Census, U.S. Department of Commerce, *Historical Statistics of the United States: Colonial Times to 1970*, Part I (Washington: Bureau of the Census, 1975), p. 52.

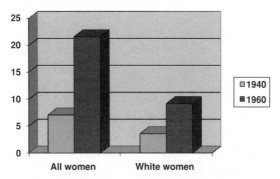

GRAPH 3.1. Rate of premaritally conceived babies per 1,000 white women annual average

compared to the period between 1940 and 1960, it is clear that the rate of growth had somewhat decreased.[18]

In all candor, there are limitations associated with the use of vital statistics. Even when broken down by race and age group, rates of single motherhood do not address such crucial sociological categories as income, religion, and educational background. In addition, although vital statistics relating to unwed motherhood can provide a baseline, or establish a minimum level of premarital sex in a given year, they do not reveal the actual level of premarital sex. However, because rates of single motherhood focus on what people have done, as opposed to what people claim to have done (or claim not to have done), they are significantly more reliable than either subject interviews or polling data. As such, they provide scholars who are engaged in the history of sexuality with the best empirical foundation. And for all of their limitations, vital statistics relating to unwed motherhood indicate that premarital intercourse probably was increasing, and increasing rapidly, during the 1940s and 1950s. After all, it seems reasonable to conclude that significant increases in the level of unwed motherhood probably reflect significant increases in premarital sex.

The Sexual Revolution

Admittedly, it would be a mistake to equate the sexual revolution merely with the increasing prevalence of premarital intercourse. John D'Emilio,

[18] Kurian, George Thomas. *Datapedia of the United States, 1790–2000* (Lanham, Maryland: Bernan Press, 1994), p. 40.

Estelle Freedman, and Beth Bailey have shown in their work that the
commodification of sex, the heavy emphasis on sexual fulfillment, the
"resexualization of women in popular and scholarly thought," and, correspondingly, the elimination – or, at least, the decline – of the double
standard proved to be important developments in the sexual revolution.[19]
Yet surely the proliferation of premarital sex remains no less significant
a social indicator. In fact, one of the reasons academics have lavished so
much attention on petting during the forties and fifties is that, having
already assumed that premarital sex was not on the rise, the practice
of petting has enabled scholars to explore some of the sexual rumblings
beneath the alleged stability of the period.[20] Equally significant, the most
important works on the sexual revolution have made a point of denying
that premarital female intercourse was on the rise during the forties and
fifties.[21]

Even Alfred Kinsey (see Figure 3.1), the most influential scholar to
write about sexuality in the twentieth century, denied that female premarital sex was rising rapidly after World War II. Although Kinsey's
data shocked American readers – especially his claims that nearly half of
women had premarital intercourse, 62 percent had masturbated, and a
quarter of married women had, at some point, engaged in extramarital
sex – he believed the big leap in female premarital intercourse took place
between 1916 and 1930.[22] Any increases after 1930, he reported, had
been "only minor."[23] Although released in 1953, and based on some
interviews that Kinsey and his staff conducted during the late 1940s, his
book *Sexual Behavior in the Human Female* did not cover the entire
decade of the 1950s. Thus, the question of whether female premarital sex
was rising or falling in the fifteen years after World War II would be left to
a later generation of researchers who would draw upon the methodology
that Alfred Kinsey pioneered. Overwhelmingly, these researchers would
conclude that female premarital intercourse remained fairly stable during

[19] D'Emilio and Freedman, *Intimate Matters*; Bailey, Beth, "Sexual Revolution(s)," in
Farber, David (ed.), *The Sixties: From Memory to History* (Chapel Hill: University
of North Carolina Press, 1994), pp. 235–62.

[20] Bailey, Beth L. *From Front Porch to Back Seat: Courtship in Twentieth-Century America*,
(Baltimore: Johns Hopkins Press, 1988), p. 80.

[21] See D'Emilio and Freedman, *Intimate Matters*, p. 117; Skolnick, *Embattled Paradise*,
p. 87; May, *Homeward Bound*, p. 117.

[22] Jones, James H. *Alfred C. Kinsey: A Public/Private Life* (New York: W. W. Norton,
1997), p. 689.

[23] Kinsey, Alfred C., Pomery, Wardell B., Martin, Clyde E., and Gebhard, Paul H. *Sexual
Behavior in the Human Female* (Philadelphia: W. B. Saunders, 1953), p. 300.

FIGURE 3.1. Alfred Kinsey, pioneering sex researcher, conducting a mock interview, 1953. (Photographer: William Dellenback, reproduced by permission of The Kinsey Institute for Research in Sex, Gender, and Reproduction, Inc.)

the forties and fifties and only began its sharp climb sometime during the late sixties or early seventies.[24]

The apparent surge in single motherhood is all the more remarkable when one considers that the 1950s were a time when couples were exchanging wedding vows at ever-earlier ages. During the Eisenhower era, the average age of marriage for men was twenty-two years; for women, it was only twenty years.[25] When it came to sexual intercourse, says cultural historian Stephanie Coontz, "Young people were not taught how to 'say no' – they were simply handed wedding rings."[26] Although Coontz's remarks wrongly imply that sex outside of marriage was not rising briskly

[24] Bell, Robert R., and Chaskes, Jay B. "Premarital Sexual Experience Among Coeds, 1958 and 1968," *Journal of Marriage and the Family* (February 1970), pp. 81–4; Christensen, Harold T., and Gregg, Christina F. "Changing Sex Norms in America and Scandinavia," *Journal of Marriage and the Family* (November 1970), pp. 616–27; Miller, Patricia Y., and Simon, William. "Adolescent Sexual Behavior: Context and Change," *Social Problems* (October 1974), pp. 58–74.

[25] Diggins, John Patrick. *The Proud Decades: America in War and Peace, 1941–1960* (New York: W. W. Norton & Company, 1989), p. 212.

[26] Ibid.

FIGURE 3.2. Kinsey (at podium, right) addressing students at the University of California, Berkeley. (Reproduced by permission of The Kinsey Institute for Research in Sex, Gender, and Reproduction, Inc.)

during the 1950s, she is correct in arguing that the trend toward these earlier first marriages effectively reduced the level of premarital sex from where it would have otherwise stood.

There were other forces capable of skewing the postwar rates of single motherhood. A greater reliance on contraception could have the effect of understating the true levels of premarital sex. For instance, were we to assume that there was a growing dependence on birth control in the fifteen years following World War II, the central argument of this chapter – that prior to the 1960s premarital sex was on the rise – would be strengthened further. This means the overall frequency of premarital sex was rising so briskly during the Truman and Eisenhower years it was able to overcome the suppressive effects of birth control, and still force illegitimacy rates to soar.

Due to data limitations it is impossible to know whether contraceptive use among the unmarried was rising or falling during the 1950s, but there exists a good deal of evidence suggesting birth control was at least becoming more culturally acceptable. On the eve of World War II, most states had laws in place restricting the advertisement and dissemination of birth control. However, by the end of the fifties only two states – Massachusetts and Connecticut – retained these restrictions.[27] As historian Donald Critchlow has shown, Gunnar Myrdal's book *An*

---

[27] May, *Homeward Bound*, p. 151. For a fuller explanation of the growing acceptance of birth control during the 1950s, see the opening chapter of Critchlow, Donald T., *Intended Consequences: Birth Control, Abortion, and the Federal Government in Modern America* (New York: Oxford University Press, 1999).

American Dilemma (1944) noted "birth control is taboo as a subject for public polite conversation." Yet by the mid-1950s the social atmosphere had clearly changed as a number of prominent organizations, including the Ford Foundation and the Rockefeller Brothers Fund, were actively promoting contraception.[28]

The rising fortunes of the Planned Parenthood Federation of America, the nation's foremost proponent of birth control, are equally revealing. In 1939, when Planned Parenthood tried to recruit doctors to provide contraceptive assistance to underserviced communities in the country, the campaign was met with only modest success. Of the approximately 1,400 physicians who were contacted, 210 came forward to offer their services. It would seem that the top officials at Planned Parenthood were very pleased with the responses, as they trumpeted the results in their annual report. However, these successes in 1939 would pale in comparison to the gains of later years. Thanks in part to the demise of the Comstock laws – legislation that discouraged public discussion of birth control – by 1955 more than twenty-two hundred doctors and medical students, and some six thousand nurses, were receiving training at Planned Parenthood clinics.[29]

In addition to the emergence of a more tolerant attitude toward birth control, there are good reasons to believe that the effective use of condoms – then, the most popular form of birth control among single people – was on the rise.[30] As a result of a test case in 1957, foreign manufacturers of condoms were allowed access to the U.S. market, thereby providing fresh competition.[31] Manufacturers also began to market condoms more aggressively during this time. Traditionally, condoms had been a specialty item – hidden behind the drugstore counter and available only upon request – but during the mid-1950s some drugstores began setting up

[28] Critchlow, *Intended Consequences*, pp. 35–6.
[29] Birth Control Federation of America, Inc. Annual Report 1939, box 101, Planned Parenthood Federation of America Archives, Sophia Smith Collection, Smith College Library Archives (hereafter cited as Planned Parenthood Archives).
[30] In fact, the first major survey of birth-control habits of sexually active teenagers, conducted in 1971, found the condom to be the most popular form of contraceptives. See Katner, John F., and Zelnik, Melvin, "Contraception and Pregnancy: Experience of Young Unmarried Women in the United States," *Family Planning Perspectives*, Vol. 5 (Winter 1973), pp. 21–35.
[31] Butts, Harry E. "Legal Requirements for Condoms Under the Federal Food, Drug, and Cosmetic Act," in Redford, Myron H., Duncan, Gordon W., and Prager, Denis J. (eds.), *The Condom: Increasing Utilization in the United States* (San Francisco: San Francisco Press, 1974), p. 208.

displays.[32] Moreover, drugstores proliferated during the 1950s, driven by the twin forces of suburbanization and chain retailing. As the primary vehicle for the sale of prophylactics, drugstores brought condoms within the reach of increasing numbers of American males.

Unfortunately, all the evidence pointing to the greater use of condoms is indirect due to a lack of data: no sales figures are available. However, the effectiveness of condoms as a product was fast improving during the Eisenhower years. As Harry Butts, a former senior official with the Food and Drug Administration (FDA) noted, once prophylactics came under close FDA scrutiny in the late 1940s, the quality of condoms improved greatly.[33] Two forces drove this development: more stringent FDA requirements and more advanced manufacturing processes.[34]

In light of the foregoing developments – namely, the more aggressive marketing of birth control, the receding taboo against contraceptives, and the superior quality of condoms themselves – the proposition that effective birth control was becoming more common among the unmarried during the 1950s would seem quite reasonable. These changes notwithstanding, it appears the rising rates of premarital sex were still able to overwhelm these contraceptive countermeasures in the twenty years after Pearl Harbor.

A final innovation that facilitated still higher levels of premarital sex was the mass production of the so-called "miracle" drug penicillin. Although discovered by Sir Alexander Fleming in 1928, it was not until World War II that scientists – having learned how to mass-produce penicillin – succeeded in bringing the drug to the general masses. With it came the ability to battle the potentially ravaging effects of venereal disease. As Allen Brandt reports in his book *No Magic Bullet: A Social History of Venereal Disease in the United States Since 1880*, by 1949 the United States was producing some 650 billion units of penicillin per month. Accordingly, the price of penicillin fell from $20 per vial of 100,000 units in 1943, to less than a dollar by 1945, to only about 30 cents by 1947.[35] Not surprisingly, the widespread availability of penicillin rendered venereal diseases far less hazardous. In 1940, the death rate from syphilis stood at more than 10.7 per 100,000; by 1955 the syphilis death rate had tumbled to about 2.5 per 100,000 – a decrease of more than 75 percent.

[32] Baker, Samuel A. "Advertising Male Contraceptives," in *The Condom: Increasing Utilization in the United States*, pp. 116, 117.
[33] Butts, "Legal Requirements," pp. 206–7.
[34] Ibid.
[35] Brandt, Allen. *No Magic Bullet: A Social History of Venereal Disease in the United States Since 1880*, (New York: Oxford University Press, 1985), p. 170.

Equally telling, *The American Journal of Syphilis* had ceased publication by 1955.[36] As the debilitating effects of venereal disease receded, an important deterrent to illicit sex lost much of its dreaded sting.

One variable that cannot be fully accounted for is the incidence of abortion. As with contraceptives, changes in the frequency of abortions are capable of affecting the official levels of illegitimacy. Illegitimacy rates are propelled upward when the number of abortions is comparatively low, and held down when the quantity of abortions is comparatively high. However, due to its criminal status in the days prior to *Roe v. Wade* (1973), it is impossible to know or even guess at the actual levels of abortion during the Truman and Eisenhower years. Therefore, it is theoretically possible the surging rates of illegitimacy from 1940 to 1960 were due more to the decreasing incidence of abortion than to rising levels of premarital sex. However, given the less traditional nature of American life, the sexualization of the popular culture, the greater sense of autonomy enjoyed by young people, and the increasing sense of shame* surrounding single-motherhood, it is difficult to conceive how the frequency of abortions could have headed downward, and not upward, during this period.

What Statistics Say about Premarital Sex

The portrait of increased premarital sex painted by vital statistics is further corroborated with fertility data compiled by the U.S. Census Bureau. By asking samples of women a series of questions, including the date of their marriage and the date of the birth of their first child, the Census Bureau has been able to gather a significant amount of information about premarital pregnancies. Unlike the rate relating to single motherhood, premarital pregnancies include babies born to unwed mothers and those born to parents who – although single at the time of conception – were married by the time of birth. By combining both groups, the premarital pregnancy rate offers the fullest possible picture of the levels of premarital sex that ultimately resulted in pregnancy. An examination of these data, compiled by the Fertility Statistics Branch, and recalculated for the purposes of this chapter (drawn from ratios and raw numbers provided by the Census Bureau's Fertility Statistics Branch relating to premarital pregnancy rates), reveals a sharp increase in premarital pregnancies over time. For example, between 1939 and 1942, there were 8.5 premarital pregnancies for every 1,000 white single women between the ages of 15

[36] Ibid, pp. 170–1.
* This "increasing sense of shame," reflected in higher rates of "shotgun" marriages, will be discussed later in this chapter."

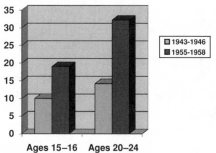

GRAPH 3.2. Rate of premaritally conceived babies per 1,000 white women by age

and nineteen. In the period between 1955 and 1958, that figure had more than doubled (to nineteen pregnancies per 1,000).[37]

For single white women between the ages of twenty and twenty-four, a significant increase also took place. Between 1943 and 1946 (the first year such numbers could be calculated), the premarital pregnancy rate stood at 14.2 pregnancies for every 1,000 unwed white women between the ages of twenty and twenty-four. Twelve years later, in the period between 1955 and 1958, that premarital pregnancy rate had risen to 32.2 per 1,000 (see Graph 3.2).[38]

When the two age-groups are combined, what emerges is a picture of considerable growth. For the period 1943 to 1946, there were 11.9 newborns for every 1,000 single white women between ages fifteen and twenty-four. Between the years 1955 and 1958, the premarital pregnancy rate had climbed to 25.3 pregnancies per 1,000 white women between ages fifteen and twenty-four – more than doubling over twelve years.[39]

[37] Rates are based on numbers derived from O'Connell, Martin, and Moore, Maurice J. "The Legitimacy Status of First Births to U.S. Women Aged 15–24, 1939–1978," *Family Planning Perspectives* (January/February 1980), pp. 16–25. At the time of the article's publication, O'Connell was a statistician and Moore was the head of Fertility Statistics Branch of the Population Division of the U.S. Census Bureau. Later, O'Connell would follow Moore as the head of the Fertility Statistics Branch. Table 3, p. 20 of O'Connell and Moore's article reveals the illegitimacy rate for never-married black and white women between ages fifteen to twenty-four. Table 5, p. 22, reveals "legitimated" or "shotgun" marriages, as a percentage of all premaritally conceived pregnancies for the years in question. From the material in Tables 3 and 5, the illegitimacy rate and the shotgun marriage rate are provided. Because the premarital pregnancy rate is equal to the shotgun marriage rate plus the illegitimacy rate, and because Table 3 provides the illegitimacy rate while Table 5 provides information that enables one to arrive at the shotgun marriage rate (called "legitimated" rate), it was essentially a matter of addition to arrive at premarital pregnancy rate. See p. 20 (for Table 3) and p. 22 (for Table 5) of O'Connell and Moore, "The Legitimacy Status of First Births To U.S. Women Aged 15–24, 1939–1978," *Family Planning Perspectives* (January/February 1980), pp. 16–25.
[38] Ibid.
[39] Ibid.

Among African American women, the growth rate was slower than whites, but the base was also much higher. Between 1939 and 1942, for example, the premarital pregnancy rate among black teens stood at 58.3 per 1,000 black single women between the ages of fifteen and nineteen. Sixteen years later (for the period between 1955 and 1958), the premarital pregnancy rate had climbed to 87.8 per 1,000 single black women between the ages of fifteen and nineteen.[40] Although the rate of acceleration among white teens was higher than the rate of acceleration among blacks, an unmarried African American teenager was more than four times more likely to become pregnant in the late 1950s than her white counterpart.

It is difficult to measure these trends within sexual behavior with a great deal of precision. To begin with, the narrow stream of published data made it impossible to determine premarital pregnancy rates for older groups of women (between the ages of twenty-five to forty-five). In addition, in its calculation, the Census Bureau found that its sample size for each given year was too small to stand on its own. Accordingly, the Census Bureau combined its samples, basing its estimates on four-year cohorts. However, for all of their limitations, the census data enjoy some important advantages over sexual surveys. Although dependent on self-reporting, the census data, unlike sexual surveys, are not morally weighted. Hidden in a series of mundane questions that covered various facets of their economic and social livelihood, respondents probably were less likely to regard queries relating to the date of their marriage – as well as the date of the birth of their first child – with suspicion. Moreover, coming from an official government agency with a deserved reputation for assuring confidentiality, respondents were probably more inclined to be forthcoming.

Although there is much that the fertility data failed to reveal, their upward trend is undeniable. What seems to have occurred here is more than a statistical blip. Just as the forties and fifties experienced a sharp increase in unwed motherhood, likewise there seems to have been a significant upswing in premarital pregnancies during this same period of time. Here, vital statistics and census data, two different sources of evidence collected through very different research approaches, tend toward the same conclusion.

So what do all of these figures reveal? They indicate that both Elaine Tyler May's assertion that the rate of "premarital sexual intercourse" was "stable from the 1920s, to the 1960s," and D'Emilio and Freedman's claim that from the 1920s the "incidence of (female) premarital

[40] Ibid.

intercourse ... remained relatively constant until the late 1960s," are not corroborated by the best empirical data.[41] Instead, the evidence suggests that far from being quiescent, the forties and fifties experienced a prodigious increase in the frequency of premarital intercourse. To argue otherwise one would need to somehow reconcile the evidence of a dramatic increase in premarital pregnancies, the more than doubling of white illegitimacy, and the more than tripling of all out-of-wedlock births with the claim that sex outside of marriage was not rising during the Truman and Eisenhower years.

The Commoditization of Sex

The portrayal of the 1950s as a decade of increased sexual candidness instead of increased permissiveness appears mistaken; however, it is wrong for more than the obvious reason. Implicit in this standard interpretation is the belief that during the postwar period changes in popular culture preceded changes in sexual behavior. As this argument goes, popular culture molded popular attitudes, which in turn, helped shape popular behavior. In accordance with this view, many scholars have argued that while the 1950s did not experience a sharp rise in premarital sexual behavior, it did witness the emergence of an increasingly sexualized popular culture. From there they have gone on to claim – albeit, more tacitly than explicitly – that the commoditization of sex helped pave the way for the "less sexually inhibited" era of the 1960s. "The amount of attention that the media devoted to sex in the fifties may be misleading since there is reason to doubt significant changes in behavior actually occurred," observes historian John Patrick Diggins. "Sex was then an emotion more felt than fulfilled."[42]

In his book *Bad Habits: Drinking, Smoking, Taking Drugs, Gambling, Sexual Misbehavior, and Swearing in American History,* historian John C. Burnham extended this argument, maintaining that when it came to premarital sexual behavior, "the media invented and promoted as much as it described change." The media's intense focus on "personal fulfillment," he continued, "fueled increases in premarital sexual activity."[43] Probably the boldest authors who have sought to harmonize the sexualization of

[41] May, *Homeward Bound*, p. 117; D'Emilio and Freedman, *Intimate Matters*, p. 256.
[42] Diggins, *The Proud Decades*, p. 204.
[43] Burnham, John C. *Bad Habits: Drinking, Smoking, Taking Drugs, Gambling, Sexual Misbehavior, and Swearing in American History* (New York: New York University Press, 1993), p. 193.

the public sphere with the sexual permissiveness of the private sphere are John D'Emilio and Estelle Freedman. By the end of the 1960s, they argued, the proposition that marriage could satisfy the quest for a sexually fulfilling life no longer seemed credible for many. In *Intimate Matters: A History of Sexuality in America* they wrote: "Aided by the values of a consumer culture and *encouraged by the growing visibility of sex in the public realm*, [Italics added] many Americans came to accept sexual pleasure as a legitimate, necessary component of their lives, unbounded by older ideals of marital fidelity and permanence."[44]

The problem with this reading of the sexual revolution is that placing changes in sexual behavior after those in the consumer culture – or, in other words, putting Elvis and Hefner before mass changes in behavior – essentially puts the cart before the horse. A high level of sexual candor in the popular culture did not characterize the 1950s, and the 1960s did not experience a sudden upswing in premarital intercourse. If anything, the reverse would be closer to the truth. Although the best evidence suggests that at midcentury a significant rise in premarital sexual activity took place, Americans during the fifties were not candid enough with themselves to recognize this important development. By contrast, 1960 saw pioneering sexologist Ira L. Reiss predicting the arrival of a sexual revolution. "America is very close to the saturation point in terms of our sexual customs," wrote Reiss, "and, therefore, change should come soon."[45] Within five years of that statement, *Time, The Christian Century, Esquire, The Nation, Mademoiselle,* and *Newsweek* had featured articles that explored the possible arrival of a new sexual revolution.[46]

The crucial distinction between the fifties and sixties lay in word, not in deed. During the 1960s, Americans were simply more willing to acknowledge the extracurricular activities of their youth than they had been during the previous decade. Perhaps these changes were largely attributable to the burgeoning population of college students, an increasingly sexualized popular culture, growing concerns over the ramifications

---

[44] D'Emilio and Freedman, *Intimate Matters*, p. 327.

[45] Reiss, Ira L. *Premarital Sexual Standards in America: A Sociological Investigation of the Relative Sociological and Cultural Integration of America's Sexual Standards* (Illinois: The Free Press, 1960), p. 249.

[46] "Second Sexual Revolution," *Time* (January 24, 1964); "David Susskind's Banned Program; Sexual Revolution in America," *Mademoiselle* (October 1963); "Dialogue on the Moral Crisis," *The Christian Century* (May 27, 1964); Failure of the Sexual Revolution in Southern California, *Esquire* (August 1964); "Morals Revolution on the U.S. Campus," *Newsweek*, (April 6, 1964); "Sexual Revolution," *America* (April 20, 1963).

of the Pill, or the steadily rising level of premarital sexual behavior. Whatever the reasons, attitudes were undoubtedly changing.

Throughout the sixties, one sees in the popular culture a bolder, less
reticent representation of sexuality. Whereas, during the late fifties, the
television characters of Ricky and Lucy Ricardo chastely slept in different
beds, by the mid-1960s the Motion Picture Association officially ended its
reliance on censors. This move assured the production of sexually candid
films, and, by the close of the decade, a number of successful motion
pictures – from *Romeo and Juliet* to *I Am Curious (Yellow)*, and *Midnight
Cowboy* – were depicting nudity and sexual intercourse on screen.[47]

Probably more than any other single development, the success of Playboy Clubs bespoke the emergence of a bolder, less reticent culture during
the early sixties. When the first Playboy Club opened its doors in Chicago
on February 29, 1960, hundreds of aspiring patrons were lined up around
the block.[48] In the weeks that followed, these long lines would become
a nightly ritual, inspiring a New York reporter to compare the crowds
outside the Playboy Club to the daily crowds outside Radio City Music
Hall.[49] By 1961, Chicago's Playboy Club had become the most popular
nightspot in town, selling more food and drinks than any other club or
restaurant in the Windy City.[50]

Technically speaking, Playboy Clubs were not open to the public. To
gain entry, one had to buy a key at a price of $25 or $50 (depending
on where one lived). Within a year of opening, Chicago's Playboy Club
boasted more than one hundred thousand key holders. Equally impressive
was Hefner's success in New York. By the end of 1961, Hefner had
collected nearly $400,000 in key sales from New Yorkers even though
the club was not planning to open its doors until the fall of 1962.[51]

On the literary front, *Playboy* magazine also showed signs of acquiring greater respectability within the culture at large. In September 1962,
Hefner unveiled the "Playboy Interview," which quickly became a publication success. Within a year of its debut, such prominent figures
as Teamster President Jimmy Hoffa, British philosopher Bertrand Russell, Indian prime minister Jawaharlal Nehru, and humanitarian Albert

[47] Allyn, David. *Make Love Not War: The Sexual Revolution: An Unfettered History*
(New York: Little, Brown & Company, 2000), p. 130; Mintz and Kellogg, *Domestic
Revolutions*, p. 209.
[48] Miller, Russell. *Bunny: The Real Story of Playboy* (New York: Holt, Reinhart & Winston, 1984), p. 76.
[49] Ibid.
[50] Cited from reprinted article in *Variety* (February 7, 1962) reproduced in Miller, *Bunny*,
p. 83.
[51] Ibid.

FIGURE 3.3. Hefner surrounded by "bunnies" at one of his many Playboy Clubs. (Reproduced by permission of Playboy Enterprises.)

Schweitzer had granted *Playboy* in-depth interviews. During this same period, *Playboy* received additional contributions from such prominent figures in American life and letters as William F. Buckley, Norman Mailer, Ray Bradbury, Carl Sandburg, and John Paul Getty.[52] These contributions imbued the magazine with an air of sophistication, offering

[52] "Playboy Interview: Bertrand Russell," *Playboy* (March 1963); Getty, J. Paul. "How I Made My First Billion," *Playboy* (October 1961); "Playboy Interview: Jawaharlal Nehru," *Playboy* (October 1963); "Playboy Interview: Albert Schweitzer," *Playboy* (December 1963); Adler, Mortimer. "How to Read a Book Superficially," *Playboy* (December 1963); "Playboy Interview: James Hoffa," *Playboy* (November 1963); Fleming, Ian. "The Hildebrand Rarity," *Playboy* (March 1960); "Playboy Interview: Malcolm X," *Playboy* (May 1963); Bradbury, Ray. "Machineries of Joy," *Playboy* (December 1962); Buchwald, Art. "Great Stories from Showbiz," *Playboy* (December 1962); Mailer, Norman, and Buckley Jr., William F. "A Debate: A Head-Clash over American Politics and Policies Today," *Playboy* (February 1963).

FIGURE 3.4. *Playboy* founder Hugh Hefner at work on his first issue, 1952. (Reproduced by permission of Playboy Enterprises.)

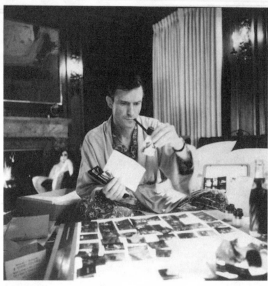

FIGURE 3.5. Hefner scrutinizing photographs on a light table in his bedroom. (Reproduced by permission of Playboy Enterprises.)

some plausibility to the claim that one could buy *Playboy* for the articles.[53]

As the preceding examples show, the popular culture of the 1950s brought an unprecedented openness to sexual issues. Nonetheless, public inhibitions remained high, especially when compared to the 1960s. After all, although Elvis appeared three times on *The Ed Sullivan Show*, the camera never fell below his waist for fear of broadcasting pictures of his gyrating hips to millions of adoring fans.[54] Similarly, although the lesbian rights group Daughters of Bilitis and the Los Angeles-based homosexual rights organization the Mattachine Society were operational during the 1950s, there was little more than a fledgling gay rights movement until the late 1960s.[55] Indeed, by the close of the fifties the combined membership of the Mattachine Society and the Daughters of Bilitis stood below four hundred.[56]

The liberalization of public attitudes toward sex affected women as well as men. In her book *Sex and the Single Girl* (1962; originally titled *Sex for the Single Girl*), Helen Gurley Brown brought the provocative message of "sex for fun" to the growing ranks of young, unmarried women.[57] The modern woman, she wrote, ought to "reconsider the idea that sex without marriage is dirty." Brown went so far as to characterize marriage as merely "insurance for the worst years of your life."[58] Brown's historical significance rested on her celebration of the single woman's life. During the 1950s, the culture placed a great premium on married and family life, but now a sophisticated writer was urging American women to enjoy the single life and "play the field." The book proved to be such a success that it was made into a Hollywood movie starring Natalie Wood, Tony Curtis, and Henry Fonda.[59] Not long after the publication

[53] According to a 1966 study by Arnold Rogow, 34 percent of psychiatrists and 37 percent of psychoanalysts admitted to being "regular or occasional readers of *Playboy*." See Rogow, Arnold A. *The Psychiatrists* (New York: Dell Publishing Company, 1970), p. 60.
[54] Bailey, "Sexual Revolution(s)," p. 235.
[55] Patterson, James T. *Grand Expectations: The United States, 1945–1974* (New York: Oxford University Press, 1996), p. 357; Esterberg, Kristen G. "From Accommodation to Liberation: A Social Movement Analysis of Lesbians in the Homophile Movement," *Gender and Society*, Vol. 8 (September 1994), pp. 424–43.
[56] D'Emilio, John. *Sexual Politics, Sexual Communities: The Making of a Homosexual Minority in the United States, 1940–1970* (Chicago: University of Chicago Press, 1983), p. 115.
[57] "Playboy Interview: Helen Gurley Brown," *Playboy* (April, 1963), pp. 53–61.
[58] Cited from D'Emilio and Freedman, *Intimate Matters*, pp. 303–4.
[59] Stern, Jane and Michael. *Sixties People* (New York: Knopf, 1990), p. 19.

of her best-seller in 1962, Helen Gurley Brown assumed the editorship of *Cosmopolitan*, and quickly succeeded in turning it into the magazine of choice for modern single women.[60]

Given the persistence of these sentiments in the popular and political culture, and in light of the rapidly rising levels of unwed motherhood and premarital pregnancies, it would appear that the old meta-narrative confuses cause with effect. Instead of private conduct lagging behind the popular culture, an increasingly sexualized culture was trailing behind a sharp, although unacknowledged surge in illicit sexual behavior. Accordingly, between the unveiling of the Marshall Plan (1947) and the publication of Allen Ginsberg's poem "Howl" (1956), the rate of single motherhood climbed by 68.5 percent. Between the beginning of World War II (1941) and the inaugural issue of *Playboy* (1953), the overall rate of single motherhood had more than doubled.[61] Far from being an era of sexual candor, it was precisely the absence of such candor that helped obscure the exploding levels of premarital sex during the 1940s and 1950s.

The recollections of writer Lynn Ferrin, as documented in Joan and Robert K. Morrison's book *From Camelot to Kent State: The Sixties Experience in the Words of Those Who Lived It*, shed additional light on the issue of sexual candor. "In the early Sixties," Ferrin recalled, "people were not open about their sex lives... Nobody was a virgin but nobody admitted it. I remember when I'd spent the night with a boyfriend, I'd either try to get back that night so my roommate wouldn't know what I was doing, or I'd just lie to her: 'Well, I stayed at Barry's house, but I slept on his couch.'"[62]

The key phrase in Ferrin's account was her observation that "nobody was a virgin, but nobody admitted it." Contained in these remarks lies the crucial distinction between convention and conduct, between norm and behavior. As informal codes that are enforced by "fear of external nonlegal sanctions," social norms tend to be durable.[63] In other words, unlike the products of the popular culture, social norms do not bend easily to transient tastes or the latest fads. Yet for all of its stability,

---

[60] Ibid, p. 20.
[61] Bureau of the Census, U.S. Department of Commerce. *Historical Statistics of the United States: Colonial Times to 1970, Part I*, p. 52.
[62] Morrison, Joan, and Morrison, Robert K. *From Camelot to Kent State: The Sixties Experience in the Words of Those Who Lived It* (New York: Times Books, 1982), pp. 175–6.
[63] McAdams, Richard H. "The Origin, Development, and Regulation of Norms," *Michigan Law Review*, Vol. 96 (November 1997).

if noncompliance with prevailing norms became frequent enough, and for long enough, one of three possible outcomes will ensue: the norm will be enfeebled, eroding the stigma or social sanctions associated with violating the norm; the norm will be modified; or the norm will eventually be replaced.

Creations of the popular culture were capable of reinforcing or undermining norms, depending on whether one was listening to Ricky Nelson and Pat Boone – both of whom tended to reaffirm prevailing standards – or the flamboyant Little Richard and Elvis Presley – both of whom tended to challenge them.[64] However, because sweeping changes in behavior anticipated the sexualization of the culture, it would appear that the commodification of sex was but a secondary consideration in the loosening of sexual behavior.

Finally, after twenty years of liberalized sexual behavior and following a decade of Hugh Hefner, rock 'n' roll, steamy novels, and racy ads, noticeable changes in social norms began appearing during the 1960s. At first these changes were subtle and ambiguous – which helps explain how the reticence of Lynn Ferrin and her contemporaries could coexist with the proliferation of Playboy Clubs. Yet as the sixties progressed, less inhibited public attitudes toward sex emerged. By the early 1970s, general attitudes toward sex had undergone a virtual sea change. In a survey conducted by the National Opinion Research Center in 1972, 23 percent of Americans thought premarital sex was "wrong only sometimes," while another 26 percent of Americans replied that premarital sex was "not wrong at all." By contrast, only nine years earlier in 1963, more than seven out of ten respondents said they would "strongly disagree" with the statement that sex before marriage was acceptable if the woman was in love.[65] At last, changes in the popular culture and, more importantly, sustained changes in mass behavior had begun to transform social norms.

The general failure to acknowledge the extent to which sexual behavior liberalized during the middle decades of the twentieth century is, in part,

[64] As Chapter 5 will show, Pat Boone's effect in reinforcing old-fashioned standards is considerably more complicated than suggested here.
[65] Survey by National Opinion Research Center, University of Chicago, February 1972. Retrieved August 20, 2008, from the iPOLL Databank, The Roper Center for Public Opinion Research, University of Connecticut. Online at: http://www.ropercenter.uconn.edu/ipoll.html. Also see Survey by Ira Reiss and National Opinion Research Center, University of Chicago, April 1963. Retrieved August 20, 2008, from the iPOLL Databank, The Roper Center for Public Opinion Research, University of Connecticut. Online at: http://www.ropercenter.uconn.edu/ipoll.html.

due to ideological factors. Over the past two decades, conservative intellectuals have created a virtual cottage industry in bashing the 1960s. "Few
would deny that the rates of abortion, divorce, family breakdown, wife
and child abuse, venereal disease, and out-of-wedlock births have mas-
sively increased since the mid-1960s," observed Roman Catholic Archbishop Charles J. Chaput, in *First Things*, a conservative religious journal
based out of New York City. "Obviously, the birth control pill has not
been the only factor in this unraveling. But it has played a major role."[66] In
his essay "The Legacy of the Late 1960s," written for the book *Reassessing the Sixties: Debating the Political and Cultural Legacy*, Harvard
political scientist Harvey Mansfield included the sexual revolution and
the collapse of the family on his short list of the six most destructive
legacies of that decade.[67] Conservative columnist Mona Charen and former Education Secretary William Bennett have each provided a similar analysis. In fact, in his book *Index of Leading Cultural Indicators*,
Bennett, like former federal judge Robert Bork in *Sloughing to Gomorrah*, refrains from mentioning the frequency of single motherhood until
the year 1960.[68]

In the minds of most conservatives, the immoral sixties are in contrast
with the more traditional 1950s. Whereas the free love, counterculture,
and campus unrest of the Johnson years are believed to have produced so-
called bad results, the flag-waving patriotism and cultural conservatism
generally associated with the Eisenhower years are credited with having produced so-called good results. However, in their understanding of
the sexual revolution, the Bennetts and the Borks, the Chaputs and the
Charens repeat the same mistake that the majority of Americans committed during the 1950s; they have confused popular cultural imagery with
the hard empirical reality of things.

---

[66] Chaput, Charles J. "Contraception: A Symposium," *First Things* (December 1988),
pp. 19–20.
[67] Mansfield, Harvey. "The Legacy of the Late 1960s," in Macedo, Steven (ed.), *Reassessing
the Sixties: Debating the Political and Cultural Legacy* (New York: W. W. Norton, 1997),
pp. 21–31.
[68] Charen, Mona. "Paying Dues for the Sexual Revolution," *Newsday* (January 22, 1990),
p. 46; Bennett, William. *Index of Leading Cultural Indicators: Facts and Figures on
the State of American Society* (New York: Simon & Schuster), pp. 44–51. Bork,
Robert. *Sloughing to Gomorrah: Modern Liberalism and American Decline* (New York:
Regan Books, 1996); also see Himmelfarb, Gertrude, "A De-Moralized Society: The
British/American Experience," in Gerson, Mark (ed.), *The Essential Neo-Conservative
Reader* (New York: Addison-Wesley Publishing, 1996), pp. 412–13.

The Rise of Shotgun Marriages

Although norms are very different from values and behavior, playing a strictly secondary role in shaping the moral order, they are sometimes capable of shaping behavior in a significant way. One especially strong example of such influence can be seen by examining the rates of "shotgun" marriages, which were steadily rising during the 1950s. As counterintuitive as it might sound, while the rates of premarital pregnancies and single motherhood were climbing throughout the Eisenhower years, so too were the rates of shotgun marriages. In other words, when a young man impregnated his girlfriend, he was much more likely to marry her at the end of the decade than at its beginning*. Apparently, the social stigma surrounding single motherhood was becoming so odious, and – conversely – the convention of marriage was so strong that couples were more likely to tie the knot than to allow their offspring to grow up in a single-parent household.

It is important to reiterate that not only did the sheer numbers of shotgun marriages increase during the fifties, but the rate also rose. What this tells us is that during the early Cold War years, the moral state of affairs was truly in a condition of upheaval. More single people were having sex. More single women were becoming pregnant and, accordingly, a great deal more children were born out of wedlock. Each of these developments is rightly characterized as antithetical to the socially conservative moral vision. However, at the same time, because of the saliency of certain traditional norms, a higher proportion of single men were marrying their pregnant girlfriends.

The Rise of the Urban Poor

That a sexual revolution, at least on a behavioral level, was unfolding during the 1940s and 1950s has some broad implications – especially as far as the explanations pertaining to the causes of urban poverty are concerned. Today, most liberals and conservatives alike maintain that the elevated rates of single motherhood – especially among African Americans – is key to explaining the rise of what during the 1980s and the first half of the 1990s was labeled the underclass, and today is more commonly

---

* O'Connell, Martin and Moore, Maurice J. "The Legitimacy Status of First Births to U.S. Women Aged 15–24, 1939–1978," *Family Planning Perspectives* (January/February 1980), pp. 16–25.

referred to as simply the urban poor. According to the standard explanation, the proliferation of single motherhood led to the formation of entire communities consisting of fragile families where absentee fathers are not the exception but the norm. Lacking a male breadwinner, the children in such families are likely to grow up impoverished and, thereby, repeat the cycle of illegitimacy, poverty, and public assistance.

Where conservatives and liberals typically diverge is on the thorny issue of causation. To conservatives in the mode of policy analyst Charles Murray, the culprit is to be found in the social welfare programs of the Great Society. As the conservative scholar Robert Gordon puts it, thoughtful observers must regard "welfare provisions as a major influence in the decline in the two-adult households in American cities." Other conservatives have focused on the liberalization of time-honored values and norms. They argue that during the 1960s, changing attitudes toward premarital sex, the institution of marriage, and the nuclear family had devastating effects upon the black urban poor.

Liberals have taken a different approach. Instead of focusing on the relaxation of traditional values, their emphasis falls on structural forces – more specifically, the decline in manufacturing jobs. As sociologist William Julius Wilson maintains in his book *The Truly Disadvantaged: The Inner City, the Underclass, and Public Policy*, the diminishing job prospects of black men, coupled with climbing rates of incarceration, had the effect of shrinking the "pool" of marriageable black males and, by so doing, led to the higher frequency of female-headed households.[69] "The development of an underclass," stated the historian David Barlet, "is directly linked to the emergence of a post-industrial economy in our cities."

Yet for all of the differences separating liberals and conservatives, both factions view the problem of single motherhood and black urban poverty as primarily a phenomenon beginning in the 1960s and the 1970s. For conservatives, the culprit is either the liberalizing values of the sixties or the supposedly extravagant social spending of the Johnson years. For liberals, the problem is economic transformation – in particular, deindustrialization – that was gathering steam during the 1960s, but began in earnest during the 1970s. In both cases, however, the 1940s and 1950s are either ignored or marginalized. However, because a sexual revolution was unfolding during the 1940s and 1950s, and given the fact single motherhood and premarital pregnancies were significantly higher among

---

[69] Wilson, William Julius. *The Truly Disadvantaged: The Inner City, the Underclass, and Public Policy* (Chicago: The University of Chicago Press, 1987), pp. 82–3.

African Americans than among whites, it is safe to say that the problem of black single motherhood predates the causes most liberal and conservative scholars have regarded as preeminent.

The Pill

Besides undermining the explanations many liberals and conservatives have invoked to explain the persistence of urban poverty, the steadily climbing rates of single motherhood during the middle decades of the twentieth century cast considerable doubt upon another article of faith: the significance of the oral contraceptive. As we noted earlier in this chapter, many journalists and scholars have seen a causal connection between the birth control pill and the sexual revolution. "The Pill – it probably launched the sexual revolution a generation ago," asserted Jane Pauley in her introduction to a news story for *Dateline NBC*. [70] In celebrating the thirtieth anniversary of the oral contraceptive, *The Ladies Home Journal* was nothing short of gushing. "It's easy to forget how truly liberating the Pill seemed to be in 1960. Nothing else in this century – perhaps, not even winning the right to vote – made such an immediate difference in women's lives."[71] The timing of the Pill's introduction reinforced this explanation. Coming onto the market in the summer of 1960, the Pill fit perfectly into the standard periodization of the sexual revolution.[72] As historian Mary Ryan writes in *Mysteries of Sex: Tracing Women and Men Through American History*, "Rates of premarital sexuality began to increase along with the wide availability of reliable birth control in the form of oral contraceptives."[73]

However, there are good reasons to be skeptical of this interpretation. First, there is the problem of timing. As rising levels of single motherhood

---

[70] See "His Turn: Male Contraception Pill Being Developed," *Dateline NBC Transcript* (September 15, 1998).

[71] Cited from Asbell, Bernard. *The Pill: A Biography of the Drug that Changed the World* (New York: Random House, 1995), p. 179.

[72] In addition to journalists, some prominent scholars have drawn a causal connection between the birth control pill and the sexual revolution. For example, in *Masters and Johnson's Sex and Human Loving*, the famous sex therapists William H. Masters and Virginia E. Johnson state that the "availability of the pill provided a sense of freedom for many women and probably contributed more to changing sexual behavior than has generally been imagined." Cited from Reiss, Ira L. *An End to Shame: Shaping Our Next Sexual Revolution* (Buffalo: Prometheus Books, 1990), p. 93. Also see Evans, Sara. *Born for Liberty: A History of Women in America* (New York: The Free Press, 1989), pp. 265–6, 281–2.

[73] Ryan, Mary P. *Mysteries of Sex: Tracing Women and Men Through American History* (Chapel Hill: The University of North Carolina Press, 2006), p. 263.

and premarital pregnancies reveal, by the time the Pill hit the market the proverbial horse had already left the barn. What is more, from the moment they hit the market, oral contraceptives were not readily accessible to young single women. At an initial cost of $11 per month, oral contraceptives were simply too expensive for the masses of single women. And although the price quickly came down – by 1966 the cost of a monthly supply was only about $2.50 – other obstacles also impeded the widespread accessibility of the Pill to the young and the unattached.[74] For example, unlike condoms, the Pill required a prescription and a return to the doctor's office every six months for refills.[75] Ultimately, the effort and expense associated with such visits was discouraging for single women until a period substantially after the Pill was made publicly available.

That said, for young unmarried women the most formidable obstacle to obtaining the Pill was probably the general attitudes of physicians themselves. As Beth Bailey reports, "In the early 1960s when the pill was introduced, only a small minority of physicians would prescribe oral contraceptives to unmarried women." Bailey further noted, "Many believed, along with a large majority of the American public, that it was wrong for unmarried women to engage in sexual intercourse. Therefore, a significant change had to take place before the Pill could play any role in the sexual behavior of young, single women as a group."[76]

The considerable reluctance on the part of doctors to prescribe the Pill is illustrated by an incident that occurred at middecade. In September 1965, *The Brown Daily Herald* reported that the director of health services at Brown University had prescribed the Pill for two female students. Almost overnight, a bitter controversy erupted, attracting national media attention. After surveying the practices of other schools, *Newsweek* described Brown as being in "the vanguard" with respect to its progressive policy on contraception.[77] However, while being "out in front" of most other university physicians, Dr. Roswell Johnson, the director of health services at Brown, had prescribed the Pill within some fairly

[74] "Contraception: Freedom from Fear," *Time* (April 7, 1967), p. 82.
[75] Brody, Jane E. "The Pill: Revolution in Birth Control," *The New York Times* (May 31, 1966), pp. 1, 34.
[76] Bailey, Beth. "Prescribing The Pill: Politics, Culture, and the Sexual Revolution in America's Heartland," *Journal of Social History*, Vol. 30 (Summer 1997), p. 823. Other scholars who have questioned the effect of the Pill on the sexual revolution are Reiss, *An End to Shame*; and Watkins, Elizabeth Siegel, *On The Pill: A Social History of Oral Contraceptives, 1950–1970* (Baltimore: John Hopkins University Press, 1998).
[77] "The Pill on Campus," *Newsweek* (October 11, 1965), p. 93.

narrow circumstances: both women had consulted their ministers first, both women were over twenty-one, and each intended to marry their boyfriends.[78]

In addition to the problems of cost, convenience, and the sexual conservatism of physicians, yet another obstacle discouraged single women from using the Pill: a widespread aversion to long-term planning. Compared to married couples, sex among single people in general, and teenagers in particular, is less likely to be regularized and more likely to be spontaneous. Accordingly, the kind of long-range planning associated with the use of oral contraceptives did not resonate among the young and single. By contrast, condoms – the one form of contraception that, historically, has been the responsibility of males – were inexpensive, convenient, and involved little if any planning. As birth-control advocate Philip Harvey writes, "The condom can be carried by the male partner with no opprobrium (indeed, peer-group pressures tend to reinforce carrying a condom in the wallet as a sign of sexual success) and it can be made available spontaneously just prior to the coital act rather than as part of a 'plan' on the part of the girl."[79] The inability of the Pill to be used spontaneously, or even intermittently, limited its appeal among unmarried women during the 1960s.

Ironically, the most compelling evidence disentangling the Pill from the sexual revolution is also the most problematic from a methodological standpoint. According to the first survey ever to examine the birth-control practices of single teenage women, the Pill was not an especially popular form of contraception. In fact, at the time of the study (1971), only about 10 percent of sexually active single women between the ages of fifteen and nineteen even admitted to "being on the Pill."[80] This figure is quite startling. If only one in ten sexually experienced single teenage girls was using oral contraceptives in 1971, what would the situation have been during the early and mid-1960s when the Pill was far less accessible?[81]

[78] "'Pill' Controversy: The Second Day," *Brown Daily Herald* (September 29, 1965), p. 1. Also see Veiner, Stephen T., "Brown Health Center Prescribes Birth Control Pills, Administration Shows Tacit Approval," *Pembroke Record* (September 28, 1965), p. 1.
[79] Harvey, "Condoms in America," p. 37.
[80] Katner, John F. and Zelnik, Melvin. "Contraception and Pregnancy: Experience of Young Unmarried Women in the United States," *Family Planning Perspectives*, Vol. 5 (Winter 1973), pp. 21–35.
[81] Snider, "The Pill: 30 Years of Safety Concerns," *FDA Consumer*, p. 8. According to Snider's estimates, the number of American women on the birth control pill rose from about 1.2 million in 1962 to approximately 5 million in 1965, to approximately 10 million by 1973.

The preceding information on the accessibility and the general usage of the Pill leads us to a larger question: if scientists had never developed oral contraceptives in the first place, or if the FDA had never approved it, would the sexual revolution have continued apace during the 1960s? Given the earlier surge in premarital intercourse during the forties and fifties, the increasingly aggressive marketing of sex, and the coming of age of the baby boom generation, it seems probable that events would have unfolded in much the same way with or without the advent of oral contraceptives.

Cultural Changes Stemming from World War II

If changes in the popular culture did not ignite the sexual revolution, and if the 1960 introduction of the birth control pill did not cause or significantly accelerate the sexual revolution, then what was responsible for the liberalization of sexual behavior? Part of the answer lies in World War II. By introducing an estimated four million women into the workforce to compensate for the approximately twelve million men in uniform, the war wrought enormous cultural change on the domestic front. One such change seems to have been a sharp upswing in the level of premarital sex. During the war years, numerous newspaper and magazine articles reported on the sexual favors that young women – popularly known as "victory girls" or "khacky-wackies" – freely bestowed upon American servicemen.[82] Besides subverting public morals, government officials believed that these "loose" young women were the primary agents behind the high levels of venereal disease among American servicemen. Encouraged by the U.S. War Department, cities across the country cracked down on female "sex delinquents" – arresting some, compelling many to be tested for venereal disease and forcing others into counseling. Despite these zealous efforts, the overall rate of single motherhood climbed sharply during the first half of the 1940s, from 7.1 to 10.1 newborns per 1,000 unmarried women of childbearing age – an increase of more than 40 percent in only five years.[83]

In a certain sense, the higher wartime rates of single motherhood would appear to be counterintuitive. The fact that increasing numbers of single

[82] Anderson, Karen. *Wartime Women: Sex Roles, Family Relations, and the Status of Women During World War II* (Westport, Connecticut: Greenwood Press, 1981), pp. 103–11.
[83] *Historical Statistics of the United States: Colonial Times to 1970, Part I*, p. 52.

men, in uniform and away from home, would engage in premarital sex is hardly surprising. Yet on the home front, where the requirements of war diminished the total number of available young men, one would likely expect to find lower levels of single motherhood and premarital sex. After all, with millions of absent single men in America – as was the case during World War II – there would presumably be fewer opportunities for sex outside of marriage. How are we then to explain the exploding rates of single motherhood – and, by extension, the soaring rates of premarital sex – with the undeniable fact that during the war years the pool of single men living in the United States was appreciably smaller?

The answer to this question may be located less in the collective lust of single men than the collective willingness of single women. As a result of the sweeping social changes unfolding during the war years, it appears higher percentages of single women were willing to lose their virginity. Of course, one reason for the emergence of these more liberal attitudes stemmed from the increased independence that wartime employment gave to single women. Like the young working women who resided in lodging houses away from the watchful eyes of family members at the turn of the century, higher levels of personal independence brought with it a greater sense of personal autonomy that in turn brought forth a wider sphere of sexual freedom.[84] As one man who worked in a factory as a teenager during World War II recalled, "The plant and town were just full of working girls who were on the make. Where I was, a male worker became the center of loose morality. It was a sex paradise."[85]

By turning briefly to the discipline of economics, and by drawing on the insights of rational choice theory, it is possible to see that the acute shortage of single men could, ironically, be another reason for the increasingly liberal wartime attitudes. In an environment where there are many single women and comparatively few eligible males, the general terms of the relationship will probably shift in favor of the man. Both parties will know that for purely demographic reasons, in the event of a breakup, the man will likely enjoy a wider range of romantic options than his female counterpart. "In sex," states anthropologist Lionel Tiger, "Women are

[84] Meyerowitz, Joanne. "Sexual Geography and Gender Economy: The Furnished-Room Districts of Chicago, 1890–1930," in Ruiz, Vicki L., and DuBois, Ellen Carol (eds.), *Unequal Sisters: A Multicultural Reader in U.S. Women's History* (New York: Routledge, 2000), pp. 307–23.
[85] D'Emilio and Freedman, *Intimate Matters*, p. 260.

the gatekeepers."[86] It would seem, therefore, that due to the wartime man shortage, fewer males gathered outside the "gates." However, because of this same wartime man shortage, more males than usual were allowed entry. In short, with single women in great supply, and single men in high demand, American males on the home front could be more insistent in their demands for sex.

Conditions of a decade earlier intensified this process. During the Great Depression, hard times caused the marriage rate to tumble and, as a result, by the time of World War II there was already what economists would call a "surplus" of single women, resulting in what is commonly called a "buyers market."[87] The upshot, of course, was that single men on the home front became even more highly prized than they would have been otherwise. And these conditions provided unattached males with even greater bargaining power in their quest for sex.

Whatever the exact origins, World War II clearly helped usher in an era of increased sexual liberalism. However, as a causative agent, the war experience can only be pushed so far. Yes, the war helped facilitate a rise in premarital sex; but in the years immediately following the war the rate of single motherhood did not fall to prewar levels, or even plateau at the peak wartime rate. Instead, the rates of single motherhood – and, by inference, rates of premarital sex – continued to climb throughout the 1940s and into the decade of the 1950s. In fact, if we isolate the years between 1945 and 1950, we see a considerable surge in the frequency of single motherhood, rising from 10.1 to 14.1 newborns per 1,000 single women of childbearing age – a 39 percent increase (which was only slightly slower than the 44 percent increase that took place during the first half of the 1940s).[88] Why did this happen? Why was there not a return to normalcy? With the war finally over, what could have perpetuated these postwar gains in the frequency of premarital sex?

The answer to this question lies not in the empirical world of vital statistics but, rather, within the slippery realm of culture. More specifically, it is located in the critical role mental health experts played in persuading Americans to relinquish a more rigid and traditional worldview. According to the leading psychologists and psychiatrists at midcentury, sexual repression was a major source of human neurosis. In their writings,

---

[86] Cited from John Leo, "The Sexual Revolution is Over," in Francoeur, Robert T. (ed.), *Taking Sides: Clashing Views on Controversial Issues in Human Sexuality* (Guilford, Connecticut: Dushkin Publishing Group, 1987), p. 301.

[87] *Historical Statistics: Part I*, p. 64.

[88] Ibid, p. 52.

a virtual battery of psychological experts – ranging from Erich Fromm, Theodore Adorno, and Harry Stack Sullivan to Carl Rogers, Gordon Allport, and Abraham Maslow – were critical of the conservative sexual morality that, at least on a surface level, seemed so dominant during the age of Eisenhower.

These concerns went well beyond the monographs of academic psychologists. In an age when religious explanations were losing their hold, and modern philosophy had largely abandoned the study of ethics, elites increasingly turned to the new science of psychology. In such a world, psychologists served as secular priests to a nation's educated classes. Hence, throughout the culture of the 1950s, Americans were being urged to ease up sexually. In books and on Broadway, in music and in movies, a more accepting attitude toward sex was detectable. Thus, in *The Common Sense Book of Baby and Child Care* (1946), Benjamin Spock advised parents not to become alarmed by their children's masturbation. And by 1950, as we have seen, even the politically conservative Norman Vincent Peale was warning his readers about the dangers of sexual repression. In a word, at the heart of the concerns of Spock, Peale, and a phalanx of psychologists was the belief that a more accepting attitude toward the self – with all of its impulses and all of its drives – would lead ultimately to a healthier, less guilt-ridden person. In the end, it was the behavior of these more secular, more expressive, less guilt-oriented individuals that sustained and intensified the sexual revolution.

Shifting the timing of the sexual revolution from the 1960s to the 1940s has some broad implications. Not only does it relegate the birth control pill to a secondary role at best, it also suggests that many of the much-heralded cultural developments of the 1950s – from the founding of *Playboy* magazine to the rise of rock 'n' roll – did little more than provide momentum to a process that was already well under way. Thus, it would seem that the scandal that engulfed Elizabeth Taylor and Eddie Fisher reflected as much as it anticipated the emergence of a new sexual morality. For all the grief the scandal caused her at the time, Elizabeth Taylor – now with eight husbands behind her – would probably have never guessed that her indiscretion and the public reaction to it stood as a barometer of the monumental change in the popular morality that we now call the sexual revolution.

4

Feminism

The Rising Status of Women in the Age of Eisenhower

In few places is the difference between the putatively staid fifties and the culturally tumultuous sixties more pronounced than in the scholarship dealing with the rise of feminism. Today, most contemporary scholars, following the lead of Betty Friedan's *The Feminine Mystique*, see the 1950s as a time when the stay-at-home wife was the cultural ideal and gender roles stood firm. However, in complicating this standard narrative, historians like Joanne Meyerowitz have explored a sizable body of literature in popular magazines that celebrated female achievement in the world of work. In her extensive examination of periodicals at midcentury, Meyerowitz found that all of the magazines she sampled "advocated both the domestic and the nondomestic, sometimes in the same sentence."[1]

Yet even Meyerowitz characterizes such proto-feminist rumblings as an "oppositional discourse" that, although resonant among many women, ran against prevailing social norms. In fact, so entrenched was the reigning patriarchal consensus, asserts Meyerowitz, that even feminist icon Betty Friedan did not "question women's responsibility for home and children" and she, moreover, "encouraged marriage and femininity, disparaged homosexuality, and expressed fears that neurotic, overbearing mothers ruined their children."[2] More recently, historians contending with such diverse topics as children's toys, cookbooks, the consumer

---

[1] Meyerowitz, Joanne. "Beyond the Feminine Mystique: A Reassessment of Postwar Mass Culture, 1946–1958," *The Journal of American History* (March 1993), p. 1458.
[2] Ibid, p. 1481.

culture, nursery cooperatives, and the G.I. Bill have joined Friedan in depicting the 1950s as a time when gender roles were becoming increasingly rigid.[3]

On a somewhat different front, an emerging body of scholarship has highlighted the rise of assertive women in labor organizations and various minority communities during the middle decades of the twentieth century. Although these female activists may not have called themselves feminists, through their conduct and rhetoric they challenged the social constraints that the wider culture imposed on women. However, for all of their success in providing greater texture and nuance to our understanding of the 1950s, these works focus on groups of women – usually nonwhite, nonsuburban, and working class – who fell well outside of the mainstream.[4] As such, these narratives have tended to bolster rather than challenge the traditional interpretation of gender relations during the early Cold War years – an interpretation that describes the general status of women as deteriorating or, at best, remaining stagnant. Simply put, few scholars today would quarrel with Eli Zaretski's characterization of the postwar era as a "fount of homophobia, misogyny, and conservatism."[5] Given these assumptions, one would not expect to see the decline of the patriarchal family, or the steady erosion of sexist attitudes, or sizable advances by women in the realm of politics. However, as this chapter

[3] Muncy, Robyn. "Cooperative Motherhood and Democratic Civic Culture in Postwar Suburbia," *Journal of Social History* (Fall 2004), pp. 285–310; Schwartz, Helen S. "When Barbie Dated G. I. Joe: Analyzing the Toys of the Early Cold War Era," *Material History Review* (Spring 1997), pp. 38–50; Oldenziel, Ruth. "Boys and Their Toys: The Fisher Body Craftsman's Guild, 1930–1968, and the Making of a Male Technical Domain," *Technology and Culture* (1997), pp. 60–96; Canaday, Margot. "Building a Straight State: Sexuality and Social Citizenship Under the 1944 G. I. Bill," *Journal of American History* (2003), pp. 935–57.

[4] Bao, Xiaolan. "When Women Arrived: The Transformation of New York's Chinatown," in Meyerowitz, Joanne (ed.), *Not June Cleaver: Women and Gender in Postwar America, 1945–1960* (Philadelphia: Temple University Press, 1994), pp. 19–36; Rose, Margaret. "Gender and Civic Activism in Mexican-American Barrios in California," in Meyerowitz, Joanne (ed.), *Not June Cleaver*; Cobble, Dorothy Sue. *The Other Women's Movement: Workplace Justice and Social Rights in Modern America* (Princeton, NJ: Princeton University Press, 2004); Frystak, Shannon L. "Elite White Female Activism and Civil Rights in New Orleans," in Murray, Gail S. (ed.), *Throwing Off the Cloak of Privilege: White Southern Women Activists in the Civil Rights Era* (Gainesville, Florida: University Press of Florida, 2004), pp. 181–203; Nasstrom, Kathryn L. "Down to Now: Memory, Narrative, and Women's Leadership in the Civil Rights Movement in Atlanta," *Gender & History* (April 1999), pp. 113–44.

[5] Zaretsky, Eli. "Charisma or Rationalization? Domesticity and Psychoanalysis in the United States in the 1950s," *Critical Inquiry* 26 (Winter 2000), p. 328.

will show, these and other challenges to prevailing gender hierarchies were rapidly unfolding during the age of Eisenhower.

The problem with the received narrative is not that it is in error, only incomplete. Betty Friedan's criticism of a public culture that greatly limited the options of women was largely right. Likewise, Meyerowitz was correct in detecting an "oppositional discourse" that approved of female accomplishment outside the roles of mother and housewife. However, during the 1950s, the greatest challenge to the subordination of women – a challenge that would generate the sweeping changes that emerged during the late sixties and early seventies – was occurring, not in the realm of popular discourse, but within the presumably conservative strongholds of the home, the church, the college campus, and the therapists' office.

The Husband–Wife Relationship

Contrary to popular belief, the patriarchal household was not rising during the age of Eisenhower. The husband may have persisted in his traditional role of breadwinner, but his status as the "head" of the household was clearly undermined by the increased democratization of the husband–wife relationship. Since the 1920s, sociologists and family experts had been predicting the advent of the "companionate family" where relations between husbands and wives would be rooted in friendship and compatibility.[6] Yet even though there may have been some movement in the direction of the companionate family, the scant evidence that exists for the 1940s suggests that most husbands continued to "wear the pants" in the family.[7]

Sometime during the 1950s, however, the distribution of power within the typical marriage appears to have shifted. By the close of the decade, the most reliable sociological studies indicated that patterns of authority within the typical Caucasian family were changing rapidly. One 1959 survey, based on more than one thousand respondents, found that only

---

[6] Mintz, Steven, and Kellogg, Susan. *Domestic Revolutions: A Social History of American Family Life* (New York: The Free Press, 1988).

[7] For example, F. D. Alexander's examination of 161 Tennessee families found that three-quarters (75%) of the wives felt husbands should be the head of the home. (See Alexander, F. D., "Family Life in a Rural Community," *Social Forces* 18. [March 1940], pp. 392–402.) Also, Reuben Hill's 1949 report on 135 Iowa couples – the majority of whom came from middle- and lower-income backgrounds – found that families were more than three times more likely to be patriarchal (21%) than matriarchal (13%). See Hill, Rubin. *Families Under Stress* (New York: Harper, 1949).

15 percent of families were dominated by the husband.[8] A second study that year examined the power dynamics within four hundred families in the Washington, D.C. area. Researchers interviewed every mother in addition to every fourth child and father. In the end, the study found that irrespective of class, day-to-day decisions – such as what the child should wear to school and what the family would eat for dinner – tended to be made by the mother. However, when it came to major family decisions, the author found that in four out of five instances, these decisions rested not solely with the man, but were made jointly by both husband and wife.[9]

A third report, one prepared by sociologists Robert Blood and Donald Wolfe in 1960, was probably the most authoritative study of the lot. In his close examination of the patterns of authority among more than six hundred and fifty families in the Greater Detroit area, Wolfe found wives dominating family decisions just as often as husbands (22 percent of the time). However, twice as frequent as either the "husband-dominant" or the "wife-dominant" model was an "equalitarian" pattern – where each spouse was allotted roughly equivalent power in the making of important family decisions. Equally impressive, Wolfe found that the egalitarian pattern of a true partnership between husband and wife extended well beyond the middle class. As Wolfe stated in the conclusion of his report, "Neither the farm families, nor Catholic families, nor the older generation, nor poorly educated families adhere to a patriarchal way of life."[10]

Of course, the sociological methods of the 1950s were much cruder than their successors today. Although scholars at the time were generally sensitive to the concerns of sample bias and the incorrect selection of pre-determined variables, by contemporary standards, the studies referenced were not very sophisticated. Taken individually, such studies must be approached with a good measure of skepticism; taken in totem, however, they are more difficult to ignore because they point, time and again, to an emergent shift in the status of women.

Some of the prescriptive literature seemed to have anticipated these changes. In journals and conferences, marriage counselors depicted the

---

[8] Johannis, Jr., T. B., and Rollins, J. M. "Teenager Perception of Family Decision-making," *The Coordinator* (June 1959), pp. 70–4.

[9] Kohn, M. L. "Social Class and the Exercise of Parental Authority," *American Sociological Review* (June 1959), pp. 352–66.

[10] Blood, Jr., Robert O., and Wolfe, Donald M. *Husbands and Wives: The Dynamics of Married Living* (Glencoe, Ill.: The Free Press, 1960).

healthy husband–wife relationship as an equal partnership. As Eleanor
Luckey and Gerhard Neubeek argued in a 1956 article, the latest research
lent support to the proposition that marriage depended on "intimate
communication; sympathetic understanding; [and] mutual respect on the
basis of equality."[11]

Indeed, this normative shift away from the patriarchal model had
become so pronounced that even the least likely of suspects, those with
a strong religious bent, claimed to accept these egalitarian ideals. In fall
1955, two sociologists surveyed three hundred single students and one
hundred married couples who were enrolled in classes at Brigham Young
University. More than 95 percent of the survey's participants were members of the Church of Jesus Christ of the Latter-day Saints – better known
as the Mormon Church – one of the most conservative of Christian sects.
In the areas of child rearing and family decision-making, the study suggested that egalitarian norms were becoming institutionalized.

By a margin of 60 percent or more, all the subgroups – men and women,
those married and single – said that they believed the husband and wife
should play an equal role in such areas as "disciplining children," "determining and supervising games children may play," and "being children's
playmate." When it came to family decision-making, the picture was a little cloudier because majorities of men and women answered "husband"
when asked, "Who should be head of family?" However, upon closer
inspection it becomes clear that the term *head of family* was more a formal designation than a functional description. By a margin of at least
60 percent, all the subgroups spoke of an equal partnership when it came
to "who should be boss of the family," "who should determine the family
budget and money matters," "who should determine the type and number of recreational activities," and, perhaps most important of all, "who
should have final word in family decisions."[12]

The one area where traditionalism continued to reign was in the performance of family chores. Apparently, most of the men and women associated certain tasks – such as "general housecleaning," "making beds,"
"washing clothes," and "planning and cooking meals," with the wife;
whereas "(f)or the men, doing heavier jobs generally fell in their division
of labor." In brief, the study found that among respondents there was

[11] Cited from Lasch, Christopher, *Haven in a Heartless World: The Family Besieged* (New
York: Basic Books, 1977), p. 108.
[12] Dyer, William G., and Urban, Dick. "The Institutionalization of Equalitarian Family
Norms," *Marriage and Family Living* (February 1958), pp. 53–8.

generally an egalitarian attitude toward power relations within the marriage. However, the data also pointed to traditional attitudes "towards a division of labor of men's and women's work."[13]

This division of work along gender lines has contributed to the mistaken image of the 1950s as a time when the patriarchal family reigned supreme and unchallenged. By all outward appearances, the traditional family model – with husband as provider and wife as the keeper of the home – remained very much intact. However, underneath the conservative exterior of the traditional nuclear family, the roles of husband and wife were being redefined.[14] In the case of most new families during the 1950s, marriage was in the process of evolving into a partnership, even as it remained very traditional in terms of gender roles. As Pat Boone crooned in his 1958 hit, marriage was now a "fifty-fifty deal."[15]

Historians tend to downplay the rise of the egalitarian marriage. "Marital partnership," writes Steven Mintz and Nancy Kellogg, "did not mean equality. A wife's primary role was to be her husband's ego massager, sounding board – and housekeeper . . . the fifties' ideal of a marital partnership were based on the assumption of a wife's role as hostess and consort."[16] Even more condemnatory was the analysis of feminist scholar Ruth Rosen. In her book *The World Split Open*, Rosen argues that housewives and career women shared a great deal in common during the 1950s: "Wherever they worked, whatever they did, they were both treated as subordinates."[17] Writing in *The Almanac of American History*, James Miller and Hugh Ambrose echo this standard line with little variation. For American women during the fifties, they write, "staying home, raising a brood of well-adjusted children, and being a loving but subordinate partner to a busy husband were the ideals."[18] Virtually identical sentiments were expressed by Rosalind Rosenberg in *Divided Lives*.[19] However, in

---

[13] Ibid.

[14] In the classic fifties sitcom *The Honeymooners*, the character of Ralph Kramden (played by Jackie Gleason), was the breadwinner, while his spouse Alice (played by Audrey Meadows) tended to the home. In one sense, the Kramdens were a very traditional household. However, when it came to power within the family, Alice was no pushover because she enjoyed just as much authority as her husband.

[15] Mintz and Kellogg, *Domestic Revolutions*.

[16] Ibid, pp. 186–7.

[17] Rosen, Ruth. *The World Split Open: How the Modern Women's Movement Changed America* (New York: Viking Press, 2000).

[18] Miller, James, and Ambrose, Hugh. *Almanac of American History* (Washington, D.C.: National Geographic, 2005), p. 274.

[19] In the 1950s, writes Rosenberg, women "felt torn between the egalitarian ideals taught in school and the reality of their subordination in the home." See Rosenberg, Rosalind,

their casual dismissal of the egalitarian family, Mintz, Kellogg, Rosen, Miller, Ambrose, and Rosenberg appear to rely on conventional wisdom or the personal anecdote. What they have failed to do is consult, much less engage, a sizable body of sociological research suggesting that marriages in America were moving toward the "democratic" model.

One scholar who has tried to use sociological data to argue that American marriages in the 1950s showed few signs of liberalizing is Liz Cohen. In *A Consumer's Republic: The Politics of Mass Consumption in Postwar America*, Cohen cites two *Journal of Marketing* studies – the first one released in 1956, the second published in 1958 – that, according to Cohen, highlight the "growing importance of men's authority over the family purse."[20] As Cohen makes clear, the first study showed that in big ticket items, such as the purchase of cars and insurance, men played the dominant role. Women continued to play a more prominent part in the buying of groceries, but even in that realm "men were playing a surprisingly significant role." As for the latter study, it showed that American couples had "moderated that stance a bit." In the buying of appliances women took the lead, but wives continued to have little authority when it came to the more expensive purchase of automobiles.[21]

However, a careful reading of each study Cohen cites indicates husband–wife relationships were far more egalitarian than Cohen's *A Consumer's Republic* would have readers believe.[22] For example, although the 1956 study showed that men played more prominent roles than women in deciding what cars to buy, the data also indicated that when it came to the grandest of all big ticket items, the family's house or apartment, the decision was arrived at in a more democratic fashion. In 58 percent of the time, the decision of where to live was made jointly by husband and wife. However, on those occasions when one spouse played a more

---

Divided Lives: American Women in the Twentieth Century (New York: Hill & Wang, 1992), p. 156.

[20] Cohen, Lizabeth. *A Consumers' Republic: The Politics of Mass Consumption in Postwar America* (New York: Vintage Books, 2003), p. 148.

[21] Ibid.

[22] Cohen actually cites a third study – Mirra Komarovsky's *Blue Collar Marriage*. However, Komarovsky's book does not speak directly to the question of power relations within the typical 1950s' marriage. It fails to do this for two reasons: first, its focus is on marriages during the early 1960s. Second, and more importantly, it is not looking at the typical marriage, but at the white, working-class marriage. Thus, of the fifty-eight men interviewed, a firm majority were either semi-skilled or unskilled. Moreover, only eighteen of the husbands interviewed had completed college. See Komarovsky, Mirra. *Blue Collar Marriage* (New York: Vintage Books, 1967). See especially "Description of the Families" in the Appendix, on pp. 356–7.

dominant role in deciding where to reside, it was the wife (18 percent), not the husband (12 percent) who had the greater say.

In Cohen's synopsis of the second study, published in 1958, she once again downplayed the authority housewives enjoyed in making purchasing decisions. Whereas Cohen accurately reported that husbands played a more prominent role in deciding what cars to buy, she ignored data suggesting women had as much influence – indeed, perhaps even greater influence – in actually deciding when to buy the family car. In a section subtitled "Whose Plans Are Best Fulfilled?" the study's author interviewed husbands and wives separately, and asked them about their future plans in four areas:

1. plans to make a car purchase
2. plans to pay for additions and repairs to the family home
3. plans to buy a major appliance
4. plans to buy a television set.

Twelve to eighteen months later, when the couples were re-interviewed, the author discovered that in every category, including car purchases, the wife's plans were more likely to have been fulfilled than the husband's plans.[23]

The results of the 1958 study can be summed up quite briefly. In some areas, such as the selection of cars and the purchase of insurance, husbands tended to exert greater authority. In other areas, such as the acquisition of appliances and the handling of savings, wives tended to hold greater sway. However, in the decisions of when and when not to make major family purchases, wives seemed to have enjoyed levels of influence that were equivalent to that of their husbands. In fact, given the data, one could make the argument that the influence of women in this second area tended to be somewhat greater than the influence of their husbands. In short, when all of the elements of the 1958 study are synthesized – the very report Cohen invokes to substantiate her claim that the patriarchal family model prevailed during the Eisenhower years – the picture that emerges is not one of husband dominance, but that of a financial partnership between man and wife, a partnership where husbands and wives played different roles but with neither one subservient to the other. As Elizabeth Wolgast – Cohen's very authority – writes in the conclusion of her 1958 marketing study: "In the American family, economic decisions are most

---

[23] Wolgast, Elizabeth H. "Do Husbands or Wives Make the Purchasing Decisions?" *Journal of Marketing* (October 1958), pp. 151–8.

commonly made jointly by husbands and wives. There is no support in the data for the notion that the economic affairs of American families are primarily the province of the husbands."[24]

Although Wolgast's *Journal of Marketing* study is compatible with the proposition that marriages were becoming more democratic during the 1950s, we must be careful to avoid assigning too much importance to such reports. A nationally representative survey conducted in 1962 pointed to the persistence of traditional attitudes toward marriage.[25] More significantly, in the absence of comparable studies for the 1930s or the 1940s, it is impossible to ascertain whether the financial influence of married women was rising, falling, or remaining more or less stable during the 1950s. Furthermore, the ability of housewives to make a wide range of purchasing decisions on their own is not altogether incompatible with the existence of husband-dominated families. As various scholars have noted, in Japanese families today, wives frequently take control of their husbands' paychecks. Yet most scholars are inclined to see these Japanese families as falling firmly within the patriarchical range.[26]

In contrast to marketing studies and polling data, the sociological scholarship that look more broadly at patterns of authority within families enjoy two important advantages. First, because they cast their net more widely, such studies are able to assess a wider array of behaviors that directly pertain to the relative power of husbands and wives. Second, since there were a handful of sociological studies conducted during the 1940s, it is possible to construct a benchmark. Therefore, it is possible to make very general comparisons between the mostly husband-dominated families that seemed to have prevailed during the 1930s and the 1940s, and the more democratically oriented families that were on the rise during the 1950s.

Of course, during the 1950s as today, there were more than a few patriarchal households in America. However, the best evidence suggests that husband-dominated families were becoming less and less prevalent, especially among the recently married. By the end of the decade, a new understanding of what it meant to be a husband and father strongly

---

[24] Ibid. p. 157. For a limited but more balanced review of the literature, see Wiss, Jessica, *To Have and to Hold: Marriage, the Baby Boom, and Social Change* (Chicago: The University of Chicago Press, 2000), pp. 43–5.

[25] By the term *traditional*, the author is referring to attitudes conducive to persistence of husband-dominated marriages.

[26] Imamura, Anne E. "The Japanese Family Faces Twenty-First Century Challenges," *Education About Asia* (Fall 2003), pp. 30–2.

resonated among young men and women alike. For example, a 1959 survey of 436 high school seniors in Louisiana unearthed some surprisingly progressive attitudes among the respondents. Although the preponderance of the young men and women subscribed to a rather traditional view of marriage – where husbands worked and the wives tended to the home – both groups seemed to hold a more modern conception of parenthood.

A majority of both male and female respondents believed that when the father is at home, he should feel just as responsible as his wife for the children. In addition, eight out of ten of the female respondents and nine out of ten of the male respondents expected the husband to manage his time in such a way as to ensure that he was able to share in the care of the children. The survey also indicated only one-third of the male respondents expected the husband to be "boss," suggesting that among the young an egalitarian conception of marriage was fast becoming the norm.[27]

In terms of discerning power relations within the typical American marriage, the assessment of wives is no less important than the expectations of would-be husbands. In 1962, the Gallup Organization, at the behest of *The Saturday Evening Post*, asked a nationally representative sample of married women the following question: "Does your husband take a more active part in running the house than your father did, or does your husband take a less active part?" In their answers, 63 percent of respondents indicated that they believed their husbands were more helpful around the house than their fathers had been, while 33 percent of respondents said their husbands were actually less active around the house.[28] Although the findings of the Gallup survey are fully consistent with the continuation – and even prevalence – of husband-dominated families, it does not support the perspective of those who would deny that American families were moving in a more democratic direction in the years immediately preceding the publication of *The Feminine Mystique*.

If we were to dip into the vast reservoir of American popular culture, the typical household during the fifties would appear to follow the Kramden family model. As television fans will remember, in the 1950s' sitcom *The Honeymooners*, loudmouth Ralph Kramden – played by Jackie Gleason – is the provider for the family. Ralph earns his living by driving

---

[27] Dunn, Marie S. "Marriage Role Expectations of Adolescents," *Marriage and Family Planning* (May 1960), pp. 99–111.
[28] Survey by *The Saturday Evening Post* and Gallup Organization, June, 1962. Retrieved August 17, 2008, from the iPOLL Databank, The Roper Center for Public Opinion Research, University of Connecticut. Online at: http://www.ropercenter.uconn.edu/ipoll. html.

a bus, while his wife Alice tends to the home. Yet while Ralph Kramden might be the breadwinner in his household, he is not by any means the boss. As virtually every episode demonstrates, Alice has every bit as much power in the household as her husband Ralph.

As we survey the postwar era, the question is not whether the patriarchal family existed at the end of the fifties – it surely did. However, the real issue is whether the husband-dominated family was becoming more or less prevalent – or, to state the matter a little differently, whether the number of Alice Kramdens were rising or falling.

Using the informal Alice Kramden Index, the best evidence suggests that families were becoming more democratic. Most children who grew up in this time saw mothers and fathers performing very different tasks. Lines of demarcation clearly existed. However, in increasing numbers, children did not see one parent subordinate to the other. With growing regularity, when mothers and fathers quarreled, little girls and little boys saw mommy prevail just as often as daddy. These changes were important in two respects: they reflected a more equitable distribution of power within the marriage, and they influenced the next generation of parents, encouraging daughters and sons to be even more predisposed toward a true partnership between wife and husband.

Women and the Church

During the 1950s, the rising status of women went beyond the home. Within many Protestant denominations there was more than a demure whisper of gender equity. Although few women were able to – or even desired to – enter the ministry, an increasing number of churches changed their internal rules and opened up their denomination to more meaningful female participation.

Under pressure from progressive forces, the United Methodist Church – the nation's second largest Protestant denomination at the time – opened up its clergy to women in 1956. The Presbyterian Church soon followed suit.[29] Two years later, in 1958, the General Synod of the Reformed Church in America called on its semiautonomous districts to approve the ordination of female ministers.[30] In addition, although the Episcopalian Church did not begin ordaining women until the 1970s, the Episcopalian

[29] Weart, William G. "Women in Clergy Voted by Church," *The New York Times* (March 1956), p. 25.
[30] "Church Acts On Ban: Reformed Groups Plan Would Let Women Hold Office," *The New York Times* (June 10, 1958), p. 30.

Dioceses in Washington, Vermont, Philadelphia, and New York began allowing women to serve as delegates to diocesan conventions during the 1950s.[31]

Almost as revealing as the new openness to the sight of women wearing collars was the changing rhetoric of those opposed to this trend. The issue of female ordination first reached the General Conference of the Methodist Church in 1940. Then, church leaders had been openly dismissive of the principle of sexual equality, especially in clerical affairs. One delegate from New Jersey complained about all of the attention given to the principle of full rights. "We are talking about full clergy rights as if the ministry were a sphere of economic activity to which any aspirant had a right to demand admission," he said. The position of minister, he continued, was not a secular privilege but a divine vocation: "We ought never to allow the ministry of the Christian Church to be degraded to a mere opportunity to earn one's living and express one's self." Orien Fifer, a delegate from Indiana, voiced similar objections. "A call to preach," he declared, "is not identical with a command of the Church to provide a place to preach."[32] Sentiments such as these struck a responsive chord among Methodist delegates, as a decisive majority voted to deny women full ministerial rights.

By 1956, however, the mood among Methodists had radically changed. Compared to 1940, the delegates in the mid 1950s were more willing to frame the question of equal clergy rights in moral terms. As Ohio Delegate Lynn Radcliffe put it, "The principle is, does Jesus Christ treat women as a child of God, entitled to the same privileges and rights as a man?" The Reverend Henry Lyle Lambdin, a delegate from Newark, echoed these sentiments. "Are we prepared to say that no woman regardless of her qualification is not fit to be a member of an Annual (Ministerial) Conference? This is the question before us."[33] In the wake of these arguments, and of the more than twenty-five hundred petitions urging denominational leaders to halt discrimination on the basis of gender, the motion providing Methodist women with full ministerial rights won full approval.

The Methodist Church was not the largest religious body to push for greater gender equity. In the decades following World War II, the nation's largest para-religious organizations – the Federal Council of

---

[31] Dugan, George. "First Women Vote at Church Parley," *The New York Times* (May 14, 1958), p. 27.

[32] Ibid, p. 27.

[33] *Daily Christian Advocate* (May 7, 1954), p. 524.

Churches (FCC) and its successor the National Council of Churches (NCC) – joined a growing number of Protestant denominations in supporting an expanded role for women in church governance. In 1948, the FCC issued a well-publicized study entitled "Women in American Church Life." In the foreword to the report, the president of the Federal Council of Churches acknowledged that the purpose of the study was to "raise the level of leadership within the church by encouraging Christians of outstanding abilities, irrespective of sex, to make their fullest contribution to the church."[34] Toward that larger goal, the study sought to achieve three ends: it attempted to highlight the contributions church women were already making; it drew attention to the additional gains that could be realized if churches took full advantage of the talents of capable women; and, citing passages from scripture, it sought to refute the claim that the Bible forbade women from assuming positions in church leadership.[35] Two years later, when Protestant leaders reorganized the FCC into the NCC, the General Department of United Church Women (UCW) was created as a semiautonomous branch setting its own agenda and controlled its own budget.[36]

From its very beginning, the UCW – an ecumenical federation composed of an estimated ten million women – had adopted an activist stance. In the tradition of the Social Gospel, their principal goals included the alleviation of suffering and the promotion of social justice. However, as an examination of *The Church Woman*, the organization's official publication, makes clear, improving the status of women was also a leading concern. An article appearing in 1952, for instance, lamented the scarcity of women in positions of real power. "Let's face a VERY SIMPLE fact," began the article, "American women are second-class citizens when it comes to having any part in shaping the diplomatic and military policies" of the country. The author continued, "No woman has an important policy-making position in the State Department, the Mutual Security Administration, the North Atlantic Treaty Organization, or the National Security Council ... No woman is an adviser to the president." The author then went on to argue that due to this absence of powerful women, the nation was being deprived of a leadership style that would bring to the table a "keener awareness" of the horrors of war, along

[34] Cavert, Inez M. *Women in American Church Life* (New York: Friendship Press, 1948), p. 48.
[35] Ibid, pp. 21–4.
[36] Calkins, Gladys Gilkey. *Follow Those Women: Church Women in the Ecumenical Movement* (New York: National Council of Churches, 1961).

with a greater degree of compassion for one's fellow human beings. The solution, she proposed, was pretty straightforward. She suggested that "capable women be admitted to partnership with men in formulating American military and diplomatic policies."[37]

An even more compelling sign of this nascent feminism that was forming among religious women was the Women's Leadership Conference that took place in April 1952. Held over a three-day period, the Florida conference attracted approximately one hundred and fifty leading female activists from across the country. Attendees included two leading figures from the UCW; an assortment of female attorneys, journalists, educators, and businesswomen; a member of the Cleveland City Council, Helen Gagan Douglas; a former congresswoman from California, a representative from the Congress of Industrial Organizations; female clerics; senior personnel from both the Republican and Democratic parties; and senior officials from both the League of Women Voters and the National Council of Jewish Women.[38]

No less impressive than the prominent attendees was the proto-feminist message that emerged from the conference. Although the initial purpose of the gathering was to promote peace and freedom, once the conference was under way, the need for equality – racial as well as sexual – quickly emerged as a leading theme. For example, an afternoon panel dealing with fairness in the world of work focused on three related issues: "prevailing prejudice against women," "prevailing prejudice against Negroes," and businesses' general hesitancy of "take(ing) women into some jobs."[39]

Another session, held the following morning, was titled "STRENGTHENING THE FORCES OF FREEDOM AND DEMOCRACY IN GOVERNMENT." In its summary of the "most interesting points," the conference proceedings noted that at the session, participants lavished praise on Susan B. Anthony and other early feminists who "blazed a trail of political activity that only now is being exploited to its fullest."[40]

Nor were these sentiments aberrations. Time and again, conference participants emphasized the need for women to become more engaged in

[37] Frederick, Pauline. "The Silent Sex," *The Church Woman* (November 1952), pp. 5–8.
[38] Mary McLeod Bethune Papers Part 1, Reel 18, "Who's Who at the Conference," pp. 403–11.
[39] Mary McLeod Bethune Papers Part 1, Reel 18, "Proceedings for the Women's Conference," p. 191.
[40] Mary McLeod Bethune Papers Part 1, Reel 18, Mrs. Henry L. Killen National Board League of Women Voters.

public affairs. Bertha Adkins, executive director of the women's division of the Republican National Committee, urged the audience to become more involved in the political process, even though that might entail offending the sensibilities of some men. "It's not going to be easy," she warned. "They'll be barriers in your way. There's still that feeling that women haven't quite the ability men have."[41] India Edwards, the Democratic counterpart to Bertha Adkins, exuded even more cynicism. "The men," she declared, "don't want women messing around in politics. They would much rather have you give a tea where the candidates can shake hands... if I weren't a crusader I'd say the hell with the whole thing and go home."[42]

In its official "Statement of Findings," the delegates to the conference reaffirmed the need for the women of America to do a better job in "obtain(ing) representation in government and a voice in policy-making," as well as the need to "wipe out discrimination against women and minorities." Perhaps most surprising was the call for "democratic living" in the family – which in the context of the early fifties was a not-so-subtle assault on the husband-dominated household.[43] That Jane Calvert, a prominent church woman, co-chaired the conference, that senior UCW leaders participated in the conference, and that *The Church Woman* reprinted the conference's "Statement of Findings" in its entirety was an indication of two progressive developments: the increased willingness of church women to confront sexual discrimination in the 1950s and, concomitantly, a willingness on the part of church women to forge bonds with groups of female activists of a similar vision.

Although Protestants were more receptive than Catholics to an expanded religious role for women, within the American Catholic Church, there were progressive developments unfolding during the 1950s. Within the field of Catholic education, the nuns staffing the countless parochial schools and the more than one hundred women's colleges at midcentury became increasingly assertive – and increasingly successful – in pressing church leaders to provide more equitable training for themselves and their students. The creation of the Sister Formation Conference in 1954, a nun-dominated organization operating as something akin to a

[41] "Top Lady Politicos Ask Others to Join Despite Male Sneers," *The Washington Post* (April 6, 1952), p. C20.
[42] Ibid.
[43] Mary McLeod Bethune Papers Part 1, Reel 18, "Official Statement of Findings," pp. 256–8.

pressure group within the world of American Catholic education, empow-ered Sisters in their struggles with male clerical authorities.[44] Besides serving as an advocacy arm, the Sister Formation Conference facilitated a greater sense of intellectual autonomy among its members through its journal *The Sister Formation Bulletin.*

From the very outset, the *Bulletin* was candid about its larger objec-tives. An important goal of the movement, declared Mary Emil Penet, was to form a Sister "who can think for herself, who is able to continue her education independently, through reading and study, and who has a love and appreciation of the things of the mind." As the journal took up questions of practice and theology, and as the movement itself brought different orders of nuns into contact with one another, Sisters decreasingly turned to the male ecclesiastic establishment, and, with greater regularity, looked either inward or to one another for the answers to their most pressing questions.

As luck would have it, two developments aided the Sisters in their timely battles against the conservative American Catholic hierarchy. The first, ironically, was a new attitude originating from the Vatican that, in the early 1950s, began encouraging nuns and the students they taught to be no less educated than the larger culture from whose ranks they were drawn.[45] In addition to Pope Pius XII's injunction, the Sisters were aided by what could loosely be called an intellectual inferiority complex among Catholics in America. During the 1950s, as more and more American Catholics settled into the ranks of the middle class, there was a growing concern over what many regarded as the Catholics' modest contribution to American intellectual life. John Tracy Ellis' famous address before the Catholic Commission for Intellectual and Cultural Affairs in 1955 – remarks that became the basis of a vigorous discussion among leading Catholic intellectuals – best articulated these anxieties.[46] For their part, the Sister Formation Conference wasted little time in using the attention Ellis' remarks had drawn to further their cause.[47]

---

[44] Morey, Melanie M., and Piderit, John J. *Catholic Higher Education: A Culture in Crisis* (New York: Oxford University Press, 2006), p. 249.

[45] Gleason, Philip. *Contending with Modernity: Catholic Higher Education in the Twenti-eth Century* (New York: Oxford University Press, 1995), p. 229.

[46] Ibid, pp. 288–9.

[47] If the intellectual attitude that Father Ellis wrote about "has deeply affected clerical thinking and cut off the channels of intellectual proficiency among the laity," proclaimed an article in *The Sister Formation Bulletin*, "then what has been the effect of these views on the 92,000 teaching Sisters, who stand at such a crucial point in the forming and passing on of traditions and values in the schools?" See Bradley, Sister Ritamary, "Man

The increasing involvement of Catholic women in lay organizations, a development that was in the works during the forties and fifties, was another way the status of women was able to rise within the American Catholic Church. Not only did Catholic women participate vigorously in such causes as the Grail movement, the Catholic Workers movement, and the Christian Family movement, but positions of leadership were open to them as well.[48] In addition, women became staff writers and even senior editors at a number of prominent Catholic journals – such as *Jubilee*, *Cross Currents*, *Integrity*, and *Commonweal* – during the 1950s.[49] Although these Catholic women remained outside of the Church hierarchy – which, as today, was the domain of an all-male clergy – they nonetheless succeeded in acquiring a more prominent voice in Catholic life and, thereby challenged traditional roles of female subservience. Given these developments, it should not come as a surprise that when Friedan's *The Feminine Mystique* first came out, it received a favorable review in *Commonweal* magazine.[50]

In acknowledging the rise of church women, we must take great pains to avoid overstating the degree of transformation. Among both Protestants and Catholics, traditional attitudes predominated during the fifties. Lay Catholic women – like Dorothy Day and Catherine de Hueck Doherty – may have become more visible actors on the cultural stage, but ecclesiastic power remained exclusively in the hands of men. Similarly, the church women who participated in the Women's Leadership Conference may have tried to carve out a larger public role for women, but they commonly addressed each other by the names of their husbands – thus Jeanne Cavert was referred to as Mrs. Samuel McCrea Cavert, and Mossie Wyker, the head of UCW, identified herself on her letterhead as "Mrs. James D. Wyker."[51] By the standards of today, these progressive

Thinking and the Conventional World," *Sister Formation Bulletin* (December 1955), p. 17 as cited in Eby, Judith Ann, "A Little Squabble Among Nuns? The Sister Formation Crisis and the Patterns of Authority and Obedience Among American Women Religious, 1954–1971," doctoral dissertation from Saint Louis University, 2000, pp. 66.

[48] Burns, Jeffery M. "Catholic Laywomen in the Culture of American Catholicism in the 1950s," *U.S. Catholic Historian* (Summer/Fall 1986), pp. 391–2.

[49] Kenneally, James J. *The History of American Catholic Women* (New York: Crossroads Publishing Company, 1990), p. 196

[50] Hozhauer, Jean. "Doing Daddy In," *Commonweal* (October 18, 1963), pp. 100–2.

[51] Mary McLeod Bethune Papers Part 1, Reel 18, Women's Conference Correspondence, Mrs. James D. Wyker to Mary McLeod Bethune, February 14, 1952, Women's Conference Registrants, pp. 29, 313.

women conformed to very old-fashioned sexual norms. For their time, however, they were indeed trailblazers who helped redefine the roles of women, both in the church and the wider culture.

Reflecting the ascendance of church women, a number of religious institutions took symbolic steps that appeared to sanction the expanding role of female congregants. In 1952, for example, a woman was elected president to the New York Council of Churches. In addition, the Washington Cathedral, breaking precedent, named two women to its board.[52] Three years later, Harvard University's Divinity School broke a 319-year tradition and began allowing women to enroll as regular students.[53] Moreover, in the fifteen years after World War II, several religious bodies, such as the Christian Scientists, the Evangelical and Reformed Church, and the General Council of Congregational Churches selected women to serve as the heads of their denominations.[54]

The most important sign of the rising status of women, however, was to be found neither in grand gestures nor in the decisions being reached at the level of the General Conference. Instead, the clearest indication that women were acquiring a stronger voice in church affairs was most visible on a local level. Among Christians in general, and Protestants in particular, religious life is most profoundly shaped at the congregational level. So, not surprisingly, it was in congregations, at the level of the local church, where the influence of women was most pronounced.

In 1953, *The Washington Post* looked at congregational leadership within a number of leading Protestant denominations. They included the Methodists, Presbyterians, and Baptists, as well as the United Brethren and the Disciples of Christ. In the end, the report found "increases from 20 to 60 percent in the number of women on church boards within the last decade."[55] To be sure, during the 1950s – as today – men continued to dominate at all levels of church governance. Yet what these changes reveal is church women were beginning to break out of their subordinate roles in a very real sense. Among most mainline Protestants, it was no

---

[52] "2 Women Put on Church Board," *The Washington Post* (November 25, 1952), p. 48.
[53] "Harvard Divinity School to Admit Women for all Theology Degrees," *The New York Times* (January 19, 1955), p. 29.
[54] "Woman is Elected Church Moderator," *The New York Times* (July 2, 1959), p. 27; "Congregationalists Pick Woman Leader," *The New York Times* (February 17, 1950), p. 5; "Boston Woman Heads Christian Scientists," *The Washington Post* (June 9, 1959), p. A11.
[55] Cornell, George W. "Women Win Church Posts," *The Washington Post* (September 4, 1953), p. 37.

longer sufficient to channel the energies of the womenfolk into separate
female organizations within the church.

Women and Psychology

As historians look back to the middle decades of the twentieth century,
it is commonly regarded as the golden age of psychoanalysis. Such a
description makes plenty of sense, as even a cursory examination of public
discourse reveals Freudian analysis loomed very large within American
culture during the 1950s. As Alfred Kazin noted in a famous article
written in 1956: "It is impossible to think of the greatest names in modern
literature and art – Thomas Mann, James Joyce, Franz Kafka, T. S. Elliot,
Ernest Hemingway, William Faulkner, Pablo Picasso, Paul Klee – without
realizing our debt to Freud's exploration of dreams, myths, symbols, and
the imaginative profundity of man's inner life."[56] Kazin's analysis was
no doubt true. However, Freud's appeal at midcentury extended beyond
the coffeehouse banter of the intelligentsia. In Cold War America, such
terms as *penis envy, superego, anal retentive, repressive, phallic symbol,*
and *Oedipus complex* entered the everyday language of ordinary citizens.

The popularity of Freud has given credence to the claim the 1950s
were a time when the roles of women became increasingly circumscribed
and their general status was, for the most part, in decline. The writings of
Freud, after all, could very easily be regarded as disparaging of women.
With the abandonment of his seduction theory in the early 1890s, Freud
himself exhorted therapists to dismiss the claims of molestation or incest
coming from female patients. Such claims, he argued, typically arose
from the failure of women to resolve the unconscious desire they had as
girls to have intercourse with their fathers. Similarly, it was Freud who
asserted that "penis envy" was a necessary component of the psycho-
sexual development of a woman, because it helped lead girls to identify
with the role of mother (as a form of compensation).[57] It is little wonder
that feminist advocates like Betty Friedan in *The Feminine Mystique* and
Kate Millett in *Sexual Politics* spent a good deal of time critiquing Freud's
condescending treatment of women.[58]

---

[56] Kazin, Alfred. "The Freudian Revolution Analyzed," *The New York Times Magazine*
(May 6, 1956), p. 22.

[57] For a discussion of the sexism inherent in Freudian theory, see Young-Bruehl, Elisabeth
(ed.), *Freud On Women: A Reader* (New York: W. W. Norton & Company, 1990).

[58] Millett, Kate. *Sexual Politics* (New York: Touchstone Books, 1970), pp. 176–220;
Friedan, *The Feminine Mystique*, pp. 105, 113, 116–17.

FIGURE 4.1. Feminist Betty Friedan (right), author of *The Feminine Mystique*, talking to a small group of women. (Reproduced by permission of the Schlesinger Library, Radcliffe Institute, Harvard University.)

What is more, some of Freud's most visible disciples used psychoanalytic theory to stigmatize those women who bucked convention by flouting traditional gender roles. During the early postwar years, it was not unusual to label career women, especially those who were single or childless, as neurotic personality types. Thus, in Ferdinand Lundberg and Marynia Farnham's *Modern Women: The Lost Sex* (1947) the authors argue that in seeking independence, the career woman was turning her back on her biological imperative. It was in a woman's nature, they insisted, to be embedded in a web of dependence. For psychologically healthy women, asserted these champions of traditionalism, the role of wife and mother accounted for "almost their whole inner feeling of personal well-being." Thus, women who refused to marry or have children were attempting to resolve some psychological trauma that they had experienced during their childhood.[59]

That conservatives used psychology to enforce traditional gender roles is well supported, but – Freud's misogyny notwithstanding – psychology exerted a more salutary effect upon the status of women than many

[59] For a solid analysis of *Modern Women: The Lost Sex*, see Chafe, *The American Woman*, pp. 202–6.

feminist scholars have recognized. Rather than reinforcing the subordination of women, the net effect of psychology in the fifties was to frame an
ethic of individualism that helped breathe life into the feminist movement.

The critic Donald Kaplan once noted that Sigmund Freud "remains
the most widely recognized name in the flourishing mental-health movement and the couch its leading symbol; but while there is now a stu-
pendous amount of psychotherapy going on of all kinds, the kind going
on least of all – indeed, in vanishing proportion to all the others – is
psychoanalysis."[60] Although Kaplan's observations were published in
1965, they could just as easily have been written in 1955. As a cultural
phenomenon, Freud was enormous; but as a school of psychology, the
influence of Freudianism waned during the 1950s. This decline was due to
some stiff competition. Outside of the world of psychological counseling,
Freudian analysis was outstripped by the towering success of psychotropic
drugs – a phenomenon discussed in Chapter 1. Within the world of psychotherapy, the challenge came from the expanding appeal of humanistic
psychology.

By the mid-1960s, Carl Rogers and Abraham Maslow had become
widely known public figures, but a decade earlier, the former had already
developed a sizable following among therapists. Many of Rogers' fellow
psychologists who had elected him president of the American Psychological Association (APA) in 1947 found the Rogerian approach provocative
and refreshing. In the fifteen years after World War II, Rogers' methods, commonly referred to as *nondirective counseling* or *client-centered
therapy*, were described and discussed in numerous articles and conferences. However, the bulk of Rogers' followers came from within the
ranks of the pastoral counseling movement. As Chapter 3 documented,
during the 1940s and 1950s ministerial training was revolutionized in
the United States as a majority of Protestant seminaries became favorably
disposed to the discipline of psychology. Significantly, it was not Sigmund
Freud but Carl Rogers who proved to be the leading light in the pastoral
counseling movement. Rogers' emphasis on the individual's innate goodness seemed to resonate among pastoral counselors. Thus, while hardly
a religious man, Rogers sat on the board of *Pastoral Psychology*, the
leading journal of the movement. Moreover, during the 1950s the leading textbooks used in the seminaries drew heavily on the client-centered
approach.

[60] Kaplan, Donald M. "Psychoanalysis: The Decline of a Golden Craft," *Harper's Magazine*
(February 1967), p. 41.

Because of its emphasis on growth and self-fulfillment, humanistic psychology tended to be a good deal more sympathetic toward women than Freudian analysis. It is little wonder, therefore, that Betty Friedan, whose *Feminine Mystique* did so much to spur the feminist movement, drew heavily from the writings of Rogers and Maslow. In urging women to reach their full potential by entering the workforce, her language reads as if it came directly out of a humanistic psychology playbook. For example, in a chapter entitled "The Forfeited Self," Friedan contrasted the emotionally stunted housewife with the self-actualized person. Rejecting Freud as her authority, Friedan repeatedly turned to Abraham Maslow, citing him to show self-actualized women were more likely to be career oriented, self-confident, independent thinking, self-expressive, honest, spontaneous, and capable of achieving sexual satisfaction.[61]

Although it would be an exaggeration to call Maslow a feminist, it would certainly be accurate to say that some of his ideas were very friendly to the cause of feminism. As early as 1939, Maslow had penned an article, based on his interviews and observations of approximately one hundred and thirty subjects, that contrasted high-dominance women to low-dominance women. According to Maslow, low-dominance types had internalized traditional gender roles, and they accordingly tended to exhibit feminine traits such as shyness, conventionality, and ready embarrassment. By contrast, high-dominance women tended to disdain many of the supposedly feminine qualities. As Maslow observed, "Many of the qualities that are considered to be 'manly' are seen in them in a high degree." These high-dominance women, he continued, "prefer to be treated 'like a person, not like a woman.' They prefer to be independent, stand on their own two feet, and generally do not care for concessions that imply they are inferior, weak, or that they need special attention and cannot take care of themselves."[62]

From even a quick survey of the article, it is clear that Maslow found high-dominance women quite noble and appealing. In the text of the article, those falling within the high-dominance category are described as "strong," "purposeful," possessing "good self-confidence," having "strength of character," and having enjoyed "emancipation from trivialities." By contrast, Maslow sees the "feminine," low-dominance women as most likely to possess such qualities as "envy," "jealousy," "suspicion,"

---

[61] Friedan, *The Feminine Mystique*, pp. 310–37.

[62] Maslow, Abraham H. "Dominance, Personality, and Social Behavior in Women," *The Journal of Social Psychology* (February 1939), pp. 3–38.

FIGURE 4.2. Abraham Maslow was one of the leading figures of the humanistic psychology movement. His work influenced Betty Friedan. (Reproduced by permission of the AHAP collection at The University of Akron.)

low self-esteem, "distrust," and "moodiness."[63] Written nearly a quarter of a century before the publication of *The Feminine Mystique*, Maslow's article betrays his feminist inclinations, and anticipates arguments that would later be employed by second-wave feminists.

During the final phase of the 1960s' upheaval, radical feminists would take up the cause of consciousness-raising groups (often referred to as *CR groups*) and by so doing, supersede Betty Friedan in their embrace of humanistic psychology. Briefly stated, radical feminists believed that if women were able to discuss their personal problems with other women in a warm, receptive environment, they would come to recognize their individual struggles as part of a larger pattern of sexual oppression. It is no overstatement to say that during the late 1960s and early 1970s, consciousness-raising groups, sometimes referred to as *rap groups, support groups*, – and even, by some hostile observers, as *bitch sessions* – became the building blocks of women's liberation. The first edition of *Ms. Magazine* provided in-depth instructions on how to organize and conduct a consciousness-raising group.[64] Consistent with the ideology of

[63] Ibid.
[64] Brownmiller, Susan. *In Our Time: Memoir of a Revolution* (New York: Dial Press, 1999).

the New Left, CR groups sought to demonstrate how the "personal is political."[65]

Although CR groups saw themselves as political vehicles, they seemed to have borrowed a great deal from Rogerian methods. Like Rogers, CR groups discouraged participants from judging one another: "Criticism inhibits and makes it more difficult to realize the goal of increased self-understanding." Women were also urged to avoid asking any questions beyond questions of clarification. As one guide explained, "Be sensitive to the possibility that to ask may be to pressure." Finally, CR groups, like client-centered psychotherapy, were supposed to be leaderless, shunning any figure "who determines the content or is presumed to be the final authority."[66] The emphasis CR groups placed on personal growth, the need to provide an affirming, nonjudgmental environment, and the belief the answer to one's problems rested within oneself strongly echoed the Rogerian approach to counseling.[67]

Needless to say, CR groups did not exist during the 1950s, and *The Feminine Mystique* had yet to be written. However, the essential thrust of humanistic psychology – the basic assumptions it held, the questions it raised, the general goals it set, and its emphasis on growth and fulfillment – was not compatible with patriarchal authority. On the contrary, humanistic psychology tended to be suspicious of virtually any form of external authority because the ultimate guide to psychic healing and self-improvement was to unleash the actualizing tendency.

A brief anecdote about Carl Rogers helps demonstrate this rejection of external authority. In 1966, a small order of nuns based in Southern California invited a team of Rogerian therapists to provide counseling to its members. This was all part of a larger project of Rogers, who was

---

[65] In her memoirs, feminist icon Susan Brownmiller recalled the importance of CR groups in her own development as a radical feminist. In time, she wrote, "many original perceptions that the pioneering consciousness-raising groups had struggled to express would become received information, routine and unexceptional." Yet despite its seemingly pedestrian insights, "I can attest that in New York during the late sixties and early seventies, nothing was more exciting, or more intellectually stimulating, than to sit in a room with a bunch of women who were working to uncover their collective truths." Ibid.

[66] The Women's Collective, "Consciousness Raising," from the CWLU Herstory website. Online at: http://www.cwluherstory.com.

[67] In retrospect, it is not so surprising that second-wave feminists would turn to psychology as a source of inspiration. Similar to the way nineteenth-century feminists such as Margaret Fuller and Julia Ward Howe found encouragement from transcendentalism, and much the way the thinking of Simone De Beauvoir had been nourished by existentialism, feminists in postwar America were drawn to a scholarly literature that encouraged introspection.

attempting to show that once so-called "normals" were exposed to the principles of humanistic psychology, they would be more productive in their work and generally happier in their lives. Encouraged to explore their most basic feelings, numerous nuns deferred to their inner voice and yielded to the temptations of the flesh, initiating sexual affairs with their priests, the laity, their therapists, and even with each other.[68] When Rogers learned that a number of therapists working under his tutelage had become sexually involved with their patients, he was at a loss to stop them. As William Coulson, Roger's close friend and top deputy, recalled: "Rogers didn't get people involved in sex games, but he couldn't prevent his followers from doing it, because all he could say was 'I don't do that.'" Then his followers would explain, "'Well, of course you don't do that, because you grew up in an earlier era; but we do, and it's marvelous: you have set us free to be ourselves and not carbon copies of you.'" The Sisters' experimentation with Rogerian methods wreaked havoc on the order. "There were 560 nuns when we began," recalled Coulson. "Within a year after our interventions, 300 of them were petitioning Rome to get out of their vows."[69]

Unfortunately for the Sisters of the Immaculate Heart of St. Mary (IHM), the crisis did not end with the mass exodus of disenchanted nuns. Those choosing to remain found it increasingly difficult to submit to the authority of their cardinal. Consequently, a bitter conflict arose between the Sisters and the church hierarchy, with the dispute eventually reaching the Vatican. Along the way, a group of Franciscan priests and brothers from the Theological Seminary of Santa Barbara, the editors of both *Commonweal* and the *National Catholic Reporter*, and approximately three thousand U.S. nuns registered their support for the Immaculate Heart Sisters. In addition, an assortment of prominent Protestant figures including Reinhold Niebuhr, Harvard University's Harvey Cox, *Christian Century* editor Martin Marty, and Episcopal Bishop Arthur Lichtenberger weighed in on the side of the rebellious Sisters.[70] Alas, it was all to no avail. In the end, the nuns lost their case as well as their teaching positions at several dozen parochial schools in the greater Los Angeles area. In addition, Immaculate Heart College, a small liberal arts institution the nuns had supervised for decades, closed its doors forever. Finally, the

[68] "We Overcame Their Traditions, We Overcame Their Faith," (interview with Dr. William Coulson). *The Latin Mass* (Special Edition, 1997), pp. 12–17.
[69] Ibid.
[70] Weber, Francis J. *His Eminence of Los Angeles: James Francis Cardinal McIntyre* (Mission Hills, Calif.: Saint Francis Historical Society, 1997), pp. 417–41.

Sisters of the Immaculate Heart of St. Mary ceased functioning as an active religious order and, for all intents and purposes, disbanded.[71]

In encouraging people to develop their full potential, and in emphasizing growth and autonomy, humanistic psychology helped cultivate the very attitudes that helped spawn the feminist movement. However, for those interested in the history of psychology, as well as the history of feminism, Rogerian therapy was more than just an alternative approach to Freud. According to a 1957 study sponsored by the Joint Commission on Mental Illness and Health, those open to professional psychological counseling were more than three times as likely to cite a minister as the first person they would consult rather than a psychiatrist or psychologist.[72] Another survey, conducted by George Gallup in the mid-1950s, yielded similar results.[73] Freudianism may have been the dominant philosophy among trained psychologists, but within the pastoral counseling movement – which, from a clinical standpoint, was considerably larger than the world occupied by psychologists and psychiatrists – it was Carl Rogers who reigned supreme.

Psychology at midcentury did not bring about a sudden transformation in gender roles. Yet in lauding the goal of self-actualization, and questioning traditional authority, psychology laid the psychic basis from whence the feminist revolution would later emerge.

Politics

Surprisingly, even in the arena of politics – the one area where we would expect traditional attitudes toward women to persist the longest – women were coming to play a more important role during the 1950s. For instance, during the 1944 general elections, nine women were elected to the U.S. Congress, but by 1957 – the very height of the baby boom – the number of women serving in Congress had climbed to seventeen.[74] At the state level, women also posted gains: in 1945, 236 women were elected to state

---

[71] Ibid.

[72] Gurin, Gerald, Veroff, Joseph, and Feld, Sheila. *Americans View Their Mental Health* (New York: Basic Books, 1960), p. 121.

[73] Cited from Myers-Shirk, Susan E. "'To Be Fully Human': U.S. Protestant Psychotherapeutic Culture and the Subversion of the Domestic Ideal, 1945–1965," *Journal of Women's History* 12 (2000), p. 115.

[74] In the fall of that year (1944), New Jersey Congresswoman Mary T. Norton publicly stated that she doubted that, within her lifetime, the number of women serving in the U.S. Congress would ever reach twelve. The reason for her pessimism was simple. As she put it, "Women won't vote for women." See Eads, Jane, "It's 'Woman's Year'

legislatures; by 1957, that figure had climbed to 317 – an increase of more than one-third.[75] And by the end of the decade, there were 341 women serving in state legislatures, a 44 percent increase from 1945.[76]

Nor were these gains an aberration unconnected to larger cultural currents. In November 1945, only three months after the surrender of Japan, George Gallup asked fifteen hundred Americans if they could support a woman for president of the United States "if she seemed best qualified for the job." Only 33 percent, or one-third of the respondents, said they could; while 55 percent said they could not. What is more, majorities of women as well as men indicated that they could not back a female candidate for president regardless of her qualifications. In 1959, when Gallup returned to the question of a female president, he found that attitudes had significantly changed. Fifty-seven percent of respondents replied that they could support a woman for president, while 39 percent said they could not. Moreover, majorities of both men and women indicated that, in principle, they could back a woman for the highest office in the land.[77] In short, by the close of the 1950s, Americans were more than 70 percent more open to the possibility of a female president than they had been in 1945.

The point here is not that the 1950s was a time when women were making enormous political strides, but rather that it was a time when women were making more than modest political gains. In fact, by the end of the 1950s, not only were there significantly more women serving as state legislators than at the end of World War II or at the close of the 1940s, but there were slightly more women serving in state legislatures than at the close of the 1960s.[78] In addition, women succeeded in becoming mayors in a handful of communities during the late forties and fifties. When Dorothy McCullough Lee, a forty-seven-year-old mother of two, won Portland's mayoral race in May 1948, she became the nation's

But – Men Still Top Ballot if Not Voting Power," *The Washington Post* (November 5, 1944), p. B3.

[75] Cox, Elizabeth M. *Women, State and Territorial Legislators, 1895–1999* (North Carolina: McFarland & Company), pp. 327–8.

[76] Ibid, p. 328.

[77] Survey by Gallup Organization, December 10–15, 1959. Retrieved April 2006, from the iPOLL Databank, The Roper Center for Public Opinion Research, University of Connecticut. Online at: http://www.ropercenter.uconn.edu/ipoll.html. Data analysis provided by John Bowblis of Rutgers University's Institute for Health, Health Care Policy, and Aging Research.

[78] Cox, *Women, State and Territorial Legislators*, p. 328.

first woman to head a city with a population in excess of five hundred thousand people.[79]

In her book *Born to Liberty*, Sara Evans argues that because of the conservatism of the culture, women during the 1950s were relegated to the "sidelines of political life," occupying "less than 5 percent of political offices, even locally." This is an important point because it helps demonstrate the degree to which conservative attitudes limited the options of women. However, if it is legitimate for Evans to underscore the comparatively small number of elected officials who were women during the early Cold War years, it is equally incumbent upon scholars to recognize those small numbers represented a sizable increase from where it had been thirty, twenty, or even ten years earlier.

Although not tantamount to political involvement, jury service speaks directly to the larger question of civic responsibility. Both during and after World War II there was a growing sense that, except for service in the armed forces, the civic demands made on women should be no less than those made on men. As the historian Alan Rogers has documented, in the period between 1943 and 1947 eight states repealed laws that prevented women from serving on juries, and with the League of Women Voters sounding the charge, these reforms continued into the 1950s.[80] Between the years 1950 and 1959, the number of states barring women from jury duty fell from thirteen to three.[81] "The reverberating phrase – 'twelve good men and true' – is being modified more and more," wrote *New York Times* writer Gertrude Samuels, "by the parade of good and true women into the jury box."[82] In short, while officially sanctioned discrimination persisted into the 1960s and beyond – with a handful of states prohibiting women from serving on juries, and a number of other states rendering jury service for women optional while it was mandatory

[79] "Woman Far in Lead for Portland Mayor," *The Los Angeles Times* (May 22, 1948), p. 1; "Maurine Neuberger, "Portland's First Lady," *The New York Times* (November 21, 1948), p. SM 33; "Six Women Named for Press Awards," *The New York Times* (April 17, 1949), p. 58; Hoyt, Isabell Murray. "Women Needed in Public Service, Says Mayor-Elect of Portland, Oregon," *The New York Times* (June 9, 1948), p. 10.

[80] For an excellent discussion of the issue of women serving on juries, see Kerber, Linda, *No Constitutional Rights to Be Ladies: Women and the Obligations of Citizenship* (New York: Hill & Wang, 1998), pp. 124–220.

[81] Taylor, Grace Elizabeth. "Jury Service for Women," *University of Florida Law Review* (Summer 1959), p. 228.

[82] Samuels, Gertrude. "The Verdict on Women Jurors," *The New York Times Magazine* (May 7, 1950), p. 186.

for men – in the main, the nation's courts were moving toward greater gender equality during the Truman and Eisenhower years.

Of course, the most impressive advances in sexual equality were made in the private realm of the family. Yet it is noteworthy that even within the world of politics, impressive gains were taking place during the supposedly dark years of the 1950s. If American women during the Eisenhower years were so politically complacent compared to the women of World War II, then why were female voters flocking to the polls in ever-greater numbers? Equally significant, if the status of women was declining, or simply stagnating, then why would increasing numbers of Americans be willing to chose a capable woman to represent them in their state capitals or in Washington, D.C.?

Part of the confusion concerning the status of women during the 1950s revolves around the failure to distinguish sufficiently between private choices and general attitudes. During the postwar period, more women chose to confine themselves to the private sphere while Americans were also beginning to feel more and more comfortable with the idea of women assuming prominent roles in public life. On a personal level, many of the same women and men who embraced the traditional model of the working husband and the stay-at-home wife were simultaneously accepting the presence of a strong, independent woman operating in the public domain.

Education as a Secularizing Force

Various surveys demonstrate the increasing acceptance of women not just in the world of politics, but also in the public sphere. However, a more thorough examination of some of these polls – analyses requiring scholars to first obtain the survey's original data set, and then mine it for additional information not previously released – reveals something else: during the 1940s and 1950s, progressive attitudes toward women were highly correlated with education. As a rule of thumb, the more schooling an individual possessed, the more inclined she was to be favorable to the liberation of women. Conversely, the less education, the less amenable she tended to be toward loosening traditional constraints on women. For example, although majorities of both men and women in 1945 indicated that they could not back a woman for president, opinions differed greatly for those holding a bachelor's degree. Fifty-seven percent of college-educated women claimed they could support a female for president, while only 40 percent said they could not. Among males, the numbers were similar, with 55 percent of college-educated men receptive to sending a qualified woman to the White House, and 38 percent opposed.[83]

Another survey conducted in 1953 explored popular attitudes toward a segment of the population generally thought of as "loose" women. In the poll, nearly thirteen hundred people were asked if they agreed with the statement: "No decent man can respect a woman who has had sex relations before marriage." According to the findings, 33 percent of all respondents agreed with the statement, while 59 percent disagreed, and 8 percent could not decide.[84] However, when the survey's data set is closely scrutinized, some of the findings as they relate to education dovetail with Gallup's earlier poll on a female presidential candidate. As in the earlier survey, college-educated respondents were more liberal than their less-educated counterparts. In fact, those with a college degree were nearly half as likely as high school-educated respondents, and almost one-third as likely as those having no more than a sixth-grade education, to agree with the statement that "no decent man" could possibly "respect" a single woman who had lost her virginity.[85]

What these figures point to was an emergent trend that made a significant contribution to the elevated status of women. This agent of change was the expansion of education during the 1940s and 1950s. Education caused people to adopt more progressive views on a variety of areas – including the status of women. This, in turn, proved crucial to challenging – as Betty Friedan aptly phrased it – "standards of feminine normality, feminine adjustment, feminine fulfillment, and feminine maturity."[86]

Figures from *Historical Statistics of the United States* tell much of the story. Where less than 20 percent of eighteen- to twenty-one-year-old women were enrolled in college during the 1949–50 school year, a decade later, more than 33 percent of eighteen- to twenty-one-year-old women were attending college – an increase of more than 50 percent.[87] During this same ten-year period, the proportion of female college students rose from 31.6 to 37.1 percent of total students. As a result of the increasing population of all college students, and especially female students, the

[83] Survey by Gallup Organization, November 23–28, 1945. Retrieved July 27, 2008, from the iPOLL Databank, The Roper Center for Public Opinion Research, University of Connecticut. Online at: http://www.ropercenter.uconn.edu/ipoll.html.

[84] Ibid.

[85] Ibid.

[86] Friedan, *The Feminine Mystique*, p. 31.

[87] Bureau of the Census, U.S. Department of Commerce, *Historical Statistics of the United States: Colonial Times to 1970*, Part I (Washington, D.C.: Bureau of the Census, 1975).

number of women in college doubled in the fifteen years after World War II.[88] Equally significant, this expansion of the college experience was occurring during a time when the secularization of the university – a process described by historian George Marsden in brilliant detail – was well under way.[89]

A careful analysis of raw polling data provides us with another important finding: schools shaped attitudes more than work. For most women, education was more highly correlated with a proto-feminist outlook than with employment status. For the purposes of this chapter, we further probed the 1945 survey relating to a female presidential candidate. As we previously noted, college-educated women indicated that they could support a female presidential candidate by a margin of 57 percent, compared to 49 percent of women with a high school education, and 30 percent with only an eighth-grade education. Thus, the data point to a strong correlation between educational attainment and having progressive views toward women.

However, the same data set also reveals that when people with equivalent levels of education are examined, employment status mattered only slightly. Among men and women with four years of high school, there was not a statistically significant divergence of opinion between those who worked and those who did not. When the impact of other variables – specifically race, gender, marital status, urbanicity, religion, education, and labor-force participation – are held constant, the results also indicate that education mattered a great deal while employment status was not an important factor. As Graph 4.1 shows, in 1945 the average marginal effect of having a college degree stood at 23.6 percent.[90]

In other words, those with four years of college were nearly 25 percent more likely to be receptive to a female presidential candidate than those without. The effect of secondary schooling was noticeable, but dwarfed when compared with that of college. Once adjusted for other variables, people with a high school diploma were approximately 8 percent more likely to be open to backing a qualified woman for president than those lacking a degree. By contrast, the average marginal effect for employment

[88] Eisenmann, Linda. *Higher Education for Women in Postwar America* (Baltimore: Johns Hopkins University Press, 2006), p. 172.

[89] Marsden, George. *The Soul of the American University: From Protestant Establishment to Established Non-Belief* (New York: Oxford University Press, 1994).

[90] Ibid. Data analysis is provided by economist John Bowblis, formerly of Rutgers University's Institute for Health, Health Care Policy, and Aging Research and, at the time of publication, an assistant professor of economics at Miami University–Ohio.

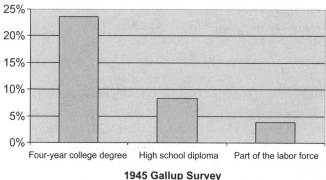

1945 Gallup Survey

GRAPH 4.1. 1945 Gallup survey, percentage of population receptive to supporting a female for president

was only 3.8 percent – and lacking statistical significance, this figure could very possibly be inflated.[91]

Gallup's 1953 survey, which probed popular attitudes toward sexually active single women, supports our earlier hypothesis regarding the role of education in influencing gender attitudes. According to the survey's data set, women with four years of college were almost half as likely as those with only a high school diploma (15.8 versus 31.4 percent), and nearly one-third as likely as women with less than a high school education (15.8 versus 44.6 percent) to agree with the traditional sentiment, "No decent man could respect a woman who had sex relations before marriage."[92]

When it came to general attitudes toward women having sex before marriage, employment status had some effect on attitudes, but in relative terms the influence was modest. According to the data, nonworking women who had failed to complete high school were only slightly more likely to agree with the pollster's statement than working women who had failed to finish high school (45.7 versus 42.9 percent). Among those who had either graduated high school or attended college, working women were roughly one-sixth less inclined to agree with the pollster's statement than nonworking women (25 versus 31.7 percent).[93]

When the polling data are scrutinized further and a logit regression is performed, the influence of education and employment becomes even

---

[91] Ibid.
[92] Survey by National Opinion Research Center, University of Chicago, June 1953. Retrieved July 27, 2008, from the iPOLL Databank, The Roper Center for Public Opinion Research, University of Connecticut. Online at: http://www.ropercenter.uconn.edu/ipoll.html.
[93] Ibid.

clearer. Once race, gender, age, religion, and work status are held constant, the average marginal effect of a college degree registered at −18.9 percent. In other words, when accounting for other variables, a person with four years of college was almost one-fifth less likely to agree with the pollster's statement ("No decent man could respect a woman who had sex relations before marriage") than a person who was without a bachelor's degree. As one might predict, the influence of high school was less than that of the full impact of college. Once other variables are held constant, the average marginal effect of a high school degree was −9 percent – half the effect of college, but still greater than the effect of employment status, which stood at − 6.8 percent.[94]

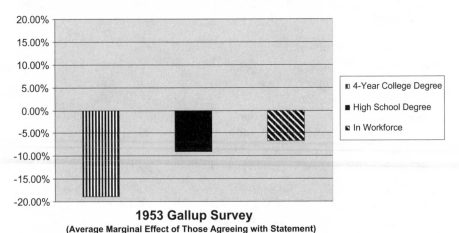

1953 Gallup Survey
(Average Marginal Effect of Those Agreeing with Statement)

GRAPH 4.2. 1953 Gallup survey, average marginal effect of those agreeing with statement: "No decent man can respect a woman who has had sex relations before marriage"

Among most historians and sociologists, the great emphasis on working women is predicated upon the belief that traditional gender roles beget traditional gender attitudes. According to this line of thinking, as long as homemakers remained absorbed in their worlds of babies and bottles, of garden clubs and Tupperware parties, it is doubtful they would ever seriously critique their predicament or fully realize their potential. "A woman cannot find her identity through others – her husband, her children," remarked Friedan in *The Feminine Mystique*. "She cannot find it in the dull routine of housework." Instead, the road to self-realization

[94] Ibid. Data analysis is provided by economist John Bowblis, formerly of Rutgers University's Institute for Health, Health Care Policy, and Aging Research and, at the time of publication, an assistant professor of economics at Miami University–Ohio.

rested outside of the home and family. "Work," Friedan insisted, "can now be seen as the key to the problem that has no name."[95] For the most part, scholars have been sympathetic to Friedan's analysis, believing that a woman's entry into the workforce is likely to offer her new challenges, instill new confidence, open up new possibilities, and facilitate her independence. However, the survey data from the 1940s and 1950s require us to develop a more nuanced analysis, mindful that the salience of work may have changed dramatically over time.

To their credit, the feminists' critique of housewives progressively became subtler and less strident. Among most movement feminists, the emphasis shifted from maximizing the numbers of women working in the professions to extending the range of options for women. As Amy Richards, author of *Manifesta: Young Women, Feminism, and the Future* and a regular contributor to the website feminist.com, explains when she is asked to define *feminism* she usually will first turn to the dictionary, which defines the term as "the movement toward the full social, political, and economic equality of all people." Richard then observes, "In my own life I like to add on: that every person have access to enough information to be able to make choices in their own lives. By that I mean, it's not so much about what choices you make, but that we have the freedom to make them. For instance, do you want to be a homemaker, a teacher, a dentist?"[96]

Most noteworthy about Richards' remarks was her willingness to treat the role of homemaker as every bit as legitimate a vocation – provided it was a free and informed decision – as the profession of teaching or dentistry. To many feminists like Amy Richards, the crucial issue is no longer whether one remains in the home or enters the workforce. Rather, it is about empowering people with free choices instead of forcing them into presumed roles.

According to Richards, the growth of lesbian couples raising their own children has forced movement feminists such as themselves to revisit earlier assumptions. "I know of a few cases," recalled Richards in an interview with National Public Radio, "where the biological mother is not the stay-at-home parent, but the nonbiological mother is. It proves that yes, there is a need for somebody to be the primary caregiver, but it does

---

[95] From Friedan's *The Feminine Mystique* as cited from Albrecht, Gloria H. *Hitting Home: Feminist Ethics, Women's Work, and the Betrayal of "Family Values"* (New York: Continuum Publishing, 2002), p. 57.

[96] See Amy Richard's "Ask Amy" column at www.feminist.com. The specific entry can be found under the heading of "feminism." Online at: www.feminist.com/askamy/feminism/fem187.

not need to be determined by biology." In the same interview, Richards spoke of a larger responsibility "as feminists who may or may not be homemakers" to ensure that those who choose to become a housewife or a stay-at-home dad be treated as "a valuable choice that both men and women can make."[97]

There is some indication that by the mid-1970s, the feminist movement was beginning to reconsider its traditional stance toward career – a position that tended to regard the stay-at-home housewives as a vocation that was ill suited for capable, intelligent women. An indication of this shifting attitude was the decision of the National Organization for Women (NOW) in 1977 to choose Eleanor Smeal – a self-described homemaker and mother of two – as its new president.

Unfortunately, this more balanced tone has not, for the greater part, been significantly integrated into the historical scholarship. Wedded to the received narrative, many academics have continued to equate the role of homemaker with tradition, conservatism, and passivity – conditions one does not normally associate with increased female assertiveness. And because the homemaker ideal was so strong during the 1950s, it is understandable that historians would continue to regard the early Cold War period as a dark age for the cause of gender equality, and fail to seriously grapple with the possibility that a proto-feminist consciousness could have emerged among politically conservative suburban housewives during the Eisenhower years.

It is plausible, perhaps even compelling, that among leading feminists during the 1960s – people like Betty Friedan, Gloria Steinem, Kathie Sarachild, and Kate Millett – the experience of work proved essential to their intellectual and ideological development. It is also plausible that sometime during the 1960s, and perhaps even the late 1950s, employment did begin to play an important role in shaping gender attitudes. However, in terms of explaining the decline of sexist views within the general population, it would appear that in the decade immediately following World War II – a time when popular attitudes toward women became more progressive – the influence of employment status was actually quite modest.

Charting Changing Attitudes

Surveys relating to the public's receptivity to a female presidential candidate reveal a great deal about liberalizing attitudes in the wake of World

---

[97] *Transcript of National Public Radio,* "Feminism Today and How it Evolved Since the Beginning of the Fight for Women's Rights," on *Talk of the Nation,* hosted by Juan Williams (October 3, 2000).

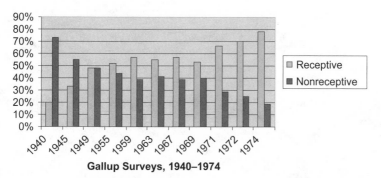

Gallup Surveys, 1940–1974

GRAPH 4.3. 1940–1974 Gallup survey, percentage receptive to supporting a qualified female presidential candidate

War II. However, these surveys are capable of achieving something even greater; they enable scholars to compare (albeit in the crudest of ways) World War II with the postwar period in promoting a progressive view of women.

During the 1940s and 1950s, many of the questions leading pollsters such as George Gallup, Elmo Roper, and Lou Harris put to the public were asked only once or twice. Yet on the issue of a female presidential candidate, Americans were queried on no less than eleven separate occasions over the course of thirty-five years. The regularity of these polls, conducted over a span of more than three decades, allow historians to chart the speed with which popular attitudes toward women were changing.

As the figures in Graph 4.3 indicate, the public's receptivity to a female presidential candidate grew rapidly, from only 20 percent in 1940 to 57 percent in 1959 – an increase of nearly threefold.

As Graph 4.3 reveals, a disproportionate share of the gains took place between 1940 and 1945, a period dominated by World War II. In fact, the percentage of Americans open to the candidacy of a qualified female presidential candidate was rising at more than twice the speed during the first six years of the 1940s than in the fifteen years following World War II.

Nevertheless, the findings of Gallup should not be accepted at face value. The fact that nearly six out of ten Americans in 1959 claimed that they could back a qualified woman for president does not mean they were truly open to such a prospect. Given the sheer magnitude of change between 1940 and 1959, it is probable that private beliefs did indeed shift. However, in all likelihood, some of the respondents were professing

FIGURE 4.3. Author and activist Gloria Steinem (center, with glasses) at a women's consciousness-raising session, circa 1970. (Reproduced by permission of the Sophia Smith Collection, Smith College.)

opinions publicly that they did not hold privately – or, in other words, they were simply saying what they thought they should be saying.[98] These survey results are therefore as much a reflection of shifting norms as they are of changing values. Although an imperfect reflection of people's true beliefs, this normative shift remains important. What it tells us is that during the 1950s, societal norms, or prevailing social conventions, were evolving in such a way that it became increasingly taboo to openly deny the principle of equal opportunity to women.

All in all, the picture painted by the survey numbers both supports and challenges important elements of the standard narrative. On one hand, it corroborates the claim World War II altered the way Americans approached the issue of gender in a profound way. Apparently, something about the World War II experience had an effect on gender attitudes. On

[98] The survey results reported here were obtained from searches of the iPOLL Databank and other resources provided by the Roper Center for Public Opinion Research, University of Connecticut.

the other hand, however, the polling figures suggest that far from being a dormant period, or a time when a conservative backlash materialized, the 1950s was a decade when the status of women was rising, and rising briskly – although at a pace somewhat slower than during the war years.

Finally, the polling numbers do not support the assertion that the 1960s reshaped popular attitudes to any appreciable extent. Certainly, the publication of Betty Friedan's *The Feminine Mystique*, the passage of both the Equal Pay Act of 1963 and the Civil Rights Act of 1964, the creation of NOW, and the rise of radical feminism galvanized female activists. Yet once we look beyond the relatively small circle of partisans and examine, more broadly, attitudes toward women on a macro level, it becomes clear that the 1960s did not represent a sharp break from the 1950s. Indeed, in the years 1959, 1963, and 1967, there was no statistically significant difference in the proportion of Americans who were either receptive or hostile to the prospect of a female presidential candidate. During the 1970s, however, the proportion of Americans open to a female candidate began to surge once again, as upwards of two-thirds of respondents indicated that they could vote for a woman for president.

A final survey, this one on the question of equal pay between the sexes, paints a picture similar in its general outlines to the surveys relating to a female presidential candidate. In 1954 and 1962, Gallup asked respondents if they believed men and women should receive the same pay for performing the same job.[99] A similar question was asked by *Fortune* magazine in 1946.[100] The results of the survey are presented in Table 4.1.

[99] Survey by Gallup Organization, June 28–July 3, 1962. Retrieved July 27, 2008, from the iPOLL Databank, The Roper Center for Public Opinion Research, University of Connecticut. Online at: http://www.ropercenter.uconn.edu/ipoll.html. Also see Gallup Organization, May 2–7, 1954. Retrieved July 27, 2008, from the iPOLL Databank, The Roper Center for Public Opinion Research, University of Connecticut. Online at: http://www.ropercenter.uconn.edu/ipoll.html; and Survey by Fortune and Roper Organization, April 12–30, 1946. Retrieved July 27, 2008, from the iPOLL Databank, The Roper Center for Public Opinion Research, University of Connecticut. Online at: http://www.ropercenter.uconn.edu/ipoll.html. The exact wording of the question posed in the 1946 survey was: "Sometimes women get paid less than men for doing exactly the same jobs. Do you think there is often a good reason for this, or that women should always be paid the same as men?"

[100] In the *Fortune* magazine poll, the exact wording of the question read: "Sometimes women get paid less than men for doing exactly the same jobs. Do you think there is often a good reason for this, or that women should always be paid the same as men?" In their responses, 24 percent said "Often good reason," 70 percent said men and women doing exactly the same job should "Always get paid same," and 7 percent answered "Don't know."

TABLE 4.1. *1946, 1954, and 1962 Gallup survey responses to the question: Would you approve or disapprove of paying women the same salaries as men if they are doing the same work?*

Year	Approve	Disapprove	No Opinion	Disapproval/No Opinion
1946	70%	*	*	*
1954	87%	*	*	13%
1962	88%	10%	2%	*

Unfortunately, 1962 appears to be the last year Gallup asked the question of equal pay for equal work to a nationally representative sample. Due to these data limitations, we are required to confine our analysis to the late 1940s through the early 1960s. As Table 4.1 shows, the emerging trend during this seventeen-year period is a fairly familiar one. Rising from a 77 percent approval rate in 1946 to 87 percent in 1954, the higher levels of support given to the principle of equal pay for equal work suggests that the liberalization of attitudes was alive and well during the late 1940s through the first half of the 1950s. However, for the next eight years or so, public opinion remained essentially flat. Accordingly, when Americans were re-polled in 1962, their answers were nearly identical to where they had stood eight years earlier.

FIGURE 4.4. Unheard of ten years earlier, women's demonstrations began to fill city streets by the late 1960s. (Photographer: Diana Davies. Reproduced by permission of the Sophia Smith Collection, Smith College.)

With respect to popular attitudes toward the role of women in society, the best evidence from scientific surveys suggests that the 1960s were far more conservative, and the 1950s considerably more progressive, than is oftentimes assumed by journalists and academics. It would seem that the importance of the 1960s rested less in its success in changing the hearts and minds of the general public than in its ability to mobilize a new generation of committed feminist leaders. In periodizing the rise of feminism in post–World War II America, the fifties should be imagined as a time when attitudes toward women were steadily changing; the sixties as primarily a period of organization-building and antidiscriminatory legislation; and the seventies as the decade when the feminist revolution came into full bloom.

Conclusion

In most scholarly accounts, the 1950s continue to be seen as a rather grim time for the cause of gender equality. According to the received narrative, World War II opened up a great many opportunities for women, as wartime employment pulled millions of women into the workplace. However, at the war's end, women were forced back into the home. And although female employment rose steadily from the sharp dip taken in the immediate aftermath of the war, these were primarily pink-collar jobs that did little to challenge the relative powerlessness of women. Moreover, thanks to the Cold War and the celebration of the domestic ideal, the social position of women deteriorated – or, at the very least, failed to improve. As Sara Evans put it, "The postwar era's emphasis on suburban domesticity, early marriage, consumerism, and high fertility produced a generation of women only vaguely aware that there were issues worthy of discussion regarding the true place of women in society."[101]

William Chafe expressed the opinion of most scholars when he wrote, "Although the actual content of women's roles had changed dramatically in the years after World War II," by the close of the 1950s "there had been little substantive progress toward (gender) equality and almost no indication of a mass movement to protest that fact."[102] These sentiments are echoed by Emily Rosenberg, who sees a "remasculinization" of domestic

[101] Evans, Sara M. *Tidal Wave: How Women Changed America at Century's End* (New York: The Free Press, 2003), p. 18.
[102] Chafe, William H. *The Unfinished Journey: America Since World War II* (New York: Oxford University Press, 1991), pp. 328–9.

culture following World War II. During the 1950s, she writes, "Personal, familial, national, and international stability depended on strong men drawing lines and setting limits on women who supported male strength and showed patriotism by conforming to a domestic ideology of female subordination."[103]

Perhaps the most colorful description of the subordination of women in the 1950s comes from the pen of Lizabeth Cohen. "An episode from the Donna Reed show," she writes, "dramatized the shifting terrain of what constituted acceptable female behavior from wartime home front to postwar homemaking: Donna runs for town council and then cheerfully abandons the campaign as soon as her doctor husband complains that he needs her more than her potential constituents."[104]

Textbooks have disseminated this message to a larger audience of undergraduates. In McGraw-Hill's *Women and the American Experience*, Nancy Woloch attributes "the domestic ideology of the 1950s" to the "backlash against women and fear of female competition that followed the war."[105] In Bedford/St. Martin's *Through Women's Eyes: An American History with Documents*, Ellen DuBois and Lynn Dumenil provide a similar interpretation. As they tell the story, the anxiety and conformity that emerged from the Cold War combined with the affluence of the postwar era fostered a "repressive social and political climate" that effectively "reinforced traditional notions of women's place in the home."[106] Elsewhere, Jo Reger characterizes the late 1940s and the early 1950s as a time when "the domestic role of women dominated American culture putting the (feminist) movement into a state of doldrums."[107] And for her part, Joanne Meyerowitz argues that although "not inconsequential," the "movements for women's rights" were "small" during the fifties, "faint counterpoints perhaps to the more conservative clamor."[108]

---

[103] Rosenberg, Emily S. "'Foreign Affairs' After World War II: Connecting Sexual and International Politics," *Diplomatic History* (Winter 1994), p. 69.

[104] Cohen, *A Consumer's Republic.*

[105] Woloch, Nancy. *Women and the American Experience*, fourth edition, (New York: McGraw-Hill, 2006), p. 498.

[106] DuBois, Ellen Carol, and Dumenil, Lynn. *Through Women's Eyes: An American History with Documents* (Boston: Bedford/St. Martin's, 2005), pp. 554–5.

[107] Reger, Jo. "Women's Movement," in Kurian, George T. et al. (eds.), *Encyclopedia of American Studies*, Volume 4 (New York: Grolier Educational, 2001), p. 348.

[108] Meyerowitz, Joanne. "Sex, Gender, and the Cold War Language of Reform," in Kuznick, Peter J., and Gilbert, James (eds.), *Rethinking Cold War Culture* (Washington, D.C.: Smithsonian Institution, 2001), p. 116.

The problem with these and similar interpretations is that their analyses of gender equality rely too heavily on advances in the public realm. Emphasizing paid employment, Chafe argues that the feminist impulse came primarily from those who worked. In their writings, both Friedan and Meyerowitz focus on the representation of gender in magazines, believing the feminist impulse arose out of popular discourse. And in *Tidal Wave*, Sara Evans emphasizes "second-wave" feminists, maintaining that the move toward gender equality occurred as a result of a new generation of female activists who became engaged during the 1960s. Although partially true, these explanations are incomplete because they fail to appreciate the important changes that were occurring within the domestic realm, the religious sphere, the therapist's office, and the college classroom.

Historians are quite right in seeing the family and church as conservative institutions. After all, during the 1940s and 1950s, churches fanned the flames of anticommunism and, by so doing, contributed to the ascendancy of a conservative politics. However, at the same time, families and churches were undergoing an internal process of liberalization whereby more and more power was being accorded to women.

Part of the reason the status of women was rising in the family, churches, and discipline of psychology was because of postwar pluralism. In the aftermath of World War II, it became part of the American creed to denounce the subservience of any one group of people to another. Actively contrasting themselves with the Nazis and Communists, Americans exalted their culture as the fulfillment of democratic ideals. This meant treating people as individuals, recognizing their capabilities without regard to their race, religion, or ethnic background. Thus, as the work of Mark Silk shows, during the latter half of the 1940s the term *Judeo-Christian ethic* came into currency. As an inclusive phrase, Judeo-Christian was intended to bring American Jews and Roman Catholics into the national fold.[109] In addition, in court rulings, congressional debates, news stories, and blue ribbon reports the second-class status accorded to African Americans became the source of much distress. Accordingly, in a myriad of ads aimed at combating racial and religious prejudice, the Ad Council in the early 1950s adopted as its slogan: "Accept or reject people on their individual worth."

Gender, it is true, was not part of this official discourse. However, it is not hard to see how the principle of recognizing individual worth went

---

[109] Silk, Mark. *Spiritual Politics: Religion and America Since World War II* (New York: Simon & Schuster, 1988), pp. 54–69.

beyond the fair treatment of Catholics, Jews, and African Americans – and
also applied to women. This shift toward universalistic principles could
be seen in the celebration of Equal Opportunity Day. Sponsored by the
National Urban League, Equal Opportunity Day sought to highlight the
advances African Americans had made, and the lengths the country had
yet to go, to provide black people in America with full citizenship.[110] First
celebrated in 1956, Equal Opportunity Day became an occasion of some
note, spreading so quickly that by 1958, thirty of the nation's governors
had issued proclamations of support. Even President Eisenhower followed
suit, meeting with several representatives from the National Urban League
and issuing a public statement on its behalf.[111]

As the decade drew to a close, however, a number of the celebrants
sought to apply the principle of equal opportunity more generally. They
wanted Equal Opportunity Day to continue to serve as a reminder of the
unjust racial barriers facing African Americans, but they also sought to
use the day to address the issue of equal opportunity more broadly. Thus,
in 1958, the Lucy Stone League, a self-described "organization devoted
to the advancement of women," sent a telegram to President Eisenhower.
In it, the group requested that he "revise" his statement honoring Equal
Opportunity Day "to include 'sex' in addition to 'race, color, and creed'
so that Lincoln's words 'equality for all' may be truly interpreted."[112]
Although Eisenhower did not accept the suggestion of the Lucy Stone
League, the statement Eisenhower provided – his call for every American
to "join in the effort to abolish all artificial discrimination which hinders
the right of each American to advance in accordance with his merits as
a human being" – was a message opponents of gender discrimination
would almost certainly have found encouraging.[113]

In its celebration of Equal Opportunity Day, *The New York Times*
adopted language that was even more to the liking of the Lucy Stone
League. As it stated in a 1959 editorial, "The primary purpose of the
observance is to direct national attention to the established American

[110] "Equal Opportunity Day Set," *The New York Times* (November 18, 1957), p. 33;
"Epitome of the 'Dream,'" *The Christian Science Monitor* (October 17, 1958), p. 20.
[111] "Ike is Given Equality Day Declarations," *The Washington Post* (November 19, 1958),
p. B12.
[112] From the Papers of Jane Grant, Special Collections and University Archives, University
of Oregon Libraries. Copy of telegram appears on the institution's website online at:
http://libweb.uoregon.uedu//ec/exhibits/janegrant/lucy/gallery3.html.
[113] *Public Papers of the Presidents of the United States: Dwight D. Eisenhower, 1957*
(Washington, D.C.: U.S. Government Printing Office, 1957), p. 823.

idea of giving a decent and fair chance to all men and women in the 'race of life.'"[114]

Outside the struggle for civil rights, various actors were more explicit in their efforts to elevate the status of women. In the psychological literature, for example, one sees the patriarchal family, which family experts roundly criticized, contrasted with the healthy democratic family. Likewise, within the realm of religion, the question of female participation in church governance was frequently cast as an issue of equal rights or unjust discrimination. As these examples demonstrate, many of the goals of feminism were aided by the political culture of the early Cold War years with its rhetoric of democracy and universal inclusion.

To be sure, traditional attitudes during the 1950s remained a potent force in American life. Although the subordination of women had been challenged in many quarters, the formulation of such concepts as patriarchy, gender oppression, and consciousness raising was still a number of years away. Most activists lacked the vocabulary to describe, much less dissect, the inhibiting conditions in which they were situated. When movies like John Wayne's *The Quiet Man* or sitcoms like *I Love Lucy* showed frustrated husbands, swatting – physically abusing – their misbehaving wives, no discernable outcry was forthcoming from the general public. Feminism, in other words, was less a movement than a sentiment, more an amorphous set of attitudes than an ideology or a doctrine. Although there was not much of a movement culture afoot during the 1950s, in many ways and on many fronts, the principle of sexual equality was pressing forward.

What one sees, therefore, in the 1950s is the advancement of feminist principles in the absence of a mass feminist movement. In understanding the rising status of women in the two decades following World War II, a concentration on the genealogy of feminism or on the numbers of women entering the workforce is insufficient. Rather than a feminist movement driving change, a combination of social processes was transforming cultural practices. The majority of women adopting these new attitudes did not come from trade unions or professional women's organizations. They were not, for the most part, communists or fellow travelers. Instead, they were what journalist Joseph Kraft called "Middle America": conservative, churchgoing and, not infrequently, suburban. The primary challenge to the subservience of women came not from the culture's periphery but from its very core, not from pockets of resistance but from the larger culture.

[114] "Equal Opportunity Day," *The New York Times* (November 16, 1959), p. 30.

The liberalizing impulse of the 1950s was not a tidal wave overpowering everything in its path. Some of the changes in the 1950s were occurring slowly, even imperceptibly. Yet as developments in the family, psychology, religion, politics, and public opinion show, women were not losing ground or simply running in place. Instead, the status of women was advancing – and advancing in earnest – in the fifteen years following World War II.

5

Youth Culture

Rock 'n' Roll, Blue Jeans, and the Myth of Opposition

According to many historical accounts of the 1950s, the youth culture was among the few significant subgroups challenging the values of the larger culture. The accepted narrative argues the prosperity of the 1950s – and with it the rise of juvenile pictures, hot rods, blue jeans, and rock 'n' roll – provided inspiration for young people to question and defy many of the rules and assumptions that their parents had long taken for granted.[1] Through this nascent critique, the teenagers of the 1950s helped pave the way to the dramatic changes that transformed the social landscape of the late 1960s and early 1970s.

There is much legitimacy to this analysis; however, it tends to overstate the challenge teens posed to the values of the larger society. As an examination of rock 'n' roll, blue jeans, public opinion data, sexual mores, and changing attitudes toward teenage rebellion will show clearly, young people in the 1950s were flouting the social norms and the moral style of the older generation. However, on a deeper level, youth culture was marching in lockstep with the ascendant values of the age.

Although an identifiable youth culture predated World War II, what most distinguished the postwar decade was that the culture of its young people became oppositional. In a surprisingly short period of time, Americans in their teens and early twenties became openly resistant to and defiant of prevailing social norms. Through the embrace of new music

---

[1] See Fischer, Klaus P. *America in White, Black, and Gray: The Stormy 1960s* (New York: Continuum International Publishing Group, 2006), p. 65; Palladino, Grace. *Teenagers: An American History* (New York: Harper-Collins, 1996), p. 5; Diggins, John Patrick. *The Proud Decades: America in War And Peace, 1941–1960* (New York: W. W. Norton and Company), p. 201.

and the adoption of new fashions, young people signaled a desire to differentiate themselves from their parents' generation. However, as a closer interrogation of the evidence reveals, the actual divide between the generations was somewhat smaller in its dimensions than one would expect.

In few places was this chasm between the young and old more evident than in the divergent representations of Frank Sinatra and Elvis Presley. On a superficial level, the two singers shared a good deal of common ground: both men hailed from humble backgrounds; each had tremendous appeal among teenage girls at the outset of their careers; both enjoyed success in Las Vegas as well as Hollywood; and for each entertainer the ticket to fame was not in singing his own compositions, but in covering the songs of others. Notwithstanding these similarities, there was a great deal of difference between the personae of Sinatra and Presley. With his greased-back hair, wide sideburns, gyrating hips, and sexualized lyrics, Elvis exuded an undeniable air of defiance and eroticism. Not surprisingly, middle-class adults were slow to embrace him. John Crosby, the television critic for *The Washington Post*, dismissed Elvis as "unspeakably untalented and vulgar."[2] Journalist Baker E. Morten, writing in *The Chicago Defender*, described Presley as a "young upstart with the embarrassing body contortions."[3] And while an article in *Look* magazine acknowledged Presley's talent, it concluded that as a result of his leers and sexually suggestive "gyrations," he was "mostly a nightmare."[4]

By contrast, the young Sinatra – whom *The Washington Post* described during World War II as the "Number 1 'pin-up boy' for America's feminine contingent" – was seen by the cultural establishment in a far more positive light.[5] With his big break as the lead singer for Harry James and later Benny Goodman coming in the late thirties and early forties, Sinatra functioned within the parameters of respectable big band entertainment. According to *The New York Times*, when he performed in Central Park during summer 1943, an event hosted by the American Legion, the "gyrations of the youngsters had the policemen on the sidelines," not scowling in disapproval, but "stomping their feet in accompaniment." As some

[2] Crosby, John. "Could Elvis Mean End of Rock 'n' Roll Craze?" *The Washington Post* (June 18, 1956), p. 33.
[3] Morten, Baker E. "'Blue Suede' Shoes to Pink Cadillacs – A Yarn," *The Chicago Defender* (June 23, 1956), p. 14.
[4] "Elvis Presley...He Can't Be...But He Is," *Look* (August 7, 1956), p. 82.
[5] "Sinatra, No. 1 Pin-up Boy, to Sing at Watergate Event," *The Washington Post* (July 23, 1943), p. B1.

journalists at the time noted, many of Sinatra's admirers were a generation older than his throngs of teenage fans.[6] In addition, in such early Sinatra hits as "Laura" and "I'm Glad This is You," there was little audible in Sinatra's lyrics or visible in his performance that might have proved threatening or offensive to prevailing social norms.

As it turns out, one of the harshest critics of rock 'n' roll – at least during its early years – was none other than Frank Sinatra. In an interview with a European newspaper in 1956, he insisted that rock 'n' roll was "for the most part," performed by "cretinous goons," and consisted of "sly, lewd, in plain fact, dirty lyrics." Moreover, he described the whole rock 'n' roll scene as the "martial music of every side-burned delinquent on the face of the earth."[7] In associating rock 'n' roll with "dirty lyrics" and teenage delinquency, Sinatra's scathing assessment reflected a sentiment widespread among the adult population. During the mid-1950s, a long list of cities, including Boston, Newark, Jersey City, New Britain, Connecticut, and Troy, New York, either cancelled or outright banned rock 'n' roll performances for fear of violence or vandalism. For example, after learning that more than a dozen people, including two young girls, had been brutally attacked by youths following a rock concert in Boston, the indignant New Haven police chief in 1956 blocked Alan Freed from hosting a concert in his town.[8]

The association of rock 'n' roll with mayhem and delinquency turned out to be only a fraction of its troubles. Even more disturbing to white middle-class Americans was its inextricable link with sex. As one Midwestern mother complained, "I think this primitive kind of music, if you can call it that, is lewd." Another parent from Cincinnati seemed less concerned by its beat than by the intimate dancing rock 'n' roll encouraged. "It looks like a Roman orgy when those kids get together," she remarked.[9] Arguably, the most prominent of the critics was celebrity

---

[6] "Let Sinatra 'open in his mouth in song,'" wrote *New York Times* reporter Louis Calta, "and the effects are disastrous. On those occasions, teenage girls are apt to grow as hysterical as mature ladies, all to the general bewilderment of sociologists and psychiatrists." See Galta, Louis. "News of Night Clubs: Frank Sinatra, or 'The Voice,' Scores at the Wedgwood Room – Other Café Notes," *The New York Times* (October 10, 1943), p. X5.

[7] Associated Press. "Frank Sinatra Blasts Goony Rock 'n' Roll," *Reno Evening Gazette* (October 28, 1957), p. 1.

[8] See Goodsell, James Nelson, "Rock 'n' Roll Opposition Rises," *The Christian Science Monitor* (May 8, 1958), p. 3.

[9] Gilbert, Eugene. "Rock And Roll, A Menace or Harmless Teenage Fun," *Alton Evening Telegraph* (August 9, 1956), p. 18.

journalist Vance Packard, the author of the best-selling book *The Hidden Persuaders* (1957). In his 1958 testimony before a Senate subcommittee, Packard warned lawmakers rock 'n' roll's "heavy unrelenting beat, and raw savage tone," would ignite "the animal instincts in modern teenagers."[10] That same year, when a teenager asked Rev. Martin Luther King, Jr. if it was sinful to listen to rock 'n' roll, King replied that whether or not it was sinful, rock 'n' roll "often plunges men's minds into degrading and immoral depths."[11] The obvious androgyny of stars like Little Richard, the sexual innuendo present in countless rock 'n' roll songs, and the sexual scandals that engulfed such marquee names as Jerry Lee Lewis and Chuck Berry reinforced the belief that rock 'n' roll sought to undermine existing sexual standards.[12]

In spite of the avalanche of negative publicity, by the close of the 1950s rock 'n' roll had grown so popular, its legions of fans had become so plentiful, its once formidable critics were in full retreat. The acceptance of rock 'n' roll as a legitimate staple of youth culture is attributable to a number of developments, but probably none is more illuminating than the meteoric rise of Pat Boone. As much as any rock 'n' roll artist who performed during the 1950s, Pat Boone – a direct descendant of the legendary pioneer Daniel Boone – personified the clean-cut, wholesome, all-American ideal. In an age of flamboyant celebrities, Pat Boone was as bland as they came. As he admitted to a reporter in 1958, "My personal life is completely colorless. I don't climb mountains. I don't chase women. I have no fascinating hobbies except my four daughters. I'm terribly in love with my wife, and I'm pretty religious."[13] In keeping with this pattern of clean living, Boone refrained from drinking, smoking, gambling, and swearing. He sang in his church choir, taught Sunday school, and occasionally took to the pulpit.[14] An article in *The Economist* was especially revealing. It reported that during the 1950s, Pat Boone was such a "stickler for correct language that he even tried to get the title of one of his songs changed from "Ain't that a Shame" to "Isn't that a Shame.""[15]

---

[10] Lawson, Steven F. "Race, Rock and Roll, and the Rigged Society: The Payola Scandal and the Political Culture of the 1950s," in Chafe, William H. (ed.), *The Liberal Moment: The New Deal and Its Legacies* (New York: Columbia University Press, 2002), pp. 216–17.

[11] Ibid, p. 209.

[12] Szatmary, David P. *Rockin In Time: A Social History of Rock-and-Roll* (New Jersey: Prentice-Hall, 1996), p. 22.

[13] Shearer, Lloyd. "Pat Boone: A Nice Guy Can Become a Millionaire," *Parade* (September 28, 1958), p. 10.

[14] Ibid.

[15] "Pat Boone in Hell," *The Economist* (March 1, 1997), p. 35.

Far from being a creation of Madison Avenue, Boone's straightlaced demeanor was evidently genuine. During the late 1950s, Boone turned down an opportunity to star opposite Marilyn Monroe – a role that would have, almost certainly, taken his career to still greater heights – because he believed the prospective role, which entailed his character having an illicit affair with an older woman, might have sent the wrong message to young viewers.[16] In another famous incident, while in the midst of filming the movie *April Love*, Boone rebuffed the suggestion of his director that he deliver an on-screen kiss to his leading lady, Shirley Jones. Boone's reason? Before he could proceed with such an overt display of passion, he first needed to discuss the scene with his wife. Not surprisingly, among many adults across the country, Boone was lionized as a shining example of what young people might become. In a famous *New Yorker* article in 1958, social critic Dwight McDonald trashed Elvis Presley, rock 'n' roll, *MAD* magazine, teenage movies, and youth culture more generally, but for all of his displeasure with the contemporary social scene, in his brief discussion of Pat Boone, McDonald had only good things to say.[17] *Time's* description of Pat Boone was even more laudatory than McDonald's, for it credited the young singer with having "confounded the swamp dwellers of the music world because he leads a blameless home life, and he has delighted parents of teenagers because, although he sometimes sings rock 'n' roll, he sings it in a damply pleasant voice, and he does not keep time with pelvic spasms."[18]

Despite his mild style – or, perhaps because of it – Pat Boone attained a sustained level of success that few singers have been able to approach. Between 1955 and 1959, Pat Boone sold more than twenty-one million records – a figure greater than any rock 'n' roll performer with the exception of Elvis Presley.[19] Equally impressive, for two hundred and twenty consecutive weeks between 1955 and 1958, Boone had a least one hit on the billboard charts. No singer, either before or since, has enjoyed a streak of such duration.[20]

Movie and television executives were quick to take notice. According to the thirty-sixth annual survey of theater owners, only two actors in

[16] Interview with Boone by the author on March 15, 2008.
[17] McDonald, Dwight. "Profiles: A Caste, A Culture, A Market II," *New Yorker* (November 29, 1958), pp. 57–107.
[18] "The Clean-Cut Kid," *Time* (June 9, 1958).
[19] Tingle, Hoard. "Musically Yours," *The Salisbury Times*, Maryland (June 13, 1959), p. 15.
[20] Boone, Pat. *Pat Boone's America: 50 Years* (Nashville, Tenn.: B&H Publishing Group, 2006), p. 53.

FIGURE 5.1. Pat Boone backstage with the other teen icon of the fifties, Elvis
Presley. (Reproduced by permission of Pat Boone.)

1957 – Rock Hudson and John Wayne – surpassed Boone in popularity.
Today, more than half a century later, it is easy to forget how, in such
movies as *Bernadine* and *April Love*, Boone was able to parlay his success
on stage into box office gold. As a result of this broad-based appeal, the
ABC network provided Boone with his own variety show, broadcast
during prime time, which ran for three years.[21] Equally impressive was
Boone's appearance on the cover of *Life* magazine in 1959.[22] However,
the most telling sign of Boone's celebrity was his success as an author.
Boone's *Twixt, Twelve, and Twenty*, an advice book directed at teenagers,
became the second best-selling nonfiction book in 1958. And in 1959, the
year J. C. Penney named Boone "Father of the Year," his book continued
to sell rapidly, becoming the year's all-around best-seller for nonfiction.[23]

---

[21] Ibid, p. 53; *Chicago Tribune* (November 17, 1957), p. A14 (Chevy ad promoting "Pat
Boone's Chevy Showroom").
[22] "Big Boom in Boone," *Life* (February 2, 1959), cover and pp. 75–80.
[23] "Singer Pat Boone '59 Father of the Year" *Pasadena Independent* (June 12, 1959),
p. A-9.

Yet for all of Boone's appeal to the cultural establishment, it is essential to remember that Boone's path to fame and fortune was through the then controversial medium of rock 'n' roll. Like the typical teenager, Boone's millions of fans were tearing up the carpet, bumping and grinding to his plethora of hit songs. And although many of Boone's hits were *covers*, or tamer versions of racier songs other artists (usually black) had already recorded, his music still fell well within the standard rock 'n' roll genre. Interestingly, while Little Richard's earlier rendition of "Tutti Frutti" was more risqué than the incarnation sung by Boone, there remained an undeniable element of sexual suggestion in Boone's version ("Got me a Gal named Sue/She knows just what to do"). Nor was "Tutti Frutti" an aberration. A host of other songs performed by Pat Boone were replete with sexual innuendo. For example, Boone's 1958 cover of "Blueberry Hill," featured a not-so-subtle allusion to sexual intercourse ("I found my thrill on Blueberry Hill/On Blueberry Hill where I found you"). The same could also be said of Boone's 1957 song titled "Don't Forbid Me" ("Let me fill your little heart with fire/cause it's cold, so cold, so don't forbid my desire...it so cold/So don't forbid my desire") as well as his 1958 hit "Bernadine" ("Say you'll wait for me out by the rocket base/And we'll both blast off into outer space/At oh, oh, oh-oh Bernadine").

The effort to separate Boone's music from the sensual elements within rock 'n' roll neglects another important fact: throughout the 1950s, it was quite common for multiple acts to be featured on the same rock 'n' roll bill – with the most prominent performer usually appearing toward the end of the program. One of the advantages of this format was that it enabled the biggest names to attract new listeners for up-and-coming artists. As one of the industry's early stars, Pat Boone frequently functioned as the big draw at these concerts. In fact, the first meeting between Boone and Elvis Presley occurred at a Cleveland concert in October 1955, where Pat Boone was the headliner and a relatively unknown Elvis Presley – still six months before his first breakout hit, "Heartbreak Hotel," topped the Billboard charts – served as Boone's "warm-up act."[24] Thus, in coming to see Boone, thousands of fans were exposed to other artists, such as Elvis Presley, whose styles of music were oftentimes more raucous and racy. To the culture's gatekeepers during the mid- and late 1950s, Pat Boone may have seemed "safe" and respectable. In reality, however, he was much more than the unthreatening, desexualized, homogenized caricature that historians and journalists have so frequently painted. The

[24] Boone, *Pat Boone's America: 50 Years*, pp. 48–9.

sexual innuendo occurring in Boone's lyrics, and his ability as a marquee performer to introduce thousands of fans to other rock 'n' roll acts,
abetted the forces of liberalization.

However, of course, Boone's most significant contribution was his role
in persuading parents and the establishment culture to embrace what they
had been hesitant to countenance previously. Whereas in the mid-1950s,
many clericals were active decriers of rock 'n' roll, by the closing years
of the decade attitudes had so shifted that in the summer of 1958, two
hundred members of the Catholic Youth Organization (CYO), accompanied by four priests, traveled to New York City to attend a Pat Boone
performance, whereupon they presented Boone with an award for his
"edifying influence on youth."[25] Over the following two years, Boone
received accolades from a number of other respectable organizations
such as North Central Christian College, an institution affiliated with the
Church of Christ; the Baltimore chapters of B'Nai B'rith and the Knights
of Columbus; the National Father's Day Committee; and the National
Conference of Christians and Jews.[26] On the surface, in its valorization
of Pat Boone, the culture affirmed his wholesome personal qualities as
evinced by Boone's polished appearance and professed lifestyle. On a
deeper level, however, they were embracing something less innocent.

In *The Adolescent Society*, a penetrating study of American high school
life, James Coleman argued that young people in the 1950s used music
as part of a larger process of identity construction. Among the more
than eight thousand Midwestern students queried, Coleman found that
an outright majority of the people cited either Presley or Boone as their
favorite singer. By a better than a two to one margin, however, the students preferred Pat Boone over Elvis Presley.[27] According to Coleman's
research, those students who were most likely to have plans for college,
and who believed it was important to maintain a "good reputation,"
tended to like Boone and, at the same time, were the least likely to be fans
of Elvis Presley.[28] Conversely, among female high school students who
were the most defiant of adult authority, Elvis was generally preferred. As

[25] Gregory, Carol. "Local CYOers Visit Pat Boone, Present Him with Plaque," *The Bridge-
port Sunday Post* (June 15, 1958), p. B9.
[26] Material from the internal files of Pat Boone's business office. Emailed to author on April
22, 2008.
[27] Coleman, James S. *The Adolescent Society: The Social Life of the Teenager and its
Impact on Education* (New York: The Free Press, 1961), pp. 22–3. Although published
in the early 1960s, the book was based on research conducted in 1957 and 1958.
[28] Ibid, p. 126.

Coleman noted, "Their black 'rock 'n' roll' jacket is a symbol in this school of orientation to a good time, cars, music, the skating rink, and unconcern with school."[29]

Complementing Coleman's findings was the research of John Johnstone, a close associate of Coleman. In his examination of students in ten Illinois high schools during the 1957–8 academic year, Johnstone found those students choosing Elvis Presley and Tommy Sands as their favorite rock 'n' roll performers tended to come from lower socioeconomic backgrounds. Moreover, in contrast to Boone fans, they did not feel very connected to the social scene in their school – or, as Johnstone phrased it, they tended to find themselves "'on the outside' rather than on the 'inside' of high school social activities."[30]

The market research of Eugene Gilbert – impressionistic though it was – lent support to Coleman and Johnstone's findings. It was found that the fans of Presley were less likely to participate in high school activities than the fans of Boone. It also discovered that, from the standpoint of academic achievement, Presley enthusiasts tended to obtain C averages, whereas Boone admirers tended to earn B averages. Hence, when students were asked how important it was to perform well academically, three in ten Boone fans claimed they attempted to "earn the highest possible grade," while only one in ten Presley buffs admitted to having tried their hardest.[31] In other words, among Elvis fans, their strong identification with Presley was an indication of their rebellion against parental authority. For the less rebellious high school students, their preference for Pat Boone was partially attributable to the fact that Boone was adored by parents, and generally perceived by the culture's gatekeepers as a safe and "wholesome choice."[32]

It is here, in the culture's willingness – indeed, its eagerness – to interpret rock 'n' roll, at least the brand dispensed by Pat Boone, as a phenomenon devoid of rebellion and deviance that enabled it to advance so quickly during the latter half of the 1950s. In identifying with Boone, parents and teenagers seemed unaware of the simple fact that as a genre, rock 'n' roll possessed a style, an energy, and not infrequently a message that transcended the individual performer. As Todd Gitlin noted, "Even the tamed stuff repackaged by clean-cut, crew-cut white bands went right

---

[29] Ibid, p. 205.
[30] Johnstone, John W. C. "Social Structure and Patterns of Mass Media Consumption," (University of Chicago: doctoral dissertation in the Social Sciences, 1961), p. 104.
[31] Ibid.
[32] Ibid.

into the body. Rock was itself a moment of abundance, energy in profusion. It was an invitation to dance, and at some fantasy level – just as the bluenoses protested – it was an invitation to make love."[33] A question no less important than the rise of Elvis is how popular sentiments underwent such a transformation that what had been widely denounced as immoral and vulgar at middecade, only three or four years later could be seen as innocuous.

Chapter I briefly touched on the notion of a *subversive consensus*. The basic idea was that it is possible for a very large swath of the general population – something approaching a consensus – to subscribe to certain practices or principles that might initially appear unthreatening, but actually present a challenge to the older, more conservative moral framework. During the 1950s, Rev. Norman Vincent Peale might be cited as an example of someone who was, paradoxically, a part of the subversive consensus. In his day, Peale was a widely admired clergyman renowned for his best-selling books, his inspirational broadcasts, his conservative politics, and his personal closeness to Eisenhower and Nixon. However, in Peale's rejection of the doctrine of Original Sin, his championing of pastoral psychology, and his advocacy of a softer approach to child-rearing practices, he challenged many of the assumptions that stood at the heart of a socially conservative vision. In a similar way, Pat Boone in the 1950s was generally associated with traditional values, but more than a few of the songs he performed and the musicians he promoted challenged the very values he privately embraced.

By the close of the 1950s, most cultural warriors had abandoned the crusade against rock 'n' roll. In its literature to teenagers, the Methodist Church was characterizing such youthful passions as rock 'n' roll and jazz as "natural" and largely harmless.[34] Family-oriented sitcoms, like *Ozzie and Harriet* and *The Donna Reed Show* depicted the children as fans of rock 'n' roll. Even Mouseketeer Annette Funicello took to singing rock 'n' roll songs with the approval and encouragement of Walt Disney himself.[35] However, by the end of the 1950s, Americans did not need to turn to their televisions to find wholesome teens who enjoyed listening to "race music." As Vice President Richard Nixon revealed during the 1960 presidential campaign, in what was an obvious effort to identify

[33] Gitlin, Todd. *The Sixties: Years of Hope, Days of Rage* (New York: Bantam Books, 1987), p. 37.
[34] Campbell, Sheila. "My Parents and Me," *Roundtable* (May 1959), p. 21.
[35] Market, Sandy. "Pickin' the Pops," *The Lima News*, Ohio (September 26, 1959), p. 7.

himself with the typical American parent, his thirteen-year-old daughter Tricia was an ardent fan of Dick Clark's *American Bandstand*.[36] Equally revealing, by 1960 the once implacable Frank Sinatra had mollified his earlier stance against rock 'n' roll, performing alongside Elvis on a CBS evening special and even singing the lyrics to a few Presley songs.[37]

Denim Jeans

Another indication of an emergent youth culture was the proliferation of blue jeans, even rivaling rock 'n' roll as a symbol of the adolescent quest for independence. Although Levi Strauss had been successfully selling denim jeans since the 1870s, only after World War II did jeans became a fashion statement of sorts among large segments of the youth population. During these years, a number of young celebrities renowned for their angst and hip defiance – actors such as James Dean, Marilyn Monroe, and Marlon Brando – assisted in this process. It would be a mistake, however, to dismiss the popularity of blue jeans as merely a phenomenon of the motion picture industry. As early as 1951 – before Brando acquired superstar status, and well before Dean became an iconic figure – a dating manual advised young men that blue jeans had become the near universal dress wear among female students at such elite northeastern colleges as Radcliffe, Smith, and Vassar. Not surprisingly, many adults reacted adversely, almost hysterically, to the fad. During the early- and mid-1950s, more than a few high schools instituted bans on blue jeans. "If you dress like a hobo you're more apt to act like a hobo," was the rationale proffered by the Board of Education in one suburban Detroit community.[38]

Mounting concerns over juvenile delinquency reinforced parental anxieties. In countless magazine and newspaper articles, and in such movies as *The Black Board Jungle* and *The Wild Ones*, jeans were the signature apparel of hooligans. "We have nothing against dungarees as such," read a 1957 editorial in *The Portsmouth Herald*, "They are perfectly suited to certain popular forms of present-day youthful diversion – like stealing gas, slashing tires, and assaulting strangers."[39] In spring 1955, a *Parade*

---

[36] Gould, Jack. "TV: A Political Telethon," *The New York Times* (November 8, 1960), p. 59.

[37] Wolters, Larry. "Presley Reclaims His Crown," *Chicago Daily Tribune* (May 13, 1960), p. D7.

[38] "Blue Jeans Banned," *The Washington Post* (July 21, 1954), p. 3.

[39] "No Place for Dungarees," *The Portsmouth Herald* (February 1, 1957), p. 4.

magazine article exploring the rising rates of delinquency among teenage girls was explicit in establishing a link between denim jeans and teenage violence. Beneath a large photograph featuring a group of jean-clad young ladies read the caption: "In a vacant lot near a Los Angeles school, four girls in blue jeans are questioned by sheriff's deputies – who know that the wearing of jeans may mean a fight is brewing."[40] The headline of a front-page article appearing in *The Chicago Sun Times* proved even more inflammatory. It read: "BLUE JEANSTER HELD; TELLS ATTACK ON TWO."[41]

As a result of this strong association between delinquency and blue jeans, Levi Strauss & Company ran into rough waters when they initiated an ad campaign in fall 1957. Featured in magazines and newspapers throughout the country, the ad showed a teenage boy, dressed in Levi jeans, walking toward a large high school. Beside the picture read the caption: "RIGHT FOR SCHOOL!"[42] The obvious purpose behind the ad was to disarm parents of their prejudice and persuade them to buy blue denims for their children. However, in the minds of many parents, blue jeans were never right for school – or, for that matter any occasion. The correspondence secretary of a parent–teacher association (PTA) chapter in the Northeast was so disturbed by the ad that she wrote to the company's headquarters in San Francisco. "We do not complain about your right to advertise but (we) do not feel this is proper attire for school. As a matter of fact, she continued, "'Levi's' or 'blue jeans' are banned by a large percentage of the schools."[43] Another complaint from a New Jersey resident made no bones about linking blue jeans to hooliganism. After scolding Levi Strauss & Company for suggesting that blue jeans were appropriate apparel, the letter concluded with the words: "Propriety and respect are good discipline rules. Let's not desecrate our schools nor promote juvenile delinquency."[44]

In addition to its association with teenage hooliganism, many adults insisted that the wearing of blue jeans clashed with age-old notions of

---

[40] Ross, Sid, and Kiester, Ed. "Tomboy with Knives: A New National Problem," *Parade* (April 17, 1955), pp. 10–11.

[41] Ibid. Photograph of *The Chicago Sun Times'* front page appeared in the *Parade* magazine article.

[42] Downey, Lynn. *Levi Strauss & Company* (Charleston, South Carolina: Arcadia Publications, 2006), p. 76.

[43] Letter dated September 19, 1957. Copy of letter provided to the author by Lynn Downey, the company historian of Levi Strauss & Company.

[44] Letter dated August 29, 1959. Copy provided to the author by Lynn Downey, the company historian of Levi Strauss & Company.

respectable femininity. It was often the case that even among those parents who tolerated blue jeans on boys, there was much opposition to the sight of blue jeans on young women. "It isn't ladylike for girls, although it's alright for young boys because the jeans are so much easier to keep clean," explained a lady from southern Ohio. "It just isn't proper," remarked another woman. "It actually doesn't hurt for boys to wear them to school, but girls – never!"[45] From the perspective of many adults, jeans would never, under any circumstances, be proper dress for women because they were either too informal or too sexually enticing. When female students at Lodi High School complained about "being pinched or patted" by their male classmates, the superintendent responded by prohibiting female students from wearing jeans to school. As the local newspaper reported, Superintendent Wilbur Wood "blamed the ban directly on the girls themselves, who, he said, 'allowed the jeans to become too tight and that invites familiarity.'"[46]

Apparently, the superintendent's indictment of tight blue jeans as sexually provocative was a common assumption during the 1950s. In a lengthy newspaper article that appeared in spring 1954, the author attempted to answer the question, "Why do so many children go wrong?" In the end, the article pointed to a number of possible factors, including the style of dress in vogue among young women. As the author put it, in paraphrasing the observations of a juvenile court judge: "Even the clothes of some teenagers is a factor in sex delinquency." The article continued: "Girls appearing before him [the presiding juvenile court judge] wear skintight blue jeans or levis. They have made them 'sexy' by wearing the jeans while sitting in a bathtub of water, then letting the jeans dry on them."[47]

Yet despite fierce resistance from schools, parents, and prominent elements of the press, blue jeans continued to gain popularity throughout the postwar period. Over the course of the 1950s, Levi Strauss, the world's largest manufacturer of blue jeans, effectively doubled its net worth.[48] Before long, the school bans against denim slackened, and blue jeans began gaining acceptance within the dominant culture. By the end of the decade, blue jeans had become so popular that some news stories by the Associated Press (AP) and United Press International (UPI) spoke of teens

[45] "Four Oppose Jeans for Girls," *The San Antonio Light* (October 16, 1952), p. 15.
[46] "'Pinched' Jean Fad Said Much Too Bad," *Pacific Stars and Stripes* (April 20, 1952), p. 4.
[47] Kennedy, Edwin. "Today's Youth: What Makes Them Go Bad," *Chicago Daily Tribune* (May 23, 1954), p. 4.
[48] Cray, Ed. *Levis* (Boston: Houghton Mifflin, 1978).

as the "blue jeans set."[49] In addition, although the complete mainstreaming of blue jeans would not occur until the early 1970s, by the close of the 1950s resistance to the denim trend evinced signs of erosion; even the vaunted Pat Boone appeared in public wearing blue jeans.[50] Publications of the United Methodist Church also featured pictures of presumably wholesome teenagers appearing in blue jeans.[51] A further indication of these shifting attitudes happened during spring 1958 when R. B. Norman, the president of the National Association of Secondary School Principals, declared that denims were "entirely acceptable" schoolwear, and blasted efforts to conflate blue jeans with hooliganism. "I feel that it is very unfair that there should be any organized effort by anyone to brand the blue jean as the 'dress of the delinquent,'" he proclaimed.[52] The following year, at the American National Exhibition held in Moscow – the site, incidentally, of the famous Nixon–Khrushchev "Kitchen Debate" – blue jeans were among the items put on display for the entire world to see.[53]

The Social Meaning of Blue Jeans and Rock 'n' Roll

Today the image of rebellious teenagers is part and parcel of most surveys of American life during the age of Eisenhower. Although the youth culture of the 1950s adopted a defiant pose, it was oppositional in only a very limited sense. While the youth culture went against the grain of prevailing norms, in a broad sense it was also moving in step with the liberalizing values of the times. For all of their hypocrisy, Americans during the 1950s were moving in a more open and democratic direction and away from a conservative, hierarchal vision. Thus, in their penchant for blue jeans, young people were doing more than merely adopting the latest fashions in clothing.

[49] See UPI story "Teenagers' Idol Getting TV Chance," *The Chronicle Telegram,* Elvria, Ohio (February 20, 1959), p. 26. Text reads: "It was only five years ago that Eddie (Fisher) had the pony tail and blue jeans set agog with squealing fervor . . ."; also see AP story "Young Posteriors May be Warmed," *The Albuquerque Tribune* (February 20, 1959); p. 1. Text reads: "The 65-word measure, sure to draw the wrath of many in the bobby sox and blue jeans set, is House Bill 193. . . ."
[50] Telephone interview with Pat Boone by the author on March 15, 2008.
[51] The covers for the May 1958 and the June 1958 editions of *Roundtable* feature teenagers in blue jeans.
[52] "Blue Jeans Acceptable School Garb for Boys," Press Release, Student Marketing Institute (February 18, 1958). Courtesy of Levi-Strauss & Company Archives.
[53] "Three Negro Models Share Spotlight with 47 Others at Moscow Exhibit," *Daily Defender* (July 27, 1959), p. 14.

Part of the appeal of blue jeans was that it had long been the dresswear of working-class Americans, especially those engaged in real physical toil. Hence, in their donning of denim, young people were "dressing down" to associate themselves with the "working man" in his noble simplicity and unpretentiousness. So palpable was the desire to identify with the working man that many teenagers went to great pains – smudging, tearing, and subjecting their denims to continuous washing – to acquire a tattered, well-worn look reminiscent of those who sweated and toiled for their daily bread. In contrast to the late 1970s, when designer jeans came into fashion, the teenagers of the fifties were taking a stand against the hierarchical nature of American society and, in the process, asserting their independence. They were saying, in effect: "We refuse to present ourselves in a way that betrays a desire to belong to a 'higher station' in society. If you wish to deal with us, you must deal with us as individuals."

Implicit in this stance was a sartorial polemic against elitism. In the wake of World War II, snobbery became a character trait increasingly held in low regard. This anti-elitist bent on the part of ordinary citizens partly accounted for the landslide losses of presidential candidate Adlai Stevenson in 1952 and 1956. With his bald, oval-shaped head and dry wit, he seemed to exude a patrician arrogance. When told by an admirer that all thinking people would vote for him in the upcoming election, Stevenson is reported to have said, "That's not enough. I need a majority." On another occasion, when a supporter tried to comfort the unflappable Stevenson by telling him that his presidential campaign, while unsuccessful, had "educated the country," Stevenson responded, "Yes, but a lot of people flunked the exam."[54] Quips like these made Stevenson the darling of intellectuals and the professoriate, but the quips alienated many Americans, President Truman included, who came to regard Stevenson as an effete scion of privilege.[55] In the wake of World War II, elitism was fast falling out of favor. The celebration of the GI soldier – a development made obvious by the election of more than five dozen World War II veterans to the U.S. House of Representatives in 1946 – as well as the valorization of democracy deepened suspicions toward those who fancied themselves, or simply appeared to think of themselves, as superior to the general population.

[54] Cited from Caplan, Ben. *The Myth of the Rational Voter: Why Democracies Choose Bad Policies* (Princeton, New Jersey: Princeton University Press, 2007); and Alterman, Eric. *Why We're Liberals: A Political Handbook for Post-Bush America* (New York: Viking, 2007).
[55] National Public Radio, "Music Cues: Adlai Stevenson," (February 5, 2000).

While anti-elitism was a widespread sentiment within the culture, it found its most fertile expression among the youth, who readily absorbed and amplified its democratizing tendencies. As David Riesman and colleagues noted in their 1950 classic *The Lonely Crowd*, "Beginning with the very young and going on from there, overt vanity is treated as one of the worst offenses...Being high-hat is forbidden."[56]

Survey data clearly indicated that anti-elitism had a great deal of resonance within the youth culture. In 1958, the University of Michigan's Institute for Social Research conducted an in-depth survey using a nationally representative sample of teenage girls. One of the tasks of the study was to identify the specific qualities possessed by the most popular girls in school. Far and away, the most frequently cited social skill was the state of being "Equalitarian" (32 percent) – or behaving in a way in which all others are treated as equals. Ranking a distant second was having a "good personality" (8 percent), and third (6 percent) was the quality of being "Lots of fun to be with."[57] Naturally, a high level of elitism and snobbery persisted into the 1950s and beyond, but because of the growing forces of democratization, it was under assault and in full retreat. To the extent blue jeans bespoke informality and an anti-elitist bent, teenagers were affirming a principle that was shared by the larger adult world.

Similarly, in their enthusiasm for rock 'n' roll, young people were not simply embracing a new, more raucous style of music. They were also affirming a musical genre that was profoundly associated with African Americans. Not only did rock 'n' roll have decidedly black roots, having evolved from the rhythm and blues of the Deep South, but a great many top performers – indeed, some of the founding fathers of rock 'n' roll, such as Chuck Berry, Fats Domino, Little Anthony, and the members of the group The Coasters – were themselves African American. Moreover, Dick Clark's enormously popular *American Bandstand*, a program frequently credited with having "whitened" the image of rock 'n' roll, regularly featured black performers and, after its first year on the air, integrated its studio audiences. Consequently, the TV-watching public, often to their amazement, saw teenagers of different races dancing to music being performed by musicians of different races. While programs like *American Bandstand* may have successfully "whitened" rock 'n' roll

[56] Riesman, David, Glazer, Nathan, and Denny, Ruel. *The Lonely Crowd: A Study of the Changing American Character* (New Haven, Connecticut: Yale University Press, 1950), p. 72.
[57] Institute for Social Research, *Adolescent Girls* (New York: Girl Scouts of America, 1956), pp. 99, 100.

and softened some of its edges, it nonetheless exposed black performers to literally millions of white teenagers.

The receptivity of white teenagers to African American culture extended beyond the music of rock 'n' roll. During the fifties, as today, young people sought to incorporate the lingo of American blacks into their own vernacular. In this process, radio disc jockeys played an indispensable role. Bearing such names as "Moon Dog" Freed, George "Hound Dog" Lorenz, and "Wolf Man Jack," these pied pipers to the young helped familiarize millions of listeners to a new hip vocabulary that drew heavily from the black experience. And although neither rock 'n' roll nor black slang was capable of providing white adolescents with anything more than a superficial glimpse of what it meant to be black in America, the teenage fascination with so-called "race music" and black idiom bespoke a greater openness to the culture and contributions of African Americans.

As one would expect, white supremacists felt threatened by the encroachment of race music. Asa Carter, a leader of Alabama's White Citizen's Council, warned of the dangers of rock 'n' roll, informing fellow whites that it was "sexualistic" and had the effect of bringing "people of both races together."[58] For all of Asa Carter's hatred and venom, his analysis was not entirely inaccurate – rock 'n' roll was (and remains) profoundly sexual, and as the many crowds at rock 'n' roll concerts showed, race music did bring people of both races together. However, for the masses of young people coming of age in the 1950s, the ability of rock 'n' roll to transcend racial barriers was not a deterrent, but all the more reason to embrace it.

From the vantage point of the early twenty-first century, as we look back to the 1950s, there is a temptation to portray the decade as an especially tumultuous time for race relations – an age when Klan membership was on the rise, and White Citizen's Councils sprouted up throughout the states of the old Confederacy. Such a portrayal contains more than a kernel of truth, but it has the danger of obscuring a larger and more important process that was unfolding simultaneously. For all of the racial prejudice endemic at the time, racial attitudes were on a decidedly liberalizing trend. Americans from all classes and regions were challenging the color line and attuning themselves to more progressive racial attitudes.

[58] Street, John. "Shock Waves: The Authoritarian Response to Popular Music," in Strinati, Dominic, and Wagg, Stephen (eds.), *Come on Down?: Popular Media Culture in Post-War Britain* (New York: Routledge, 1992) p. 305.

To be sure, racial conflict was heated and widespread, but that was primarily because the status quo was being altered – the rules of the game were being rewritten. When all is said and done, the Theodore G. Bilbos and the Strom Thurmonds, the Ku Klux Klansmen, and the Orval Faubuses were active and obstreperous, they rallied armies of reactionaries and hampered racial progress, but in the end they were steadily losing ground.

The rejection of racial hierarchies and the belief in the principle of equality was an ascendant value in the 1950s. The victory against fascism during World War II and the nation's celebration of pluralism and tolerance sounded the death knell for the very notion of racial, religious, or ethnic superiority. Of course, principle and practice are not always in harmony. As so frequently occurs when principles challenge deeply rooted customs, Americans gravitated toward the ideal of equality slowly, ambivalently, and inconsistently. Young people, however, being less burdened than their elders by traditions and customs, were able to embrace the principle of equality in a less ambivalent fashion. It should, therefore, come as little surprise that shortly after the first sit-ins, *Seventeen* magazine, in its monthly "Teens in the News" page, provided a very sympathetic write-up of Ezell Blair, an eighteen-year-old college freshman and one of the early leaders of the sit-ins.[59] While rock 'n' roll was not explicitly political – certainly, not in the same sense as the sit-ins – it had enormous psychological and symbolic significance because it was one of the means through which teenagers sought greater familiarity with African American people and culture.

If the popularity of rock 'n' roll bespoke a growing comfort with black culture, and if the rise of blue jeans suggested a growing rejection of elitism, both heralded a more relaxed attitude with respect to sex. As elevated rates of single motherhood and premarital pregnancies reveal, the incidences of sex outside of marriage soared during the 1950s.[60] Thus, to the extent young people were signaling their acceptance of a less traditional sexual code by embracing blue jeans and rock 'n' roll, they were also acting in correspondence with the liberalizing values that were afoot during the 1950s. To be sure, the decreasingly reticent behavior of young people frequently clashed with prevailing norms. Yet beneath this

[59] Cited from Green, Jr. Ronald S. "Innovation, Imitation, and Resisting Manipulation: The First Twenty Years of American Teenagers, 1941–1961" (University of Oklahoma; doctoral dissertation), p. 308.
[60] See Chapter 3 for more details on this point.

rebellious demeanor – more specifically, in young people's more accepting attitude toward their natural impulses and urges – teenagers were in general accord with the dominant trends of the period.

The Youth Culture and Sex

Although there was a great deal of parental concern surrounding sex in the 1950s, it is important to realize that even in the public realm, general attitudes toward sex were moving at cross-purposes. While parents discouraged promiscuity, they also did not want their children to become sexually repressed. Much of modern psychology at the time underscored the dangers of sexual repression, and through the flood of child-rearing literature, parents were alerted to these concerns. Apparently the advice of experts had some impact on popular behavior. According to child-rearing studies conducted during the 1950s, condemnatory attitudes toward masturbation were beginning to wane.[61] By the close of the 1950s, the work of anthropologist Margaret Mead, which was critical of the strict sexual codes often encountered in Western societies, had become familiar to millions of educated Americans.[62] Spurred by these developments, many public schools, and even some Catholic schools, began incorporating sex education into the curriculum.[63]

Revealingly, panty raids, accounts of which were scattered throughout newspapers, elicited a surprisingly lukewarm response overall. Although involving hundreds and, at times, even thousands of male college students, and despite the National Guard being mobilized on a particularly raucous occasion, the implication of the dearth of moral outrage bespeaks an indulgence on the part of the public.[64] It was illustrative of the tendency to indulge the rampant sexual hunger of healthy young men as a "normal" albeit roguish heed to the call of nature. What should have been anathema in light of the received narrative of the fifties merely elicited a wink and a nod by the very elders who were supposedly fostering a sexually

---

[61] Darby, Robert. "The Masturbation Taboo and the Rise of Routine Male Circumcision: A Review of the Historiography," *Journal of Social History* Vol. 36, No. 3. (Spring 2003), pp. 737–57.

[62] Howard, Jane. *Margaret Mead: A Life* (New York: Simon & Schuster, 1984).

[63] See, for example, "Methods of Sex Education Hit at Family Conference," *The Washington Post* (March 15, 1950), p. 13; "Tells of Sex Education: Spearer Describes Denver Diocese Program to Catholic Women," *The New York Times* (October 17, 1950), p. 40; "Catholics View Sex Education," *The Washington Post* (February 19, 1957), p. A17.

[64] Bailey, Beth. *Sex in the Heartland* (Cambridge, Mass.: Harvard University Press, 1999), p. 45–8.

repressive atmosphere. A *Coronet* magazine article published in 1959 captured the dominant mood of the country when it described panty raids as among "the latest development in the age-old quest of college students for surplus self-expression (also known to science as auxiliary hell-raising or overtime fun)."[65] It would seem that, as in earlier times, the prevailing attitude was "boys will be boys." While the taboo toward premarital sex remained high – it was probably rising during the fifties – Americans were simultaneously beginning to assume a less stodgy outward stance toward sex in general.

Evolving attitudes toward the practice of going steady provides the most compelling evidence of the gradually liberalizing attitudes of parents during the 1950s. Before World War II, the high school scene was dominated by a system of casual courting; adolescents were encouraged to "play the field" and date a variety of not-very-serious partners. However, during the 1940s and 1950s, a relatively new convention – the practice of going steady – came into vogue. Initially, parents reacted quite negatively to this new model of high school romance. As reporter Jane Whitbread explained, as parents looked back upon their own experience, they recalled their teenage years "as one long adventurous whirl in which everyone got to know scads of different kinds of people until the Right One, selected on the basis of richly assorted experience, finally came asking."[66] In addition to disrupting these earlier, more casual patterns of courtship, many parents believed that a much greater chance of sexual intimacy would likely result from the practice of going steady. Accordingly, a flurry of newspaper and magazine articles – in publications ranging from *Life* and *Ladies Home Journal* to *Teen* and *America* – minced few words in denouncing the practice.[67]

Some Catholic authorities were even more strident in their opposition to going steady than the leading journalists. In spring 1957, four students attending a Catholic high school in Bristol, Connecticut, were expelled from the school for going steady. "Parents send their children to my school

---

[65] Lardner, John. "Hanging Season on Campus," *Coronet* (November 1959), p. 37. See also Beth Bailey, *From Front Porch to Back Seat: Courtship in Twentieth-Century America* (Baltimore: Johns Hopkins University Press, 1988), and Ronald S. Green, "Innovation, Imitation, and Resisting Manipulation: The First Twenty Years of American Teenagers, 1941–1961" (Dissertation, University of Oklahoma, 1998).

[66] Whitbread, Jane. "The Case for Going Steady," *The New York Times Magazine* (July 14, 1957), p. 166.

[67] See "Going Steady, A National Problem," *Ladies Home Journal* (July 1949), pp. 44, 128, 131; Panas, Natalie. "Go Steady? A Teenager's View," *America* (September 17, 1960), p. 637; "Debate About Going Steady," *Life* (September 9, 1957), pp. 94–103.

so that they can be reared in a gentile, Christian environment," explained Father Settimio Crudele, the principal of St. Anthony's High School. "We do not consider steady dating conductive to that kind of atmosphere."[68] Elsewhere, Catholic students in Cincinnati, Ohio, Lynn, Massachusetts, and Allentown, Pennsylvania, were expressly forbidden by church authorities from engaging in serious dating.[69] As Jesuit priest Philip Mooney explained in an article, "Teenagers going steady are enkindling mutual love the same way as courting couples do . . . The resulting tension [puts] a heavy strain on the observance of God's law of chastity."[70] Father Joseph McClinchey, the principal of St. Mary's High School in Lynn, Massachusetts, was more succinct. "'Going steady,'" he proclaimed "is a menace to the purity of our youth."[71]

The sentiments of most adults, it would appear, were in general alignment with the attitudes of most Catholic officials. In 1955, when pollster George Gallup asked a nationally representative sample if they thought "boys and girls in high school should be allowed to 'go steady,' or should they date different boys and girls?," only 17 percent – or about one in six Americans – favored allowing teenagers to go steady, while 69 percent opposed it. Although large majorities of adults were hostile to the idea of going steady, Gallup found a surprisingly high level of variation along age, class, and residential lines. People residing in small towns were more likely to decry the practice of going steady than those living in large cities. The college educated were less hostile to steady dating than those hailing from a more limited educational background. And, as one might expect, respondents in their twenties were far less likely to oppose the practice of going steady than those in their thirties and forties.[72] Finally, not withstanding the fierce opposition of some Roman Catholic clerics, there was very little difference in the attitudes of Catholic and Protestant Americans.

However, by the closing years of the 1950s, adult opposition to serious dating had largely receded. Articles bearing such titles as "The Case for Going Steady" and "If You Don't Go Steady You're Different" appeared

---

[68] "School Outs 4 Pupils for 'Going Steady,'" *Chicago Daily Tribune* (February 9, 1957), p. 6.

[69] "Catholic Schools Asks 'Steady Daters' to Go," *The Washington Post* (February 10, 1957), p. A3.

[70] "Going Steady," *Time* (March 11, 1957).

[71] Curtis, Olga. "Clergy, Family Experts Worried About Teen Agers 'Going Steady,'" *Lowell Sunday Sun* (March 24, 1957).

[72] Gallup, George. "'Going Steady' Voted Down," *The Washington Post* (April 17, 1955), p. F8.

in popular magazines.[73] In 1950, the author of *Senior Scholastic*'s popular "Boy Dates Girl" column was disdainful toward the practice of going steady – suggesting that it appealed to the fickle few who were "afraid to buck open competition." Within only eight years' time, the author had assumed a dramatically different stance.[74] In column after column, Gay Head – the author of "Boy Meets Girl" – provided high school students with advice on how to catch a steady partner and how to hold onto a longtime girlfriend (or boyfriend). Going steady had become normative, a practice endorsed by the majority of teenagers (according to a 1955 survey by the Purdue Opinion Panel, 57 percent of high school students had gone or were currently going steady), and apparently accepted, if only tacitly, by the typical parent during the late 1950s.[75]

Significantly, despite all of the hand-wringing over the practice of going steady, and despite all of the concerns expressed over the dangers of petting, the romantic lives of adolescents generated a surprisingly low level of acrimony between teenagers and their parents. As the historian John Modell has documented, a survey of teenage girls conducted in 1939 found that 30 percent of respondents pointed to disagreements over their boyfriends as a source of conflict between them and their mothers and fathers. However, by 1959, only 7 percent of respondents believed likewise.[76] During the 1950s, journalists and clerics may have been preoccupied with the sexually precocious teenager, but once one exited the public square and entered the private homes of the typical American family, the evidence suggests that a less somber mood prevailed.

The growing convention of steady dating points to another important feature of the 1950s: its youth culture had a more liberating effect on young women than on young men. When it came to courtship, for example, the practice of going steady was probably more likely to safeguard the reputation of sexually active young women than the earlier practice of frequent and casual dating. As it turns out, many of the vociferous critics of steady dating were correct. The greater intimacy of "going steady" probably facilitated a higher level of sexual intercourse among the young.

[73] See Spicer, Betty Coe, "If You Don't Go Steady You're Different," *Ladies Home Journal* (December 1959), pp. 68–89, 94; Whitbread, Jane. "The Case for Going Steady," *New York Times Magazine* (July 1957), pp. 14, 36, 42.
[74] Head, Gay. "Boy Meets Girl," *Senior Scholastic* (May 3, 1950), p. 18.
[75] Beck, Joan. "Test Your Knowledge of Teens," *Chicago Daily Tribune* (December 10, 1959), p. C15.
[76] Modell, John. *Into One's Own: From Youth to Adulthood in the United States, 1920–1975* (Berkeley, Calif.: University of California Press, 1988), p. 228.

However, this greater intimacy – besides assuaging the anxieties of many parents ("Jane's boyfriend is such a nice young man. I can't see him pressuring Suzie into doing something she wouldn't want to do") – had the effect of deterring young men from bragging about their sexual conquests. In short, under the new regime of dating, there was a stronger incentive on the part of single men to protect the reputations of their girlfriends by keeping mum about how far they had gone – and this greater reticence, in the end, worked to the advantage of young women.

Teen movies, another staple of 1950s youth culture, provide an additional sign of the less constricted roles young women were coming to assume in the fifties. In such movies as *Blue Denim* (1959) and *A Summer Place* (1959), the female protagonists (Carol Lynley and Sandra Dee) played the roles of burgeoning young women who were willing to abandon their virginity in the pursuit of sexual fulfillment – all the while remaining "good girls." Such depictions would have been unheard of at the beginning of the fifties, when the very words *virgin* and *seduction* were sufficiently provocative to cause both the League of Decency and the Production Code to deny their seals of approval.[77] Yet as the success of the foregoing movies indicate – neither of which ran afoul of the censoring boards – and as the subsequent popularity of Helen Gurley Brown's *Sex and the Single Girl* (1962), the old rules were changing fast. Although the double standard continued, the emphasis on female chastity was less enforced than had been the case during earlier years.

The Common Ground Shared by Teens and Their Parents

The convergence of the youth culture with the ascendant values of the 1950s was not confined solely to blue jeans, rock 'n' roll, and the acceptance of new courting rituals. Upon closer inspection, another staple of 1950s teen culture – the delinquent film – was a good deal less oppositional than it appears at first glance. Rather than showing the divergent values between the young and old, *Rebel Without a Cause* – the movie that catapulted James Dean to iconic status, and the signature teen movie of the 1950s – depicts the defiant adolescent in revealingly meaningful moments, affirming the ideals of the larger society. As most movie buffs will recall, the character of Jim Stark (played by James Dean) moves to a new suburban school where he is harassed by a gang of delinquents.

---

[77] Harris, Jr., Albert W. "Comment: Movie Censorship and the Supreme Court: What Next?" *California Law Review* (Spring 1954), pp. 122–38.

In response to a challenge from Buzz Gunderson, the gang's leader, Jim agrees to take part in a "chickie run" – a high-speed game of chicken, where the two drivers race toward a cliff, and the first driver to jump out of the speeding vehicle is declared the loser. In all outward appearances, Jim displays the characteristic features and signs of a juvenile delinquent. He wears blue jeans, drag races, gets drunk, is continually brooding, has a history of fighting, and exhibits a great deal of disdain for the adult world. When we lift the veil, however, underneath Stark's tough exterior is a sensitive young man from a troubled home. Although well meaning, Jim's parents are self-absorbed, status-conscious, and insufficiently attentive to the emotional needs of their son. From Jim's perspective, his father is a particular source of disappointment because he is a weak man who permits himself to be bullied by his more dominant wife.

The principal source of friction between Jim Stark and his parents – and, for that matter, between Jim and the adult world – is not Jim's rejection of their principles, but the smoldering hostility toward the shallowness and self-serving hypocrisy of his elders. In one of the earliest scenes of the film, an inebriated Jim Stark erupts when his father reprimands him for drinking, while having told a police officer, only a minute earlier, that he did not "see anything so bad about taking a little drink." In one of the most famous lines in the movie, Dean accuses his parents of double-speak. "You're tearing me apart," he exclaims. "You say one thing, he says another, and then everybody changes back again!" Later in the movie, when Jim decides to do the right thing and tell the police about his role in the accidental death of Buzz, his parents do everything they can to dissuade him. "You can't be idealistic your whole life, Jim," his father exclaims. To which Jim retorts sharply, "Except to yourself!" Moments later, seeing that he is not having any success in getting Jim to change his mind, Mr. Stark admonishes his son for his naïveté, and for his refusal to tell a little white lie. "You'll learn when you get older, Jim," he explains. But Jim has none of it. "Well, I don't think that I want to live that way," he responds. At stake in this exchange, arguably the most powerful scene of the movie, is Jim's integrity – his determination, in the face of parental opposition, to act in an honorable manner for a principled reason, even if it requires him to pay a price.

At the conclusion of the film, following the tragic death of Jim's friend Plato, Mr. Stark finally extends to his boy the emotional support he had long desired. He folds his son in his arms and comforts him, providing Jim with his jacket to keep him warm, and reassuring him that things are going to be fine. The movie finally comes to a close on a mildly optimistic note, with father and son seemingly reconciled, and Jim and his girlfriend Judy (played by Natalie Wood) apparently prepared to take their place as responsible members of society.[78]

Through the struggles of the movie's lead character Jim Stark, the audience is exposed to the chasm that oftentimes arises between principle and practice. Viewers are presented with the scenario of the respectable, middle-class household, which can quickly become an incubator of confusion and torment if parents disengage from the emotional lives of their children. In the character of Jim Stark's father, portrayed by actor Jim Backus (of Thurston Howell fame on *Gilligan's Island*, and the memorable voice of Mr. Magoo), the audience is shown how a basically decent man can become enfeebled and even poisonous to the ones closest to him if steadfast principles are wanting. Finally, the viewer is made to grasp how the rhetoric of personal responsibility is essentially a meaningless notion if the individual is unwilling to or prevented from accepting the full consequences of his behavior. Although a classic teen movie, *Rebel Without a Cause* is also a morality tale. At the heart of the story is a critique of the adult world. However, it is not a critique of its ideals but, rather, the failure of adults to live up to their ideals.

For the most part, the essentially conservative message of *Rebel Without a Cause* was shared by the larger population of teenagers who came of age during the 1950s. In the way they dressed, in the music they danced to, and the slang they used, young people in the fifties went further than earlier generations in delineating a semiautonomous adolescent culture. Some historians have interpreted this youth culture as necessarily challenging the values of the adult world. "The world of teenagers and the world of adults," writes historian Klaus Fischer, "seemed increasingly to belong to two different species, especially in the postwar years when a distinct teenage subculture with attendant dress, behavior, and style of leisure could be identified."[79] Both David Halberstam and Grace Palladino apparently shared this interpretation. During the 1950s, writes Halberstam, "A new young generation of Americans was breaking away from the habits of its parents and defining itself by its music."[80] For her part, Palladino maintains that the universal high school experience provided teenagers a peer group they could turn to. "When the teenage

---

[78] See *Rebel Without a Cause* (1955). Nicholas Ray, director. Warner Brothers.
[79] Fischer, Klaus P. *America in White, Black, and Gray: The Stormy 1960s* (New York: Continuum International Publishing Group, 2006), p. 65.
[80] Halberstam, David. *The Fifties* (New York: Villard Books, 1993).

majority spent the better part of their day in high school, they learned to look to one another, and not to the adults for advice, information, and approval."[81] In his book *The Proud Decades*, John Patrick Diggins paints a picture of the fifties that is similar to the interpretations of Klaus Halberstam and Palladino. The teenagers of the fifties, he argues, were in large measure alienated from their parents. He writes, "[A]uthority seemed to have broken down in the postwar years as youth culture showed signs of unruliness and disorder."[82] Notwithstanding these analyses, the best evidence suggests that the typical teen did not turn to his peer group (or to the youth culture more generally) when grappling with the larger and more fundamental questions of meaning and value.

In the fifteen years following World War II, the most authoritative examination of the attitudes of young Americans was the Purdue Opinion Panel. With its nationally representative sample of between two and three thousand respondents, the surveys charted the opinions of teenagers on a wide range of issues over extended periods of time.[83] According to its findings, teens in the 1950s – just as their successors in contemporary times – looked to both their peers and parents, depending on the situation. When it came to leisure and fashion, young people understandably sought to imitate their friends and schoolmates. Consequently, when teenagers were asked to whom they would most likely turn when determining "what to wear to party," by more than a four to one margin, they chose their peer group over their parents. Similarly, when young people were asked whose feelings and opinions carried the most weight in determining "the clubs you join," and "how to act in the gang," teenagers by a ratio of two to one and three to one, respectively, placed the highest premium on the opinions of their friends and schoolmates.[84]

However, when the subjects moved to matters of a more personal and ideological nature, the influence of the parents rose precipitously. When young people were asked "whose feelings or opinions" they considered most important when shaping their own political outlook, teenagers were more than twice as likely to identify "parents or people their age" than their peers (54 to 21 percent). And when asked to whom they would turn for advice "on personal problems or troubles," teenagers were almost

[81] Palladino, *Teenagers: An American History*, p. 5.
[82] Diggins, *The Proud Decades: America in War and Peace, 1941–1960*, p. 201.
[83] Remmers, H. H., and Radler, D. H. *The American Teenager* (Indianapolis: Bobbs-Merrill Company, 1957).
[84] Ibid, pp. 234, 235.

five times more inclined to select their parents or some other adult over their friends and schoolmates.[85]

The separate worlds in which teenagers and their parents operated did not mean there was an estrangement in the relationship between adults and their children. In fact, there is a sound basis to postulate that on some matters – such as clothing and probably leisure – most parents thought it appropriate for children to take their cues from friends and classmates. When teens were asked if parents should "usually" determine the kinds of clothes they wear, only about 10 percent of boys and 12 percent of girls answered in the affirmative. As one would expect, teenagers wanted the freedom and space to be teenagers, but surprisingly most parents believed likewise. When teens were asked to predict the way their parents would respond – whether they, as mothers and fathers, believed they should "usually" be able to determine the kinds of clothes their adolescent children wore – only one in four teenagers said their parents held such a position. At the end of the decade, when adolescents were once again quizzed about the attitudes of their parents, only one in five teenagers said their parents frequently criticized the way they dressed.[86] In other words, if the respondents were correctly relaying the attitudes of their mothers and fathers, most parents and teenagers during the early Cold War years had arrived at a general understanding or a kind of intergenerational compact. Within the typical American family there was a commonly held belief that certain aspects of teenage life should be governed by teenagers themselves. It is little wonder, then, that in the mid-1950s when the University of Michigan's Institute for Social Research asked young men between the ages of fourteen and sixteen to rate the strictness of their parents, 5 percent responded "very strict," 29 percent said "strict," 63 percent answered "lenient," and 3 percent replied "very lenient." In the end, the respondents were nearly twice as likely to characterize their parents as "lenient" or "very lenient" (66 percent) than as "strict" or "very strict."[87]

Additional findings by the Purdue Opinion Panel go even further in undermining the proposition that the typical teen was alienated from his parents. According to these survey data, youngsters in the fifties were also conforming to another important attribute of the family: a personal

[85] Ibid, p. 235.
[86] Beck, "Test Your Knowledge of Teens," *Chicago Daily Tribune*, p. C15.
[87] Institute for Social Research, *A Study of Adolescent Boys* (New Brunswick, N.J.: Boy Scouts of America, 1955) p. 169.

belief in God. By more than a three to one margin, teenagers said they agreed with the statement: "Religious faith is better than logic for solving life's important problems" (57 percent agreed; 18 percent disagreed; and 22 percent answered, "Don't know").[88] In another question, when asked to identify the "one group of people" who "could do most to promote peace in the world," 52 percent of the teenage respondents chose religious leaders; while only 23 percent selected educators and 5 percent chose "Statesmen."[89] In short, the findings of the Purdue Opinion Panel suggest that the majority of youngsters in blue jeans, dancing to rock 'n' roll, and looking to their peers for guidance on social matters were, for the most part, subscribing to the values of the adult world.

Yet for all of the common ground adults and teenagers shared, there is no denying that young people were, at some level, asserting their autonomy by rebelling against their parents. Even if confined primarily to the realm of manners and norms, young people were rejecting the pastimes, styles, habits, and fashions of the previous generation. What are we to make of this youthful "revolt"? What does the widening cultural gulf between parent and child reveal about American life in the 1950s?

One crucial development revealed by the rise of the youth culture was the dramatic growth in consumption. Except for the use of slang and new norms in courting, virtually all of the components of the 1950s youth culture – its movies, music, fashions, and fads – depended on a vibrant youth market. Although a youth market of sorts had existed in earlier times, the combination of after-school jobs and weekly allowances endowed young people in the 1950s with an unprecedented amount of economic power in shaping the outward expressions of their own social order.

However, the autonomous world of American teenagers was not entirely autonomous. As one would expect, many entrepreneurs and corporations, aided by battalions of admen, took marked notice of the purchasing power of young Americans that, by the close of the 1950s, amounted to approximately $10 billion.[90] Capitalizing on the anxieties and desires of the nation's adolescents, business interests played a pivotal role in shaping and expanding the market for innumerable products targeted at youth: records, fast food, movies, hot rods, cosmetics, and clothing.

[88] Remmers and Radler, *The American Teenager*, p. 171.
[89] Ibid, p. 174.
[90] "A New $10 Billion Power: The U.S. Teenage Consumer," *Life* (August 31, 1959), pp. 78–85.

While acknowledging the importance of consumption in shaping youth culture, one must be careful to avoid overstating the power of the cultural industry. On plenty of occasions, American business, to its own detriment, failed to recognize the yearnings and desires of teenagers. In the case of blue jeans, for instance, the industry's leading manufacturer, Levi Strauss & Company, was slow to fathom the symbolic significance of their own signature product. Indeed, as late as the 1960s, the popularity of its 501 jeans took Levi's executives by surprise.[91] In addition, from the advertising campaigns launched during the 1950s it is clear that its executives had little grasp of the underlying reasons their jeans were so favored by teenagers. Instead of emphasizing the rebellious, outsider connotations of blue jeans, Levi Strauss attempted to prevail upon the public that denims were "Right for School" – which is to say, wholesome and unthreatening – a strategy obviously calculated to assuage parents, but one not likely to resonate very strongly among teenagers themselves, the key demographic for Levi's products. Moreover, despite the popularity of jeans among young women, Levi Strauss did not begin featuring female models in its ads until the 1960s.[92] It is probably not much of an exaggeration to say that the enormous success of Levi Strauss occurred not because of but in spite of the company's efforts to forge a more wholesome image for the public.

In a similar manner, the role of Pat Boone in sparking a high school fad for "white buck" shoes during the late 1950s was not conceived by Madison Avenue or by executive boards in the footwear industry. Rather, the craze arose from countless fans of Boone – or the aspiring boyfriends of these fans – who were drawn to the way Boone dressed and sought to emulate him. Although they were manipulated at times by the consumer culture, the teenagers of the fifties exercised free will in their quest for self-expression, just as their counterparts do today. They were not the pawns of corporations and savvy admen – or, to borrow the words of anthropologist Oscar Lewis, they were not "insubstantial and passive automatons who carry out expected behavior patterns."[93] Instead, young people were purposefully driven actors who were grasping for symbols or cultural markers that would assist them in constructing a new, more autonomous identity.

[91] Cray, *Levi's*, p. 150.

[92] Downey, *Images of Levi Strauss & Co.*, p. 82. At the time of publication, the author served as the in-house historian for Levi Strauss & Company.

[93] Lewis, Oscar. "An Anthropological Approach to Family Studies," *American Journal of Sociology* (March 1950), pp. 470–1.

FIGURE 5.2. In the early 1950s, Levi Strauss attempted to assuage parents that denims were "Right for School" – wholesome and unthreatening. (Courtesy Levi Strauss & Company Archives, San Francisco.)

Embracing Rebellion

Another development that contributed to the rise of youth culture – a development less noticeable than the burgeoning youth market, but no less important in its long-term implications – was the adoption of a lenient

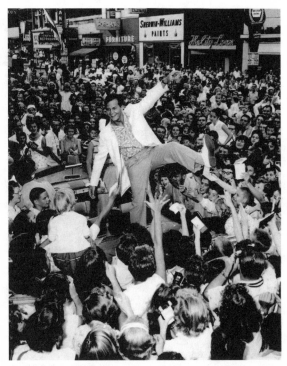

FIGURE 5.3. Pat Boone, standing in a convertible flashing his signature "white bucks" to an enthusiastic crowd in Akron, Ohio. (Reproduced by permission of Pat Boone.)

parenting strategy by the families of most teenagers. The forbearance of adults toward their adolescent children and their willingness to wink at the defiance of their teenagers reveals a great deal about the dominant ideology of the early Cold War years. Throughout the late forties and fifties, the rebelliousness of teenagers was not only tolerated by the larger culture, but was, to a surprisingly large degree, sanctioned. Although parents may not have liked the way their children dressed or the music they listened to, they tended to regard these practices as a healthy sign of growth. Time and again, parents had been assured by psychologists and pundits alike that adolescence was a time of experimentation when young men and women were attempting to fashion a new identity. Indeed, the very term *identity crisis* was coined in 1950 by émigré psychologist Erik Erickson to describe the psychic struggle teenagers underwent to progress to the next stage of their psychological development.[94] As Erickson explained it, the

94 See Erickson, Erik, *Childhood and Society* (New York: W.W. Norton, 1950).

FIGURE 5.4. High school students in the 1950s were the first generation to have sufficient income to create a vibrant youth market. (Reproduced by permission of the Mississippi Valley Collection, The University of Memphis.)

teenage years could be seen as a kind of "psychological moratorium," where it was safe and even salutary for youngsters to temporarily assume different kinds of identities – identities that typically beckoned the young to cut the apron strings and flout certain traditions and customs.

If one were a parent during the 1950s, it was not necessary to have read Erickson in order to have absorbed these lessons. Countless articles in the popular press provided adults with a more digestible version of Erickson's basic message. In its regularly syndicated columns, the Gesell Institute – headed by renowned developmental psychologist Arnold Gesell – counseled parents to be less demanding with their children. The teenager's "resentment against parents is desirable," it advised, because such resentment "is an indication that the adolescent is beginning to show the desire to achieve the independence from them that every really mature person must attain. Without it, youth would never free itself from parental domination."[95]

---

[95] The Gesell Institute, "Adolescents' Revolt Weighed by Author," *The Washington Post* (May 4, 1955), p. 37.

A 1957 article that appeared in the *National Parent–Teacher* magazine relayed a message that was virtually identical to the point raised by the Gesell Institute. "Some clashes are not only normal and inevitable," noted the article, "but actually desirable ... Children must grow up. They must emancipate themselves from their families, learn to stand upon their own feet, and pursue ways of life that makes sense for their generation."[96] This willingness to recognize generational differences that existed between teenagers and parents – and the strong tendency to regard adolescence as largely a psychological process of experimentation and growth – encouraged parents to adopt a less exacting attitude, essentially indulging many of the transgressions of teenagers.

"Adolescence: Time of the Rebel," a *New York Times* article from fall 1960, typified these popular attitudes toward teenage rebellion. As the author reported, a young woman she knew personally – the eighteen-year-old daughter of her acquaintance – had seemingly been an ideal child. "Always a happy, loving youngster, the girl gave her parents a deep sense of gratification." However, once she attained adolescence and "began to flutter her wings experimentally in her first attempts toward independence," both of her parents reacted in sheer horror. "With her first attempts at defiance, her father found himself trembling with rage, her mother began to have violent migraine headaches. Without resorting to severe punishments or rigid limits, they soon let her know what her change in attitude did to them." As a consequence, the young lady felt extremely guilty and gave up in her pursuit of autonomy. Over time, she became increasingly withdrawn from her old friends. "Helpful at home, she obeyed her parents' rules, studied hard at school, but, unfortunately, she also stopped really growing up."[97]

The underlying message of the article was clear: if parents were unbending in the demands, or insufficiently understanding of their children's desire to "flutter their wings" in their natural drive for independence, disastrous consequences would likely follow. For the sake of the psychological well-being of children, it was therefore critical parents accord teenagers a greater measure of freedom, including the freedom to be rebellious and defiant. As the widely circulated Public Affairs pamphlet "Making the Grade as Dad"(1950) remarked, "Curious as it may seem, they (teenagers) need regulations, if for no other reason than to

---

[96] Wolf, Anna W. M. "Can A Child Be Too Good," *National Parent–Teacher* (September 1958), p. 7, 8.

[97] LeShaw, Eda J. "Adolescence: Time of the Rebel," *The New York Times* (October 9, 1960), p. SM93.

rebel against them. For only as they rebel do they prove to themselves that they can be independent."[98]

This more lax attitude on the part of parents helps explain why, in the face of all the consternation and cavil about blue jeans and rock 'n' roll, parents permitted little Johnny and Suzie to wear denims and listen to rock 'n' roll records. In those cases when something akin to a hard line was pursued, adults often refrained from taking an imperial, heavy-handed approach. As historian William Graebner observed, in the battle against blue jeans and other articles of clothing deemed undesirable, the most acclaimed strategy during the mid-1950s was the so-called Buffalo Plan – an innovative approach that was first developed in Buffalo and then copied by numerous towns and cities across the nation – which called on student councils to formulate voluntary dress codes enforced through peer pressure.[99] As an article in *Senior Scholastic* acknowledged, "In most schools adopting such codes, students themselves vote on each item of the code."[100] In their eagerness to underscore the opposition to the rising youth culture, scholars have tended to focus on the reaction of conservative authorities – a widespread phenomenon and certainly the gist of an engaging narrative, but probably not characteristic of the typical family who granted their children the freedom, and in many cases the financial resources, to indulge their musical and fashion tastes.

"Wally's Comb," a 1959 installment of the popular *Leave It to Beaver* series, is illustrative of the approach recommended to the parents of teenagers. In the episode, Wally comes home with a rock 'n' roll-inspired hairdo called the jellyroll. At the urging of his wife, Ward Cleaver attempts to persuade his son to change his hairstyle, warning him that it could adversely affect his swimming times. However, Wally, fond of his new look, decides against altering it, whereupon Ward drops the issue. However, June Cleaver is undeterred in her mission. "He looks like, like a gangster!" she exclaims to her husband. "You know, the next thing, he's going to be wearing a leather jacket and motorcycle boots." At a loss as to what to do, June Cleaver drives to Mayfield High School where she asks the principal Mr. Howell to mandate that all students show up to school with normal hair styles. Despite her pleadings, the principal

---

[98] Neisser, Walter and Edith. "Making the Grade as Dad" (New York: The Public Affairs Committee, 1950).

[99] Graebner, William. *Coming of Age in Buffalo: Youth and Authority in Postwar Buffalo* (Philadelphia: Temple University Press, 1990), pp. 99–101.

[100] "Dress Codes . . . Cool or Square," *Senior Scholastic* (November 21, 1958), p. 10.

remains unconvinced. Like Ward Cleaver, the principal considers the jellyroll as little more than an innocent fad. As he patiently explains to June Cleaver, "If a boy comes to school clean and neat we don't tell him how to comb his hair. After all, its one of the first forms of self-expression." June Cleaver's disappointment, however, is short-lived. The following day, Wally finally accedes to her wishes after the Beaver, wishing to emulate his older brother, greases up his own hair in a half-baked imitation of the jellyroll hairdo.[101]

The most notable feature of this *Leave It to Beaver* episode was the nonauthoritarian approach of most of the adults. Whereas Wally's parents – especially June Cleaver – objected to his hairdo, they did not compel him to change it. Even Wally's mother, the severest critic of the jellyroll hairstyle, showed reluctance in forcing Wally to alter his new look. Her preference was to delegate the role of taskmaster to the principal. However, the principal refuses because, like Ward Cleaver, he does not find the latest teenage craze to be a legitimate source of concern. Ultimately, Wally's decision to banish the jellyroll stems less from a sense of obedience than from the realization that his hairstyle has been a source of embarrassment to his parents.

The enormous attention surrounding youth fads further marginalized the perceived challenge posed by a defiant youth culture. The notion of a fad had been in existence for more than half a century, but during the postwar years a new term – the *youth fad* or the *teen fad* – became a visible feature of public conversation. Rather than eliciting alarm, these mercurial exhibitions of youth – from panty raids to phone booth stuffings – were typically received with bemusement by adult authorities. For every June Cleaver there were several Wards who, with a sense of forbearance, identified innocuous impulses behind these juvenile excursions. Thus, despite his antipathy to rock 'n' roll, Rhode Island Senator John Pastore, head of a 1958 congressional investigation of the music industry, was willing to tolerate this new musical style as a "fashion and fad that appeals to young people." As Pastore explained to fellow committee members, apparently with a hint of embarrassment, his own fourteen-year-old daughter was a fan of the Coasters.[102] In short, fads were regarded as an innocent stage on the road to adulthood in the 1950s. To most parents they were a transient phase, no more inappropriate – or, for that

[101] See episode "Wally's Comb," from 1959 season of *Leave It to Beaver*.
[102] Lawson, Steven F. *Civil Rights Crossroads: Nation, Community, and the Black Freedom Struggle* (Lexington, Kentucky: University Press of Kentucky, 2003), p. 217.

matter, condemnatory – than a nine-year-old boy's belief that all girls have cooties.

It would seem that when it came to the treatment of young people, the parents of the 1950s were of two minds. On one hand, there were widespread concerns over juvenile delinquency as well as the excessive pampering of sons.[103] On the other hand, there was a greater sensitivity to the psychological needs of young people. These conflicting assessments – one tending to lead to a policy of greater indulgence when it came to one's own children, all the while advocating a "get tough" approach as far as those troublesome teenagers on the other side of the tracks were concerned – go far in explaining the desperate behavior of America's parents during the Eisenhower years.

Enhancing these indulgent attitudes on the part of adult authorities was the vivid memory of World War II – in particular, the image of the submissive German. As discussed in earlier chapters, in the minds of most social commentators at midcentury, Hitler's ascent to power was attributable to a German population that was conditioned to be conformist. The German people, it was posited, typically possessed a submissive personality: they too readily yielded their minds and souls to a strong leader or the governing whim of the crowd. Mindful of this, many social commentators attempted to apply the lessons of recent German history by alerting Americans to the hazards of social conformity, thereby fostering a more critical attitude toward authority. In pioneering works such as Theodor W. Adorno's *The Authoritarian Personality* (1950) and Gordon Allport's *The Nature of Prejudice* (1954), and in such best-sellers as David Riesman's *The Lonely Crowd* (1950) and William Whyte's *The Organization Man* (1956), readers were warned that a high level of conformity existed in the United States, and unless this trend was resisted, the American way of life would be in peril. A stream of articles in the popular press – like *The New York Times Magazine*'s "Portrait of the Authoritarian Man," *The Reporter*'s "Herd, the Self, and the Gulf Between," and *The Reader's Digest*'s "Danger of Being Too Well Adjusted" – hammered away at these themes. By 1947, anxieties surrounding the dangers of excessive submissiveness had reached a sufficiently high pitch so as to convince the editors of *The Reader's Guide to Periodical Literature* to begin designating a separate category to address the pressing issue of "conformity."

---

[103] For the authoritative account of the widespread concerns surrounding juvenile delinquency during the 1950s, see Gilbert, James, *A Cycle of Outrage: America's Reaction to the Juvenile Delinquent in the 1950s* (New York: Oxford University Press, 1986).

The fallout from these articles was considerable, encouraging people to resist external influences and play an active role in formulating their own values, dreams, and goals – in short, their own identities. Thus, during the 1950s, the term *identity* became a recurrent theme in American culture because it expressed and helped illuminate the challenges of autonomy and self-authorship – a process that a steadily increasing number of people seemed determined to undertake. Understandably, this emphasis on individual autonomy – the precise opposite of submissiveness – molded popular attitudes toward teenagers in the direction of greater freedom and permissiveness. Accordingly, with all of the hand-wringing over the dangers of submissiveness, many adults felt uneasily toward the "goody-goody," or an excessively compliant child.

Although acknowledging the "too good adolescent" may be "easier to live with" than his more defiant counterpart, an article in the *National Parent–Teacher* magazine characterized the complacent child as a symptom of "weakness under cover." As the author explained, "The too-good child is not really free from the hostilities and aggression that all of us harbor, to some degree, toward the people in our lives. He is merely repressing them. The ready compliance is born of an unreasoning fear that if he reveals himself he will lose the love of those he depends on for protection. With this goes unrest and a feeling of inferiority . . . he suffers a kind of emotional impoverishment." The article also argued that although the more rebellious child might tax the patience of his parents, his defiant stance – if kept within proper bounds – was a sign of psychological health. "Adolescence is a period when the average youngster, especially in the late teens, is in a state of revolt against the adult world in general and parents in particular," it explained.[104] In an age when psychology was reaching ever-greater heights of cultural influence and, as we have seen, when figures like Erik Erickson dominated the field of adolescent development, such explanations enjoyed a great deal of resonance. Operating within appropriate limits, teenage hostility was seen by most adults as developmentally healthy, and not something to be afraid of.

Desirous of dispelling the odor of sanctity surrounding him, Pat Boone and the people closest to him revealed that he too sinned as a youth – engaging in vandalism, petty theft, and underage drinking while coming of age in Nashville. Far from feeling the stain of scandal, Pat Boone's father-in-law, country singer Red Foley, seemed to welcome Boone's past

---

[104] Wolf, "Can a Child Be Too Good," pp. 7, 8.

transgressions. "Some people thought Pat was a sissy, a goody-goody all his life," Foley noted. "Well, that's not in him at all. He's a regular fellow." To Foley, as to most Americans in the fifties, it was admirable for a young man to be upright, but an unspoken assumption was that one's masculinity could be impaired by excessive virtue. As Foley further remarked, Boone needed to disclose such petty rogueries "so that people don't get the idea he's a sissy." Although integrity and fair play were necessary ingredients, the idealized male was required by convention to have a dash of mischief thrown in to ensure against any creeping suspicions of sissyhood.

Mischief, once a character flaw, seemed to slip into the realm of independence, and become a semi-virtue, a habit of mind for the self-assertive. So entrenched was the acceptance, even tacit encouragement, of mischief that newspapers ran nationwide essay contests wherein parents submitted the wilder antics of their children. Hank Ketcham, originator of the comic strip *Dennis the Menace*, would translate the winning anecdote into his character's deeds of mischief and mayhem. Often, the real-life episodes surpassed everything encountered in *Dennis the Menace* or elsewhere in comics. We hear of a boy denuding his mother at the beach; of a young lad tripping the fire alarm at a professional sporting event; and of a preadolescent Robin Hood snatching his father's wallet and distributing the contents among neighborhood scamps. To possess mischief was a salutary symptom of masculine self-determination – an early manifestation of American individualism. Thus parents beamed rather than scowled when recounting such tales of juvenile mischief.[105]

Russell Lynes, an editor for *Harper's Magazine*, expressed the prevailing sentiment. As he noted in a *New York Times* article in 1959, among young people "'rebelliousness' is, in part at least, a reflection of our fairly new belief in 'permissiveness' and in our encouraging them to make up their own minds."[106]

As one might expect, these attitudes did not only affect the behavior of parents, but helped shape the outlook of teenagers as well. For many

---

[105] Jenkins, Henry. "'The All-American Handful': Dennis the Menace, Permissive Child-rearing, and the Bad Boy Tradition," in Spigel, Lynn, and Curtin, Mike (eds.), *The Revolution Wasn't Televised: Sixties Television and Social Conflict* (New York: Rutledge, 1997). Obtained from Jenkins' website at: http://web.mit.edu/cms/People/henry3/dennis.html.

[106] Lynes, Russell. "Teen-Agers Mirror Their Parents," *The New York Times* (June 28, 1959), p. SM12.

young men, the old model of the saccharin, nonswearing all-American boy was losing some of its appeal. As we have seen, even Pat Boone was trying to shy away from this all-too-clean image. Although young men did not wish to totally cast off the values of the older generation, they did not see themselves – nor did they want to be seen by others – as "goody-two-shoes" or as the passive creations of their elders.

For young men in the 1950s, just as for young men in contemporary times, the requirements of manhood demanded that some distance be inserted between teenager and parent. As a result of these changing notions of adolescent masculinity, the Boy Scouts began losing a little of its old sparkle. We must be careful, however, to avoid overstating this point. It was not as if their membership rolls dwindled; in fact, the total number of Boy Scouts grew by 35 percent between the years 1950 and 1960.[107] Yet that expansion did not keep pace with the growth of the population, which rose by 44 percent for eleven- to seventeen-year-old males – the eligible age for Boy Scouts.[108]

The somewhat lagging fortunes of the Boy Scouts stand in stark contrast with the explosive growth experienced by the Cub Scouts. From 1945 to 1960, Cub Scout membership rose precipitately, climbing from somewhat more than three-quarters of a million (828,344) to just over 1.85 million, an increase of more than twofold. During this same period, the population of eight-, nine-, and ten-year-old males, the eligible age for Cub Scouts, grew by slightly less than 47 percent.[109] In other words, at a time when the ranks of the Boy Scouts were expanding at a slightly slower pace than the larger population, the total membership of the

[107] Membership figures provided by Pat Wellen, Research Director of Boy Scouts of America.

[108] Bureau of the Census, *United States Census of the Population 1950: Detailed Characteristics: U.S. Summary* (Washington, D.C.: 1953), p. 1–165; Bureau of the Census, *Census of the Population Volume 1. Characteristics of the Population* (Washington, D.C.: 1960), p. 1–354. A 1958 article, published by *Senior Scholastic*, acknowledged the recruiting problems the Boy Scouts were having. As the article reported, Boy Scout officials were planning to institute a series of reforms "the most sweeping in the movement's 48-year history." The reason for these initiatives? "(T)he traditional program's waning appeal to modern-minded youngsters." See "New Look for Boy Scouts," *Senior Scholastic* (October 31, 1958), p. 1.

[109] Bureau of the Census, *United States Census of the Population 1950: Detailed Characteristics: U.S. Summary* (Washington, D.C.: 1953), p. 1–165; Bureau of the Census, *Census of the Population Volume 1. Characteristics of the Population* (Washington, D.C.: 1960), p. 1–354; Membership figures provided by Pat Wellen, Research Director of Boy Scouts of America.

FIGURE 5.5. Vested in patriotism and conformity, the popularity of the Boy Scouts began to wane in the early Cold War years. (Photographer: Henri Cartier-Bresson. Reproduced by permission of Magnum Photos, Inc.)

Cub Scouts accelerated at a pace well in excess of the country's growing population.[110]

Given the explosive growth among the Cub Scouts and the strong emphasis placed on the family and country, one might have expected to see the Boy Scouts undergo a period of rapid growth during the Eisenhower years. Why did such gains in membership fail to materialize? The answer lies in the increasing tendency of young men to regard the model Boy Scout as insufficiently independent. In an age when conformism and obedience were being assessed with a more critical eye, Boy Scouts were perceived by many male teenagers as excessively compliant. It is therefore little wonder Holden Caulfield, the protagonist of J. D. Salinger's *The Catcher in the Rye*, spoke disparagingly of his brief stint with the

---

[110] Boy Scout and Cub Scout numbers provided by Pat Wellen, the Research Director of Boy Scouts. National figures for the various ages provided by the U.S. Census Bureau. See Bureau of the Census, *Census of the Population: 1960* (Washington, D.C.: U.S. Government Printing Office, 1961) p. 345; and *Detailed Characteristics: U.S. Summary* (1950 Population Report P-C1) (Washington, D.C.: U.S. Government Printing Office, 1953), p. 1-165. The idea of using Boy Scouts as a way of discerning larger cultural attitudes is borrowed from Kett, Joseph F. *Rites of Passage: Adolescence in America, 1970 to the Present* (New York: Basic Books, 1977).

Boy Scouts, equating its rules to the kind of exacting regimentation one would expect to see in that other bastion of conformity, the army.[111] Given the times, such skeptical attitudes on the part of adolescents were understandable. From its formation in 1906 to the present, scouting has been largely planned, controlled, and supervised by adults who, in effect, functioned as a voluntary "officer corps."[112]

In assessing the youthful rebellion of the 1950s, it is important to distinguish between the realm of culture and that of values. In the case of the former, young people were abandoning many of the manners and customs of their parents. In the latter case, the picture was opaque as teenagers rejected elitism and sexual prudery, all the while becoming more tolerant and democratic. The youth culture, therefore, could be seen as oppositional in only a superficial sense, and only to the extent that it challenged established manners and norms. However, on the level of values – or, in the moral outlook of the typical teen – the youth culture generally affirmed, and in some cases amplified, the principles of tolerance and freedom, of greater democracy and openness – all values that were on the rise during the Eisenhower years. Far from drawing upon a calculus all its own, the youth culture – as we see it manifested in the rise of blue jeans, teen magazines, and rock 'n' roll – ascribed to the values of the larger society. In particular, they subscribed to those values lying at the heart of the Permissive Turn. From the perspective of moral traditionalists, the youth culture was oppositional. Yet its opposition arose from the same stream – indeed, it was part of the same vein – of the liberalizing impulse that was ascending throughout the postwar years. Thus, to the extent his tattered blue jeans symbolized a tacit acceptance of an egalitarian ethos, or his taste in music betrayed less inhibited sexual attitudes, as well as a curiosity and openness toward other races, the typical teenager in the age of Eisenhower was a half step in front of where the country was already heading.

The limited level of acrimony between the generations is a testament to the rapid pace of change unfolding during the age of Eisenhower. As

---

[111] J. D. Salinger, *The Catcher in the Rye* (New York: Little Brown, 1951), p. 141.

[112] In fact, scouting's founder, Lord Robert Baden-Powell, had explicitly patterned the movement on the military – not an especially individualistic institution – in an attempt to tap into the "gang" instinct he noticed in boys while asserting control through a structure modeled on the marshal traditions of Great Britain. Hence, the organization of youngsters into troops and patrols were intended to appeal to the adolescent desire to belong while exerting the disciplined leadership, order, and control with which Baden-Powell was well familiar from his long and distinguished military career. Baden-Powell, Robert. *Lessons From the Varsity of Life* (London: C. Arthur Pearson, LLD, 1933).

we have seen, young people were adopting attitudes toward race relations, sex, and traditional authority that were in tension with significant
elements of an older moral vision – but so too were adults. And it was
because the disposition of adults was liberalizing so briskly that a ran-
corous generation gap failed to emerge. In the end, a close examination
of the 1950s youth culture should help readers appreciate two important
postwar developments that are oftentimes obscured by the received narrative: first, for all of the fears over the dangers of juvenile delinquency,
the typical parent displayed a high (and rising) level of indulgence toward
young people during the 1950s; second, by the close of the decade, the
ascendant values of the age – and correspondingly, the dominant values
of most teenagers – were rapidly diverging from an older, conservative,
and more traditional worldview.

The Glamorization of the Young

From the youth culture of the 1950s arose a development that would
prove critical in redefining the established moral order. In his famous
examination of youth culture, a critique that appeared in the pages of *The
New Yorker* in 1958, Dwight Macdonald stumbled upon a phenomenon
he seemed at a loss to explain. During the course of his research, Macdonald learned Dick Clark's hit dance show *American Bandstand* attracted
eight million viewers every weekday on ABC, half teenagers or younger –
a finding that necessarily implied the other half consisted of adults.[113] If
rock 'n' roll emerged from youth culture, and if its message and energy
had a unique appeal to the country's teenagers, then how was one to
account for these millions of adult fans?

The startling success of *MAD* magazine raised similar questions.
Founded in 1952 by a once-aspiring teacher William Gaines, *MAD* deftly
lampooned various elements of the popular culture. It was bawdy, irrev-
erent, and audacious in its jibes and general format. Yet as the most
cursory perusal of the magazine would attest, *MAD*'s brand of humor
was decidedly juvenile. However, as numerous articles at the time suggest,
adults enjoyed the magazine as well.[114] By the 1960s, four in ten high

---

[113] Macdonald, "Profiles: A Caste, A Culture, A Market II," p. 96.
[114] During the 1950s, such prominent cultural figures as Ernie Kovacs, Roger Price, and
Sid Caesar contributed to *MAD* magazine. In addition, news about *MAD* appeared in a
number of columns and articles that were obviously targeted to an adult audience. See,
for example, "Books Today," *The New York Times* (April 29, 1959), p. 27; Morten,
Baker E., "TV Star Also Hep On Army, How to Get in That is, it Appears," *The*

school students and nearly six in ten college students were reading the magazine.[115] Moreover, as its treatment in the popular press suggests, *MAD* included among its readers a substantial number of people who were well beyond their college years. Once again, the obvious question that arises is how such a lowbrow creation of the youth culture successfully attracted a mass following among those who were no longer youngsters?

The answer to this question lies in the culture's valorization of youth or in the desire of adult men and women to remain young at heart. In the indulgence society accorded youth, and the rise of a commercial culture targeted to a burgeoning youth market, the teenage years came to be seen as a halcyon, carefree time. Reinforcing this glamorization was a scourging critique of American society-at-large. As we have noted, a stream of best-selling books in the fifties indicted the adult world for its conformism, submissiveness, other-directedness, repression, hypocrisy, and callousness. The ferocity of this critique made adolescence appear to be an idyllic time of fresh experience and innocence – a period when the individual had yet to be corrupted by the cynical vices of modern life. Moreover, many of the protagonists of youth-oriented movies and books (such as Jim Stark in *Rebel Without a Cause* and Holden Caulfield in *Catcher in the Rye*) were conflicted adolescents who heroically struggled to resist the inauthentic and dehumanizing qualities of the adult world. The severe contrast between the beauty and valiant idealism of youth and the spiritually stifling fate of adulthood impelled many to resist the encroachments of Father Time and the negative qualities that come in tow. For such people, identifying with youth culture eased the discomfort they felt toward the current state of American society. And because the world of adolescents was so tightly bound to consumption, millions of adults, flush with disposable income, were able to essentially shop for identity – in other words, they were able to purchase many of the symbols and trappings of the youth culture.

As the approximately six million adult Americans who regularly watched *American Bandstand* suggest, the valorization of youth was an undeniable phenomenon during the early Cold War. Over time it grew more formidable. With the advent of the 1960s and the coming of age of

Chicago Defender (September 24, 1955), p. 7; Lyon, Herb, "Tiger Ticker," *Chicago Daily Tribune* (April 25, 1956), p. B8; Kilgallen, Dorothy, "Louis Prima Packs the House," *The Washington Post* (April 6, 1959), p. B6.

[115] Mattews, Kristin L. "A MAD Proposition in Postwar America," *The Journal of American Culture* (June 2007), p. 212.

the first baby boomers (a child born in 1946 would have been sixteen in 1962), the cult of youth attained critical mass. And as the cultural wars of the 1960s intensified, the appeal of youth gained a stronger pull among those alienated or offended by some aspect of American society – a development reflected by the literally millions of adults who aped the younger generation in their preference for blue jeans and other accoutrements of the rising generation. In the decades since the 1960s, an ever-increasing proportion of adults have deferred to their juniors not simply in their choice of music and clothing, but also in the use of slang, the brandishing of tattoos, and – in the case of some older men – in the purchase of motorcycles and the sprouting of ponytails.

The youth culture, in modern times, has fulfilled a function similar to the role played by minority and bohemian communities in earlier years. As sociologists Rolf Meyersohn and Elihu Katz pointed out in the late 1950s, in modern times, bohemian communities have become "a kind of social laboratory" for city dwellers: "Here something new can be tried out – because it is expected – without threatening either the bohemian minority and the urban population as a whole."[116] Thus, an uneasy tension persists with both groups mutually contemptuous, but each recognizing the utility of the other. In a strikingly similar process, the youth culture has become a social laboratory of sorts, where the larger community of adults are able to survey the fads among teendom, and then – depending on a combination of ephemeral factors, such as their hip quotient, the saliency of its message, and its ability to shock middle-class sensibilities – appropriates certain youth fashions as their own.

In *The Death of the Grown-up* (2007), *Washington Times* pundit Diane West was especially observant in describing the cultural seduction of grown-up Americans. "More adults, ages eighteen to forty-nine," she noted, "watch the Cartoon Network than watch CNN. Readers as old as twenty-five are buying 'young adult' fiction written expressly for teens. The average video gamester was eighteen in 1990, now he's going on thirty."[117] To be sure, much of this posturing may be attributed to the age-old quest for eternal youth. During this same period, the numbers of Americans joining health clubs or undergoing cosmetic surgery also climbed. However, at the heart of this burgeoning youth culture was not

---

[116] Meyersohn, Rolf, and Katz, Elihu. "Notes on a Natural History of Fads," *The American Journal of Sociology*, Vol. 62, No. 6 (May 1957), p. 598.
[117] West, Diane. *The Death of the Grown-up: How America's Arrested Development is Bringing Down Western Civilization* (New York: St. Martin's Press, 2007).

just a nostalgic longing for the days of yore. Equally complicit was a desire on the part of these adults, or at least a significant number of adults, to align themselves with some of the more notable symbols of defiance – be they blue jeans, motorcycles, rock 'n' roll, or tattoos. By imitating the styles of defiant youth, the not-so-young registered their dissatisfaction with important aspects of American life and, in so doing, adopted an oppositional stance toward some essential features of the existing moral order.

In short, a drastically new development had burst upon the scene. Throughout the Truman and Eisenhower years youth culture, although outwardly rebellious, tended to uphold the values of the larger society, tacitly or otherwise. Thus, although rock 'n' roll may have clashed with social conventions – in its relaxed attitude toward sex and in its receptivity of African American culture – it was in harmony with the ascendant spirit of the times. By the early seventies, however, the nation's moral terrain had been reshaped dramatically and – as we will see in the final chapter – in challenging prevailing norms, the youth culture had also challenged the prevailing moral order.

6

The Self

From Original Sin to Self-Actualization – Jackson Pollock, Charlie Parker, and New Notions of Identity in Postwar America

Considering the shifts in child rearing, psychology, religion, and sex, it would not be much of an exaggeration to say that Americans at mid-century had a new sense of themselves and the wider world around them. The enormous popularity of Mahatma Gandhi is perhaps the most illustrative example of this new understanding of the self. Gandhi had been the focus of enormous media attention before his death – appearing three times on the cover of *Time* magazine. As with the assassination of John F. Kennedy, Gandhi's martyrdom elevated him from admired figure to celebrated icon. Thus, when the chancellor of the University of Chicago was asked to compile a list of the ten greatest people of his time, he placed Gandhi at the top of his rankings, describing him as "the man who most represents Christ in the last 2,000 years." *Life* magazine declared that with Gandhi's death, the world had "lost its greatest apostle of peace and the brotherhood of man." *The Christian Century* was equally laudatory: according to one of its unsigned editorials, "Gandhi was the greatest man" of the twentieth century, surpassing even the likes of Roosevelt, Churchill, and Woodrow Wilson.[1]

What is clear in the adulation of Gandhi is that for the first time in the nation's history, masses of Americans came to regard a contemporary figure who was non-Western and non-Christian as a towering moral authority. How then did this wizened brown man of the East attain such

---

[1] "India Loses Her Greatest Soul," *Life* (February 9, 1948), pp. 27–31; "Gandhi Belongs to Tomorrow," *The Christian Century* (February 18, 1948), pp. 201–2; Also see Bishop G. Bromely Oxnam, "Saint as Reformer," *Saturday Review of Literature* (January 7, 1950).

FIGURE 6.1. Mahatma Gandhi was one of the most admired figures of the postwar era. For many Americans, his asceticism was seen as a corrective for Western materialism. (Reproduced by permission of the Sophia Smith Collection, Smith College.)

prominence and approbation in the American mind? As this chapter will show, it was all part of a new emphasis on the self that, in the early Cold War years, became the preoccupation of leading thinkers on the American scene. Thus, in the fifteen years following World War II, R. D. Laing wrote *The Divided Self*, literary critic Lionel Trilling authored *The Opposing Self*, psychoanalyst Erich Fromm penned *Man For Himself*, and theologian Reinhold Niebuhr composed *The Self and the Dramas of History*. During this same period, *authenticity* became a popular buzzword thanks to the writings of existentialist philosophers and Gestalt therapists. Moreover, refugee scholar Erik Erikson coined the term *identity crisis*, while psychologists Abraham Maslow and Carl Rogers popularized the term *self-actualization*. It would be no exaggeration to state that, during the early Cold War years, issues pertaining to the self stood among the most important concerns of the day.

In order for values to liberalize to any appreciable extent, such a shift had to occur. As long as there was a dominant personality type that looked upon impulses with suspicion and hostility, who took seriously the notion of Original Sin, and who placed a greater value on self-mastery than self-expression, the very saliency of the Permissive Turn – the extent to which behavioral codes could loosen – would be severely limited. Although it might not have been immediately apparent at the time, social attitudes became less rigid during the middle decades of the twentieth century. In a very general sense, these changes were attributable to several separate developments, all of which touch directly on modern notions of the self. They were: a rejection of the belief in the innate depravity of mankind, the celebration of spontaneity, and a pronounced turn toward self-awareness. While seemingly disconnected, these three developments effectively eroded and gave rise – on an unprecedented scale – to a more secularized notion of the individual.

The Decline and Fall of Original Sin

In the fifteen years following World War II, Americans increasingly saw human nature as intrinsically good. According to this more modern perspective, those qualities that emanated from the self – specifically, one's inner drives and spontaneous impulses – were typically to be embraced, whereas those qualities that constrained one's inner drives were to be discarded as unnecessary obstructions. The Permissive Turn, therefore, not only pertained to the loosening of behavioral codes but, on a deeper level still, involved a particular evaluation of the human personality – one that rejected, either in its overtly religious form or in its secularized variant – the very notion of Original Sin.

The Reverend William Andrew, writing in the late 1940s, captured this attitude well. "Each child," he insisted, "has his own rhythms about all physiological tensions and needs, such as eating, sleeping, elimination, sex. These biological rhythms are God-given, normal, and necessary to healthy productive lives... They are not a source of danger and anti-social behavior, unless they are treated with shame, disgust, or hostility." Elsewhere in the article, Andrew blasted those who "believe more in the child's original sin than in his original virtue." He went on to insist that what taints the innocence and inner beauty of a child is the "attitude of the parent, who can only see defilement in the child's body and in his innate desires."[2]

Best-selling author Harry Overstreet, a philosophy professor at the City College of New York, echoed these sentiments. In *The Mature Mind* (1949), Overstreet challenged traditional Christian teachings concerning man's fall. As he explained, the venerated St. Augustine of Hippo, the man most responsible for the formulation of the doctrine of Original Sin, "denied to our species the healthy blessing of self-respect." Overstreet argued that the Augustinian vision of Christianity, with its heavy emphasis on human depravity, essentially declared man "to be basically impotent to work out his psychological salvation. Instead of encouraging him to develop all of the characteristically human powers within him, and so overcome inner contradictions and outer obstacles, it encouraged him to distrust himself and malign himself... In short, it encouraged the individual to remain a dependent child."[3] The response to Overstreet's book was enthusiastic. Positive reviews flowed from the *Library Journal*, *Kirkus Reviews*, *The Saturday Evening Post*, *The Christian Century*, and *The New York Times*. In 1950, *The Mature Mind* reigned at the top of *The New York Times* nonfiction best-seller list for sixteen consecutive weeks and posted Book-of-the-Month Club sales of 247,000.[4]

This cultural rejection of Original Sin – reflected in the writings of Andrews and Overstreet – corresponds perfectly with the most widely read parenting advice of the postwar period. As we saw in Chapter 2, Spock's child-rearing philosophy placed a great deal of weight on the instinctual nature of children. Naturally, such an emphasis countenanced permissiveness on the part of mothers and fathers because there was little need to ride herd over a child's impulses and urges if such inclinations were generally positive. On a deeper level, however, Spock's glorification of human instinct was actually a glorification of human nature. "Your baby is born to be a reasonable, friendly human being," declared Spock. "If you treat him nicely, he won't take advantage of you." Elsewhere in *The Common Sense Book*, Spock insisted that the child's "desire to get along with other people happily and considerately develops within him as part of the unfolding of his nature, provided he grows up with loving, self-respecting parents."

[2] Andrew, William R. "Studies in the Foundations of Character," *Journal of Clinical Pastoral Work* (Winter 1947), pp. 4–5.
[3] Overstreet, Harry. *The Mature Mind* (New York: W. W. Norton & Company, 1949) pp. 261, 263.
[4] Hackett, Alice Payne. *70 Years of Best-Sellers* (New York: R. R. Bowker Company, 1967).

The bristling optimism of *The Common Sense Book* has not escaped scholarly scrutiny. Social historian Michael Zuckerman found its buoyant tone to be more than a trifle problematic. "The success of a book based on premises such as these is more than a little puzzling," he remarked. "Ascetic civilizations do not display such acceptance of instinct. Competitive cultures do not so eagerly embrace a conception of human nature so amiable and mild. And yet Benjamin Spock breaks precisely with that dominant tradition in America which has considered children as scaled-down savages."[5]

In a similar vein, psychologist Carl Rogers, whose notion of the "actualizing tendency" is premised on a positive evaluation of the individual's innate capacity, was openly disdainful toward the doctrine of Original Sin. Traditional Christianity, he stated in 1952, "has permeated our culture with the concept that man is basically sinful, and only by something approaching a miracle can his sinful nature be negated."[6] Such a doctrine, he continued, is fundamentally wrong because at "the innermost core of man's nature, the deepest layers of his personality, the base of his 'animal nature,' is positive in nature – is basically socialized, forward-looking, rational, and realistic."[7]

Given his glowing assessment of the self, it naturally follows that Rogers regarded impulses as generally positive and, at the worst, innocuous. Human consciousness, he declared, "instead of being the watchman over a dangerous and unpredictable lot of impulses," becomes instead the "comfortable inhabitant of a richly varied society of impulses" that are "self-governing" and therefore do not need to be "fearfully guarded."[8]

Not surprisingly, the pastoral counseling movement, over which the figure of Carl Rogers loomed very large, was eager to discredit any such lingering belief in the innate depravity of human beings. This softening of traditional Christian doctrine was on full display in 1953 at the fourth National Conference on Clinical Pastoral Education. There, an especially revealing conversation occurred among a handful of prominent ministers. Responding to a paper delivered by Ernest Bruder, the Reverend J. L. Cedarleaf stated that "theology should be a defense but a

5 Zuckerman, Michael. "Dr. Spock: The Confidence Man," in Rosenberg, Charles E. (ed.), *The Family in History* (Philadelphia: University of Pennsylvania Press, 1975), p. 186.
6 Rogers, Carl. *On Becoming a Person: A Therapist's View of Psychotherapy.* (London: Constable, 1960).
7 Maslow, Abraham H. "Our Maligned Animal Nature," *Journal of Psychology* 28 (1949), p. 277.
8 Rogers, *On Becoming a Person*, p. 119.

defense of warmth and flexibility which leads to God as a kind, loving father with an authority of understanding, not authoritarianism." Such a framework, he continued, "needs to be flexible and characterized by love. While we have a rational bent and need to make theology explicit, we need to correct it by a recognition of psychodynamics and the need to love."[9]

In addition to betraying a deeply rooted hostility toward authoritarianism, Cedarleaf's position, which the majority of his colleagues apparently shared, seemed to equate theology with the foremost values of psychotherapy. Accordingly, God was characterized less by his divine judgment than by his "warmth," "kindness," "understanding," "flexibility," and "love." What one is left with ultimately is not the wrathful God of a Jonathan Edwards, but a deified version of Barney the Purple Dinosaur. Needless to say, Cedarleaf's conception of God leaves little room for a doctrine that insists on the innate depravity of man.

To the question of whether Rogerian methods were sufficiently "Christian," the Reverend Dugald Arbucle, a member of the pastoral counseling movement, was surprisingly frank. It all rested, he explained, on one's conception of God in relation to man. "If one has an avenging God of wrath, or looks upon man as an inferior creature to condemn or forgive, he will not agree with client-centered therapy. But if he has a God of understanding love and is willing to accept man as he is with potentiality to grow, he will find client-centered therapy congenial."[10]

In articulating the superiority of the uncivilized self over the more inhibited religious vision characteristic of Calvinism, the most emphatic statement came not from J. L. Cedarleaf or even from Carl Rogers. Instead, it came from Rogers' friend and collaborator Abraham Maslow. "I can report empirically," asserted Maslow in a 1949 article, "the healthiest persons in our culture . . . are most (not least) pagan, most (not least) 'instinctive,' most (not least) accepting of their animal nature." Maslow was thus providing a not-so-subtle critique of deliberativeness, sexual restraint, and self-discipline. In other words, the struggle between Original Sin and what Andrews, Maslow, Rogers, and Cedarleaf might have called *original virtue* was a battle that pitted an ethic of self-control against an ethic of self-expression.[11]

---

[9] Hall, Charles E. *Head and Heart: The Story of the Clinical Pastoral Education Movement* (Decatur, Georgia: Journal of Pastoral Care Publications, 1992), p. 92.

[10] Arbucle, Dugald. "Therapy Is For All: Client-Centered Therapy Is Christian," *The Journal of Pastoral Care*, Vol 5, No. 4 (1952), p. 34.

[11] The author would like to thank historian David Ciepley for pointing out this distinction.

Indicative of this milder, more optimistic view of the divine was the emergence, in the 1950s, of a more approachable creator – a deity who was not to be feared like the God of Abraham, but to be loved and revered for his approachability. The middecade hit, "Have You Talked to the Man Upstairs," and other popular jukebox songs like "The Lord is a Mighty Big Man," Perry Como's "Somebody Up There Likes Me," and Elvis Presley's "Big Man in the Sky" were expressions of this new sentiment – a mood that conceived of God as something akin to a celestial buddy.[12] Perhaps most telling was a 1950s' magazine piece that focused on the faith of Hollywood celebrities. In the article, actress Jane Russell was emphatic in affirming her love of God. "And when you get to Him," she exclaimed, "you'll find He's a livin' doll!"[13]

Naturally, there were those in the 1950s who reacted harshly to the culture's humanizing of God and deemphasis of sin. However, here too we see the diminishing salience of a traditional Christian vision. In the America of the 1950s, the foremost proponent of a perspective that stressed the sinfulness of man's nature belonged to the theologian Reinhold Niebuhr. Through the many books and articles he authored, Niebuhr exercised a great influence on a long list of public figures including Adlai Stevenson, Lewis Mumford, Will Herberg, Martin Luther King, Jr., Perry Miller, Hans Morganthau, James Reston, and Arthur M. Schlesinger, Jr.

While Niebuhr was quick to underscore the limitations of individuals, his exploration of man's sinful nature was decidedly less gloomy than the theology of most Christian conservatives. With his great penchant for ambiguity and paradox, what Niebuhr took with one hand he partially gave back with the other. Thus, while highlighting the universality of sin, Niebuhr sought to temper this bleak portrait with the countervailing doctrine of "original righteousness" – the belief that notwithstanding the ravages of sin, a spark of the divine resided at the core of each and every person. According to Niebuhr, man's "true essence" – the original good he possessed before the Fall – was not entirely forfeit. "Sin," he wrote, "is a corruption of man's true essence but not its destruction."[14]

A similarly nuanced position could be seen in Niebuhr's assessment of John Calvin, one of the leading figures of the Reformation. In his theological writings, Calvin maintained that in the aftermath of the Fall,

---

[12] Cornell, George W. "Religious Song Appeal," *The Kerrville Times* (Kerrville County, Texas) (March 31, 1957), p. 1.

[13] "New Cults, Strange Gods," *The Letherbridge Herald* (October 2, 1959), p. 4.

[14] Niebuhr, Reinhold. *The Nature and Destiny of Man: Volume 1: Human Nature* (New York: Charles Scribner's Sons, 1941), p. 269.

the world had become engulfed in sin. As a result, the things of this world – its pleasures and indulgences – were inherently evil. As we noted in the second chapter, one magazine targeting Seventh-Day Adventist teenagers sought to convey the complete depravity of this fallen, earthly realm. "The pleasures of this world," it warned, "has Satan in every corner."[15] According to this Calvinist-tainted perspective, sin was so pervasive that it corrupted everything around us. Reinhold Niebuhr, by contrast, had an assessment of the world that was far more optimistic than Calvin. Just as the Fall had "corrupted" but not "destroyed" man's original righteousness, Niebuhr believed that the Fall had not transformed the world into an entirely depraved and evil realm. Put simply, in the theology of Niebuhr, the world was not all good, but neither was it irredeemably bad.

A final example of the way Niebuhr's thinking diverged from traditional Christian theologians involved his evaluation of sin. In Niebuhr's mind the greatest threat to the soul of man was his vaunted sense of pride, a quality he believed arose from the anxiety humans felt as "finite" beings who, as a result of their freedom and reason, were still capable of grasping the infinite. However, with Reinhold Niebuhr, and his inclination toward irony, few things were either "black" or "white." While warning against the spiritual dangers that sprang from human anxiety, Niebuhr was also quick to underscore the admirable human qualities – such as invention and creativity – which arose from this same state of anxiety. Man's anxiety, Niebuhr explained, was both "the source of creativity and a temptation to sin."[16] Elsewhere, in his famous analysis of the Tower of Babel, Niebuhr wrote of "the inevitable and inescapable pride involved in every human enterprise, even in the highest most perfect or, more correctly, particularly in the highest and noblest human enterprise."[17] Hence, man's natural state of anxiety – the source of pride and creativity – was not to be regarded as either all good or all bad but, rather, as an amalgam of both elements.

Compared to the orthodox Christian perspective, the theology of Niebuhr was more nuanced and less gloomy in three important ways: first, owing to his belief in original righteousness, Niebuhr believed man was less depraved than those holding to a traditional Christian outlook;

---

[15] Fonn, Bel. "Dancing Feet," *The Youth's Instructor* (May 22, 1956), p. 14.

[16] Niebuhr, *The Nature and Destiny of Man*, p. 183.

[17] Rasmussen, Larry, (ed.), *Reinhold Niebuhr: Theologian of Public Life* (Minneapolis: Fortress Press, 1991), pp. 83, 86.

second, due to his rejection of Calvinism, and its renunciation of the things of this world, Niebuhr believed sin was less pervasive than those in the conservative Protestant tradition; and, third, because he believed man's inevitable state of anxiety was not only the source of sin but also the seedbed of human greatness, he had a less condemnatory stance toward the innate qualities of human beings than those subscribing to the traditional Christian position. That Reinhold Niebuhr, widely recognized during the fifties as the nation's leading advocate for reemphasizing human depravity, had so significantly softened the orthodox Christian perspective on the issue of sin, testifies to the great length Calvinism had receded in postwar American thought.

In concert, the general deemphasis of Original Sin, Spock's favorable treatment of human instinct, and the actualizing tendency of Carl Rogers all reflected the postwar ascendancy of the self. In formulating a client-centered approach to counseling, the humanistic school of psychology not only altered the relationship between doctor and client, but as the source of the "actualizing tendency," the self was elevated in status. In advising mothers and fathers to place more faith in the instinctual nature of their children, child-rearing experts not only encouraged greater permissiveness, but they also promoted a more benevolent assessment of human nature. And in altering the general depiction of God from a wrathful father to a God of understanding love, the proponents of pastoral counseling not only succeeded in altering the image of God, but the status of man and the moral status of the self also changed.

Yet how do we know these changes were culturally resonant? How can we be sure that this more positive evaluation of the self was a widespread phenomenon that affected more than a tiny elite? The answer lies in sociological studies (with respect to permissive parenting), survey data, and explosive market demand (with respect to the democratization of psychology), and climbing rates of both single motherhood and premarital pregnancies (with respect to sexual behavior). That greater numbers of Americans were willing to defy prevailing norms as they related to religion, sex, and even child rearing suggests that what was at play during the 1950s went well beyond a small cadre of intellectual elites, and instead involved the values of tens of millions of people. At the center of midcentury American culture stood the Permissive Turn, and at the heart of the Permissive Turn was not just a relaxation of traditional constraints, but of even greater significance, there stood a new, decidedly more positive vision of the self.

The Celebration of Spontaneity

While the rejection of original sin signified a step away from the pessimistic evaluation of man that had long been part of a Calvinist worldview, it also led to the affirmation of the uninhibited self within the wider culture. As one readily gleans from a survey of the arts, there was indeed a new valuation placed on spontaneity during the Cold War years as Americans no longer sought to control and confine their inner urges, but instead looked to them as the true source of artistic inspiration. In painting, this celebration of natural feelings and impulsiveness could be seen in the works of such abstract expressionist painters as Robert Motherwell and Jackson Pollock. At the heart of these artistic innovations was an improvisational style that, as cultural historian Daniel Belgrad put it, "privileges the unpremeditated act."[18] Instead of scripting one's work in advance through a dispassionate, deliberative process, artists sought to look inward and, in a spontaneous moment, tap into the vast resources of their subjective subconscious in a creative act of improvisation. "At the time of making a picture," recalled the artist Hans Hoffman, "I want not to know what I'm doing; a picture should be made with feeling, not knowing." Robert Motherwell was even more explicit, claiming his art resulted from a "quickened state of subjectivity – freedom from conscious notions."

However, the most compelling illustration of the central role spontaneity played with abstract expressionists were to be found not in words but rather in the physical actions of Jackson Pollock. As he perfected his famous "drip" technique, Pollock stood at the very middle of the canvas, a cigarette dangling from his mouth, and with the help of a brush or stick he dripped, flung, smeared, or splattered paint all around him. This exercise more closely resembled an extemporaneous dance performance than a carefully planned drawing. By his own admission, Pollock sought to represent his art to others as the product of improvisation. "When I'm in my painting," relayed Pollock to a reporter from *Life* magazine, "I'm not aware of what I'm doing." The end result was a picture that instead of being representational of the outside world, seemed to reflect the inner world of the artist himself. As Pollock recalled in a 1950 interview, "There was a reviewer who wrote that my pictures didn't have any

[18] Belgrad, Daniel. *The Culture of Spontaneity: Improvisation and the Arts in Postwar America* (Chicago: The University of Chicago Press, 1998).

FIGURE 6.2. Jackson Pollock working on a large canvas as his wife looks on. The spontaneity of his technique established him as one of the leading artists of his era. (Reproduced by permission of the Pollock-Krasner House and Study Center, Stony Brook University, State University of New York.)

beginning or end. He didn't mean it as a compliment, but it was. It was a fine compliment."[19]

In a manner analogous to abstract expressionism, bebop music personified the aesthetic of spontaneity. A reaction against the tight structure and regimentation of the large swing bands, bebop burst onto the jazz scene in the immediate postwar years. As a rebellion against calcified jazz conventions, bebop brought forth in the musician an unprecedented level of inventiveness. Instead of forcing an adherence to a carefully formulated script, no two songs sounded the same as musicians were encouraged to improvise. Initially, some older jazz musicians expressed skepticism, believing bebop's emphasis on spontaneity was excessive and would lead to an absence of musical structure. Louis Armstrong, a proponent of this view, disparagingly referred to bebop as "Chinese music."[20] Yet in

[19] "Jackson Pollock: Is He the Greatest Living Painter in the United States?," *Life* (August 8, 1949), p. 45.
[20] Freedman, Samuel G. "A Jazzman's Fountain of Youth," *The New York Times* (October 8, 1989), Section 2, page 23.

spite of its many critics, bebop quickly developed an enthusiastic following among jazz aficionados. By the latter half of the 1940s, bebop had
emerged as an important musical form, featured in such prestigious New
York nightspots as the Onyx Club and the Three Deuces. Dizzy Gillespie's
"New 52nd Street Jazz," the first bebop recording by a major recording
company, became the top-selling jazz album of 1946.[21]

Among the pioneers of bebop were trumpeter Dizzy Gillespie, bassist
Oscar Pettiford, drummer Max Roach, and pianists Bud Powell and
Thelonious Monk. Unquestionably, bebop's greatest figure was the legendary alto saxophone player Charlie "Bird" Parker. Saxophonist Sonny
Criss recalled the only musical maxim ever given to him by Parker: "Don't
think. Quit thinking," he advised during a 1947 performance.[22] Miles
Davis, who in his youth played with Parker, was especially impressed
with the latter's uncanny improvisational style. "He didn't conform to
the Western ways of musical group interplay by organizing everything,"
recalled Davis. "Bird was a great improviser and that's where he thought
great music came from and what great musicians were about . . . just the
opposite of the Western concept of notated music."

Beatnik writers Jack Kerouac and Allen Ginsberg were so entranced
by bebop that they fashioned a new literary style – what they called *beat
poetry* – in a direct imitation of improvisational jazz. Adopting Charlie
Parker as their hero, beatnik writers attempted to capture the spontaneity
and raw energy of bebop. In the briefest of terms, the basic idea was to get
the writer in a cognitive state where his words would flow freely, with as
little deliberation as possible. As Kerouac advised in his essay "Elements
of Spontaneous Prose," the writer should avoid being overly deliberative
at all costs. The ultimate objective of the author, poet, or essayist is to
"write 'without consciousness'" in a "semi-trance" state allowing the
subconscious to pronounce "what conscious art would censor."[23] For
Kerouac and his contemporaries, the use of amphetamines and alcohol
were frequent aids used to achieve such a state of mind.

None of this is to suggest that beat poetry, abstract expressionism,
and bebop were devoid of any forethought. In each case, improvisation
occurred within more structured and formalized parameters. Nor is this
to deny that earlier genres of art were devoid of improvisation. However,

---

[21] Stump, Roger W. "Place and Innovation in Popular Music: The Bebop Revolution in
Jazz," *Journal of Cultural Geography*, Vol. 18 (Fall/Winter 2000).

[22] Belgrad, *The Culture of Spontaneity*, p. 184.

[23] Kerouac, Jack. "Elements of Spontaneous Prose," *Evergreen Review* (Summer 1958),
p. 72.

FIGURE 6.3. Charlie Parker (right), preeminent practitioner of bebop, on sax jamming with Miles Davis (left) and drummer Roy Haynes, circa 1947–8. (Reproduced by permission of The Institute of Jazz Studies, Rutgers University.)

with an aesthetic of spontaneity there was a deliberate cultivation of the spontaneous self, enabling improvisation and impulse to play the defining role in the creative process. The assortment of artists who valorized spontaneity believed that at his vital center, the self was the font of creativity and insight – a kind of actualizing tendency for the artistically inclined.

Spontaneity in Mental Health

It would be a mistake to dismiss the celebration of spontaneity as an oppositional impulse primarily confined to artists. As a broad cultural phenomenon reflecting the spirit of the times, the postwar embrace of improvisation went beyond the avant-garde. In psychology itself – arguably the most influential of the social science disciplines – spontaneity became widely celebrated. Time after time, psychologists equated spontaneity with mental health, in effect arguing that cultural practices could usually be judged positively if they facilitated spontaneity, and assessed negatively if they thwarted its full expression.

In his article "The Great American Neurosis," for example, John Gustin complained that the nation's "obsessional character structure" led to a "lack of spontaneity" and freedom.[24] Another 1950s study of child-rearing practices concluded that permissive parenting was superior to the more traditional approach characterized by strict discipline. Although finding little difference in self-control or happiness, the study concluded that permissive homes fostered "less inner hostility and more friendliness, and higher levels of spontaneity and originality."[25] It would appear that both studies took for granted the belief that higher levels of spontaneity was a natural good.

Of all the mental health experts, psychiatrist Harold H. Anderson was probably the least constrained in his celebration of spontaneity. "The aim of psychotherapy," asserted Anderson, "is to increase the child's spontaneity and his harmony with others." In another article, Anderson defined *domination* – a condition mental health experts roundly detested – as "behavior that attacks the spontaneity of another."[26]

In all likelihood, the majority of mental health experts did not regard spontaneity as a virtue in itself, but they did see it as an outward sign of well-being. Because Americans at midcentury were coming to view the self as a boundless reservoir of inherent goodness and potentiality, the spontaneous person could be seen as someone who was in touch with his so-called "true" self. Accordingly, it was not necessary for such an individual to pause and reflect before continuing his behavior. Thus, even before the 1950s and prior to the dawn of the twentieth century, the leading literary figures who comprised the movement in Romanticism revered spontaneity. As Ralph Waldo Emerson proclaimed, "The vision of genius comes by renouncing the too officious activity of the understanding and giving leave and the amplest privilege to the spontaneous sentiment."[27] Elsewhere, in "Self-Reliance," perhaps his most famous essay, Emerson insisted that his inquiry "leads us to that

[24] Gustin, John C. "The Great American Neurosis," *Psychoanalysis* I (1952), pp. 48–61.

[25] Watson, Goodwin. "Some Personality Differences in Children Related to Strict or Permissive Parental Discipline," *Journal of Psychology* 44 (1957), pp. 227–49. The study was based on questionnaires sent to some seventy-eight homes.

[26] Anderson, Harold H. "Socially Integrative Behavior," *Journal of Abnormal & Social Psychology* 41 (1946), pp. 379–84; and Anderson, H. H. "Studies in Dominative and Socially Integrative Behavior," *American Journal of Orthopsychiatry* 15 (1945), pp. 133–9.

[27] Emerson, Ralph Waldo. "Literary Ethics: An Oration Delivered Before the Literary Societies, Dartmouth College," (July 24, 1838).

source, at once the essence of genius, the essence of virtue, the essence of life, which we call Spontaneity or Instinct."

In the mind of Emerson, and virtually all of the Romantics, spontaneity was not necessarily irrational, but it was opposed to cool and measured deliberation – that which Freud called the "procrastinating factor of thought."[28] Psychologist Abraham Maslow was particularly insightful in describing the relationship between spontaneity and cool reason. "Pure spontaneity," he wrote, "consists of free, uninhibited expression of the self, i.e., of the psychiatric forces with minimal interference by consciousness. Control, will, caution, self-criticism, measure, deliberativeness, are the breaks upon this."[29] Needless to say, Maslow and the entire school of humanistic psychology revered spontaneity because being autonomous and self-actualized meant possessing the ability to act naturally, without regard to stifling social conventions, or having to rely on self-censorship.

In an earlier time, when Calvinism enjoyed a stronger hold over the American mind, the virtuous, upstanding citizen would have been equated with the stoical qualities of self-mastery and self-control. Being a healthy, mature person meant being able to put away childish things, and although seen as refreshing and vibrant, spontaneity – like the stereotypical image of African Americans – had the connotation of being impulsive and juvenile. However, in the postwar era, when people increasingly regarded the self as a wellspring of creativity and goodness, spontaneity leapt forward and the old attributes of "self-command" and "self-mastery" slipped imperceptibly into the shadows.

The Inward Turn

While the rejection of Original Sin led to the enthusiastic acceptance of instinct and urge in the cultural realm, it also pointed toward a new focus on self-awareness and introspection in the realm of the personal. Here, the faint echoes of Romanticism are audible once again. Yet rather than being a primary cause, this inward focus was a secondary effect. It was, as it were, a mere "pit stop" on a journey of self-discovery. Preceding the turn inward was the rejection of external standards. In concrete terms, this meant that the truths derived from tradition, scripture, natural law,

[28] Quote cited from Grana, Cesar. *Bohemian versus Bourgeois: French Society and the French Man of Letters in the Nineteenth Century* (New York: Basic Books, 1964), p. 185.
[29] Maslow, Abraham H. *Toward a Psychology of Being* (New York: Van Nostrand Reinhold, 1962), p. 107.

or some other source of authority external to ourselves were deemed to be simplistic, artificial, and fundamentally misguided. So instead of looking outward to the objective world to find truth and meaning, the individual was encouraged to turn inward.

At a psychology conference in Cincinnati during fall 1959, Abraham Maslow sought to explain this process. In his penetrating remarks, Maslow spoke of the "total collapse of all sources of values outside the individual." He then went on to argue that with the demise of authority, and the realization that neither economic prosperity nor political democracy is able to provide life with value and meaning, "there is no place else to turn but inward, to the self, as the locus of values."[30]

An equally powerful articulation of these sentiments was penned by Carl Rogers during the early 1950s. In his description of self-actualized people – or, as he put it, "the person who is living the process of the good life" – Rogers found that such individuals did not depend on the judgment of others or their past behavior, nor did they "rely upon guiding principles." Instead, Rogers noticed that there was a strong tendency on the part of the self-actualized to look within. "I find that increasingly such individuals are able to trust their total organismic reaction to a new situation because they discover to an ever-increasing degree that if they are open to their experience, doing what 'feels right' proves to be a competent and trustworthy guide to behavior which is truly satisfying."[31]

The horrors of World War II, the anxieties of the Cold War, and the growing disillusionment with the increasingly materialistic and bureaucratic nature of modern society convinced many that the answers to life's big questions could only be found by turning inward. Truth, in other words, resides in the soul, and cannot be accessed through sacred texts, Sunday school, or an amorphous set of norms commonly known as "the American Way." As for science, it enjoyed an unprecedented level of prestige during the 1950s, but the prevailing belief at the time was that although science was capable of answering questions of fact, it had little to impart about meaning or truth. Sociologist Leonard Krieger was able to describe this new stance toward truth and authority in a very compelling way, one that helps explain an increasing skepticism toward objective truth, as well as the rise of a Rogerian approach among mental health counselors. The "loss of belief in any valid authority between

[30] Maslow, Abraham H. "Existential Psychology: What's In It For Us," in May, Rollo (ed.), *Existential Psychology* (New York: Random House, 1960), pp. 50–1.
[31] Rogers, *On Becoming a Person*, p. 189.

individuals," wrote Krieger in *Ideas and Events*, "is being compensated by a growing belief of a valid authority among the drives within individuals."[32]

American literature reflected this trend and grew more introspective after the war. Between 1945 and 1960, the first-person narrative quickly became the default setting for leading novelists. During the interwar years, the novel had looked very different. While there were occasional experimentations with the use of first-person narration, virtually all of the great writers at the time – Hemingway, Faulkner, Hurston, Thomas Wolfe, Pearl Buck, Sinclair Lewis, and so on – wrote in the customary third person. In the aftermath of the war, however, the American novel changed. The list of authors adopting the first-person narrative during the forties and fifties reads like a who's who of American literature and comprises such luminaries as Norman Mailer, Ralph Ellison, Philip Roth, Gore Vidal, John Updike, Robert Heinlein, Jack Kerouac, Raymond Chandler, and Saul Bellow.[33] In an age of introspection, the first-person narrative seemed to go hand in hand with the primacy of subjective experience.

However, the most compelling sign of an enhanced self-awareness was to be found in the religious critique of authoritarianism. Due to the World War II experience, Americans sought to define themselves against the stereotypical image of the submissive, obedient German. As a result, the culture soon came to assign a greater importance to the principles of democracy, diversity, and individual autonomy. Within the realm of religion, this critique of authority gave momentum to other secularizing forces that were afoot at midcentury.

For many liberal Protestants, guilt and the authoritarian impulse were related concerns in that the former helped produce the latter. As the line of reasoning went, an individual's misplaced feelings of guilt and self-loathing led him to become excessively submissive in his religious, political, and social life. The Reverend Ernest Bruder, a prominent figure in the pastoral care movement, subscribed to this line of thinking. In 1954, in a scathing review of Monsignor Fulton Sheen's *Peace of Soul*, Bruder pilloried the conservative priest for advocating an approach to religion that was too rigid and unforgiving. According to Bruder, "It could well

[32] Krieger, Leonard. *Ideas and Events: Professing History* (Chicago: The University of Chicago Press, 1992), p. 51.
[33] Schaub, Thomas Hill. *American Fiction in the Cold War* (Madison, Wisconsin: The University of Wisconsin Press, 1991). Also see Dickstein, Morris. *Leopards in the Temple: The Transformation of American Fiction, 1945–1970* (Cambridge, Mass.: Harvard University Press, 2002).

be said that the author gives one the impression that 'peace of soul' is that state in which the individual has been able to accept the arbitrary thinking and dictates of others." The result, Bruder continued, "may not necessarily be 'peace' but rather an unhealthy resignation to authority. This attitude would glorify and perpetuate individual immaturity, as well as enhance dependence upon some external group, and as such would be seriously suspect, and highly unacceptable, to all who seek to strengthen individual freedom and responsibility."[34]

To Bruder and many other clerics, the culprit in the perpetuation of a submissive stance in spiritual matters was not so much religious leaders as it was religious doctrine. Instead of encouraging people to consult their own consciences, they argued, antiquated edicts and outdated prohibitions caused parishioners to look to codified rules – or to ministers who themselves relied on these rules – to direct their moral decision-making. According to Bruder and his compatriots, the problem with this approach was that it lacked faith in the ability of the individual to look inward and discover for himself the correct moral path. Hence, in the twenty years after World War II, many mainline Protestants attempted to curb what they saw as the authoritarian proclivities of traditional religious practices. Rather than relying on the Law – that is, external principles encapsulated in scripture or philosophy – these opponents of legalism called on Christians to look inward and, with the help of the Holy Spirit, discern the divine handwriting that exists within every person. As Robert Gleason put it, "The distinctive claim in this new school of ethics is that it aims at placing man, in the uniqueness of the given moment, before God his Father in an I–Thou relationship of love. Given that relationship the decision that is proper in the unique set of circumstances should inevitably follow for the sincere Christian, guided as he is by an Inner Light."[35]

By the time Eisenhower became president, theologians ranging from Paul Tillich and H. Richard Niebuhr to Paul Lehmann and Joseph Fletcher were imploring Americans to develop a nonauthoritarian moral code by looking inward and submitting to God's love. They did this not to advance some version of moral relativism, but rather to challenge the legitimacy of natural law and the universality of moral principles. "Legalism in the sense of legal formalism can become, like certain types of logic, a

---

[34] Bruder, Ernest E. "Reviews and Abstracts," *Journal of Clinical Pastoral Work* (Autumn 1949), p. 164.

[35] Gleason, Robert W. "Situational Morality," *Thought* Vol. XXXII (Winter, 1957–8), p. 90.

kind of play with pure forms, consistent in itself, detached from life,"
wrote Paul Tillich. "If applied to life, this play can turn into a destructive
reality...from our point of view, legal formalism and totalitarian sup-
pression are intimately related." In other writings, Tillich expounded on
the idea of a "transmoral conscience," a faculty capable of superseding
or transcending all moral laws.[36] Years later, in what proved to be his
last writing, Tillich restated this basic position, but in a more accessible
way:

> Let us suppose that a student comes to me faced with a difficult moral decision.
> In counseling him I don't quote the Ten Commandments, or the words of Jesus
> in the Sermon on the Mount, or any humanistic ethics. Instead, I tell him to find
> out what the commandment of *agape* in his situation is, and then decide for it
> even if traditions and conventions stand against his decision.[37]

According to Tillich, Fletcher, and a whole battery of theologians who
railed against moral legalism, in the realm of ethics there was but one
absolute: the law of love. Dispensing with external rules, the one axiom
was to follow the commandment of *agape*, or the law of love.

Although the revolt against legalism gained steam throughout the
1950s, it had already established a firm foothold by the close of the 1940s.
In large part, this antilegalism was an expression of the antiauthoritarian
ethos of the period. "Most of the leading Protestant and Jewish theologians," observed *Pastoral Psychology* editor Seward Hiltner in 1950,
"are as antimoralistic or antilegalistic as any psychoanalyst."[38] Of course,
tensions between the rigid law and the more flexible conscience long predated World War II. However, reflecting the antiauthoritarian mood of
the early Cold War era, the efforts to undermine inflexible rules held
enormous currency among liberal Protestants. "By the 1950s," observed
the religious historian E. Brooks Holifield, "the mainline American theological schools were becoming outposts in a battle against 'absolute moral
laws.'"[39]

In religious circles during the 1950s, leading theologians began promoting *situation ethics* as an alternative to legalism. Relatively few

[36] Cooper, Terry D. *Paul Tillich and Psychology: Historic Explorations in Theology, Psychotherapy, and Ethics* (Georgia: Mercer University Press, 2006), pp. 165–6.
[37] Cited from Hiltner, Seward, and Southard, Samuel. "Paul Tillich and Pastoral Psychology," *Pastoral Psychology* Vol. 16 (December 1965).
[38] Hiltner, Seward. "Religion and Psychoanalysis," *Journal of Pastoral Care* 4 (1950),
p. 35.
[39] Holifield. A History of Pastoral Care in America, p. 279.

Americans, however, were familiar with the term until the following decade, when the Reverend Joseph Fletcher wrote a scathing critique of legalism in 1966. With the publication of *Situation Ethics: The New Morality*, Fletcher was catapulted to the first ranks of academic celebrity. Upwards of 150,000 copies of his book sold within the first two years. Articles about Fletcher appeared in *Playboy* and *Time*. And soon after the publication of *Situation Ethics*, at least three other books and innumerable articles were written in response to his argument. Today *situation ethics* is a commonly recognized term, but historically it was a product of the theological revolt against legalism that was unfolding during the 1950s.

The turn inward marked the apotheosis of the optimistic appraisal of the self. With the decline of the doctrine of Original Sin, the individual ceased to be seen as an inherently depraved being; what emerged in its place was a modern-day avatar of the fifth-century heresy of Pelagianism. Under this new rationale, the self was inclined to be neither good nor evil; it simply became what one made of it. However, the celebration of spontaneity went beyond this strict neutrality. Among artists and art enthusiasts who hailed improvisation, there was a belief – many times unarticulated – that the self was the source of creativity and artistic insight, and even if one were incapable of creating art, the telltale sign of the sensitivity of the soul was whether one was able to appreciate the product of an artist's spontaneity. With the turn inward, however, we see a wholly unprecedented level of optimism. In urging people to be inwardly focused, American proponents of existentialism, Eastern mysticism, Third Force psychology, and situation ethics presented the inner self as the gateway to truth. Like the Romantic movement in literature and art, the turn inward had profound epistemological implications because it held human intuition – not tradition or divine edicts, not natural law or instrumental reason – was the primary means through which truth could be discovered and meaning could be discerned. With the turn inward, millions felt obligated to – in the words of Norman Mailer – "set out on that unchartered journey into the rebellious imperatives of the self."[40]

It is essential that we see the abandonment of the doctrine of innate human depravity, the celebration of spontaneity, and the renewed emphasis on introspection not simply as related developments. They were also,

[40] Mailer, Norman. "The White Negro," *Dissent* (Spring 1957), pp. 276–93.

more importantly, progressive stages in an evolutionary process. Each step, beginning with the rejection of Original Sin and culminating with the turn inward, took the individual further away from the goal of self-mastery and closer to the Romantic ideal of being unrepressed and unencumbered.

The Reaction to the Rise of Science

In what may be the ultimate in irony, the turn inward to introspection and the resultant emphasis on intuition was driven in large measure by the exalted status of postwar science, the old enemy of things unseen and beliefs unconfirmed. In the 1950s, an age when science enjoyed an unprecedented level of prestige, Americans became increasingly inclined to the belief – indeed, by the close of the decade it had become cliché – that the greatest challenges facing man fell beyond the reach of science. Had not Nazi Germany, with its world-renowned physicists and its first-class team of engineers, been a scientifically advanced country? The argument was not that science was wicked or sinful; rather, it was limited and therefore incapable of speaking to life's biggest questions. Given these assumptions, it followed that an overreliance on instrumental reason not only neglected the spiritual dimension of man, but it also fostered an attitude of mind that impeded the ability of the individual to access the deeper and richer truths of life.

This brings us back to Gandhi, whose enormous prominence was illustrative of this growing weariness toward a calculating, dispassionate reason. Following his death in 1948, Gandhi joined the pantheon of heroes of American culture who were hailed by both mainline Protestants and religious conservatives. However, for most Americans during the fifties, a time when the consumer culture was ascending to ever-greater heights, the beatification of Gandhi was attributable less to what he had actually said or written than to what he had come to symbolize: an alternative to the calculating, repressive worldview that we generally associate with a Calvinist outlook. It is hard to see how a Gandhi – preaching an identical message of love and nonviolence, but clothed in a fashionable sports jacket, sporting a Swiss watch, and wearing the 1940's equivalent of a power tie – could have generated a comparable level of moral authority in the West.

On a deeper level, Gandhi, with his preference for the loincloth over the business suit, the wooden staff over the Malacca cane, and the makeshift sandal over the exquisitely crafted leather shoe, came to symbolize certain values that seemed imperiled by modern life. Where the West was scientifically driven, Gandhi was ascetically oriented; where modern man was "other-directed," Gandhi was introspective, urging his followers to "turn the searchlight within"; where Americans were avidly acquisitive, Gandhi was steadfastly antimaterialistic. However, as romantically unconventional as he may have appeared, Gandhi's otherness was not entirely alien to most Americans. In the celebrated tradition of saints, prophets, and especially Christ, Gandhi's embrace of simplicity seemed to reflect an otherworldliness, a profound appreciation for truths that exist beyond the reach of instrumental reason.[41]

During the 1930s and the first half of the 1940s, Gandhi had enjoyed a small but enthusiastic following in the United States. These admirers, for the most part, were Christian pacifists who, in addition to embracing the principles of nonviolence, had a withering critique of the increasingly depersonalized and materialistic nature of modern life. At conferences of religiously inspired pacifists held during fall 1944 and winter 1945, pacifists justified their call for political action by invoking the teachings of Christ and Gandhi. Moreover, they challenged the "prevailing materialism of our time," as well as "the erroneous notion" that "rational thought alone could comprehend the nature of reality."[42] In the aftermath of World War II, as the materialism of American society soared, the relevance of Gandhi's message grew exponentially. Accordingly, it was during this period when Gandhi became an enduring cultural icon.

This ambivalence toward instrumental reason and modern science – a stance that helps account for Gandhi's tremendous appeal in the West – was not advanced exclusively by religious figures or social conservatives. Instead, this was a mainstream view that allowed people, in a certain sense, to have their cake and eat it too. In other words, it enabled Americans to applaud science while simultaneously recognizing the limitations

[41] In 1949, in his review of Vincent Sheean's biography of Gandhi, critic Sterling North, who works for *The Washington Post*, seemed to raise this very point. "Those of us who continue to cherish elements of our scientific skepticism," he wrote, "are yet increasingly aware that materialism is not enough, and that the science which has given us the atom bomb and bacteriological warfare may eventually destroy the human race. Like Vincent Sheean, most of us are groping for some faith, some code of ethics which will reestablish human dignity. Maybe Gandhi offers the answer." See North, Sterling, "Sheean's Magnificent Testament," *The Washington Post* (July 31, 1949), p. B6.
[42] Danielson, Leilah. "It is a Day of Judgment: Peacemakers, Religion, and Radicalism in Cold War America," *Religion and American Culture: A Journal of Interpretation*. Vol. 18, No. 2 (Summer 2008), pp. 215–48.

of science. Nowhere was this viewpoint better expressed than by Hayward Keniston, a dean at the University of Michigan. "We have become so enthralled with the scientific way," he complained, "that we forget that there is another road to truth – the immediate experience of reality which we call intuition. This intuitive understanding is the only access we have to the deepest and highest aspects of our individual and collective lives. Truth, beauty, loyalty, courage, faith – these are the realities by which men live in the fullest sense; through them we come to the knowledge of good and evil."[43] It is worthy to note that in his call for an intuitive understanding of the nature of beauty and the knowledge of the good Keniston's outlook had a great deal of overlap with Joseph Fletcher and situation ethics.

Merle Tuve, one of the scientists who helped develop radar, was more laconic than Keniston, describing the content of higher education in the 1950s as "so much technology and so little self-knowledge."[44] Even Albert Einstein was quick to acknowledge the limitations of science and the greatness of Gandhi. Of the former, Einstein noted "objective knowledge provides us with the powerful instruments for the achievement of certain ends, but the ultimate goal itself and the longing to reach it must come from another source."[45] In addition, Einstein characterized Gandhi as "a role model for generations to come,"[46] and, in his earlier years, Einstein had actually written Gandhi a personal letter in which he expressed his desire to someday meet the Indian leader. Equally telling, at his residence in Princeton, New Jersey, Einstein displayed the pictures of four great men in his office – only one of them a nonscientist. They were Sir Isaac Newton, James Clerk Maxwell, Michael Faraday, and Mahatma Gandhi.[47]

Although it may not be readily apparent, the lionization of Gandhi reflected a more positive assessment of the individual. In elevating the humility that Gandhi personified, Americans were in effect declaring that instrumental reason had its limits, and as important as the latest scientific

---

[43] Keniston, Hayward. "The Humanities in a Scientific World," *The Annals of the American Academy of Political and Social Science* (January 1947), p. 161.

[44] "Stress on Esthetics in Colleges is Urged," *The New York Times* (December 31, 1949), p. 13.

[45] Einstein, Albert. *Out of My Later Years* (New York: Philosophical Library, 1950).

[46] Singh, Rama. "International Day of Non-Violence," *The Hamilton Spectator* (October 2, 2007). Online at: www.thespec.com/opinions/article/257744.

[47] Isaacson, Walter. *Einstein: His Life and Universe* (New York: Simon & Schuster, 2007), p. 438.

breakthrough may be, the perspective of people who look inward to their hearts for moral guidance provides us with the best hope for the future of humankind. Simply put, the quest for wisdom and self-knowledge, objectives that seemed all the more necessary by the heightened pace of scientific achievement, helps explain the culture's preoccupation with the self, and of Mahatma Gandhi, during the middle decades of the twentieth century.

Conclusion

One final factor that must be recognized if we are to understand the increased orientation to the self in modern times is the expansion of modern psychology – a cause so obvious as to be easily overlooked. As Harvard University psychiatrist Robert Coles has remarked in his survey of the field, psychology has come to connote "a concentration, persistent, if not feverish, upon one's thoughts, feelings, wishes, worries – bordering on, if not embracing, solipsism: the self as the only or main form of (existential) reality."[48] Although perhaps a little exaggerated, this observation does contain a kernel of truth. In highlighting the dangers of repression, Sigmund Freud and his followers encouraged people to interrogate their emotions, confront their deepest fears, scour their distant memories, and identify their hidden desires. Humanistic psychology, with its elevation of the actualizing tendency, went even further than Freudian analysis in its efforts to banish repression. Together, these two competing schools of psychology succeeded in creating a therapeutic ethos that established the sustained inward focus as a signature feature of modern life.

In summation, during the early Cold War years the decline of the doctrine of Original Sin, the valorization of spontaneity, the turn inward toward a heightened self-awareness, the reaction to the rise of science, and the growing influence of psychology were swirling about the culture with an unprecedented level of intensity. Each of these developments bespoke a more optimistic evaluation of the self – a belief that the resources innate to the individual are generally positive, creative, forward-looking, and constructive. They each also rejected, root and branch, the pessimism

---

[48] Bellah, Robert N. "The Quest for the Self: Individualism, Morality, Politics," in Capps, Donald, and Fenn, Richard K. (eds.), *Individualism Reconsidered: Readings On the Endangered Self in Modern Society* (Princeton: Princeton Theological Studies, 1992), p. 118. Coles, a child psychologist, is a member of the faculty at Harvard University.

one would normally associate with a Calvinist outlook. As a consequence, there emerged in postwar America a new "cast of mind," or sense of self, one that made reticence, restraint, guilt, and self-mastery – qualities we generally associate with a religiously conservative vision – increasingly difficult to maintain.

7

Denouement

The Normative Lag and the Role of Religion
in the Transformation of American Culture

The behavior that was hidden in the 1950s finally exploded into public view the following decade. By the end of the 1960s, Americans had few reservations about expressing their innermost beliefs. What the nation experienced was a classic instance of norms coming into line with values. Because norms and conventions are public by definition, they have received the most attention from scholars and journalists. Whether it is fidelity to one's spouse, opening the door for old ladies, or refusing to date one's first cousin, prevailing norms – that is, behavior that is socially expected and publicly respectable – are easily identifiable and thus not very difficult to write about. By contrast, private values and behavior – especially those at odds with prevailing norms – are often concealed from public view, and thus elude the grasp of rigorous inquiry. As a result of this academic bias, it is easy to conflate norms and values, or to believe that the liberalization of one entails the relaxation of the other.

In the field of sociology, one of the classic studies distinguishing between norms and values is Richard La Pierre's famous exploration of anti-Asian bigotry. During the early 1930s, La Pierre accompanied a Chinese couple as they journeyed throughout the American West. Over the course of two years and approximately ten thousand miles, the three traveled to 184 restaurants and 67 hotels. La Pierre found only one establishment that refused to accommodate its prospective Chinese guests.[1]

Six months after La Pierre returned from his Western odyssey, he dispatched a questionnaire to each of the establishments he and his Chinese friends had visited. To his astonishment, in response to the question "Will

[1] La Pierre, Richard T. "Attitudes vs. Actions," *Social Forces* (3), 1934, pp. 231–2.

you accept members of the Chinese race as guests?" 92 percent of restaurant and hotel managers answered no. "What I am trying to say," wrote La Pierre, "is that in only one out of 251 instances in which we purchased goods or services necessitating intimate human relationships did the fact that my companions were Chinese adversely affect us."[2]

What the La Pierre study illustrates is the sizable chasm that sometimes exists between social norms and personal values. Throughout much of the West in the 1930s, entrenched notions of white superiority carried with it a high level of anti-Chinese sentiment. Consequently, on the West Coast, a region with a centurylong familiarity with Asians, a proscriptive norm developed that withdrew hospitality from people of Japanese and Chinese descent. Despite these probable beliefs of Asian inferiority, many Westerners were simply unwilling to act in accordance with existing norms. In all likelihood, they would still have expressed their approval of these conventions to their neighbors. Yet when faced directly with the choice of either serving Chinese guests or turning them away, many of the people – in fact, more than 99 percent of the respondents – were willing to defy those same conventions. Had La Pierre confined his study solely to the verbal responses of restaurant and hotel managers, it would have revealed something about norms alone, but by expanding the scope of the study and examining human action, he discovered something very different about behavior and values.

As in La Pierre's study, norms and values in postwar America were not in perfect alignment, but what proved to be so unusual about the 1950s was that in certain cases norms and values moved in opposite directions. Under the pressures of the Cold War, the conservatism of some norms intensified. The anxieties of the time, buttressed by the need to distinguish Americans from godless communists abroad, led the public to the door of religion, which, in turn, caused more people than ever to attend church. Thus, in the 1950s we see the hyperpatriotic American Legion buying billboards on highways, exhorting passersby to go to church on Sundays, and similarly, the Advertising Council attempted to promote piety with the slogan "The family that prays together stays together."[3] Meanwhile, FBI Director J. Edgar Hoover – one of the country's foremost crusaders against the Red Menace – underscored the importance of religion in his message to young people: "The teenager today has drifted away from

---

[2] Ibid, pp. 233–4.
[3] Boyer, Paul. "The Chameleon with Nine Lives: American Religion in the Twentieth Century," in Sitkoff, Harvard (ed.), *Perspectives on Modern America: Making Sense of the Twentieth Century* (New York: Oxford University Press, 2001), p. 263.

the old-time religion. If our nation is to survive, the high school students must get back to the thing that our nation was founded on, the Bible."[4]

Postwar psychology followed this same pattern of seeming conservative in a normative sense, but actually being quite liberal on the level of values. As a number of scholars have pointed out, cultural conservatives used psychology to reinforce traditional gender roles during the 1940s and 1950s.[5] In magazines such as the *Saturday Review* and *Ladies Home Journal*, readers learned that women who placed career over family, or who sought to compete against men in the rough-and-tumble world of commerce, were psychologically deficient in important ways.[6] Similarly, during the postwar years, homosexuality became a growing concern among mental health professionals. In 1952, for example, the American Psychological Association (APA) described homosexuality as a "psychopathic personality disorder" and, throughout the middle decades of the twentieth century, many psychologists sought to cure patients of their sexual orientation.[7]

In contrast to the 1960s – with the founding of the *Journal of Humanistic Psychology*, the celebration of peak experiences, the popularity of group-encounter therapy, and the virtual explosion of consciousness-raising groups – psychology at midcentury appeared staid and conservative. For instance, in his classic work *The Cultural Contradictions of Capitalism*, Daniel Bell asserted that the decisive turn toward the therapeutic occurred not at midcentury, but during the 1960s.[8] Likewise, in *New Rules: Searching for Self-Fulfillment in a World Turned Upside Down*, Daniel Yankelovich argued that the preoccupation with self-fulfillment "started on the nation's campuses during the sixties but spread to the rest of the population in the seventies."[9] And, finally, in *The Culture of Narcissism*, Christopher Lasch attributes the rise of the "new narcissist"

---

[4] Bergler, Thomas. "Christian Youth Groups and Cultural Crisis in America, 1930–1965" (Doctoral dissertation, University of Notre Dame, 2002), p. 142.

[5] Zaretsky, Eli. "Charisma or Rationalization: Domesticity and Psychoanalysis in the United States in the 1950s," *Critical Review* (Winter 2000), pp. 328–54; Chafe, William H. *The American Woman: Her Changing Social, Economic, and Political Roles, 1920–1970* (New York: Oxford University Press, 1972), pp. 201–17.

[6] Buhle, Mari Jo. *Feminism and Its Discontents: A Century of Struggle with Psychoanalysis* (Cambridge: Harvard University Press, 1998), pp. 173–4, 194, 271. "By the 1940s," writes Buhle, "ego psychologists were leading a relentless assault on feminism quo careerism and managed to silence all but the most steadfast" (p. 271).

[7] Zaretsky, "Charisma or Rationalization," pp. 336–7.

[8] Bell, Daniel. *The Cultural Contradictions of Capitalism* (New York: Basic Books, 1973), pp. 143–4.

[9] Yankelovich, Daniel. *New Rules: Searching for Self-Fulfillment in a World Turned Upside Down* (New York: Bantam Books, 1981), p. 172.

to a combination of conditions that took shape not in the 1950s, but during the late 1960s, at the height of the counterculture and the antiwar movement.[10]

Yet again we see that appearances are not always an accurate reflection of what is happening on the ground. As Chapter 2 demonstrates, notwithstanding the contributions made by mental health professionals in fostering social conformity and in encouraging conservative norms, psychology played a crucial role – perhaps, the crucial role – in the postwar liberalization of values. Correspondingly, the growth of progressive child rearing, the medicalization of alcoholism, and religion's embrace of the therapeutic – all developments unfolding during the late 1940s and 1950s – were driven, in large measure, by the rise of psychology.

A similar discrepancy between private practice and public pronouncements is evident in the field of child rearing. Despite the popularity of the *Common Sense Book*, most Americans said they believed the country needed to take a harder line against unruly children. This tough stance was due in part to growing concerns over juvenile delinquency, as well as to the fear of momism – the belief that the feminization and excessive pampering of American boys were turning out a generation of weak-kneed neurotics.[11] A 1949 survey by George Gallup found that 50 percent of Americans answered "parents too soft" or "children have it too easy" when they were asked, "What would you say is the main fault of parents in raising children nowadays?" By contrast, only 5 percent were of the opinion that parents lacked sufficient sympathy, patience, or tolerance.[12] Another survey, taken in the fall of 1954, goes even further in revealing the conservative outlook of many Americans toward child rearing. When a nationally representative sample of fifteen hundred people were asked, "Do you think discipline in most homes is too strict or not strict enough?" only a meager 1 percent answered "too strict," while more than four out of five respondents (83 percent) proclaimed, "Not strict enough."[13]

---

[10] Lasch, Christopher. *The Culture of Narcissism: American Life in an Age of Diminishing Expectations* (New York: W. W. Norton & Company, 1978), pp. xiii, xvi.

[11] Wylie, Philip. *Generation of Vipers* (New York: Farrar & Rinehart, 1942).

[12] Survey by Gallup Organization, January 23–January 28, 1949. Retrieved August 20, 2008, from the iPOLL Databank, The Roper Center for Public Opinion Research, University of Connecticut. Online at: http://www.ropercenter.uconn.edu/ipoll.html.

[13] Survey by Gallup Organization, October 15–October 20, 1954. Retrieved August 20, 2008, from the iPOLL Databank, The Roper Center for Public Opinion Research, University of Connecticut. Online at: http://www.ropercenter.uconn.edu/ipoll.html.

In short, at midcentury an overwhelming majority of Americans seemed to believe that families were becoming overly indulgent with their sons and daughters. However, despite these expressed sentiments, a wealth of studies reveals that during these supposedly conservative years, child-rearing practices were becoming less rigid and more flexible in the aggregate. When a nationally representative sample of mothers were asked, "Are your children being raised (have they been raised) more strictly or less strictly than you were raised by your parents?" mothers, by a margin of better than two to one (59 to 23 percent), stated that their children were being raised "less strictly."[14] Yes, people may have decried the laxness of their neighbors, pointing their fingers sternly at one another. However, insofar as their own child-rearing practices were concerned, Americans were fast abandoning the rod in favor of a strong scolding, or a simple "time out."

Finally, during the Truman and Eisenhower years, it would appear that sexual norms had become increasingly conservative, at least in some areas. On the political front, efforts to root out disloyalty at home led many to associate sexual deviancy with political subversion. As with the general perception of the much-despised communist subversive, many suspected gays of leading double lives. On the one hand, they were generally anonymous and appeared normal; on the other, however, they seemed to secretly scorn everything that was good and wholesome about the American way of life. In an age when sinister forces were thought to be dwelling incognito among us, it was not too great a stretch to lump communists and homosexuals under the same generic categories of subversive and un-American. "Communists, deviants – they are one and the same," remarked Senator Clyde Hoey of North Carolina.[15] Nebraska Senator Kenneth Wherry was equally critical. "I don't say every homosexual is a subversive, and I don't say every subversive is a homosexual. But a man of low morality is a menace to the government, whatever he is, and they are tied up together."[16]

In examining the intersection between McCarthyism and homophobia, historian John D'Emilio observes, "There was congruence between

---

[14] Survey by *Saturday Evening Post* and Gallup Organization, June, 1962. Retrieved August 20, 2008, from the iPOLL Databank, The Roper Center for Public Opinion Research, University of Connecticut. Online at: http://www.ropercenter.uconn.edu/ipoll.html.

[15] Cited from Peterson, James R. "Playboy's History of the Sexual Revolution: Something Cool; Part VI, 1950–1959," *Playboy* (February 1998), p. 72.

[16] Whitfield, Stephen J. *The Culture of the Cold War* (Baltimore: The Johns Hopkins University Press, 1991), p. 43.

anti-Communism in the sphere of politics and social concern over homosexuality. Attempts to suppress sexual deviance paralleled and reinforced the efforts to squash political dissent."[17] In the midst of the second Red Scare, it was assumed that to deviate from the political mainstream or to defy sexual conventions was more than simply weird; it was morally suspect.

Yet while seizing nominal control of the public sphere, the conservative mood of the 1950s was not able to significantly shape morals. As Chapters 2 and 3 attempted to show, while society grew more religious, the population itself became more secular; and although sexual norms remained conservative, sexual behavior liberalized, becoming less constrained.[18] Indeed, it was during the 1950s – at the very moment the stigma surrounding homosexuality was strengthening – that gay enclaves in New York, Chicago, and San Francisco and underground gay bars in a number of other cities, were quietly forming.

The fact that the Cold War was unable to prevent this process of liberalization does not mean that the Cold War was irrelevant. By pulling norms in a conservative direction, the midcentury crusade against "fifth columnists" at home and communism overseas probably limited the extent to which moral constraints loosened. Naturally, the conservative drift of social norms did not affect everyone. As is to be expected, America had its share of hypocrites who said one thing in public while doing something very different in private. However, there are always the conformists who, in taking their cues from friends and neighbors, internalized society's prevailing norms. In *The Lonely Crowd* (1950), sociologist David Riesman called such folks "other-directed," William Whyte preferred to term this modern prototype the "Organization Man."[19]

---

[17] D'Emilio, John. "The Homosexual Menace: The Politics of Sexuality in Cold War America," in Peiss, Kathy, and Simmons, Christina (eds.), *Passion and Power: Sexuality in History* (Philadelphia: Temple University Press, 1989), p. 236.

[18] It should be noted that it was after World War II, as sexual norms were becoming more constrained, that homosexual communities in a number of large cities – most notably New York and San Francisco – began to take shape. See D'Emilio, John. *Sexual Politics, Sexual Communities: The Making of a Homosexual Community, 1940–1970* (Chicago: University of Chicago Press, 1983); Chauncey, Jr., George. "The Postwar Sex Crime Panic," in *True Stories from the American Past*, Graebner, William (ed.) (New York: McGraw-Hill, 1993), p. 176.

[19] Riesman, David, Glazer, Nathan, and Denney, Reuel. *The Lonely Crowd: A Study of the Changing American Character* (Garden City, N.Y.: Doubleday & Company, 1950); Whyte, Jr., William H. *The Organization Man* (New York: Simon & Schuster, 1956). For a fuller discussion of Riesman and Whyte's ideas, see McClay, Wilfred M. *The Masterless: Self and Society in Modern America* (Chapel Hill, N.C.: University of North Carolina Press, 1994), pp. 269–95.

In addition to the submissive personality structure as described by Riesman, Whyte, and Erich Fromm, there were probably still larger numbers of people who, although not personally supportive of conservative norms, were careful not to defy them. Therefore, it would be reasonable to say that in the absence of the Cold War and the conservative norms fostered by it, the personal behavior of Americans would most likely have loosened even further. However, the larger point is that values, despite this Cold War conservatism, were losing ground in the face of changing trends in psychology, sexual behavior, religion, child rearing, the youth culture, as well as public attitudes toward alcohol addiction and the appearance of a new, more secular evaluation of the self.

Pressures to conform probably contributed to the normative gap. To the extent the 1950s were a time of social conformity, the compelling need of Americans to fit in only helped widen the breach between norms and values. In trying to adhere to the conservative, middle-class ideal, millions of Americans at midcentury did exactly what they were supposed to: they flocked en masse to suburbia, begat large families, regularly attended church, and eschewed radical politics. However, in those private corners of their lives that are not easily scrutinized by prying parents or nosy neighbors – in their personal attitudes toward sex, parenting, or religion – more and more Americans were personally rejecting a traditionally conservative moral framework.

The increasing gulf between norms and values may not be as paradoxical as it first appears. Although the Cold War contributed to the value-normative gap, it is also possible, even likely, that norms were responding to behavioral change. During the 1950s, as experts, social commentators, clerics, and other guardians of public morality surveyed the American scene, they probably sensed significant moral change. In all likelihood, they saw signs of secularization or ruefully noticed a decline in sexual modesty. Yet instead of appreciating the full magnitude of these subtle shifts in the way people deported themselves, most interpreted these behavioral changes as mere undercurrents that, however disturbing, were not representative of a larger trend. Thus, for all the distress over the perversity of the much vilified Kinsey Reports, there seemed to be little concern for or awareness of the increasing frequency of premarital intercourse. Similarly, for all the outrage over the defamation of the Lord's Day, opponents of Sunday shopping seemed oblivious to the new pact between religion and the therapeutic, or to the churches' general deemphasis of proselytizing. While not fully cognizant of the scope of behavioral change, many traditionalists felt sufficiently provoked to respond, constricting social norms in retaliation to the mass loosening of personal values. In other words, the liberalization of values helped give rise to its own antithesis. Conventions moved "rightward" because behaviors were moving "leftward."

This countermobilization against liberalizing values was not entirely driven by elites. In order for norms to tighten appreciably, the messages of elite agitators – the people sociologist Harold Becker termed *moral entrepreneurs* – would have needed to resonate strongly among large swathes of the general population.[20] Therefore, it is likely that on a grassroots level a great many Americans detected behavioral changes that they detested, and that they correctly believed ran counter to established values. Thus, when elites sought to reverse the permissive trend, they found plenty of popular support. Yet at the end of the day, these agitators and their grassroots supporters succeeded only in tightening social conventions, which further widened the gap between values and norms.

There are those who upon surveying the national scene would have us think of the 1950s as a time of moral panics. From scares over comic books and juvenile crime, to panics over child molestation and communist subversion, America in the 1950s is frequently portrayed as a frightened nation in pursuit of ghosts – ghosts who, more than anything, were figments of the collective imagination.[21] Although operative in certain instances, moral panics do not accurately characterize the era. The perceived threat to conservative values was hardly the product of mass paranoia. Not only was the challenge to an older morality concretely real, but it was also a far more formidable phenomenon than what most critics at the time had ever imagined.

The failure of social conservatives to comprehend the extent to which values were being transformed was not due to a lack of perceptiveness on their part. In fact, the social crusaders who sought to uphold the

---

[20] By *moral entrepreneur* Becker was referring to moralists, or social do-gooders, who sought to preserve conservative values. See Becker, Howard S., *Outsiders: Studies in the Sociology of Deviance* (New York: Free Press, 1963).

[21] Thompson, Kenneth. *Moral Panics* (London: Routledge, 1998); Gilbert, James B. *A Cycle of Outrage: America's Reaction to the Juvenile Delinquent in the 1950s* (New York: Oxford University Press, 1986); Cohen, Ronald D. "The Delinquents: Censorship and Youth Culture in Recent U.S. History," *History of Education Quarterly* (Autumn 1997), pp. 257–8; Goode, Erich, and Ben-Yehuda, Nachman. "Moral Panics: Culture, Politics, and Social Construction," *Annual Review of Sociology* Vol. 20 (1994), pp. 149–71; Ben-Yehuda, Nachman. "The Sociology of Moral Panics: Toward a New Synthesis," *Sociological Quarterly* Vol. 27 (1986), pp. 495–513; Chauncey, Jr., George. "The Postwar Sex Crime Panic," in Graebner, William (ed.), *True Stories From the American Past* (New York: McGraw-Hill, 1993), pp. 160–78.

traditional moral order seemed to have a greater awareness of moral change than the majority of scholars who write about the 1950s today. At present, most historians and sociologists persist in viewing the fifties as an essentially conservative era in which religion was becoming stronger and sexuality was held in check. During the 1950s, however, conservative critics tended to be less sanguine about the moral state of affairs. Their inability to grasp the magnitude of behavioral change was attributable to the same set of factors that hamper today's academics: private behavior is often concealed, and nonnormative behavior is frequently hidden, which makes it difficult to determine whether society's values are tightening, loosening, or remaining relatively stable at any given point in time.

In determining the scope and nature of change the moral crusaders of the 1950s were by and large wrong, but in discerning the direction of behavioral change these same crusaders were generally right. Their judgment was not based on a systematic analysis, but on an intuition most likely grounded in amorphous trends or the occasional anecdote. In their attempts to resist a threat that they felt but could not touch, a danger they sensed but could not see, conservatives often found themselves boxing at shadows. With little idea of just what they were fighting, they swung wildly – even blindly – praying that someway, somehow, something would connect. Because these outraged conservative agitators possessed only a vague understanding of what they were battling, their counterattacks were doomed before they began. For example, the pillorying of Alfred Kinsey and the vilification of homosexuals proved to be futile counters to the mass liberalization of sexual behavior – a phenomenon that was affecting black and white alike. Likewise, the censoring of comic books and the popular fears surrounding juvenile delinquency were clumsy responses to the rise of progressive parenting and the decline of patriarchal authority.

In isolation, the strong reactions to Alfred Kinsey and kiddy comics, to sexual deviants and teenage delinquents, probably would strike the average person today as bizarre, excessive, and somewhat paranoid. However, when analyzed more broadly, these moral campaigns can be seen as the ineffective efforts by social conservatives to police the boundaries of a rapidly changing moral order. In the end, of course, such efforts proved unsuccessful: instead of fostering traditional values, the countermobilization merely postponed the day of reckoning, when norms were forced to liberalize.

In brief, the defining feature of the 1960s was not the liberalization of values, but the loosening of social conventions. To be sure, values liberalized during the 1960s. The sexual revolution continued its advance and old-style religious piety, although still vibrant in many respects, continued its retreat. Values were merely following a firmly established pattern that had been set during the previous decade – or, to borrow a famous colloquialism, the tracks had already been greased. What unfolded, in other words, did not signify a rupture with the prevailing values of the past, or – like the Permissive Turn of the 1940s – represent a significant acceleration of preexisting trends. Instead, what took place during the 1960s was the closing of a gap, the resolving of a discrepancy. People's notions of what behaviors were publicly respectable shifted dramatically – and like a tightly stretched rubber band that is abruptly released, the distance between norms and values suddenly closed.

New Movements and New Organizations

The normative revolution of the late 1960s institutionalized the challenge to the traditional moral framework. With it, there arose a new set of movements and organizations that sought to transform the larger culture. An example of this process was the phalanx of environmentalist organizations such as the Environmental Defense Fund (EDF), Friends of the Earth, and Zero Population Growth (ZPG) that burst onto the scene during the late 1960s. Although these new groups were populated by middle-class liberals, they actually were extremely critical of the materialist values that stood at the heart of the bourgeois ethic – values that were indispensable to the continuation of a mass consumer society.[22]

Besides bringing new structures into existence, the revolution in norms caused some established organizations, such as Students for a Democratic Society (SDS) and the Student Nonviolent Coordinating Committee (SNCC), to jettison their liberalism and adopt a radicalized agenda. On a deeper level, this political radicalization was more than a mere shift in ideology, as it involved the rejection of the dominant values of the larger culture. Black militancy, for example, involved more than the dismissal of integration and creative nonviolence. As Stokely Carmichael, the foremost purveyor of the slogan "Black Power" noted, "The goal of black people must not be to assimilate into middle-class America, for that class – as a whole – is without a viable conscience as regards humanity . . . the values

---

[22] Cotgrove, Stephen, and Duff, Andrew. "Environmentalism, Values, and Social Change," *The British Journal of Sociology* Vol. 32, No. 1. (March 1981), pp. 92–110.

FIGURE 7.1. During the late sixties and early seventies, a variety of movements challenged the values of middle-class America. (Photographer: Diana Davies. Reproduced by permission of the Sophia Smith Collection, Smith College.)

of that class," he continued, "are based on material aggrandizement, not the expansion of humanity."[23] Similarly, "radical feminism" – the brand of feminism adopted by the New Left during the late sixties and early seventies – involved more than the effort to achieve equal pay for equal work. At the heart of its campaign was a deeply rooted antagonism toward the individualistic and aggressive qualities that leading theorists equated with patriarchy. In both cases, it was the repudiation of certain core principles – values that could be characterized as religiously conservative and temperamentally bourgeois – that gave rise to a radical political stance. Thus, on a very basic level, the ethical became the political. With

---

[23] Carmichael, Stokely, and Hamilton, Charles V. *Black Power: The Politics of Liberation in America* (Toronto: Vintage Books, 1967), p. 40.

FIGURE 7.2. An antiwar protest on the University of Florida campus, 1968.
(Reproduced by permission of the Special Collections Archives, Smathers Library,
University of Florida.)

FIGURE 7.3. During the late 1960s, black militancy had more to do with rejecting
the wider culture than seeking acceptance into it. (Reproduced by permission of
the Special Collections Archives, Smathers Library, University of Florida.)

FIGURE 7.4. Feminists Gloria Steinem and Pamela Hughes giving the "Black Power" salute, 1972. (Photographer: Dan Wynn. Reproduced by permission of Farmani Gallery and the Sophia Smith Collection, Smith College.)

the mainstreaming of oppositional values came the partial mainstreaming of an oppositional politics.

There is perhaps no example that more vividly demonstrates the extent to which oppositional politics had become institutionalized than the rise of the new institution than the Federal Employees for a Democratic Society (FEDS). Inspired by SDS – its younger, more famous counterpart – FEDS was comprised of hundreds of federal bureaucrats who during the late sixties and early seventies challenged the policies of the Nixon administration. Among the activities it undertook were initiating petition drives, as well as protesting the war in Vietnam and resisting President Nixon's Anti-Ballistic Missile (ABM) System. In 1970, it signed onto a statement that characterized the United States as a society that "condones violence and practices genocide" against "brown people at home" and "third world populations abroad."

Instead of meeting clandestinely or otherwise operating in the shadows, FEDS was open about its activities. The largest chapter of FEDS, one that operated within the Department of Health, Education, and Welfare (HEW), held weekly discussions on government premises where they mulled over such issues as draft avoidance, the feasibility of employing sit-ins and slowdowns to oppose administration policies, and opposition to the Anti-Ballistic Missile program. When senior officials at HEW sought to prohibit such meetings from being held on government premises, FEDS refused to yield. It sued the department in federal court – and ultimately prevailed.

On the religious front, the nation's mainline Protestant churches that, throughout the forties and fifties had been veering away from an other-worldly orientation, became brazenly secular during the 1960s. With the remarkable success of such books as Joseph Fletcher's *Situation Ethics*, Peter Berger's *The Sacred Canopy*, and Harvey Cox's *The Secular City* – works that questioned either the relevance or the desirability of a conservative Christian vision – few observers of the 1960s could honestly say they were living in an age of increasing religious fervor. Expressing this new mood was the National Council of Churches (NCC), which in the sixties popularized the slogan, "The world sets the agenda for the church."[24]

In the charged atmosphere of the 1960s, the level of social change reached ever-greater heights as conventions ceased to function as a drag on shifting values. Whereas at the close of the 1950s norms trailed liberalizing behavior, a decade later the tables had reversed and it was now behavior that trailed liberalizing norms. As a consequence, norms tended to overstate the extent of behavioral change. The so-called Woodstock generation may have garnered an enormous amount of attention at the close of the 1960s, but comparatively few Americans, including young people, considered themselves part of the counterculture. In a similar vein, George and Nina O'Neil's *Open Marriage: A New Lifestyle for Couples* may have been a phenomenal success in 1973, ranking third on the list of best-selling books, but for all of the changes ushered in by the sexual revolution, wife-swapping was not an especially commonplace practice at this time.[25]

The remarkable speed with which norms were moving during the late 1960s led many to believe the culture was at the dawn of a new age. In *The Greening of America*, Charles Reich wrote of the impending arrival of a social revolution that "will originate with the individual and with culture, and will change the political structure only as its final act ... It promises a higher reason, a more human community, and a new and

[24] Edward, T., and Oakes, S. J. "The Missionary Pope: John Paul II and the New Evangelization," *Crisis* (May 25, 2005).

[25] Secrest, Meryle. "The New Marriage; Studying the Dynamics of the New Marriage," *The Washington Post* (September 17, 1972), pp. G1, G4; Dullea, George. "Open Marriage Isn't a Closed Book," *The New York Times* (October 5, 1977), pp. 58, C5.

liberated individual." He continued: "Its ultimate creation will be a new and enduring wholeness and beauty – a renewed relationship of man to himself, to other men, to society, to nature, and to the land."[26] Although Reich exaggerated the extent of cultural transformation, the liberalization of norms enabled values and behavior to change with more rapidity. If, instead of outpacing behavior, the social conventions of the late sixties had simply lagged behind values (as had been the case throughout the 1950s) then the extent of behavioral change would almost certainly have been more modest.

Another accelerant to the changes of the late sixties and early seventies was the vast multitudes of baby boomers coming of age. Although their parents had been profoundly affected by the cultural winds blowing throughout the forties and fifties, their exposure to a more conservative past – combined with the durability of traditional norms – partially blunted the degree of transformation. As the historian James T. Patterson points out:

What the restless young still lacked in the 1950s was the greatly magnified sense of possibility – of open-ended entitlement – that was to give them greater energy and hope in the 1960s. Instead, they still encountered strong cultural norms that prescribed traditional roles for "growing up": "girls" were to become wives and homemakers, "boys" were to enter the armed services and then become breadwinners. Few young men, (Elvis) Presley included, imagined that they should avoid the draft: half of young men coming of age between 1953 and 1960 ended up in uniform, most for two years or more.[27]

Those who became adolescents or entered their twenties during the Truman and Eisenhower years witnessed immense social change as attitudes liberalized. However, among those who came of age during the 1960s – those baby boomers who had been born into an era when psychology was on the march and Benjamin Spock was on the rise, when sin was in retreat and the college experience was becoming democratized – the extent of change was far greater. It was not so much the level of moral change within people as the sense of possibility existing between people that best distinguishes the 1960s from the previous decade.

---

[26] Cited from Jenkins, Philip. *Decade of Nightmares: The End of the Sixties and the Making of Eighties America* (New York: Oxford University Press, 2006), p. 25.

[27] Patterson, James T. *Grand Expectations: The United States, 1945–1974* (New York: Oxford University Press, 1996), p. 374.

By the time Richard Nixon became president, the pace of change at the grassroots level was actually accelerating. This was partly the result of: (1) liberalizing norms were effectively pulling behavior further away from a traditionally conservative standard; (2) institutionalized opposition that challenged the older moral framework openly and systematically; (3) a youth culture that – as a result of the antiwar movement and a widening generation gap – was increasingly defiant of traditional authority; and (4) the cumulative changes that had been simmering for a quarter of a century. Hence, in the areas of psychology, religion, sexuality, and gender significant changes were well under way during the Nixon years. For example, within the field of pastoral counseling, the therapeutic impulse was so strong that by the early 1970s the conservative evangelical movement was not simply embracing the tenets of modern psychology – something it had already done by the early 1950s – but many of their leading voices were prepared to banish religious faith and explicit references to God from the counseling session altogether. As David Harrington Watt pointed out in *A Transforming Faith: Explorations of Twentieth-Century American Evangelicalism*, during the early 1970s, in a column appearing in *The Moody Monthly*, the official organ of the conservative Moody Bible Institute, readers received warnings to the effect that it was not simply ineffective, but from the standpoint of psychological health, it was actually dangerous to pray over one's emotional problems.[28] Even more surprising, during the early Nixon years the link between pastoral counseling and the traditional Christian message had become so tenuous that even the conservative Fuller Theological Seminary considered luring the famed therapist Rollo May into the ranks of its faculty. A leading figure of the movement in humanistic psychology, Rollo May was a collaborator with Rogers and Maslow, an enthusiastic proponent of existentialism, and despite early seminary training, an avowed atheist.[29]

Within the secular world of psychology and psychiatry, the most vibrant force during the 1970s was the pharmacological revolution that had been ignited by the introduction of the tranquilizer Miltown in 1955. However, notwithstanding the preeminence of psychotropic drugs, psychotherapy – derided by its critics as the "talking cure" – continued to flourish throughout the 1960s and 1970s. Two government surveys – the first one completed in 1957 and the second conducted in 1976 – attest

[28] Watt, David Harrington. *A Transforming Faith: Explorations of Twentieth-Century American Evangelicalism* (New Jersey: Rutgers University Press, 1991), p. 152.
[29] Ibid, p. 152.

to the steadily rising cultural influence of psychological counseling. In the twenty-year period between the two surveys, the percentage of adults believing that they would always handle personal problems on their own without having to turn to outside help fell from 44 to 35 percent, a reduction of one-fifth.[30] More significantly, the proportion of Americans who reported consulting a professional for a serious personal problem nearly doubled, rising from one-seventh to one-fourth of the adult population.[31] Although psychotherapy became a prominent feature of American culture at midcentury, the best evidence shows that its influence continued to climb during the 1960s and 1970s.

The changing status of women proved to be no less sweeping than the advances posted by the movement in psychological counseling. As Chapter 5 related, the percentage of Americans who indicated that they could support a qualified female candidate for president rose rapidly during the 1970s, jumping from 53 percent in 1969 to 78 percent in 1974.[32] That 50 percent increase over a period of a few years exceeded the 33 percent gain that had occurred over the 1950s, and easily outpaced the ensuing decade when the level of support for a female presidential candidate remained fairly stable.

As one surveys the late 1960s and early 1970s, another important development begins to come into focus. As Chapter 2 relayed, the medicalization of alcoholism – that is, the view that alcoholism is a disease as opposed to a moral failing – made great advances in the decade following World War II. In 1944, only about one in eighteen Americans considered alcoholism to be an illness: by 1954, six out of ten Americans characterized it as a disease. By the early 1970s, however, the disease model was not exclusively applied to alcohol abuse, but it was also being used to explain a host of compulsive behaviors such as gambling, child abuse, and drug addiction. In earlier times, such behavior would have been labeled evil or sinful, but during the sixties and seventies the language of sin was fast becoming antiquated.

---

[30] Veroff, Joseph, Kulka, Richard A., and Douvan, Elizabeth. *Mental Health in America: Patterns of Help-Seeking from 1957 to 1976* (New York: Basic Books, 1981), p. 79.

[31] Ibid.

[32] See Survey by Gallup Organization, March 12–March 17, 1969. Retrieved August 20, 2008, from the iPOLL Databank, The Roper Center for Public Opinion Research, University of Connecticut. Online at: http://www.ropercenter.uconn.edu/ipoll.html. Also see Survey by National Opinion Research Center, University of Chicago, February 1974. Retrieved August 20, 2008, from the iPOLL Databank, The Roper Center for Public Opinion Research, University of Connecticut. Online at: http://www.ropercenter.uconn.edu/ipoll.html.

Probably the surest sign of the general acceptance of the disease model was the Nixon administration's promotion of the potent narcotic methadone. Touted as a way of combating heroin addiction, methadone clinics sprouted up in major cities across the nation during the late 1960s and early 1970s. At the height of its acclaim, the Nixon administration sought to create a network of methadone maintenance programs capable of treating between 150,000 to 175,000 addicts, approximately two-thirds of the estimated population of heroin users in the country.[33] Toward that end, President Nixon created by executive order a special office within the White House selecting physician Jerome Jaffe to be his new "Drug Czar," and then sought to endow this new agency with approximately one billion dollars in funding over a three-year period.[34]

Predictably, these progressive reforms on the part of Nixon brought about a conservative reaction. "It's substituting one addiction for another," complained the director of a drug rehabilitation center in Philadelphia. "Heroin was created to stop morphine use and now methadone is supposed to stop heroin use. It's an endless cycle."[35] These concerns were shared by George Wilson, a special assistant to Michigan's mental health director. "What's bothering me," he told a reporter from the Associated Press, "is that we may be on the verge of creating a new generation of methadone addicts."[36] Despite these and similar criticisms, Nixon pressed on with his methadone maintenance program until 1974 whereupon public support began to evaporate amid a flurry of news stories that reported a rash of methadone overdoses, the emergence of a methadone black market, and the horrors of methadone-addicted babies.

In its willingness to substitute one narcotic for another, the Nixon White House was, in essence, dispensing altogether with the goal of abstinence and, in its place, endorsing the proposition that a person's dependency on heroin could most effectively be broken through medical intervention. This strategy differed from the medicalization of alcoholism in two important ways: first, in the case of problem drinking, there was the demand to go cold turkey. The expectation was for the recovering

---

[33] Associated Press, "Methadone: Heroin Substitute, and Peril," *The Lima News* (October 24, 1971), p. D1.

[34] Conrad, Peter, and Schneider, Joseph W. *Deviance and Medicalization: From Badness to Sickness* (St. Louis: C.V. Mosby Company), p. 246.

[35] Associated Press. "Methadone Addiction Up," *Daily Capital News* (Jefferson City, Missouri) (December 20, 1972), p. 8.

[36] Stowell, John. "Crackdown Eyed On Methadone Use as Heroin Substitute," *The Daily Tribune* (Wisconsin Rapids, Wisconsin) (December 23, 1972), p. 14.

alcoholic to refrain from the consumption of liquor altogether. Second, with their reliance on group support and the twelve-step program, neither Mary Mann nor AA founder Bill Wilson demanded that the recovering alcoholic seek professional help. By contrast, in the case of methadone maintenance, the allure of addiction was regarded as so overpowering, and the efficacy of willpower was seen as so enfeebled, that maintenance instead of abstinence became the ruling paradigm, and with this shift professional medicine moved to the forefront of the recovery process.

In the end, the application of the disease model to problem drinking, heroin addiction, compulsive gambling, and child abuse had the effect of reducing blame and social stigma and, by so doing, encouraging troubled people to seek outside help. As sociologists Peter Conrad and Joseph Schneider explained, the medicalization of nonnormative behavior "is related to a longtime humanitarian trend in the conception and control of deviance . . . it is not retributive or punitive, but at least ideally, therapeutic."[37] In addition to these qualities, medicalization could be seen as, at once, mild, innovative, progressive, and scientific – attributes in accord with an increasingly liberal social order. Needless to say, in its rejection of moralizing and, concomitantly, in its abandonment of a punitive approach, the medicalization of deviancy pulled the culture further away from a traditionally Christian perspective.

Judaism, Liberal Protestantism, and the Permissive Turn

Although easy to overstate, it would appear that as far as the liberalization of values is concerned, Jewish Americans were well "ahead of the curve." Throughout the 1950s the attitudes of the general population were drifting closer and closer to the more progressive outlook held by a disproportionate number of American Jews. In *Science, Jews, and Secular Culture*, David Hollinger takes up the subject of Jewish exceptionalism, arguing that Jewish intellectuals played a vital role in transforming the public culture from what had been primarily Christian to what it became, and presently is: pluralistic.[38] The point we are raising here dovetails with Hollinger's, but rather than focusing on Jewish intellectuals the concentration is – for the moment – on the moral attitudes of the rank-and-file. Whether one is looking at the rise of modern psychology or the advancing

---

[37] Ibid, p. 138.
[38] Hollinger, David A. *Science, Jews, and Secular Culture: Studies in Mid-Twentieth-Century American Intellectual History* (Princeton: Princeton University Press, 1996), pp. 3–16.

forces of secularization, the liberalizing tendencies afoot during the postwar period seemed to be especially resonant among Americans of Jewish descent. As we saw in Chapter 2, an exhaustive examination of young people's attitudes during the 1950s revealed that Jewish teenagers were less than half as likely as their Catholic and Protestant counterparts to believe a person's fate in the "hereafter" was contingent on "how we behaved on earth." Similarly, Catholic and Protestant teenagers were more than twice as likely as their Jewish counterparts to believe "religious faith is better than logic for solving life's important problems."[39]

When the issue turned from religion to psychology, American Jews once again exhibited attitudes that tended to be markedly more progressive than those of their Protestant and Catholic neighbors. According to a federally sponsored study, conducted by the University of Michigan in 1957, Jews had a more positive view of psychological counseling than their contemporaries. For example, the study found that Jewish Americans were fully one-third more likely than Methodists or Lutherans, and nearly twice as likely as Baptists, to have sought professional help in dealing with a problem of a psychological nature.[40]

To be sure, some of the differences in the worldview of Christians and Jews were attributable to the social position of each group. Compared to Protestants and Catholics, Jewish Americans were more likely to have attended college and less likely to have resided in rural areas. There was also a greater tendency for Jews to be employed in the professions.[41] Thus, to the extent the United States was modernizing – and its people were becoming less rural, more educated, and increasingly white collar – the worldview of Christian Americans was likely to liberalize, and more closely approximate the moral outlook of American Jews. During the 1950s, as today, one's larger vision was shaped in large part by the class position one occupied.

However, on this question of Jewish exceptionalism demography does not quite explain everything. The Jewish embrace of a more secular worldview seems to have extended beyond what their higher levels of income and education would have dictated. There were few studies in the 1950s that directly address this issue by performing a multivariate

[39] Remmers, H. H., and Radler, D. H. *The American Teenager* (Indianapolis: Bobbs-Merrill Company, 1957), p. 171.
[40] Veroff, Joseph, Kulka, Richard A., and Douvan, Elizabeth. *Mental Health in America: Patterns of Help-Seeking from 1957–1976* (New York: Basic Books, 1981), p. 172.
[41] Veroff, Joseph, Kulka, Richard A., and Douvan, Elizabeth. *The Inner American: A Self-Portrait from 1957–1976* (New York: Basic Books, 1981), p. 439.

analysis of survey data. However, more recent scholarship has been able to unearth attitudinal differences between Christians and Jews, even when accounting for social class. For example, survey data compiled in 1976 found "low income Jews" were "high users" of professional psychiatrists and psychologists compared to Protestants of similar social standing, and comparatively low users of counseling services provided by clerics.[42] Another study, based on extensive survey data compiled from 1972 to 1980, found that Jewish American families – even when one controlled for education and income – were more likely than Christians to place a high value on the self-direction and autonomy of their children and, correspondingly, assign less importance to the value of conformity (such as displaying good manners).[43]

Although there was a dearth of such comparative studies during the 1950s, by examining the data sets of public opinion surveys conducted many decades ago it is possible to examine the influence of various demographic factors on controversial issues. In other words, it is possible to look at a variety of demographic categories – such as religion, race, sex, income, education, and geographical region – and determine the influence these discrete factors exercised in shaping public opinion at midcentury.

Thus, as we saw earlier, education appears to have played a much more important role than employment in shaping popular attitudes toward the role of women in society. In 1945, when Gallup asked a nationally representative sample if they could vote for a qualified woman for president, people with different demographic profiles were likely to provide very different answers. Although a majority of Americans indicated that they would not be willing to vote for a "qualified" female presidential candidate, among those with a bachelor's degree, some 57 percent of college-educated women and 55 percent of college-educated men indicated they could support a woman for president.[44] When a multivariate analysis was performed, and a host of other variables – such as race, residential location, gender, and labor-force participation – were considered, it found that respondents with four years of college were nearly 25 percent more likely to be receptive to a female presidential candidate than those

---

[42] Veroff, Joseph, et al., *Mental Health in America*, p. 179.

[43] Cherlin, Andrew, and Celebuski, Carin. "Are Jewish Families Different? Some Evidence from the General Social Survey," *Journal of Marriage and the Family* Vol. 45, No. 4 (November 1983), pp. 903–10.

[44] *Survey by Gallup Organization, November 23–November 28, 1945.* Retrieved July 27, 2008, from the iPOLL Databank, The Roper Center for Public Opinion Research, University of Connecticut. Online at: http://www.ropercenter.uconn.edu/ipoll.html.

270 The Permissive Society

without. By contrast, individuals in the labor force were only modestly more likely to support a female presidential candidate than similarly situated people who did not hold down jobs.[45]

The same method of analysis we used to analyze the effects of education and job status can also be employed to study the effects of religion. When a multivariate analysis was performed on the same 1945 survey, it found that Jewish Americans – even when one accounted for such variables as education and residential location – were 15 percent more likely to support a female presidential candidate than non-Jews from similar backgrounds.[46] Stated plainly, quite apart from their higher levels of income and education, the experience of being Jewish in America facilitated more progressive attitudes toward the status of women in society.

When the inquiry was expanded and the question shifted from a female presidential candidate to the willingness of Americans to regard alcoholism as a "disease," the results were strikingly similar as Jews were far more likely to regard alcoholism as a disease than non-Jews. According to the 1954 survey, some 84 percent of the Jewish respondents – compared to 62 percent of non-Jewish respondents – regarded alcoholism as a disease. Once the numbers are further scrutinized and a logit regression is performed, it reveals that when education, race, job status, and residential location are held constant, Jews were 20 percent more likely to believe that alcoholism was a "disease."[47] In summation, Gallup's 1945 poll on the prospect of a female presidential candidate, and the 1954 survey on whether alcoholism is a disease, substantiate later studies that strongly suggest that American Jews, even when accounting for their higher class status, were more likely to hold socially liberal views than either their Catholic or Protestant neighbors.

That American Jewry during the late forties and fifties was at the forefront of the Permissive Turn – and that they, in more recent times, have been more likely to embrace progressive social values than their neighbors – should not come as a great surprise. Besides being a product of their higher social position, the forerunner status of American Jews

---

45 Ibid.
46 Ibid.
47 Survey by *Gallup Organization, December 2–December 7, 1954.* Retrieved March 3, 2009, from the iPOLL Databank, The Roper Center for Public Opinion Research, University of Connecticut. Online at: http://www.ropercenter.uconn.edu.proxy.lib.fsu.edu/ipoll.html. Technical assistance provided by Florida State University Economics graduate student William Doerner.

helps illustrate an important truth that is easily overlooked: what we have referred to in these pages as the "traditional moral framework" was, at its base, a *traditionally Christian* moral framework. The worldview it helped foster – whether it be a hostile stance toward modern psychology, progressive child rearing, or the disease model – was driven by a particular evaluation of human beings, one that stressed human limitations and the pervasiveness of sin.

Although Jews were a conspicuous part of the liberalizing social changes unfolding at midcentury, they were not its chief architects. That role belongs to a varied crew who fell within the liberal Protestant tradition. They included such figures as psychologists Carl Rogers and Rollo May, child-rearing experts Benjamin Spock and Arnold Gesell, religious figures Paul Tillich and the Norman Vincent Peale, and alcoholics' defenders Marty Mann and Bill Wilson – all people who, in one way or another, challenged the cultural dominance of a traditional Christian perspective. Instead of emphasizing Original Sin, this brand of Protestantism subscribed to the notion of "original righteousness." Instead of turning to scripture as its principal moral guide, it called on people to consult their individual consciences, and – rather than emphasizing life in the hereafter – its adherents placed tremendous importance on achieving justice here and now, in the temporal world they inhabited in the flesh.

Due to their critical stance toward both the authority of scripture and the pronouncements of Natural Law, the proponents of this brand of liberal Protestantism were inclined to accept a certain level of opaqueness and ambiguity in their quest for truth. The reason for this acceptance in pretty straightforward: if the truth was to be accessed by looking within, then the downplaying of doctrine and the elevation of one's personal subjective religious experience would necessarily follow. One of the implications of this perspective is that it tends to deemphasize dogma and facilitate the belief that there are a variety of paths leading to truth. Correspondingly, we see within the leading liberal denominations a declining emphasis on proselytizing during the middle decades of the twentieth century. As a percentage of church income, less and less money was being directed to "spreading the Word."[48] In fact, many Protestant ministers were hailing Gandhi – someone they might have seen as merely a "virtuous pagan" in an earlier era – as one of the moral giants of our time. Even theologian Reinhold Niebuhr, the most prominent religious

[48] Study cited in Landis, Benson Y. *Yearbook of American Churches: Edition for 1955* (New York: National Council of Churches, 1954), pp. 297–8.

thinker of the 1950s, would assert in 1958 that it was unnecessary – and inappropriate – to convert Jews to Christ.[49]

Natural law was just one of the issues that divided liberal Protestants from their more conservative fellow Christians. As in the case of Judaism, liberal Protestants tended to reject – root and branch – Calvinist notions of human depravity. However, that was just the start. Within the Protestant Liberal tradition there exists a strain that goes well beyond the rejection of Calvin by elevating the individual to unprecedented heights. The epitome of this kind of optimism can be found among the Universalist Unitarians, a denomination that believes that every man and woman – possessing, as they do, a spark of the divine at the core of their very being – will ultimately achieve salvation. The Holiness movement, a term used to describe some of the followers of John Wesley, also exuded high levels of hopefulness. According to its central doctrine, by fully embracing the Holy Spirit it was possible to experience "entire sanctification." Once the pious achieved this "perfected" state they would be able to "walk as Christ walked," freed from the inclination to sin. While most Christians, including liberal Protestants, regard the Unitarian Universalists and the present-day heirs to the Holiness movement as excessively upbeat, the kind of optimism that suffuses their theology was in important ways similar to the moral vision that became ascendant during the early Cold War years.

This extreme optimism can be seen most clearly in the rise of humanistic psychology. During the early 1950s – a full decade before Carl Rogers became a guru of sorts to a generation of secular therapists – psychological counseling had become a thriving field within the nation's Protestant seminaries, and the figure who loomed largest in the whole pastoral counseling movement was none other than Carl Rogers.[50] The churches' clear preference for Rogers over Freud tells us volumes of the general mood prevailing at the time within most mainline Protestant seminaries: despite the horrors of World War II, there was a yearning to cast human beings in a more positive light. While Freud believed repression could be psychologically unhealthy, he also believed that some repression – a good dose of it in fact – was needed to keep the base impulses of humans in check. Carl Rogers, however, saw the matter quite differently. If humans were – at their very core – good, then repression of our natural impulses

---

49 Nieburh, Reinhold. *Pious and Secular America* (New York: Scribner's, 1958), p. 108.
50 Holifield, E. Brooks. *A History of Pastoral Care in America* (Nashville: Abingdon Press, 1983), p. 300.

was – as a general rule – bad. As Rogers explained, instead of repressing their impulses, self-actualized people would tend to follow their internal promptings, seeing them as reliable guides to leading wholesome, productive, and meaningful lives.[51]

Carl Rogers' evaluation of the human condition was a radical departure from the more gloomy assessment of Freud, but it also differed sharply from the appraisal of Abraham Maslow – someone who, along with Rogers, is regarded as the founding father of humanistic psychology. For purposes of analysis Rogers could be seen as representative of the liberal Protestant tradition, while Jewish psychologist Abraham Maslow could be seen as representative of the Hebraic tradition. As with Rogers, Maslow utilized the notion of an "actualizing tendency." However, in contrast to Carl Rogers, Maslow believed only a small percentage of people could ever become self-actualized in the fullest sense.[52] In this respect, Maslow was less inclusive than Rogers, who had been adamant in the claim that self-actualization could be achieved by virtually everyone.

There was another important area where Maslow and Rogers differed, and that was on the nature of evil. Ever the eternal optimist, Rogers believed evil was not an integral part of man's basic nature. In 1951, in a dialogue with Jewish philosopher Martin Buber, Rogers had stated, "Man is basically good," to which Buber gently retorted, "Man is basically good – and evil."[53] Like Buber, Maslow's view of human nature was more chastened than Rogers'. It cannot be said Maslow vilified man, as the actualizing tendency he espoused precluded such an interpretation. However, with his memory of Jewish suffering, Maslow was not able to ignore altogether the evil impulses dwelling within the bosom of every person. As Andrew Heinze points out in his award-winning book *Jews and the American Soul*, toward the end of his life Maslow told *Psychology Today* that he intended to launch a study that examined the nature of evil. "Both the all-good theory of self and the all-bad theory of self are inadequate," he remarked.[54]

---

[51] Evans, Richard. *Carl Rogers: The Man and His Ideas* (New York: E. P. Dutton & Company, 1975), p. 73; and see Rogers, Carl, *On Becoming a Person: A Therapist's View of Psychotherapy* (Boston: Houghton Mifflin Company, 1961).

[52] According to Maslow's famous "hierarchy of needs," a very small percentage of the population (less than 2 percent) could be expected to reach the highest stage of psychological development.

[53] Cited from May, Rollo. "The Problem of Evil: An Open Letter to Carl Rogers," *Journal of Humanistic Psychology* Vol. 22 (Summer 1982), p. 18.

[54] Heinze, Andrew. *Jews and the American Soul: Human Nature in the Twentieth Century* (Princeton: Princeton University Press, 2004), p. 289.

In the formulation of humanistic psychology, there were a couple of factors – quite central to the Jewish experience – that limited the Judaic influence. First, and most obviously, there was the recognition of the human capacity for evil. Among psychological and social theorists of Jewish linage, the leading figures during the early postwar years – people like Erich Fromm, Theodor Adorno, Max Horkeimer, Bruno Bettelheim, Herbert Marcuse, Hannah Arendt, Abraham Maslow, and Erik Erikson – made the Holocaust, or the social forces behind it, either an important theme in their scholarship or the source of much reflection.[55] Such an intellectual orientation made it difficult to devise a theory of human nature that downplayed evil to the degree of Carl Rogers.

A second, more complex factor involves the importance of community within the Jewish tradition. As scholars as far back as Émile Durkheim have noted, the importance of belonging to a larger community of fellow Jews has been central to the maintenance and perpetuation of Jewish identity over the centuries. In fact, one of the reasons rituals are such an important feature in Jewish life today is because in the absence of strong belief – and in recent times there have been a great many Jews, especially in the Reform movement, who do not possess an abundance of faith in the supernatural – rites and rituals have become a way of fostering group identity. However, the clarion call to interiority – the attempt to cast one's gaze internally and access the power of the actualizing tendency – is a largely solitary affair that facilitates a kind of isolated individualism easily detached from a larger sense of community. Apparently, the danger of excessive individualism – triggered by the attempts of people to turn inward and self-actualize – became a concern for Maslow. As Heinze recounts, Maslow jotted down some thoughts to himself in his notebooks that revealed a desire to reconcile an inward, introspective focus with a commitment to community. "To integrate and become serene at cost of giving up world, escaping and avoiding it, is a sort of phoniness," he observed. "One condition of comprehensive inner peace is the peace of other people ... Much harder job but very necessary."[56] It is worth noting that on the issue of excessive

---

[55] See Fromm, Erich, *Man for Himself: An Inquiry into the Psychology of Ethics* (New York: Holt, Rinehart & Winston, 1947); and Fromm, Erich, *Escape from Freedom* (New York: Farrar & Rinehart, 1941); Arendt, Hannah, *The Origins of Totalitarianism* (New York: Harcourt & Brace, 1951); Marcuse, Herbert, *Eros and Civilization: A Philosophical Inquiry into Freud* (Boston: Beacon Press, 1955); Erikson, Erik H., *Childhood and Society* (New York: Norton, 1950); Bettelheim, Bruno, *The Informed Heart: Autonomy in a Mass Age* (Glencoe, Illinois: Free Press, 1960); Adorno, Theodor W. et. al. *The Authoritarian Personality* (New York: Harper, 1950).

[56] Heinze, Andrew. *Jews and the American Soul*, p. 288.

individualism, Rogers did not seem terribly concerned, as he had very little to say on the matter.

In the rise of humanistic psychology – and here it is important to note that it was Rogers' version, not the more somber vision of Maslow, which resonated most strongly among those providing counseling – one witnesses the influence of a liberal Protestant ethos. Roger's articulation of the "actualizing tendency" can be seen as a secularized version of the Quaker notion of the "Inner Light," or Lutheran mystic Jacob Boehme's belief that the "sacred spark of the divine" resided at the core of every person. Likewise, Rogers' claim to universality, his insistence that the masses of ordinary men and women could someday become self-actualized and thereby achieve a sort of nirvana on earth was akin to the Unitarian doctrine of universal salvation. Little wonder, therefore, that prior to the sixties the strongholds of Rogerian thought were to be found in Protestant seminaries. In fact, Rogers himself had been a student at Union Theological Seminary, a bastion of liberal Protestantism.[57]

What one sees in the rise of Rogerian counseling is an intensified challenge to traditional authority and – within the field of psychology itself – a pronounced deference to what Rogers called "the authority within." These developments, which went well beyond what Freudians countenanced, were made possible by liberal Protestantism.

Important as it was, the rise of humanistic psychology was one of a number of early postwar developments that led to the demise of the traditional moral framework. In the area of moral decision-making – and, more specifically, in the rise of situation ethics – we once again see the unique imprint of liberal Protestantism. As the work of E. Brooks Holifield has shown, it would be only a slight exaggeration to state that during the 1950s the debate surrounding situation ethics was the exclusive preserve of theologians, most of whom were Protestant. It was only in 1966, when Episcopalian cleric Joseph Fletcher wrote the best-selling book *Situation Ethics: The New Morality* – an expanded version of his 1959 article, "The New Look in Christian Ethics" – that the phrase "situation ethics" become a popular term among the general public.[58] In what could be seen as a corollary to the doctrine of "original righteousness," liberal Protestants like Fletcher argued that humans had the ability to

[57] Evans, Richard. *Carl Rogers: The Man and His Ideas* (New York: E. P. Dutton & Company, 1975), p. 73; and Rogers, Carl R. *A Way of Being* (Boston: Houghton Mifflin, 1980).

[58] Long, Edward LeRoy. "The History and Literature of 'The New Morality,'" in Cox, Harvey (ed.), *The Situation Ethics Debate* (Philadelphia: The Westminster Press, 1968), pp. 105–6.

turn inward and – with the help of the Holy Spirit – determine the correct moral course of action in a concrete situation. They could do this, argued Fletcher, without having to rely on biblical edicts or natural law. All they needed to do was consult their hearts, and apply the principle of love to each moral situation. "The situationist," declared Fletcher, "follows a moral law or violates it depending on love's need."[59]

No doubt, even before the debate surrounding situation ethics first attracted Christian theologians, millions of Americans had refused to subscribe to an absolute and unchanging moral code. In addition to the increasing heterogeneity of American society, the rise of pragmatism in the late nineteenth century, and its continued popularity in the twentieth – as well as the influence of existentialism during the late forties and fifties – ensured the growth of such dissent.[60] Nonetheless, situation ethics gave theologians in the late forties and fifties, and the general public in the sixties and seventies, the language, the rational, and even the biblical basis to break from the classical Christian moralist position with its championing of a binding and absolute universal law. More pertinent to this discussion, after the Holy Office in 1956 condemned situation ethics as a form of subjectivism it became the crusade of liberal Protestants in particular – people such as James Gustafson of the Yale Divinity School, Joseph Fletcher of the Episcopal Theological School in Cambridge, Massachusetts, Anglican Bishop John Robinson, Union Theological Seminary's Paul Tillich, and Paul Lehmann, the Parkman Professor of Theology at Harvard Divinity School.

It is especially telling that in 1966 and 1967, a time when many in the Christian press wrestled with the issue of situation ethics, leading Jewish journals such as *Judaism, Conservative Judaism*, and *Tradition* were essentially silent on the matter.[61] Finally, in the Winter 1968 issue of *Conservative Judaism*, an article appeared – but it was quick to portray situation ethics as a uniquely Christian phenomenon, referring to its champions as "the new Christian moralists" and characterizing the Christian treatment of moral law as lacking "the absolute character and the seriousness which it has in Judaism."[62]

[59] Fletcher, Joseph. *Situation Ethics: The New Morality* (Philadelphia: Westminister Press, 1966), p. 26.
[60] Cotkin, George. *Existential American* (Baltimore: The Johns Hopkins University Press, 2003).
[61] Based on review of all of the 1966 and 1967 issues of *Judaism, Conservative Judaism*, and *Tradition*.
[62] Schultz, Joseph. "Reflections on the New Morality," *Conservative Judaism* (Winter 1958), p. 51.

The advent of situation ethics reveals an easily overlooked phenomenon: the crucial role liberal Protestantism played in steering the larger culture in a less traditional and more culturally progressive direction. At bottom, this is a story of appropriation. By incorporating what some would view as an "insight" – and others as folly – of liberal Protestant theology, the larger culture was to acquire a new panoply of intellectual armor in its struggle against the Moral Absolute.

One possible reason for liberal Protestantism's intimate connection to both humanistic psychology and situation ethics involves the importance it traditionally ascribed to the Holy Spirit. In Roman Catholicism and conservative Protestantism, the transformative powers of the Holy Spirit have been largely held in check; in each case, the seeming appearance of the Holy Spirit is filtered through and constrained by doctrine and natural law. Among Southern Baptists, for example, the Holy Spirit is closely tied to scripture; it is seen as providing devout Christians with the wisdom and state of heart to properly receive the Word of God. Even most Pentecostals, whose practices of being "slain in the spirit" and speaking in "tongues" are regarded as direct encounters with that most elusive member of the Trinity, are forbidden from allowing these experiences to supersede or contradict the basic teachings of the church.

However, in more liberal traditions, such as among the Quakers, Unitarians, and certain Episcopalians and Lutherans, biblical doctrines are downplayed and universal laws are seen as anachronistic. Among such believers, the promptings of the Holy Spirit, an intensely personal and subjective experience, are accorded greater deference – and for very sound reasons. How could biblical doctrines, if they are thought not to be infallible; or moral laws, if they are believed not to be universal, supersede one's direct experience with the divine? In a word, the common thread running through situation ethics, Rogerian therapy, and religiously robust notions of the Holy Spirit is the optimistic belief that the answers to life's most important questions are to be discovered by looking internally and accessing a mysterious but wonderful power at the center of our very beings.

It is no coincidence that religious groups placing particular weight on the workings of the Holy Spirit have tended to be more open than mainstream denominations to vigorous female participation. Thus, within the Holiness movement, the forerunner to modern-day Pentecostals, we see no dearth of prominent women. Indeed, a strong case could be made that the most important figure in the Holiness movement was Phoebe Palmer – the leader of the famous Tuesday Meeting for the Promotion of Holiness – the religious group that effectively launched the Holiness movement in the mid-1830s.[63]

Likewise, among the Society of Friends (the Quakers), women have historically been active and visible members of the community. As historian Larry Ingle observes, because there is no ordained clergy among Quakers, "anyone male or female, is free to minster within the simple meeting for worship as she or he is led by the Spirit of God; from the earliest days when meetings recorded the gift of ministry, they recognized women along with men."[64]

The prominence of women among Protestants who exalt the Holy Spirit requires no tedious explanation. In highlighting the "divine spark" existing within every person, denominations emphasizing the Holy Spirit contained strong democratic tendencies. The Holy Spirit, after all, is an "equal opportunity" visitant that does not draw distinctions based on race, sex, ethnicity, or social status. As one participant in the famous 1906 Azusa Street Revival declared:

We had no pope or hierarchy . . . we had no human program; the Lord himself was leading. We had no priest class . . . We did not honor men for their advantage in means or education, but rather for their God-given "gifts" . . . The Lord was liable to burst through anyone . . . Some would finally get up anointed for the message. All seemed to recognize this and gave way. It might be a child, a woman, or a man. It might be from the back or from the front. It made no difference.[65]

What mattered most to these believers was not the hierarchy and rank existing in the external world, but communing with the Holy Spirit and radiating its love outwardly toward one's own family and friends, and to neighbors and strangers alike. Accordingly, within those traditions emphasizing the Holy Spirit, the qualities most celebrated are not those of discipline, courage, assertiveness, and cunning – "masculine" traits generally associated with worldly success; but the gentler virtues of love, compassion, empathy, patience, and tenderness – qualities we associate with the Holy Spirit, as well as the maternal. Predictably, over time, as

---

[63] See Stephens, Randall J., *The Fire Spreads: Holiness and Pentecostalism in the American South* (Cambridge: Harvard University Press, 2008), pp. 29, 32–3, 35, 42, 146; and Raser, Harold B., *Phoebe Palmer: Her Life and Thought* (Lewiston, New York: Edwin Mellen, 1987).

[64] Ingle, Larry. "A Quaker Woman On Woman's Roles: Mary Penington to Friends, 1678." *Signs* Vol. 16, No. 3 (Spring 1991), pp. 587–96.

[65] Cited from Barfoot, Charles H., and Sheppard, Gerald T. "Prophetic vs. Priestly Religion: The Changing Role of Women in Classical Pentecostal Churches." *Review of Religious Research* Vol. 22, No. 1 (September 1980), p. 8.

church authorities began to impose limits on the areas the "spiritual gifts" could directly affect, the status of women began to decline.[66]

As the findings of a few landmark studies show – the first conducted in 1957, the second in 1973 – women have been more inclined than men to embrace psychological counseling.[67] Since the 1970s, this phenomenon – known in the medical literature as the low frequency of male "help-seeking" – has been the subject of numerous articles. Whether one's focus is England or the United States, Finland or Australia, the research has uniformly shown that men are less willing than women to undergo psychological counseling.[68] Apparently, there is something about the roles women have traditionally assumed as mothers and nurturers that have made them less reluctant than men to embrace the kind of inner probing and emotional vulnerability intertwined with psychology's demand to turn inward. Stated a little differently, there is something about the masculine gender scripts men have traditionally followed that has idealized emotional "toughness" and cultivated an aversion to emotional vulnerability. Thus, we see the logic behind the quip of New York Times columnist Maureen Dowd that a man who has embraced his interior, emotional side is someone who has successfully "gotten in touch with his inner chick."[69]

A similar process appears to have unfolded in the Christian quest to commune with the Holy Spirit. In such an endeavor, the requirements for the devout was to "let go" and surrender to the Holy Spirit. In other words, control and the pride accompanying it were forced to give way to humility and submission. In each of the areas we have been discussing – psychological counseling and Protestant spirituality – women have stood out because the social roles they have historically assumed made them particularly receptive to the requisite cognitive style – an outlook that ranks

---

[66] Barfoot, Charles H., and Sheppard, Gerald T. "Prophetic vs. Priestly Religion: The Changing Role of Women in Classical Pentecostal Churches." *Review of Religious Research* Vol. 22, No. 1 (September 1980), p. 8.

[67] For a discussion of the two studies see Veroff, Joseph et al. *The Inner American*, p. 3.

[68] See Butler, Ruth, "Determinants of Help-Seeking: Relations Between Perceived Reasons for Classroom Avoidance and Help-seeking Behaviors in an Experimental Context," *Journal of Educational Psychology* (December 1998), pp. 630–44; and Berman, Alan, "Help-Seeking Among Men: Implications for Suicide Prevention," paper prepared in 2008 for the American Association of Suicidology by a grant from the Irving and Barbara Gutin Charitable Family Foundation.

[69] Dowd, Maureen. "Quien Es Les Macho?" *The New York Times* (February 24, 2008), section: Wk, p. 12. In the article, Dowd was specifically referring to Obama's reluctance to go on the attack during Democratic presidential primaries.

love above power, mercy above justice, charitableness above frugality, spontaneity above discipline, and moral intuition above abstract reasoning. Whether it is attributable to a process of evolutionary hardwiring or to learned gender roles, the qualities Carol Gilligan has associated with an "ethic of care have been empirically shown, in quite a number of studies, to resonate more strongly among women than among men."[70] In short, during the early Cold War years and beyond, the Calvinist ideal of self-restraint and self-mastery was steadily receding in favor of a more flexible, more secular, and a less rule-based moral vision.

Changing child-rearing practices was, naturally, another important feature of the liberalizing impulse emerging after World War II. Although the rise of science – and, specifically, the authority of scientific experts – was the principal factor behind this liberalization, other forces were also afoot. Liberal Protestantism's more optimistic appraisal of the individual diminished the rationale for a stern approach toward parenting. Prior to the twentieth century, liberal Protestants had already adopted a less exacting parental strategy. Scholarship indicates that the child-rearing practices of Quakers and Unitarians in the eighteenth and nineteenth centuries were, to a surprising degree, "modern."[71] A growing tendency to exalt the angelic nature of children accounted for this new development. As religious historian Rebecca Larson recounts: "After the mid-nineteenth century, a shift from the Calvinist view (corrupted with Adam's sin) to a Romantic belief in infant innocence resulted in a new sentimentalization of childhood."[72] Once again, the issue of human depravity determined the constraints one imposed on life as it should be lived, and on children as they should be raised. An article featured in 1829, in the Unitarian newspaper the *Christian Examiner*, sought to contrast the different moral styles of conservative Christians from their more liberal counterparts. "We can often determine to which sect a man belongs by his looks, tone,

[70] For the authoritative description of an "ethic of care" see Gilligan, Carol, *In a Different Voice: Psychological Theory and Women's Development* (Cambridge, Mass.: Harvard University Press, 1982). For a survey of the literature confirming gender differences in moral reasoning, see Rothbart, Mark K., Hanley, Dean, and Albert, Marc., "Gender Differences in Moral Reasoning." *Sex Roles* Vol 15. Nos. 11/12 (1986).

[71] Hafkin Pleck, Elizabeth. *Domestic Tyranny: The Making of American Social Policy Against Family Violence from Colonial Times to the Present* (Illinois: The University of Illinois Press, 2004), pp. 37–41.

[72] Rebecca Larson. *Daughters of Light: Quaker Women, Preaching, and Prophesying in the Colonies and Abroad, 1900–1775* (North Carolina: The University of North Carolina Press, 2007), pp. 165–6.

and gait." Religious liberals "incline to the amiable and pacific virtues," while Calvinists "to the stern and self-denying virtues."[73]

Given the assumptions of liberal Protestants – assumptions that flow directly from their theological assessment of man – it is not surprising to see the Rev. Norman Vincent Peale, a politically conservative but theologically liberal minister, advising parents in 1950 about the dangers of "harsh demands," sexual repression, and "stern discipline."[74] Simply put, with the rising influence of postwar psychology, austere child-rearing strategies became more difficult to sustain and, accordingly, growing numbers of Americans came to embrace the broader worldview of liberal Protestantism with its more positive assessment of human nature and milder approach to the rearing of children.

Many Jewish Americans found the assumptions that rested at the heart of the Permissive Turn, with its embrace of Carl Rogers, and deemphasis of dogma, with its less patriarchal posture and rejection of natural law, infinitely preferable to the religious orthodoxy that had long dominated discussions of morality. The higher social positions Jews were apt to occupy, combined with a historical experience that caused many Jewish Americans to look unfavorably upon the moral style of conservative Christians, helped render Americans of Jewish descent particularly receptive to the liberalizing changes that were underway during the 1950s. However, these shifting attitudes did not amount to what David Hollinger has termed a process of "de-Christianization."[75] As we have seen, much of the liberalizing changes unfolding in the areas of child rearing and psychological counseling, in the promotion of the disease model and, in the rise of situation ethics were consistent with – and, indeed, partially inspired by – a liberal Protestant vision, with its more positive evaluation of the Self. Just as Jewish exceptionalism has been an important presence on the cultural scene, so too has Protestant particularism. In its suspicion of the law, and its exceedingly upbeat assessment of the individual – stances made possible by its unique theological outlook – liberal Protestantism played a crucial although little recognized role in transforming the moral terrain of post–World War II America.

[73] Howe, Daniel W. "John Witherspoon and the Transatlantic Enlightenment," in *The Atlantic Enlightenment*. Manning, Susan, and Cogliano, Francis D. (eds.). (Burlington, Vermont: Ashgate Publishing Company, 2008), p. 66.

[74] Peale, Norman Vincent, and Blanton, Smiley. *The Art of Real Happiness* (New York: Prentice Hall, 1950), pp. 37, 56.

[75] Hollinger, David A. *Science, Jews, and Secular Culture*, p. 17.

The Permissive Turn, therefore, was not anti-Christian per se, but it was in sharp tension with a traditional conservative Christian perspective. Understandably, a great many Jewish Americans, as well as a substantial number of liberal Protestants, were very receptive to these sweeping changes, welcoming them as a liberating alternative to an older ethic they regarded as repressive and self-righteous.

Conclusion

In examining the period between the late 1930s and the early to mid-1970s, it is possible to delineate, in an admittedly crude way, among three stages of cultural transformation. The first stage, which can be associated with the late 1930s and the early 1940s, can be thought of as a period of comparative stability. Although there was an ongoing process of liberalization – something that had been unfolding since before the turn of the century – the rate of change was slow, and values and norms were largely in alignment. However, due primarily to the World War II experience, the pace of change quickened during the Truman and Eisenhower years as values began to loosen at a more rapid tempo than norms. It was during this second stage that the Permissive Turn began to unfold in earnest. Finally, beginning in the mid- to late 1960s and proceeding throughout much of the 1970s, the nation entered the third stage in the march toward a freer and more secular culture where individual autonomy became the hallmark of the times. In this third stage, social norms evolved rapidly – not only catching up to values, but in many instances surpassing them. By so doing, norms helped pave the way to a new, more dramatic phase in the transformation of the culture – an era characterized by second-wave feminism, gay liberation, pop psychology, a more defiant youth culture, the medicalization of deviancy in a variety of forms, a burgeoning environmentalist movement, greater tolerance for "different" people and different lifestyles, and still higher levels of premarital sex. At last, the revolution had arrived, the nation was transformed, and a secularized worldview had come to dominate moral decision-making.

Archives

- American Academy of Motion Pictures Arts and Sciences; Special Collections, Hedda Hopper File
- Association of Clinical Pastoral Education Papers, Pitts Theological Library Archives, Emory University
- Benjamin Spock Papers, Syracuse University Special Collections
- Emil Lehman, National Survey on Synagogue Leadership (1953), Dorot Jewish Division, New York Public Library
- Institute of Religion Papers, Syracuse University Special Collections
- Joshua Loth Liebman Papers, Boston University Special Collections
- Levi-Strauss & Company Archives
- Marty Mann Papers, Syracuse University Special Collections
- Papers of the National Conference of Christians and Jews, Social Welfare History Archives, University of Minnesota
- Papers of the Super Market Institute (now called the Food Market Institute) Washington, D.C.
- Papers of the U.S. Ad Council. Library Archives, University of Illinois–Urbana
- Planned Parenthood Federation of America Archives, Sophia Smith Collection, Smith College Library Archives
- Southern Baptist Convention Library and History Archives
- Special Collections Archives, Smathers Library, University of Florida
- United Methodist Archives and History Center of the United Methodist Church, Drew University

Index

Abortions, 113, 124
Actualizing Tendency, 157, 228, 232, 236,
    247, 273, 274, 275
  description of, 21
  Maslow's notion of, 273
  resistance to external authority, 157,
    228
Ad Council, 175
Adorno, Theodor W, 133, 214, 274
Advertising, 6, 25, 66, 111–112, 207, 250
African Americans, 10, 24, 29, 42, 44, 50,
    115, 125–126, 175, 194–196, 223,
    238
  childrearing approach, 42
  embrace of modern psychology, 44
  rates of single motherhood, 115
  receptivity towards psychology, 194–
    195
  stereotypical image of, 238
Agnew, Spiro, 17
Alcoholics Anonymous, 45, 267
  growth of, 27
  notion of "dry drunks," 31
  resistance to disease model, 30
  see Disease model, Marty Mann and Bill
    Wilson
Allport, Gordon, 133, 214
American Bandstand, 189, 194, 220, 222
  see Clark, Dick
The American Creed (movie), 66
American Federation of Religion and
    Psychiatry (AFRP), 80–81
American Medical Association, 31

American Psychological Association (APA),
    19, 154
Anti-Elitism, 193–194
April Love (movie), 183
Armstrong, Louis, 234
Autonomy, 113, 131, 149, 159, 206, 215,
    240, 269, 274, 282
  connection to the feminist movement,
    159
  connection to identity, 215
  Jewish emphasis on, 269
  see Teenagers, need for autonomy
Azusa Street Revival, 278

Baby Boom, 47, 49, 105, 130, 159, 222,
    263
  height of, 159
Baptists, 43, 68, 89, 151, 277
Beat Poetry, 235
Bebop, 234–236
Becker, Herald, 256
Behaviorism, 21
Bell, Daniel, 47, 48
Bible (RSV), 70–75
  conservative opposition to, 71–72
  popularity of, 71
Biblical literacy, 73
Bibliolatry, 74
Bingo, 60–63
  history of, 60
  as political issue, 61–62
  popularity of, 60
  Referendums on, 62–63

Birth Control, declining taboo towards, 110–111
Birth Control Pill
  alleged importance of, 104–105, 124, 127
  distribution to college students, 128–129
  popularity among teenagers, 129
  popularity during the 1960s and early 1970s, 129
Black militancy, 258–259
Blue Denim (movie), 201
Blue Jeans, 189–194, 196, 205–208, 212, 219–220
  advertisement of, 207–208
  early history of, 189
  growing acceptance of, 192
  as signifier of informality, 194
  as symbol of defiance, 189–190
  social meaning of, 192–193
Blue Laws, 63–65
Bohemian Communities, 222
Boone, Pat, 123, 139, 187, 188, 192, 207, 209, 215–217
  clean-cut image, 182–183
  popularity as an actor, 183–184
  profile of typical fan, 186
  sexual innuendo in his songs, 185
Boy Scouts, 217–219
  decline of, 217
  also see Cub Scouts
Bronfenbrenner, Urie, 41
Brotherhood Week, 65–67
  Hollywood's promotion of, 66
Brown, Helen Gurly, 121–122, 201
Bruce, Steve, 36
Buber, Martin, 273
Buffalo Plan, 212
Burns, Arthur, 11–12

Calvinism, 229–232, 238–239, 271, 280
  Niebuhr's rejection of, 230–232
Card playing, 58, 63
Carmichael, Stokely, 258–259
Carter, Asa, 195
Catcher in the Rye, 218, 221
  also see Salinger, J.D.
Catholic
  attitudes towards psychoanalysis, 93
  attitudes towards psychology, 93–94

Catholic women's leadership in lay organizations, 150
Extra Ecclesiam Nulla Salus, 92
  intellectual inferiority complex, 149
Census Bureau, 113, 115
Childrearing, 2, 13, 15, 16, 29, 42, 43, 52, 88, 138, 227–228, 232, 237, 252, 253, 271, 280–281
  among Mormons, 138
  class differences, 41–42
  racial differences, 237–238
  religious differences, 227–228, 271, 280–281
  also see Benjamin Spock
Christianity Today, 88
Church Attendance, 3, 49, 55–57, 73, 97–98
Clark, Dick, 189, 194, 220
  also see American Bandstand
Client-centered therapy, 21, 77–78, 154, 157, 229
  compatibility with conservative Christianity, 229
  criticism of, 78–79
Cohen, Lizabeth, 140–142
Cold War, effect on conservative norms, 254–255
Coles, Robert, 247
College
  effect on attitudes towards sexually active single women, 163, 165–166, 168
  effect on attitudes towards psychology, 43
  effect on attitudes towards women running for public office, 162–164, 269–270
  growth of female student population, 163–164
Companionate marriage, 136
Complacency Narrative, 2
Complacent child, 215
Conformity, 174, 214, 218–219, 252, 255, 269
  in 1950s, 255
  Jewish resistance to, 269
  postwar fears of, 214
Condoms, 111–112
Congregationalists, 84
Consciousness raising groups, CR groups, 156–157, 170

Conservatives
  acceptance of Keynesianism, 11–12
  assessment of the 1960s, 124
  hostility to the disease model, 32
  hostility to Freud, 16–17
Council for Clinical Training, 76, 79, 81
Cub Scouts, 217–218
  also see Boy Scouts
Cushing, Richard Cardinal, 94

Dancing, 58, 60, 63, 89, 181, 194
  Southern Baptist opposition to, 53, 59
Dating
  parental attitudes towards, 199–200
  see going steady
Davis, Miles, 235, 236
Dean, James
  Rebel Without a Cause (movie)
    p. 201–203
Dennis the Menace, 216
Disc jockeys, 195
Disciples of Christ, 68, 151
Disease Model, 13, 26, 28, 30–32, 42–44,
    49–50, 52, 265–267, 281
  AA resistance to, 30–31
  popular acceptance of, 25–26, 29, 265
  implications of, 13, 31–32
  wider application of, 265
  also see Methadone
Disney, 188
Dobson, James, 17
Domesticity, 3, 47, 173
Donna Reed Show, 174, 188
Draw Sword (Bible game), 74
Dress Codes, see Buffalo Plan
Durkheim, Émile, 274

Ed Sullivan, 121
Edwards, Jonathan, 229
Einstein, Albert, 246
Eisenhower, Dwight, 49, 50, 54, 65, 67,
    89, 176, 188
Ellis, John Tracy, 149
Emerson, Ralph Waldo, 237, 238
Environmentalists, 258, 282
Episcopalian, 45, 84, 144–145, 275,
    277
Equal Opportunity Day, 176
Equal Pay Act of 1963, 171
Equal Pay for Equal work, 172, 259
Erickson, Erik, 209–210, 215

Evangelical and Reformed Church, 151
Experts, deference to, 11–13

Fads, 213–214
Falwell, Jerry, 98
Farnham, Marynia, See *Modern Women:
    The Lost Sex*
Faulkner, William, 152
Federal Council of Churches, 67, 83, 100,
    145,
Federal Employees for a Democratic
    Society, 261–262
Feeney, Leonard, 92–93
  The Feminine Mystique, 134, 143, 150,
    152–153, 155–156, 171
  reception of, 50
Feminist Movement, 154–155, 159,
    167–168, 171, 173, 177–178, 259
  causes of, 177–178
  emphasis placed on working women,
    166–168
  status movement in sixties and seventies,
    167, 173
First-person narrative, 240
Fisher, Eddie, 101–102, 133
  also see Elizabeth Taylor
Fletcher, Joseph, 77, 241–243, 248, 262,
    275–276
  also see Legalism
Food and Drug Administration (FDA),
    104, 112
Freed, Alan, 181
Freud, Sigmund, 3, 16–17, 19, 21, 25, 32,
    77, 93, 152–154, 159, 238, 247, 272
  cultural influence, 152
  visit to America, 3
  on repression, 77
  hostility to religion, 12
  opposition by Feminists, 152–153
Friedan, Betty, 124–135, 136, 150–153,
    155, 156, 163, 166, 168, 171, 175
  on importance of work, 166, 168
  reliance on psychology, 155
  also see *The Feminine Mystique*
Fromm, Erich, 19–21, 133, 255, 274
Fuller Theological Seminary, 264
Fundamentalists, 72, 74–75, 87

Gay, 121, 134, 251, 253–254, 257, 282
  equation with communism, 253–254
  status in the 1950s, 121, 254

Geertz, Clifford, 98
Gandhi, Mahatma, 224–245, 244–247,
  271
  popularity of, 244
  symbolic significance of, 244–245
Gesell, Arnold 210, 211, 271
Gilligan, Carol, 180
Ginsberg, Allen, 122, 135
God, as a buddy, 229–230
Going Steady
  advice about, 200
  Catholic opposition to, 198–199
  implications for premarital sex, 200–201
  parental opposition to, 199
  The Greening of America, 262–263
Graham, Billy, 3, 34–35, 50, 55, 57,
  85–91, 98
  moderation of message, 88–90
  New York Crusade, 87–88, 90–91
  on proselytizing to Jews, 85
  treatment of sin, 89
Guilt, 16, 25, 32, 34, 52, 133, 240,
  248

Hefner, Hugh, 52, 103, 117–120, 123
Herberg, Will, 54–55, 58, 67, 83–84, 95,
  230
Hemingway, Ernest, 152
High School, universal experience of,
  203–204
Hiltner, Seward, 76–78, 242
Hoffman, Hans, 233
Holiness Movement, 272
Hollinger, David, 267, 281
Holy Spirit, 241, 272, 276–279
Homosexuals, see Gay
Hoover, J. Edgar, 34, 250–251
Horney, Karen, 19–21
Houston, Charles, 34
Humanistic psychology, 25, 77–78,
  154–159, 238, 247, 251, 264,
  272–273, 275, 277
  also see actualizing tendency, Carl
  Rogers, Abraham Maslow, IHM
  Sisters
Husbands, the attitudes of young people
  toward role, 138, 143
  division of labor within the home, 143
  helping out at home, 143

Identity, 9, 54, 166, 186, 207, 209, 215,
  221, 225, 274

Identity Crisis, 209
  also see Erik Erickson
IHM Sisters, 157–158
Impulses, 32, 133, 197, 213, 226–228,
  272–273
Inflation during the 1940s, 48
Institute for Pastoral Care (IPC), 76,
  79–81
Intergenerational Compact, 205
Intermarriage, religious, 68–70, 92,
  94
Inward Turn, 238–244

Jewish Exceptionalism, 267–271
Jewish
  attitudes towards alcoholism, 270
  higher class status, 269
  Jewish teenagers' attitudes toward
  religion, 96–97
  study of Conservative Synagogues,
  94–96
  also see Joshua Loth Liebman
Joyce, James, 152
Judeo-Christian tradition, 82, 175
Jury Service, 161
Juvenile Delinquency, 181, 189–191, 214,
  220, 252, 257
  equation with blue jeans, 189–190
  equation with rock 'n roll, 181

Kazin, Alfred, 152
Kerouac, Jack, 1, 52, 235, 240
Keynesianism, 11–12
King, Martin Luther, 1, 182, 230
Kinsey, Alfred, 106, 108–110, 255, 257
  Also see Premarital Sex
Kramdens, Ralph and Alice, 143–144

La Pierre Study, 249–250
Labor strikes of 1946, 5
Lasch, Christopher, 251–252
Leave it to Beaver, 212–213
Lee, Dorothy McCullough, 160–161
Legalism, 241–243
Legion of Decency, 59–60
Lesbian couples, 167
Liberals
  image of 1950s, 2
  view of poverty, 126
Liberal Protestants, 45, 46, 81, 88, 240,
  242, 271–282
  attitudes toward Natural Law, 271–272

childrearing practices, 280–281
emphasis on the Holy Spirit, 277
Liebman, Joshua Loth, 32–37, 45–46, 48,
    52
    assessment of sin and guilt, 34
    critique of conservative Christianity, 46
    Peace of Mind (1946), 32, 35
Little Richard, 185
Lolita (the novel), 103
Lords Day Alliance, 65
Lucy Stone League, 176
Lundberg, Ferdinand, see *Modern Women:*
    The Lost Sex

MAD Magazine, 183, 220, 221
Mann, Marty, 29–32, 45–46, 49, 52, 267,
    271
Marriage
    average age of, 109
    power relations within, 136–144
    in Japanese households, 142
Maslow, Abraham
    contrast with Rogers, 273–274
    influence on Betty Friedan, 155
    on high dominance women, 155–156
    on importance of instinct, 229
Masturbation, 106, 133, 197
Mattachine Society, 121
May, Rollo, 21, 77, 264, 271
McCarthyism, 175, 253–254
McDonald, Dwight, 183, 220
McIntire, Carl, 72
Mead, Margaret, 197
Meat Crisis of 1946, 4–5
Medicalization of Deviancy, 267
Merton, Thomas, 94
Methodists, 59, 69, 71–72, 84–85,
    144–145, 151, 188, 192, 268
    on converting Jews, 84–85
    on ordination of women, 144–145
    on dancing, 188
    on going to movies, 59–60
Methadone, 265–267
"Middle America," notion of, 177
Middletown Study, 72–73
Miltown, see Tranquilizers
Ministry, women's entry into, 144–145
Modern Women: The Lost Sex, 153
    also see Ferdinand Lundberg
Modernization Theory, 56–57
Moral entrepreneurs, 256
Moral panics, 256

Moral Universe, 16
Mormons, 138–139
Motherwell, Robert, 233
Myrdal, Gunnar, 10, 110–111

National Association of Evangelicals,
    150
National Council of Churches (NCC), 71,
    76, 85, 89, 146, 262
National Conference of Christians and
    Jews, 65–66, 186
National Conference on Alcoholism
    (NCA), see Marty Mann
National Organization for Women, 167
National Urban League, see Equal
    Opportunity Day
Nazi, 36, 82, 175, 244
Niebuhr, H. Richard, 76, 241
Niebuhr, Reinhold, 84, 89, 158, 225,
    230–232
    anxiety, 231–232
    original righteousness, 230
    proselytizing to Jews, 84, 271–272
Nixon, Richard, 188–189, 192, 261,
    264–265
Non-directive therapy, see client-centered
    therapy
Norms, 30, 105, 122–123, 125–126, 138,
    151, 170, 179, 181, 192, 196, 206,
    219, 223, 232, 239, 249–250, 252
    durability of, 122–123
    also see Social Conventions and
    Subversive Consensus
Nudity, depiction in films, 118

Office of Price Administration (OPA), 5
Open Marriage, 262
Organization Man, 214
Original righteousness, 230–231, 271, 275
Original Sin, 19, 46, 77, 188, 226–229,
    232–233, 238, 243–244, 247, 271
Overstreet, Harry, 227

Pacifists, 245
Patterson, James T., 263
Palmer, Phoebe, see Holiness Movement
Panty Raids, 197–198, 213
Parker, Charlie, 235, 236
Pastoral Counseling, 52, 76–82, 93, 154,
    159, 228–229, 232, 264, 272
    leading journals of, 77
    Roman Catholic support of, 93

Pastoral Counselors, popularity among the General Public
Peale, Norman Vincent, 35–37, 50–52, 80, 89, 91, 133, 188, 200, 271, 281
  conservatism of, 50, 188
  progressive attitude towards childrearing, 51, 281
  theology as therapy, 36–37
Penicillin, 112–113
Pentecostals, 277–278
  Speaking in Tongues, 277
  see Azusa Street Revival
Permissive Turn, 2–3, 8, 12, 14, 16, 41, 44, 49, 52, 105, 219, 226, 232, 270, 281–282
Permissive, history of the term, 17
Peter Berger, 55, 57, 262
Planned Parenthood, 111
Playboy
  Clubs, 118
  Interview, 118–119
Pluralism, 57, 66–67, 70, 85, 92, 175, 196
  Brotherhood Week, 66–67
  as liberalizing force, 175
Pollock, Jackson, 233–234
Pope Pius XII, 93, 149
Postwar Boom, myth of, 47–49
Premarital Pregnancy, 105, 113–115
Premarital Sex, 103–108, 110, 112–118, 122–123, 126–127, 130–132, 198, 282
  Alfred Kinsey's findings, 108
  during World War II, 130–132
  presumed level of, 130
Presley, Elvis, 1, 52, 123, 180, 183–187, 189, 230, 263
  as figure of rebellion, 187
  profile of typical fan, 187
  performance with Frank Sinatra, 180–181
Proselytizing, 53, 82, 84–86, 88, 91, 99, 255, 271
Presbyterians, female clergy, 144
Psychiatry, World War II, 17–18
Psychoanalysis, comic series, 22–23
Psychology,
  Black attitudes towards, 44
  depiction in movies, 21–22
  curriculum in Seminaries, 81
  male and female attitudes towards, 43, 279–280

growth of during postwar years, 19
legitimacy given as a result of World War II, 18
also see Pastoral Psychology
Purdue Opinion Survey, 96, 200, 204–206
Puritanism, 46

Quakers
  attitudes towards childrearing, 280
  emphasis on the "inner light," 275
  prominent role of women, 278

Radical Feminism, 171, 259
Rayburn, Sam, 5
Rebel Without a Cause (movie), 201–203, 221
Religiosity, 94–95, 97
  International comparison, 97
Religious doctrine, 65, 67, 70, 91, 241
Remasculinization of American Culture, 173–174
Repression, 2, 25, 51, 77, 132–133, 197, 221, 247, 272, 281
  as facilitating unhealthy attitudes towards sex, 132–133, 197
  Freudian view of, 77, 247, 272
  liberal view of, 2
Ribicoff, Abraham, 62
Richards, Amy, 166–167
Rice, John, 87–89
Rieff, Philip, 52
Riesman, David, 20, 194, 214, 254–255
Rising Expectations, 208
Robertson, Pat, 98–99
Rock 'n roll, 1, 103, 123, 133, 171, 181–187, 189, 192, 194–196, 201, 206, 212–213, 219–220, 223
  growing acceptance of, 182–183, 185–187
  connotations of sex, 103, 123, 181–182, 186–187
  connotations of violence, 181–182
  as race music, 185, 188, 195
Rogers, Carl 19–21, 45–46, 77–79, 133, 154–155, 157–159, 225, 228–229, 232, 239, 264, 271–275, 281
  attitude towards organized religion, 46
  contrast with Freud, 19–21
  contrast with Maslow, 273–274
  IHM Nuns, 157–158

influence among pastoral and secular psychologists, 77–79
liberal Protestant background, 45
Rossellini, Roberto, 100

Salinger, J.D., 218
see Cather in the Rye
Savings, 4, 7, 141
Science
Foundation support of, 11
prestige of, 9–13
Truman's promotion of, 9
Social Sciences, 11
Science, challenge to traditional values, 12–13
Secularization Theory, 56–57
Self, 16, 21, 30–31, 224–226, 228, 232, 243, 255
Self-actualization,
implications for challenging gender roles, 155, 159
model of, 239
treatment of impulses, 273
Self-authorship, 215
Self-mastery, 226, 238, 248, 280
decline of, 238
Self-realization, 21, 82, 166
Seminary Training, 81
Sex and the Single Girl, 121
see Brown, Helen Gurly
Sexual Survey, 105–106, 115
Sex Education, 107
Sheen, Fulton, 28, 32, 34–35, 93, 240–241
attitude towards alcoholism, 28
critique of psychoanalysis, 93
criticism of, 240–241
Shell Shock, 18
Shotgun Marriages, 125
Sinatra, Frank, 180–181, 189
criticism of rock 'n roll, 181
public embrace of rock 'n roll, 189
Sister Formation Conference, 148–149
Sit Ins, 196, 261
Situation Ethics, 242–243, 246, 262, 275–276, 277, 281
also see Joseph Fletcher and Legalism
Smeal, Eleanor, 167
Snake Pit (movie), 22
Snobbery, see anti-elitism

Social conformity, 214, 252, 255
Social Conventions, 170, 223, 238, 256–257, 263
also see norms
Social Science, foundation support of, 10–11
Society of Friends, see Quakers
Southern Baptist, 68, 74, 81, 86, 89, 277
attitudes towards dancing, 53, 59,
size of, 74
seminary training, 81
Spock, Benjamin, 37–41, 44, 46, 48, 52, 133, 227–228, 263, 271
cultural influence of, 37–38
on discipline, 38–40
on importance of peer group interaction, 40
on natural goodness of children, 227
Spontaneity, 233–238
abstract expressionism, 233–234
in bebop jazz, 234–235
in mental health, 236–237
in poetry, 235
Stevenson, Adlai, 50, 193, 230
Student Non-Violent Coordinating Committee (SNCC), 258
Subversive Consensus, 52, 188
Sullivan, Harry Stack, 19–21
criticism of Freud, 20
Summer Place (movie) 201
Super Markets, 64

Taft, Charles P., 83
Taylor, Elizabeth, 101–103, 133
Technological Utopia, 7–8
Teen Movies, 201
Teenagers, 5, 8, 86, 124
conservatism of, 203–206
need for autonomy, 206, 213, 208, 211, 215
also see all of Chapter 5 (134–198)
Tillich, Paul, 77, 241–242, 272, 276
opposition to legalism, 242
connection with pastoral counseling movement, 77
Tolerance, 10, 89, 92, 196, 219, 252, 282
Traditional moral framework, 9, 47, 48, 52, 258, 271, 272

Tranquilizers, 24–25
  sales of, 24

Union Theological Seminary, 45, 84, 89,
  275–276
Unitarians, 272, 277, 280
United Brethren, 151
United Church women, 146–148,
  150
Universal Salvation, 275
Universalists, 267, 272
Urban Poor, underclass, 125

Venereal Disease, 112–113, 130
"Victory Girls", 130

Wake Forest College, 53, 58
Wallace, Henry, 49
Wayne, John, 177, 184
Wesley, John, 272
White Citizen's Council, 195
Wilson, Bill, 30–31, 45, 267, 271
Wilson, William Julius, 126

Women
  attitudes towards woman president, 160,
    162–165, 168–169, 171, 269–270
  college attendance, 163–164
  church governance, 144–145, 151
  politics, 159–161
  also see Jury Service
Women's Leadership Conference, 147–148
Work, impact on feminism, 155, 164–166,
  168, 175
World Council of Churches, 83–84, 86, 88
Worldliness, 59, 62, 99, 245

Youth culture, 3, 9, 1 03, 179, 182–183,
  186, 189, 192, 194, 197–198,
  200–204, 210–212
  effect on young women, 200–201
  and sex, 197–198
  adult emulation of, 220–223
  importance of consumption, 206
Youthful Rebellion,
  values vs. culture, 219
  as sign of *mental health*, 210–212